INDO-ARYAN ORIGINS AND OTHER VEDIC ISSUES

Indo-Aryan Origins and other Vedic Issues

Nicholas Kazanas

ADITYA PRAKASHAN
New Delhi

First published, 2009
First reprint, 2011
Second reprint, 2016
Third reprint, 2019
Reprint, 2024

ISBN 978-81-7742-115-6

Published by Aditya Prakashan, 2/18, Ansari Road, New Delhi – 110 002.

email: contact@adityaprakashan.com
website: www.adityaprakashan.com

Printed at Replika Press Pvt. Ltd.

Contents

Introduction

The basic theme of the papers in this volume is that much of the *RV* (=*Ṛgveda*) is pre-Harappan, certainly before 3200 and probably before 3800 BCE. A corollary to this idea is that the IAs (=Indoaryans) who composed and arranged the Rigvedic hymns round the old Sarasvatī river were fully indigenous to Saptasindhu, the land of the seven rivers in what is today N-W India and Pakistan. Both ideas go against the grain of the mainstream academic notion that wants the IAs to enter this area c 1700-1500 and compose the *RV* c 1200 or after. These ideas are still cherished among Western indologists but there is a distinct change of climate in favour of indigenism in Indian centres of learning. Some scholars in the West are changing too.

Except paper Two the others unfold in two lines of thought. One line is a direct presentation of the evidence for an early *RV* date and for Indoaryan indigenism and of various issues regarding Rigvedic studies, like the meaning of *pur* in paper Four. The other is polemic and attacks the various false arguments marshalled by the adherents of the AIT (=Aryan Invasion/Immigration Theory). Professor M Witzel receives the brunt of my attacks since he writes on this subject more frequently and vociferously than any other scholar: there is nothing personal. We have met and exchanged views fairly amicably, but I disagree both with his views and methods.

As the papers have an introductory paragraph summing up the issues and argument(s) involved, I shall not write much about each one of them except to indicate the Journal or other publication where each appeared.

Like other indigenists I have received attacks and critiques, some of them rather scurrilous (from my *priyatamaśatru* Witzel). Some mainstreamers accuse me of having an "agenda", which in academic parlance means that I have strong preconceptions and do not heed other views (ie those of the accusers) and am therefore incapable of being objective (as the accusers believe themselves to be). This of course is patent nonsense. All scholars without exception are prejudiced to a degree (whether in the political or religious sphere) and to that degree all their views are coloured. Even to say or think 'I have no point of view in the matter' is a point of view or an agenda. All scholars have therefore an agenda in promoting their personal pet theories; that these theories may be shared by others, or even an enormous majority, does not make them correct and does not put the scholars above an agenda. Such writers when tested, appear, I have found, wanting in good scholarship (which entails broad and detailed knowledge of the subject) and sound reasoning. They hide behind a veneer of superciliousness and one-upmanship producing heaps of writing, full of irrelevant secondary references and tedious trivia that constitute sheer pedantry and do not advance true knowledge one iota. Things are not much different in the field of positive sciences. "Much as the field purports to encourage experimental freedom, the entire structure of science, with its highly competitive grant system, coupled with the publishing and peer review system, largely depends upon individuals conforming to the accepted scientific [=mainstream] view. The system tends to encourage professionals to carry out experimentation whose purpose is primarily to confirm the existing [=received, 'orthodox'] view of things or to further develop technology for industry, rather than to serve up true innovation" (Mc Taggart 2001:13; square brackets added). Remove this last phrase "technology for industry" and you have the same situation in the humanities. Or, to cite a slightly different aspect of the same matter: "Good ideas are often very annoying to people who have built their careers around old bad ones" (Hancock 2005:214).

I am not, of course, the first scholar to deal with these issues. Most of my predecessors are frequently mentioned in these papers. As I point out in the first one 'Indigenous Indo-Aryans and the *Ṛgveda*', my own interest flared forth in 1996. I soon discovered that other scholars had been dealing with this subject for more than a century. An eye-opener was *Frontiers of the Indus Civilization* 1984, eds Gupta SP and Lal BB. Then of great help proved the book *In Search of the Cradle of Civilization* 1995 by Feuerstein G, Frawley D and Kak S, despite its several flaws. I corresponded for a period with Frawley and Kak, both of whom offered advice and aid. Another scholar who gave me generous and unstinting help is V Agarwal of Minnesota. This is an opportunity to express my gratitude to them.

The first paper was published by the *Journal of Indo-European Studies* in 2002. I had much earlier sent an article 'Indo-European Deities and the *Ṛgveda*', in which I argued for about two pages that, since the *RV* contained some 20 names of IE (=IndoEuropean) deities found scattered in twos and threes in other branches (Hittite, Greek, Italic, Slavic etc) and considering some other salient features, *the RV should be dated very much earlier than 1200*. As expected (for in those days it was unthinkable to mention such a thing in mainstream publications), I was asked to remove the offending paragraphs with the promise from the editor, J Mallory, that he would consider a full paper on the *RV* date and indigenism. In view of the future paper, the price to pay seemed small; so I removed the paragraphs and that article was published in 2001. Subsequently, Mallory said he would open a discussion with five Western and five Indian scholars commenting on my new paper. I wrote the paper and it was published in Dec 2002. One referee had commended it with two comments:

(a) "[T]he author gives different arguments against recent works by Witzel (and some other scholars) who oppose the idea of an autochthonous character of the speakers of Indo-Aryan in India. Some of these critical thoughts are quite interesting." (b) "Maybe the age of the first arrival of Indo-Europeans (or of the beginning of a cultural influence of Indo-European) in India should be pushed further back: thus important archaeoastronomical data mentioned in the article may be relevant for the definition of this time."

It is interesting that the referee did not allow the possibility of indigenism but had to have an IE influx of people or cultural elements; he/she could only think of pushing the influx further back! (Is not this an "agenda"?) And why have referees the advantage of anonymity? Under this cover they can and do commend or condemn a paper not on fairly objective criteria, but, as is often proven, on purely subjective predilections, usually reflecting mainstream views. Peer-reviewing would be truly more valuable only if the "peers" put their name down and were prepared to face criticism on their views. Anyway, nine comments on my article were published, eight of them hostile (including the only Indian one) and a neutral one by E. Bryant. In fairness to Mallory, however, he published subsequently my 'Final Reply' in which I tackled most of the important objections in those comments: this was published in the *JIES* 2003. It has not been reproduced here because it could make sense only with reference to the Comments printed in the *JIES*. Its main points have all been incorporated in the other papers.

Paper Two is a study of Vedic thought tracing the theme of One and Many and Man's Self-realization from the *RV* to the Upanishads. It is being reproduced here by the kind permission of Profs DP Chattopadhyaya general editor of the PHISPC and GC Pande editor of the volume *Golden Chain of Civilizations* (by the Centre for Studies in Civilization, Delhi) wherein it is included as part of my study *Vedic, Mesopotamian and Egyptian Religiophilosophical Thought*

(2007). In this I examine some ideas about the nature of 'civilization' and trace a unifying thread running through the *RV, AV*, Brāhmaṇas and Upanishads, ie man's return to his source which is the Supreme Godhead, Itself unmanifest but the Primal Cause of all manifestations.

Paper Three 'Diffusion of IE Theonyms' was published in a much simpler form in the *JIES* 2001, then was revised several times and finally published in its present form in the Quarterly Journal of the *Mythic Society* (Bangalore), 2006. This utilizes material used in earlier publications concerning some 20 Vedic names of gods and goddesses and their cognations in other IE branches. After some exchanges with J Mallory (editor of the *JIES*), I refute herein some of his views which may be shared tacitly or volubly with other Indoeuropeanists.

Paper Four 'Rigvedic pur' was first published in the *Adyar Library Bulletin*, 2003, then was revised and expanded and published in *Man & Environment* (Pune), 2006. In that same issue was published paper Five 'Samudra and Sarasvatī' which here appears only as 'Samudra' since the discussion on the river Sarasvatī is found in paper 1 and, again, briefer, in paper 9. In paper 3, I endeavour to show that *pur* does not mean 'fort' or 'town', as is commonly thought, but a 'magical, non-material, psychological defence'. In 'Samudra' I stress that the Vedics knew well the ocean. This was first published in a shorter version in the *QJMS*, 2004. Some years earlier Witzel and Frawley had a quarrel in *The Hindu* on the meaning of *pur* and *samudra*. I sent a letter to *The Hindu* but it was not published so I wrote these two papers.

Paper Six 'Anatolian Bull and Vedic Horse' was published in the *QJMS* (Bangalore) 2006. It argues that the Hittites do not preserve many elements from the Proto-Indo-European culture and Anatolia (=Modern Turkey) could not possibly be the original homeland.

Paper Seven 'Vedic and Mesopotamian' was first written for the *Annals of Bhandarkar Oriental Research Institute* but was not published for a long time so I had it published in *Migration and Diffusion* (Vienna), 2005. The printing there was unfortunately so bad that the Sanskrit citations were unreadable. After minor revisions it was published in the *Adyar Library Bulletin* (2007: Olcott commemorative issue) but was also incorporated in the largest article mentioned in connexion with Paper Two, in the 'Vedic, Mesopotamian and Egyptian Religiophilosophical Thought'.

Paper Eight, 'Vedic and Egyptian' also formed part of that article and was written independently for and published in the *QJMS*, 2007. In both papers, I examine the very strong possibility that the Vedic culture influenced the Mesopotamians and Egyptians early on.

Paper Nine 'Indo-European Linguistics and Indo-aryan Indigenism' was written at the request of Prof Angela Marcantonio who edited the volume *The Indo-European Language Family: Questions about its Status*, published by the Institute for the Study of Man (Washington), which publishes also the *Journal of Indo-European Studies*. Here I argue yet again that although the evidence shows there was an original ProtoIndo European language this can no longer be reconstructed and I re-collect the evidence for an early *Ṛgveda* and Indian indigenism. I incorporated much material from previous articles showing that the RV predates the Harappan or Sarasvati-Sindhu (or Indus-Sarasvati, as is generally called) civilization. I have made some minor changes in this present version.

Paper Ten, 'The mainstream model' is a thoroughly revised and recast version of a paper, 'The Establishing of a View', published in *ABORI*, 2003. It analyses the forces that go into the establishment of the mainstream view and examines some examples in the sciences where the Establishment strongly resists changes in the received dogmas. This was revised and expanded considerably and published in the *Research Bulletin* of the Vishverananda Vedic Research Institute (Hoshiarpur), 2008.

As was said, the unifying theme of the studies comprising this volume is the anteriority of Vedic over all other IE branches and its closer proximity to the mother tongue now lost irretrievably, despite the abortive efforts to "reconstruct" it (see papers 1 and 9); also the sister theme that Indoaryans are indigenous and Saptasindhu may, in fact, have been the ProtoIndoEuropean locus of diffusion, although a wide area from Saptasindhu to the Pontic Steppe seems just as feasible.

As these essays were written at different times and for different publications, very occasionally some of the material in them is repeated. The reader will consequently find some few repetitions in some articles. I beg to be forgiven for this overlapping, but it would have taken very long to make the necessary deletions and corrections in the various texts whereas the reader can quickly skip the offending repetition. In any case, I doubt whether anyone will sit and read the entire volume without frequent breaks. I recommend one paper at a time.

I wish to thank all the editors here who have given their permission for the use of articles printed in their publications. My thanks also to Koenraad Elst who encouraged me to put the papers together for this volume. Finally I must acknowledge with gratitude that all this effort would have been impossible without the help of my secretary Mrs Daphne Sakalis Oikonomou who painstakingly typed the original drafts and retyped them for this publication.

One: **Indigenous Indoaryans and the Ṛgveda**

I. Abstract

In this paper I argue that the IndoAryans (IA hereafter) are indigenous from at least 4500 (all dates are BCE except when otherwise stated) and possibly 7000. In this effort are utilized the latest archaeological finds and data from Archaeoastronomy, Anthropology and Palaeontology. I use in addition neglected cultural and linguistic evidence. I find no evidence at all for an invasion. The new term "migration" is a misnomer since a migration could not have produced the results found in that area. The *Ṛgveda* (=*RV*) is neither post-Harappan nor contemporaneous with the ISC (=Indus-Sarasvatī Culture) but much earlier, ie from the 4th millennium (with minor insignificant exceptions) and perhaps before.

II. Introduction

1. Two things must be said at the outset. First, an unambiguous decipherment of the Indus script would most probably settle the issue of the IndoAryan origin. All claims so far, whether by sanskritists (Rao et al) or by dravidianists (Parpola et al) are unconvincing as BB Lal's survey shows succinctly (1997:203-14). E Bryant's more recent survey (2001:177-84) concurs with Lal: Bryant thinks S Kak's (sanskritic) efforts promising (181-2) and mentions M Witzel's thought that the Indus script may be Munda (184). But unless finds with longer legends or other writings are unearthed, the Indus script (like the Phaistos disc of Crete) will not be deciphered easily. Consequently I shall ignore this and make the best of the other available evidence.

Second, at any time new finds may emerge (eg objects of iron from, say, 2800; large settlements in the Ganges area from 3000; tablets with recognisable Dravidian writing from 2500; or whatever else) that will change radically whatever picture we now have.

2. I am a sanskritist with a little Greek and less Latin. I am of Greek nationality (but a British subject) and although I have twice visited India for extended periods I know very little about the modern religion(s) there and practically nothing about its politics (except the unfortunate conflict over Kashmir). As an undergraduate and postgraduate at SOAS (London) in the 1960s I absorbed the mainstream "Aryan Invasion Theory" (AIT hereafter); for G Dales's work that knocked down Sir M Wheeler' s extravagant view had not yet percolated down to us. In any case I was then, and continued to be for many years afterwards, interested in Sanskrit only, the dramatic works and the Upanishads and Vedānta; I had no interest at all in the early history of India. Subsequently I taught the AIT with the South Russian Steppe as the locus of dispersal of the IndoEuropeans (IE hereafter) for 18 years and I wrote a Course of Sanskrit (in Md Greek) in which I actually concocted fictitious passages about the Aryans invading with chariots and subduing the natives who thought it prudent to accept them and cooperate! In 1987, I began to wonder about the AIT. In the same year I went to India and collected much material which took a few years to sort out and digest, since I had little acquaintance with Indian archaeology and early history. What became abundantly clear in the early 1990s (and filled me with incredulity) was the fact that there was **no evidence whatever** for any invasion (which by that time was becoming "migration"). In 1996 I abandoned the AIT in all its forms and the mainstream chronology for Sanskrit literature. The experience was doubly painful: first it was not easy to give up an idea I had taken for granted for more than 20 years; second I could not understand why mainstream indologists adhered to the AIT so passionately, since it was supported only by linguistic data that could, in any event, be interpreted in different ways.[1]

3. I shall not be dealing with the history of this issue (see Kazanas 1999 and 2001a). JP Mallory (1973) and recently E Bryant (2001) have dealt with it very fully. I shall only mention the fact that M Witzel attacked several scholars who since the early 1990s manifested support for the Indian Indigenous Origin (IIO hereafter); amid various criticisms (especially 2000:13) he used the term "revisionists" (also 2001:22), ignoring obviously that in the early 19th century many European scholars took India, on the strength of Sanskrit, to be the original homeland (Mallory 1973:26-9). Even after scholars revised their views and, rejecting India, adduced different locations from the Baltic to the Balkans and eventually rewrote Indian (pre-)history, there was a succession of Indian scholars, mainly, who maintained the IIO in one form or another (Rao 1880, Aurobindo 1914, Dhar 1930 et al, et al). The term "revisonist" is therefore inapplicable. Witzel ignores also that Copernicus, Kepler and Galileo were 'revisionists' in rejecting the geocentric system of Ptolemy (which held sway for some 1500 years) and, against an oppressive and repressive mainstream opinion (and officialdom), reinstated—with improvements—the heliocentric system of Aristarchos of Samos (3rd cent BCE).

4. E Bryant' s *The Quest for the Origins of Vedic Culture* (2001) is a long overdue study presenting the indigenist views, advocated mainly by Indians. Witzel describes it as "a balanced description and evaluation of the two century old debate" and Mallory as "not only an important work in the field of Indo-Aryan studies but a long overdue challenge for scholarly fair play" (both on the back jacket of the 2001

---

[1]I give this biographical note to forestall any suspicions that I am of Indian extraction or have any connections with India, though I do correspond with some Indian scholars.

publication). Certainly, Bryant' s work is invaluable and balanced and fair in the usual academic way but like so many other studies it makes the issue seem far more complicated than (in my view) it is by giving undue weight to arguments that do not deserve it and by ascribing undue importance to the linguistic side.[2]

The IE and IA issues are, of course, primarily linguistic but only in that the terms IE or Proto-Indo-European (PIE hereafter) refer to languages, not races or nations. This does not mean at all that scattered linguistic data and conjectures, about which there are very grave disagreements and which give no sure dates, can be taken to be the decisive arbiter in this issue. (See IX 2, 3 & 4.) *The issue is no longer a linguistic one*. The nature of IA or Vedic and its relationship to other IE languages—which are purely linguistic matters—were decided long ago, quite properly, by the discipline of Philology. Other disciplines did not intervene at any time. But today the issue is quite different: we are now concerned with the question *when and how* Vedic appeared at its historical habitat. Since Vedic and other languages did not sound of themselves in a vacuum but were spoken by human beings, these questions involve movements of peoples and their material cultures. Philology has little competence in this field; even Historical Linguistics would be trespassing since it deals with changes within language(s) in relative not absolute chronology—actual dates being derived from other sources. This is the field of History and in prehistoric

---

[2]Two different examples should suffice. Bryant adopts too lightly H Hock's view that "It seems simpler to posit one migration into India" rather than many out of it (p 146). This applies not only to India but to all other proposed urheimats and has no validity as an argument. (See below IX, 3) He also states that the Greeks and the Scandinavians "preserve no mention of their migrations into their historical territories" to counterbalance the non-mention of migration in the *RV*. Bryant's statement is untrue. Both Greeks and Scandinavians do preserve some memories of migration, wrong though they seem to us (see III, below).

times of Archaeology and related disciplines. The difficulties besetting the larger IE issue are due, I think, to the fact that linguists continue to arrogate to themselves the competence of these other disciplines. Just as experts from other sciences do not intervene in Linguistics, so linguists should not tell historians, archaeologists et al what to do or how to do it just because the latter's finds are at variance with linguistic wishes.

5. Mallory ended his overview of the "IE problem" (1973:60) with this perceptive statement: "a solution to the problem will more than likely be as dependent on a re-examination of the methodology and terminology involved as much as on the actual data themselves". The method of approach in the West has not changed since then. Methodology itself (and terminology, which may be regarded as one of its aspects) depends on the human element known as conditioning, or prejudice, which often reproduces mechanically inherited forms. And this, because scholars do not turn their attention inwards to examine the very instrument with which they do all their studying, thinking, comparing, etc. Attachment to any notion is not healthy: Plato asked of "academics" (=the students at his Academy) to let the mind (or ψυχή *psuchē* 'soul'), free of all concerns, rest periodically on its own with true, immutable Being (*Phaidōn* 79C, *Phaidros* 247C-E). Max Müller explained that his conjectural chronology of the *Ṛgveda* (*RV* hereafter; the Vedic Hymns 1200-1000, Brāhmaṇas etc 1000-800, and so on) was only a *terminus ad quem* adding "we should not forget that this is a constructive date only and that such a date does not become positive by mere repetition" (1916:34). Many scholars c 1900 CE tried to push the date of the *RV* to an earlier date, arguing that the 200-year periods are far too short for the development of these different types of literature and using such evidence as was then available, like astronomical data. Nevertheless the conjectural chronologies fell into mere repetition and became established dogma.

6. At that time (1875-1900 CE) Philology had developed considerably whereas Archaeology was in its gestation period. It was unavoidable that linguistic considerations should play an important role. As it happened, such considerations played a decisive role and the eminent linguist M. Emeneau wrote (1954:282): "At some time in the second millennium BC a band or bands of speakers of an Indo-European language, later to be called Sanskrit, entered India over the north-west passes. This is our *linguistic doctrine* which has been held now for more than a century and a half. There seems to be no reason to distrust the *arguments* for it..." (my emphasis). The statement contains a factual error since it was less than a century that this doctrine had gained currency (see § 3, above). But the important point is that Emenau makes a judgment about a historical occurrence admitting it to be a received doctrine and using the word 'arguments' in its support, not, as one might expect in a case of historical events, terms like 'evidence', 'data', 'records' or 'testimony'.

J Shaffer, archaeologist/anthropologist, wrote succinctly about this situation: "The Indo-Āryan invasion(s) as an academic concept in 18th- and 19th-century Europe reflected the cultural milieu of that period. Linguistic data were used to validate the concept that in turn was used to interpret archaeological and anthropological data. What was theory became unquestioned fact that was used to interpret and organise subsequent data. It is time to end the linguistic tyranny..." (1984:88). Let me give an example or two of the received theory being used to interpret and organise other data. Accepting the *RV* date as c 1200, Witzel examines the Near-East (NE hereafter) chariots (2000:6; 2001:47, 59ff) then foists them onto the *RV* pointing out that such chariots (those in the *RV* also) are subsequent to 1700! He disregards the few details of *RV* chariots that make them quite different from the NE ones. Another example: an old text *Jyotiṣa Vedāṅga* dealing with Astronomy, has a certain astronomical reference which was thought by some to denote a date

1370-1150 (Witzel 2001:72-3) but Witzel writes that the style of this work places it during the last centuries BC and ignores completely that the chronological scheme itself is being questioned.[3] The noted sanskritist Aklujkar (Professor at British Columbia, Canada) does not consider the mainstream chronology incontestable and writes "only *relative* chronology has been well argued for" (1996:66).

One does not begin the study of the history of a people, even a people speaking a particular language (IE in this case), with highly ambiguous and controversial linguistic considerations. As was said, these are useful in establishing relations with other members of the language family but not in establishing dates. Linguistic phenomena would have been more significant only if there had been attested in the region at least one non-IE language of equal antiquity as Vedic (like Etruscan in Italy and Basque, still alive, and Iberian in Spain). But to start with the assumption that *Vedic was an intruder when no other language of equal age was attested* was wrong method or defective scholarship. Chronologies are usually established by written records; in the absence of such documents,we turn to archaeological finds and similar datable evidence.The unreliability of the linguistic data and theories based thereon can be amply demonstrated by the very case we are investigating. The same philological data with minor variations and differences in emphasis have been examined and interpreted differently by different scholars who reach thereby different conclusions. Thus T Burrow (1973:9ff) on purely philological considerations takes central Europe as the urheimat and the date of the dispersal from middle to late

---

[3]This prejudicial approach goes far deeper and has wider implications. A Zide a priori ruled out any possibility of a sanskritic language being that of the Indus script (1979:257). GL Possehl too stated on the same subject that "Indo-Aryan is dismissed since the Fairservis position is that... [it]... arrived in the subcontinent at ca 1500 BC" (1996:153). A Hitze states "Theories according to which the Indo-Aryans would be autochthonous cannot be substantiated" (1998:139 & n 2).

3rd millennium. Gamkrelidze and Ivanov (1985, 1990, 1995) posit as the PIE urheimat the region south of Caucasus and the date of the dispersal or migrations in the early 3rd millennium. From the same data SS Misra derives dates ranging in the 5th and 6th millennium and prefers N-W India (1992). I Diakonov favours the Balkans (1985) and G Owens takes Minoan to be the first IE language, the Greeks indigenous and the Aegean the cradle of PIE culture (1999). Others again have other views. Mallory examines summarily some of these conflicting "estimates" and cries out "Will the 'real' linguist please stand up" (1997:98). No linguist is saved simply because he/she claims to have "correct" data and method. The "when" and "how" are concerns of experts other than linguists.

7. Apart from the linguistic issue, however, we have here another subtle aspect. Since there are all these different claims for the urheimat (and some more on additional criteria) from the Baltic region to the Balkans, the Pontic Steppe (Mallory et al), Anatolia (Renfrew et al), Central Asia (Sargent 1997) and N-W India-and-Pakistan, then any one location is controversial. Why mainstream scholarship should single out and ostracize only N-W-India-and-Pakistan is incomprehensible—particularly when Archaeology and Anthropology since the early 1980s stressed that there was no trace of mass invasion in this area (Jarrige & Meadow 1980; Lal & Gupta 1984:343), unlike all other locations (see III, 3, below). Thus in a recent work (2001:138-9) Mallory mentions Europe, the Pontic Steppe and Anatolia as possible urheimats but not Northwest India.

In an article of this size one clearly can't deal with all authors and all details. I shall attempt to cover all important aspects but, as I said following Mallory, my methodology will be different. I feel certain that archaeologists will think I omit important aspects of their finds. Because of my method which assigns Philology to a subordinate position and must select from the vast field of Linguistics, philologists will feel even more offended. So be it. Taking it for granted that there is an IE family of languages and without speculating about the time depth and the form and extent of the PIE, I start with historical records. Since Witzel's and Bryant's studies are most recent, I shall refer to them frequently (and to Bryant with page number only). Naturally, I shall not reproduce all the data and arguments I have used in my published articles 1999, 2000, 2001c and 2001d.

III. Historical records

1. In the *RV* (and later Indic texts) there is no hint of the Āryas coming into the Saptasindhu[4], the land of the seven rivers in North India and Pakistan (as known today). AB Keith wrote "It is certain... that the Rrgveda offers no assistance in determining the mode in which the Vedic Āryans entered India... the bulk at least [of the *RV*] seems to have been composed rather in the country round the Sarasvatī river" (1922:79). Witzel thought he found references to an immigration but admits them to be "indirect" and finally wrote that the Brāhmaṇa texts "manage to garble the evidence" (1995b:321, 340). Several scholars indulge in semantic conjurings saying that various names in the *RV* refer to places and rivers in Afghanistan, Baluchistan, Iran etc, but this is not a very honest practice since by such interpreting (turning facts into metaphors and symbols, and vice versa) one can prove anything[5].

Even Witzel admits finally (2001 § 3) that the *RV* was composed "round the Sarasvatī river", as Keith put it.

---

[4]Some may feel offended by my use of 'Saptasindhu'. In the RV we find several references to the 7 rivers: I, 32, 12 and 35, 8 *saptá síndhūn* acc pl; I, 34, 8 *síndhubhiḥ* instr pl; etc, etc. Many others before me have used 'saptasindhu': it is short and most convenient (see Kazanas 2001b, § 14).

[5]R Kochhar, an Indian astrophysicist, surpasses the staunchest Western invasionist in having most of the action in the *RV* (and the *Rāmāyaṇa*!) set in Afghanistan (2000). Curiously, he makes little use of his own science, Astronomy. He admits that there are more than 150 references in the epic *MB*, and lists several (53-7, 112-3), but thinks it "not possible to single out those verses ... contemporaneous with the battle" (but see sect V, 3, below)...

Apart from its silence on a former homeland, or immigration, the *RV* contains positive indications about the Āryas' very long presence in Saptasindhu. Hymn X, 75 gives a list of names of rivers not in the order west-to-east, as we would expect from invaders advancing in that direction, but from east-to-west, as of a people long settled and having the east as a starting point of reference. Then there are passages expressing the Aryans' strong sense of being rooted in their lands when they recall their ancestors taking their place in the sacrifice "here", like the Angiras family (IV, 1, 3) or the Vasiṣṭhas (VII, 76, 4), etc.

2. Furthermore, the Vedic texts refer to peoples being exiled or driven away from Saptasindhu. The early *Aitareya Br*[6] (VII, 33, 6 or VII, 18) writes of sage Viśvāmitra exiling his 50 disobedient sons so that, in later periods, "most of the Dasyus are the descendants of Viśvāmitra, mostly in the east" (*VI* [6], 'andhra'). In the *RV* we have at least two similar and much more informative passages. *RV* VII, 18, 16 tells how Indra helped King Sudās defeat his numerically superior enemies (the 10 Kings), many of whom were of Aryan tribes, and "scattered them far over the earth" (*párā sárdhantaṃ nunude abhí kṣā́ṃ*). In VII, 6, 3 "Agni assailed repeatedly those Dasyus and from the east turned the unholy ones to the west (*...pūrvaś-cakāra-áparāṃ...*)". Now, to take the last reference, since the Dasyus are, according to the AIT, the native Dravidians or Mundas or whatever else, they should have been driven south; yet the text says unequivocally

... and mentions only two solar eclipses Oct 955 and July 857, which BN Achar shows to be quite wrong and irrelevant (2001:4-5). He cites Erdosy 1995 but not K Kennedy's paper therein (see IV, 1 below) which denies any demographic disruptions during or after the Harappan decline (ie no immigrants c 1900-1500); nor does he cite Shaffer (also in Erdosy) who, again, denies any intrusion before 600. Witzel dismisses most of Kochhar's conclusions (2001:11, n 26) but indulges his own fancy of finding reminiscences of foreign places (ibid § 9) and criticizes Hock who denies wholly the value of such a practice (n 41).

[6]Br = Brāhmaṇa. *VI* = Vedic Index.

"west". Consequently, the *RV* text not only negates any Aryan entry and displacement of 'natives' but states explicitly that both Aryans and Dasyus were driven westward and far over the earth. Even if we allow for some hyperbole here, it does not seem out of the bounds of possibility, surely, that people moved out in numbers to Iran and the NE[7]. Some suggest that IAs moved out also to spread the Aryan culture peaceably (Frawley 2001:6, 124, 168, 231, 290)—as in X 65, 11 'you spread the Aryan laws over the earth'. When we look at the historical records of other IE peoples we find that, unlike the IAs, many of them have preserved memories of migrations.

3. The Jews record clearly the early migration of Abraham from Ur (*Genesis* 11) — to mention also a non-IE people. The Iranian *Avesta* (Fargard I) provides strong recollections: it names 16 locations, from which the Iranians passed before

[7]Witzel wrongly states that "nowhere in the Vedas do we hear of a *westward* movement" (2001:15, n 42 & text). Considering that the RV was composed and preserved not as a text for modern scholars to play with, not as an encyclopaedia of Mythology nor a text for early Indoaryan History, the two references that I give (there may be more) should be considered adequate. He also ignores that those who left would not be there to write about it.

S. Talageri traces meticulously in the RV a westward movement (2000, ch 4). I am not fully convinced yet by this, but it deserves consideration. Witzel launched a critique (2001b): the derisive title is indicative of his attitude: 'Westward ho! The incredible wander-lust of the Ṛgvedic tribes exposed by S Talageri...' But Talageri (2001) met most points in a counter-attack admitting some errors and showing that Witzel had made both errors and misrepresentations. As the conflict is extensive and the issues many, I shall take 3 points only. **a)** W accuses T of ignorance of linguistics and zoology over T's taking *Jahnāvī* to be the Ganges (post-Vedic *Jahnāvī*) and *Śiṃśumāra* the Gangetic dolphin (2000:110-1) saying *Jahnāvī* is the wife of *Jahnu* while the dolphin is of the river Indus. T points out that a woman *Jahnāvī* is totally unknown in the whole Indic literature but is twice mentioned in the *RV* while Jahnu is not mentioned once; then, that W himself identifies *śiṃśumāra* with the Gangetic dolphin in two other papers of his (1987; 1999 EJVS 5-19, p 30: *non vidi*)! See also *T 2000:465, where W's identification is spelled out in full.* This means of course that, apart from anything else, W did not read T's book in full. ...

settling down, not in strict geographical order, and among them is *haptahendu* which sounds like the *saptasindhavaḥ*, the 7 Rivers of *RV*; no doubt, there are many regions on Earth with seven rivers, but only in NW India at that time do we find an actual reference naming a land of 7 rivers. The Irish Celts record 5-6 waves of immigrations but no place of origin (MacCanna, 1983:54-63). The Scandinavians recall coming from the south-east and Sturluson gives Troy as the place of origin (*Edda* 1-5, 57-8). The Anglo-Saxons composed poetry showing clearly that "the consciousness of their origin from and the strong links with the North West Europeans continued long in the new land [ie England]" (Branston, 1993:22). The Greeks recall mainly, though not exclusively, through Herodotos (I 57-8; II 51; V 44; etc) that the Pelasgians were the autochthonous people on mainland Greece who stayed put in Attica and elsewhere, while the invading Greek-speakers moved all over and southward (for other

... **b)** W stresses (§ 7) that *RV* VI 45 is late: "Applying the principles pioneered by Oldenberg, *RV* 6.45 can be shown to be a composite hymn built of *tṛcas* at an uncertain period... Such late additions must not be used as an argument for the age of the bulk of book 6". T points out that EV Arnold, who criticizes Oldenberg on some points, places this hymn among the oldest and that Witzel himself in his 1995 paper (p 317) states that this very hymn VI 45 is "an unsuspicious hymn" that is "not suspected as an addition". **c)** W attacks (§ 9): "Iranian has none of the local Panjab and UP loanwords that are found in Vedic, which means that the Old Iranian languages cannot come from Panjab". T replies: "W claims not only to identify 'non-Indoaryan' loanwords in Vedic, he can also identify the exact regions from which these 'loanwords' were borrowed: ... Punjab... UP... Bactria... loanwords! W knows, with scientific exactitude that loanwords, from *imaginary* 'substrate languages', which are found in both Vedic and Iranian are definitely from Central Asia and not from Punjab or UP and, equally, that loanwords found only in Vedic are from Punjab or UP not because his theory suggests these locations, but because he has found actual inscriptions from *pre-RV* eras in ... non-Indo-Iranian languages where these words are actually recorded!"

Enough said. W replied to T with one page and a half of vague generalities and the accusation that T used unreliable texts. He does not explain how he knows what the local lexicon was in ancient Panjab or UP!

details, Eleutheriadou, 1997:120-59). Archaeologists are uncertain about the 'coming of the Greeks' and the date but for the proto-Greeks give c 1900 or 2200 or c 3200 (Taylour 1990:14-5; Coleman 2000; Mallory 2001:140-1); a second wave of invasions at just after 1200 is much more certain. The Romans too thought they came from Troy (in Vergil's *Aeneid*). Though early (c 1620), the Hittite writings record no immigration, but they are hardly distinguishable from those of other NE cultures; nonetheless, historians OR Guerney (1990:13) and WE Dunstan (1998:161) and J Puhvel, the eminent hittitologist and comparativist (1994), regard them as intrusive in the area.

Thus as far as historical records go (and despite the fact that most of these may be more or less mythological), in comparison with their relatives, the Vedic people have a better claim for being indigenous. We know from other sources definitely that the Balts, Celts, Romans and Slavs migrated[8] (See Elst, 1999:194-7; for details Mallory 1989, ch 3.) The same holds for the Germanic peoples (we have already mentioned the Scandinavians), though there is some uncertainty about their early movements: as their literature (except for Wulfila's biblical translation into Gothic, 4th cent CE) is very late, ie 8th century CE (Baldi, 1983:124ff), any memory of a migration could well have faded away.

4. In summing up his extended survey of linguistic evidence Witzel tells us that the mode of the IA entry is "archaeologically **still little** traced"; it is, he states, securely traced in the texts (horses, chariots, religion etc) and from linguistics and possibly from future studies of the male Y chromosome (2001:55-6). Here we have an attempt at falsification ("little" when in fact it is *none*) and wishful thinking. Neither horses and chariots nor linguistic

---

[8]Here I ignore the Baltic people's 'tradition' of descent from India since it is very late and, perhaps, based on ideas current in the early 1800s, despite arguments to the contrary (Chatterji, 1968; also Singh 1995:64-5).

phenomena, such as Witzel provides, prove any entry. They are *interpretations* of facts by a mind already coloured by the AIT. I shall deal with horses, chariots and linguistics in later sections. I do not use the epic and puranic genealogies and vast spans of time because I consider them unnecessary. At various places, but mainly § 19 (p 57), Witzel dismisses as "*worthless*" all dates based on the native tradition that has the onset of the Kaliyuga in 3102. True, the tradition, which is found in Epics, Purāṇas and astronomers, which knows nothing of an invasion but, on the contrary, has the IAs spreading out with their culture in all directions, and which places the *RV* (its arrangement) just before 3102, appears to be late, within, say, 1st-6th centuries CE. But we must not ignore the weighty evidence of the classical sources (the Megasthenes report c 312-280 BC) giving related chronologies. Arrian (*Indika* 1, 9), Pliny (VI, 21, 4) and Solinus (52, 5)—all give dates of 6000+ for Indian royal genealogies: so this aspect of the tradition is at the *very latest of the 4th century BC*. I am not claiming here that the tradition is necessarily correct in all (though it could be in most of) its aspects but only that it is not as late as it seems at first sight. The evidence provided now by Archaeoastronomy will have something to say on this matter (see sect V, below).

One final point on historical records. Grammarians (Yāska, Pāṇini, Patañjali) distinguish between sacred *mantras* and correct worldly usage and vulgar, ungrammatical speech, but not of loans from non-Sanskritic indigenous languages. In their attempt to keep Sanskrit pure they would have been doubly careful about such loans. True, loans in Vedic might well have been forgotten, but, equally true, we don't know this for a fact and the dates for the grammarians are given in the light of the AIT and should be now *sub judice*. Similarly, the Greek and the Chinese visitors' records of India mention no subject-people speaking a non-Sanskritic language. (In contrast, Herodotos states explicitly (I 58) that the Pelasgians in Attica learnt the Greek tongue and thereafter (II 51) began to consider themselves Greek. But they retained the memory of their former condition; Homer calls Zeus of Dodone 'Pelasgian' (*Iliad* 16, 233) while Aeschylus (*Suppliants* 250-9) talks of the παλαίχθων *palaichthōn* "old autochthon" Pelasgian.

The IAs had developed unrivalled mnemonic disciplines for preserving their sacred texts and culture through an oral tradition, though writing on highly perishable material cannot be ruled out altogether. I see no reason at all why they would not have preserved (as the Jews did) tales of their long trek to Saptasindhu particularly if, as the AIT has had it, the *RV* hymns were commposed soon after the arrival c 1500. So many other people are not ashamed to admit they are immigrants. Why should they—especially when they admit internecine conflicts and other unrighteous acts?... Yet they have left no statement of immigration the way other cultures have. Of course the *RV* is not a record of historical events: we call it "mythology" but it was faithfully and scrupulously preserved by the IAs because for them it was sacred Revelation. This is analogous to the Hebrew writings of the Old Testament, which was also sacred Revelation not only for the Jews but also for billions of Christians. Just as the OT contains historical events like migrations, battles, successions of kings, etc, so does the *RV*—except that it mentions no immigration.

There is, then, nothing in the "written" records that supports the AIT.

IV. Archaeology, Palaeontology, Anthropology

1. Writes JM Kenoyer, specialist in the archaeology of the Indus Valley: "[T]here is no archaeological or biological evidence for invasions or mass migrations into the Indus Valley between the end of the Harappan phase, about 1900 BC and the beginning of the Early Historic Period around 600 BC" (1998:174). Shaffer and Lichtenstein confirm this emphasizing the continuity of the indigenous culture (1999).

The absence of archaeological evidence began to be noted in the late 1960s. Jarrige and Meadow established (1980) the indigenous Mehrgarh culture with cereal cultivation c 6500 on the Bolan, north-west of Mohenjadaro and its gradual spread south-east to the Indus where it developed into the Harappan or ISC (=Indus-Sarasvati Culture) c 3000. Subsequent studies confirmed this: "The shift by Harappan groups and, perhaps, other Indus Valley cultural mosaic groups, is the only archaeologically documented west-to-east movement of human populations in South Asia before the first half of the first millennium BC" (Shaffer & Lichtenstein 1995:135).

Other investigators provide additional evidence from their own branches of research. No flow of genetic traits occurred from Bactria into Saptasindhu c 1800: "Parpola's suggestion of movement of Proto-ṚgVedic Aryan speakers into the Indus Valley by 1800 is not supported by our data. Gene flow from Bactria occurs much later and does not impact Indus Valley gene pools until the dawn of the Christian Era" (Hemphill & Christensen 1994). K Elst, who quotes this passage, explains that the later flow is apparently that of the Shaka and Kushana invasions (1999:232; also Bryant, 231). K Kennedy (in Erdosy, 1995) concurs with this view: "There is no evidence of demographic disruptions in the northwestern sector of the [Indian] subcontinent during and immediately after the decline of the Harappan culture" (again in Elst, 233; also Bryant, 231). However, Kennedy's investigation of the skeletal record does show a break at c 4500[9]. This may or may not have wider implications (see n 12).

---

[9]Personally, I distrust such finds but only because, where they indicate a flow of genes, we do not know if it was a migration, or visiting merchants, or slaves, or whatever." (Kazanas 1999:18-9). Witzel mentions the "male Y chromosome" that has not been studied yet adequately and quotes Cavalli-Sforza (2001: § 7 & n 23), but the Cavalli-Sforza work has difficulties and contradictions (1996:5, 29, 32, 210, 299, etc) and the whole discussion is full of uncertainty. Lord Renfrew pointed out that in this area there are "difficulties of methodology not yet resolved" and gave examples (1997:89).

More recent genetic studies show that this break is not indicative of an influx of new people, the IAs, and even suggest that European peoples descended from the inhabitants of SE Asia. Cavalli-Sforza and his team state that "Indian tribal and caste populations derive largely from the same genetic heritage of Pleistocene [=10000 to 3 mya] southern and western Asians and *have received limited gene flow from external regions since the Holocene* [=c 10000 to present]. The phylogeography [=neighbouring branches] of the primal mtDNA and Y-chromosome founders suggest that these southern Asian Pleistocene coastal settlers from Africa would have provided the inocula for the subsequent differentiation of the distinctive eastern and western Eurasian gene pools". (Emphasis and square brackets added; Cavalli-Sforza 2003 These data have been put in after 2003 with some revisions for this publication.)

2. Witzel admits the absence of archaeological and palaeontological evidence for an immigration: "*So far* archaeology and palaeontology, based on multi-variate analysis of skeletal features, have not found a new wave of immigration into the subcontinent after 4500 BCE (a separation between the Neolithic and Chalcolithic populations of Mehrgarh), and up to 800 BCE" (2001:9: my emphasis). In view of some linguists' disparaging remarks about Archaeology (see n 10b and n 21) please note the change from "invasion" to "(im-)migration": Archaeology of course, and not Linguistics, showed beyond doubt that the Harappan cities were simply abandoned, not destroyed by enemy-attackers. Note also the qualifier "so far". It is customary with invasionists not to be content with stating the fact of absence of evidence but to add that it is only until now implying thereby that the evidence *will* turn up. Ten years after Dales' first publications on the true causes of the collapse of the Harappans and the work of other archaeologists (eg Rao 1973), Burrow wrote: "The Aryan *invasion* of India is recorded in no written document, and it cannot *yet* be traced archaeologically, but it is nevertheless firmly established as a *historical* fact on the basis of comparative philology" (1975:21: my emphasis). The terms "invasion" and "historical fact" betray a very deep prejudice no less than the little word "yet". This is a sample of the linguistic tyranny that Shaffer mentioned (sect II, above). Today, more than 25 years later, the evidence is still not forthcoming. Edmund Leach too dismissed linguistics and the AIT: "Because of their commitment to a unilateral segmentary history of language development that needed to be mapped onto the ground, the philologists took it for granted that proto-Indo-Iranian was a language that had originated outside India or Iran... From this we derived the myth of the Aryan invasions." Leach went further: "Indo-European scholars should have scrapped all their historical reconstructions and started again from scratch. But this is not what happened. Vested interests and academic posts were involved" (Leach 1990).

R & B Allchin, British archaeologists (Cambridge), begin their 1982 study of the ISC by stressing its continuity but in ch 11 they usher in the Aryans; they also note the presence of several cultural elements in the ISC and point out their similarity with elements in "later Vedic Literature" (1982:203). Here one should note that it is **the later Vedic Literature not the *RV* itself.** In their 1997 study they again stress the continuity (p 191), then, following A. Parpola, they bring in the Aryans: "Their presence *should* therefore be in evidence archaeologically... But as yet it is **scarcely** attested in the archaeological record *...presumably because* their material culture and lifestyle were already indistinguishable from those of the existing population" (pp 221-2: my emphasis). Here we note the linguistic device subtly suggesting the existence of evidence (*...scarcely* attested) when there is none. Then there is the subtle contradiction in the pleonastic use of "as yet": for if the material culture and lifestyle were indistinguishable then obviously there will never appear any distinguishing evidence. Note also the mingling of a hypothetical explanation (...presumably because) with actual facts. The Allchins are saying that the Aryans lived in close proximity to the ISC natives, acquired their "material culture and lifestyle" (ie clothing, tools, weapons, means of transport, building methods and the like) but not their language, *nor writing* (?!), then gradually infiltrated the ISC society or entered in two waves (so Parpola), took over and imposed their own language and religion expunging the native ones from the area. I might add here Witzel's "successive waves of migrations" (1995a:337)[10] and trickling or "transhumance movements" (2001:§ 11).

---

[10]a) In this study Witzel talks of a peaceful immigration but also uses the terms "battles" and "campaigns" (324), "initial conquest" (326) and "frequent warfare" (339) thus indicating that beneath the lipservice to "migration" (which became fashionable) lurks the notion of invasion. The impression is supported by his use as an (elite) "dominance model" of the "Norman French introduced by a few knights and their followers in Anglo-Saxon England" (2001:30, n 85). He obviously does not know that the "few knights", (most of them literate, unlike the IAs) had in fact 12000 soldiers: led by William the Conqueror (no peaceful immigration with such a title), they hewed down King Harold and his loyal thanes then proceeded to destroy villages in Southern England until London accepted William as their lawful king (Trevelyan 1972:106). The example was used also in Witzel's 1997 work (p xxii).

b) I can see why Witzel mentions C Ehret (2001:12, 22) but Ehret's views, formed mostly from well documented cases in Africa are not relevant to prehistoric Saptasindhu and, in any case, I would like to see some real paradigms especially where Ehret says that the "linkage of pottery and ethnicity breaks down in class societies" (1988:572). The reference to Ehret is thus neither illuminating nor relevant. The quote from Anthony 1995 (also vague and irrelevant) cannot be traced in Witzel's Bibliography.

Witzel's n 177 (§ 0 on Archaeology) says that recently some archaeologists "tested in Papua—New Guinea what the material remains of some five different linguistic communities belonging to one particular area would look like". After a few years they dug them up "and found the same material culture! So much for the often used and alleged overlap of language and culture". In other words, archaeologists are useless and should leave all such investigations to linguists. But note that this esteemed Professor does not bother to specify who were the archaeologists, what was the area, who were the communities, what were these "material remains" and so on. ...

There are enormous gaps in the logic of the alleged IA migration. The Harappans were literate and civilized, maintaining their 1000 year old culture through peaceful means, trade and perhaps religion—rather than expansion through war and conquest. Their area is given as 1.5 million sq km (Rao 1991:1), but I suspect it was much bigger: recent archaeological finds show that Harappan wheat was cultivated in the region of Bihar (ie far to the east of Saptasindhu) at 2300 (Frawley 2001:70-71). Then c 2000-1800, because of ecological and environmental changes including the alteration of river routes and the desiccation of the old Sarasvatī, they, or many of them, began to move eastwards to the Gangetic basin. At about this time enter our illiterate Aryans, according to the AIT.

3. The end result of all this is the aryanization of North India (Witzel 1995:106). But apart from non-testable vague conjectures, no invasionist gives a reasonable explanation of how this enormous event materialized in so vast an area. Renfrew used the model of *elite dominance* not precluding conquest or some form of violence. Witzel seemed to use a similar confused model in his 1995 study but abandoned this and, like the Allchins, adopted a more sophisticated process of acculturation and infiltration (2001:§ 10-11)[10b]. But all the parallels given are not true, only approximate. I can't find a true parallel situation. The Kassites and Mitanni who came from the East and ruled Mesopotamia (Dunstan 1998) are

---

... Instead, on this vaguest of generalities he condemns the entire science of Archaeology. (For similar views, see also n 21, below.)

That this superior attitude towards other scholars and scientists is customary is shown by a brief exchange between Prof Witzel and Dr Wujastyk (*Indology* website, On Line 8/3/2000). Wujastyk writes: "I am afraid that I neither trust nor believe anything said by atomic scientists about humanistic subjects (or most other subjects). Let's try to keep this list scholarly, shall we!" And Witzel agrees(!). Thus in this steam-roller statement scientists are considered incompetent or irrelevant for "most other subjects". To be scholarly is equated with indeterminate "humanistic subjects"—and a supercilious attitude(?). It is all rather extraordinary.

thought to be "elite dominance" groups but, in fact, they lost their IE culture (preserved in some few linguistic elements, proper names and gods) and got totally engulfed by the highly developed, literate local culture(s). The Anglo-Saxons in Britain managed to drive the Celts westward and confined the Picts to the north, but they succeeded because they invaded in large numbers. When the Slavs (illiterate barbarians) made their waves of incursions into Byzantine Greece in the 8th century CE as far south as central Peloponnese, they were soon afterwards absorbed by the natives. The Vikings founded a state at Kiev in the Slav heartland and conquered Normandy but despite "elite dominance" they got absorbed into the Slavic and Latin cultures respectively. The Normans invaded England and Norman French certainly supplanted O English as the official language but they were numerous, literate and conquerors (n 10a above). We cannot find anywhere an example where an illiterate people immigrate peacefully in small waves then impose their culture on the literate civilized natives.

If there was acculturation and the Aryans had acquired the "material culture and lifestyle" of the Harappans *before* they entered into Saptasindhu, as the Allchins suggest, then the *RV* hymns ought to reflect some Harappan elements (urbanization or ruins, fixed fire-hearths, bricks, cotton, silver, etc); but it is the later Vedic texts, mainly the Brāhmaṇas and not the *RV* that do so (see § 2, above, Allchins' statement). It is impossible that while texts many centuries later than the *RV* should contain ISC aspects, the *RV* itself, although being closer to the ISC, contains no traces of these aspects. But we must also ask why the Harappans, who were moving eastward then, should abandon their language and religion and adopt those of the Aryans. It is all very well to erect theories and models and write glibly about "elite dominance" and the like, but all this does not even so much as come near the question. A second question is why would they allow and accept the renaming of their mountains, plains and rivers. This too is not in the least explained satisfactorily. When immigrants arrive in a new populous country, they may retain their own culture, their language and religion, but, especially if they come "trickling" peacebly in small numbers, they learn the local language and customs and certainly do not rename places, rivers and lakes. Such at any rate has been the behaviour of the Jews and Gypsies in all the centuries of their wandering. Where renaming has taken place, it is invariably after invasion and conquest (though even conquest does not always have this result, for Greeks retained their religion and language and place names despite 400 years of Ottoman rule)[11].

In this region of the Seven Rivers, then, we have an archaeologically well attested culture that seems to have no literature at all (other than the briefest inscriptions: no code of laws, no religious hymns or secular songs, no fables and tales), and then, in immediate succession, *an illiterate people, not archaeologically attested*, produces all the kinds of literature that the previous culture lacked. It is a most amazing paradox (first noted by D Frawley), an astonishing coincidence of space, time and people. The case of the Mycenaeans and Minoans comes to mind. But the Mycenaeans are well attested archaeologically; they produced no literature that we know of, only inventories (Ventris and Chadwick 1973), and were invaders and conquerors: so the parallel is not true.

One could of course suppose a model of cultural penetration combining technology with ideology (and perhaps religion), as English spread in the modern world. How feasible would such a model be? It would not be very

---

[11]Many Greeks became Muslims, of course, either through coercion or choice. But while many others learnt Turkish and served as advisors to the Sultan, officials and even governors in some districts (Serbia, Rumania), they abandoned neither their Greek language nor their Orthodox faith. The Jews in diaspora have in some cases behaved similarly.

accurate since (a) English was taken to North America, South Africa, Australia and New Zealand by different kinds of immigrants whereas in other countries it is only the second language, as French and German were before the 1940's; (b) today we have very fast transport and satellite communications.

The AIT is, of course, possible—just as it is possible to be struck by lightning in one's bed, or to fall from the 10th floor on the lawn below and live with only a few bruises. Many wondrous things are possible in life, but the question is—do they really happen?... And because it seems so unrealistic I refuse to accept the notion of any kind of (im)migration. If there was an Aryan entry c 1500 and "aryanization", it could only have been an invasion.

4. The supreme and overruling fact is that, despite decades of fervent search, there is not a shard of archaeological evidence (as Witzel admits, 2001:n 7 and text) of an invasion. Many have done much earth-digging and book-research but have found nothing (eg Mallory 1989:46ff, 227-9; 1997:113). It would be too tedious to refer to all this literature. Suffice it to quote Elst who has surveyed all the literature and says of B Sargent's 1997 *Genèse de l' Inde*, "the Indo-Aryan invasion doesn't get farther than Pirak in Baluchistan" (1999:320). V Sarianidi too cannot get any closer with his NE Aryan invaders (1999).

A final note on Archaeology. Much has been written about *pur* "fort, town (?)" and Witzel suggests this may refer to the Indus cities (2001:63). There is only one insuperable difficulty applying to all scholiasts he cites: there is not one mention in *RV* of *iṣṭakā* 'brick', the material of the Indus cities, which, however, appears in post-rigvedic texts (see § 2, above). The *RV* has purs of metal (!eg IV 27, 1 *ā́yasī*) and of stone (eg IV 30, 20 *aśmanmáyin*). The stone pur is understandable in our terms. But what is the metal pur?... Furthermore, in VIII 1, 8 we find an extraordinary pur—*cariṣṇu* 'mobile'—which belongs to Śuṣṇa, generally thought to be the drought-demon. Now, how mobile and metallic purs can be Indus cities, or other immobile stone-structures found in adjacent areas, is not explained by all these experts. (No, I don't know what these purs are. I don't claim to understand much in the *RV*. But now see paper Four in this volume on 'Rigvedic *pur*'.)

Personally I would be content to rest here. The linguistic complications, which are not complications, can be easily accommodated and interpreted in this scheme of things. Nonetheless, there is more evidence of very firm nature, so we may as well look at it. I shall deal with the aspects of horses, chariots and the Sarasvatī further down.

V. Archaeoastronomy

BN Narahari Achar (of Memhis, USA) has used a combination of computer programmes to generate on the screen of a computer monitor the sky formation above any given location at any given time as far back as 8000 BCE. With his "Planetarium software", as he calls his apparatus (2001:2), he has reconstructed a simulation of the ancient star positions in the sky above North India and was able to correlate various astronomical references in the ancient Indic texts with the formations (and dates) displayed in his monitor. Astronomical data have been under investigation since the early 1800s and many studies of varied results and quality were produced in the 20th century (Bryant 2001:35, 251-61; Witzel 2001:§ 29-30). I shall not be examining any of these because, (a) they are too numerous; (b) they have been examined for the most part by Bryant and Witzel; (c) they are all superceded now by Achar's Archaeoastronomy.

1. The first paper (1999, published in EJVS 5-2) dealt with a reference in *Śatapatha Br* II, 1, 2, 2-3 to the effect that the Kṛttikās/Pleiades are fixed in and do not swerve from the east. This reference has been examined, analysed, interpreted and discussed ad nauseam yielding all kinds of results according to the scholar's desires. S Kak arrived at a date 2950 (1994:35). This comes very close to what Achar finds, namely that such astronomical events could have been observed only c 3000. Achar mentions that SB Dikshit had propounded the very same idea about 100 years earlier but later Western scholars rejected it by claiming that the *ŚB* phrase "never swerve from the east" means something else. Witzel writes an introduction to Achar's article suggesting we should not really believe what the *ŚB* says and adds a long piece of his own on the Pleiades again "correcting" any "wrong" impressions we may have had from Achar's paper. All this is compressed in his 2001 study, § 29; he adds the objection, however, that as "iron" is mentioned in the *ŚB* and the iron age does not begin in India before, say, 1200, the text cannot originate at c 2950. He reiterated this objection in relation to another astronomical reference (2001:n 222). All this is hardly serious. If the Brāhmaṇa wanted to say something else, it would have done so. As for the use of "iron"—this objection will not stand. The Vedic texts (other than the *RV*) do mention a "swarthy metal" *śyāma* or *kārṣṇā-/ kṛṣṇā-/ yasa* but there are no references to smelting or other processing of this metal, only to the metal in contrast to other metals (*Vedic Index*). Since iron objects were found from 2600 in Harappan sites, Afghanistan and Baluchistan (Possehl & Gullapalli 1999:159-61), it is not remarkable that these texts should mention this metal. All this is well known to Witzel. Then, in Egypt, meteorite iron is known from 3000+. But there is another consideration probably unknown to most indologists. This "swarthy metal" could be blackened copper: to harden copper, the metal is heated up (but below melting point), then left to cool down without use of water and this blackens the copper, not with soot that can be wiped off; a similar effect is produced by oxidation with various sulfides (Hughes & Row, 1982:92, 187). Thus the verse *AV* XI 3, 7 speaks of flesh *māṃsa* being *śyāma* 'swarthy metal' and blood *lohita* being *lohita* 'red copper'; since the ṛṣis probably knew that flesh is produced from and maintained by blood, the correspondence is quite apt–reddish copper for blood and (processed) black copper for flesh. Some have claimed that all this is speculation on my part and ignore the decades of speculation that *śyāma-* or *kṛṣṇa- āyas* is "black iron"! There is no problem. Consequently I see no reason to doubt Achar's results.

2. I see no reason to doubt Achar's second paper (2000) regarding the date of *Joytiṣa Vedāṅga*. Here evidence is provided that an astronomical reference in this text is not of a date c 400 as some western scholars think, nor of c 1300 as others claim (identifying the star Dhaniṣṭha with β Delphini) but c 1800, when Dhaniṣṭha, now identified with δ Capricorn, receives sun and moon together for the winter solstice (Achar 2000:177). Witzel does not know of Achar's paper but quotes others with dates 1370 and 1150. His objection here is that the style of the *joytiṣa* is that of late epic and therefore the text cannot be earlier than the last centuries BC. This again is hardly serious. Are we to suppose then that a sober scientist is publishing fabricated evidence or that the writer of the text cast back somehow and concocted a misleading astronomical situation? And this because of the vague and variable criterion of "style"? But style and dating therefrom depend on chronologies derived from the AIT which has the IAs arriving at Saptasindhu c 1500. This whole concept is now *sub judice*. Besides, the astronomical observations could have been recorded c 1800 and the text retouched later. However, as the Indians preserved in ancient times so much of their lore through oral tradition, they could have preserved the late-epic style also for many centuries.

3. We now come to the epic *Mahābhārata* and Achar's third paper (2001). In this, Achar examined some astronomical references in Bks III, V and XIII of the *MB*. His sky map showed that of all calculations by Westerners and Indians only that of KS Raghavan (1969) was correct: the exact year for the great war of the Bharatas on the basis of all these data was 3067. In Bk V, to take some examples,

Kṛṣṇa leaves for Hastināpura on the day of the *Revatī nakṣatra* in the month *Kaumuda* (=*Kārtika*, ie Oct-Nov) and arrives there on the day of *Bharaṇī* (81, 6ff); on the day of *Puswya* Duryodhana rejects all offers of peace; Kṛṣṇa departs on the day of *uttara phālguni* and says to Kṛṣṇa that the *amāvāsyā* (day of the New Moon) will come after 7 days, then Karṇa describes the positions of some planets at that time (141, 7-10). All these data converge in agreement with Achar's sky formation only in the year 3067. Whatever other data are contained in the *MB* and whatever other dates are suggested thereby, the passages with the astronomical facts for the year 3067 remain unaffected. The ancient Indian tradition of the Purāṇas and astronomers was fairly correct in placing the onset of the Kali Yuga at 3102 and the Bharata war 35 years earlier: the disparity is only 70 years. The medieval Kashmiri historian Kalhana (and his tradition), of course, seems to have been quite right in setting the previous cycle at 3067 (Elst 1999:104).

Here however we must take into account that people begin to create tales and poetic cycles in fixed forms 2 or 3 generations after the event they celebrate when the actors have departed from the stage. So 3067 is a good date for the origin of the core of the *MBh*. It is the date when the sons and grandsons of the warriors began to recite/sing in established forms the deeds of their ancestors.

Neither Bryant nor Witzel mention this paper, so we don't know what sort of objections will be raised[12]. But, if these

---

[12]Achar's work gives a concrete terminus. The IAs are definitely in Saptasindhu by 3000. Since the RV antedates the ISC we must postulate an earlier date. As the only other indication is the break in the skeletal record c 4500 (IV, 1, end, above), we could posit a putative entry at this date. If archaeologists agree with this, then the IAs are immigrants at c 4500 but autochthons surely by 1500. My main concern since 1996 has been to show that the IA-speakers were long-settled inhabitants (*palaichthon*) in Saptasindhu and that the *RV* is pre-Harappan. I do allow the possibility that IA had come at a much earlier date.

finds are correct (and I see no reason at all to doubt them), then, obviously, there is much work ahead for the younger indologists. As Leach said, the old chronologies and matters of style and so on will have to be scrapped and a new framework established. On the basis of the astronomical data the initial core of the *MB* belongs to the early 3rd millennium; the epic developed and grew in length in the subsequent 1000 years, when, c 1800, perhaps, a new change of style, language and rearrangement of contents took place leading to the final form in the last centuries BCE. This is conjectural, of course[13].

When, in 1996, I decided to abandon the mainstream view of the AIT and its chronology, I knew very little about astronomical data beyond the works of Jacobi and Tilak (both in the 1890s). Naturally it is good to have confirmation from Archaeoastronomy since heaven does not lie. But I had then done some comparative work on mythology and language (initially between Sanskrit and Greek) which also supported what the historical and archaeological records declared.

[13]Witzel derides (2001:n 170) the idea of "kings" in the Gangetic plains of the 7th millennium "when this area was populated by a few hunter and gatherer tribes". Here again preconception projects backwards models of a later age and gives later significance to rigvedic *rājan* 'king', *sabhā* 'assemly', etc. There is nothing remarkable about a tribe of gatherers and hunters having a "monarch" in 6000+ or 60000+. If there is a group of people, someone of necessity will be "first among equals" and if his leadership proves good he is bound to pass into history/ legend.

Civilization (or culture) surely is not just technology with large buildings, fast machines and weaponry, but, more importantly, an inner state whereby people know and give to all beings that which is due. (See eg the discussion in Plato's *Republic* 369Bff, especially 372A-B.) R Rudgley cites Prof Yasuda Yoshinory who found "a marvellous principle" for civilization, that is "a respect for and co-existence with nature" and wrote further: "Civilization begins to appear when a workable system for living, that is a proper relationship between man and nature, is established in accord with the features of a given region". Yoshinory wrote this in respect of the Jōmon Culture in Japan, 10700 to 400 (Rudgley 1998:31-3).

VI. The Preservation Principle (PP, for short)

In a 2001 paper I presented the Table of Deities that follows; it was built after extensive study. The IE branches examined were Vedic, Avestan, Hittite, Greek, Roman, Slavonic, Baltic, Germanic and Celtic; also some additional evidence from the Mitanni and the Kassites in the Near East. The Germanic branch comprises some early Germanic material (reported by Roman authors), some Anglo-Saxon and the later, richer Scandinavian lore. The Celtic branch consists of early Gallic (again reported mainly by Romans), Britannic, Welsh and Irish. (Other IE branches like Armenian, Tocharian, etc, provide negligible relevant material.)

I examined the various deities starting with the Vedic ones then moving westward. If I were to start with any other branch, I would soon need to shift to a different one and then another, because very few names of non-Vedic gods have correspondences in the other branches.

Abbreviations for languages used are: Av = Avestan; E = English; Gk = Greek; Gmc = Germanic; Gth = Gothic; Ht = Hittite; Ir = Irish; L = Latin; Lth = Lithuanian; Ltt = Lettish (or Latvian); Mcn = Mycenaean; OE = Old English; OHG = Old High German; ON = Old Norse; Rs = Russian; S = Sanskrit; Sc = Scandinavian; Sl = Slavonic; V = Vedic; W = Welsh.

Vedic	**Other IE branches**
Agni	Ht *Agnis*, Rs *Ogon*, L *ignis*, Lth *ugnis*, Ltt *uguns*. (Note: even the Iranians who had Fire worship did not preserve this name, not even as a demon like Indra, Sauru etc, though the stem appears in the name *dāštāγni*.)
Aryaman	Mcn *Are-mene* and Gk *”A ϱης Ares*; Celtic *Ariomanus* (Gaul)/ *Eremon* (Ireland); Sc *Irmin*. The ar-stem in most IE languages.

Aśvin-	Celtic *Epona* (Gaul); Mcn *Iqeja* (horse deity); Gk *ἵππος hippos* (Mcn *iqo*, dialect ikkos) L *equus*, OE and Ir *eoh*, Baltic *ešva*.
Bhaga	Kassite *Bugas*; Sl *Bogu*; Phrygian *Bagaios* (Ζεύζ, *Zeus* Gk); Gk *Φοῖβος Phoibos*.
Dyaus	Ht *DSiu-s*; Gk *Ζεύς /Δία- Zeus/Dia*; Roman *Ju[s]piter*; Gmc *Tîwaz*. Lth dievas (usually 'god' cognate with S deva, √*dīv*).
Indra	Ht *Inar(a)*; Mitanni *Indara*; Kassite *Indaš*; Celtic *Andrasta /Andarta*. Gk *ἀνήρ /ανδρ- anēr/andr-*, Av *indra* (a demon).
Marut-as	Kassite *Maruttaš*; Roman *Mars*; Irish *Morrighan*. The stem *mar/mor/mer-* etc is common in all IE branches.
Apāṃ- Napāt	Roman *Neptunus*; Celtic *Nech-tan* (Irish). Gk *ἀ-νεψ(=πσ)-ίος anēpsios*; L *nep-*; OHG *nevo*, OE *nefa*, OLth nep, etc.
Parjanya	Slavic *Perunŭ*; Baltic *Perkunas* (and variants); Sc *Fjörgyn* (*-n*, Thor's mother).
Ṛbhu	Gk *'Ορφεύς Orpheus*; Gmc *Elf* (and variants). *Gth arb-aiþs*(?); OSL *rabu*, R *rabota*; L *orbu* (S *arbha*, Gk *ὀρφανός orphanos*); etc.
Sūrya	Kassite *Šuriaš*; Gk Ηλιος *Hēlios*; Roman *Sōl*. Gth *savil*, ON *sol*, W *haul*, OSl *slunice*, Rs *solnce*, Baltic *Saule*.
Uṣas	Gk *'Ηως Ēos*; Roman *Aurora*; Gmc *Ēostre*. Lth *auśra*, Ltt *ausma*, W *gwawr*, etc.

Varuṇa	Mitanni *Uruwna*; Gk *Οὐϱαός Ouranos*; Baltic *Vēlinas* (– and cf *jur-* = sea). L *ūrīna*, O N *ver* (=sea).
Vāstoṣ-pati	Gk *'Εστία Hestia*; Roman *Vesta*. Gth *wisan* 'to stay'; OHG *wist* 'inhabiting'; Toch A/B waṣt/ost 'house'.
Yama	Sc *Ymir*; Av *Yima*.
	L *gemi-nus* (=twin); Gk *ζημία zēmia* (=damage), Av *yam*.

Attn: to this table should be added S *Mitra* and AV *Miϑra* also S Śrī and L *Ceres* (Gk *Kēr*?); inadvertently Ht Agnis was omitted from the original Table (while Ht *Wurun* (?) was wrongly included with Varuṇa). For a more up-to-date Table and discussion see paper Three 'The Diffusion of Indo-European Theonyms'.

Here the upper line shows the incidence of the deities and the lower shows the cognate stems that occur in languages where the deities are not preserved. Thus it might be argued that the Rs 'Ogon' is a direct borrowing of the Vedic Agni, who is an innovation, and, less plausibly, the same for Roman *Neptunus*, Celtic *Nech-tan*, but the presence of the cognate stems in Latin and Baltic for *agn-* and in Greek and Germanic for *nep-/ nev-* nullify such arguments. Some deities, again, may be disputed (eg Gk *Οὐϱανός Ouranos* or Sl *Bogu*) and be removed, but the pattern would not change appreciably. There are many more motifs that have been preserved in Vedic as against other individual branches. In fact there is hardly a major motif common in two or more of the other branches that is not found in the *RV*.

The all-inclusiveness of Vedic is all too apparent and quite remarkable. Greek and Germanic managed to preserve only half as many deities as Vedic. Yet, to take some examples, Gmc preserves the stem *nef-/ nev-* and *savil/ sol* but not the corresponding deities which are preserved in other branches. Greek too preserves *nep-, andr-*, and *zēm-* but, again, not the deities. Just as surprising are the very meagre retentions in Baltic, Slavic and, even more, in Anatolian. This situation can arise only from loss of memory of the significance of the mythological-religious figure over a long period of time because of lengthy geographical movement and/or absorption of new elements (sometimes forcibly, perhaps, through subjection) from other culture(s). It is a well known fact of history that people on the move for a long period tend to lose elements of their culture while their language suffers changes, as they meet with other cultures and/or have little leisure to pass their lore to the new generations—much more than a people remaining sedentary (Lockwood 1969:43; Burrow 1973:10; Hock 1991:467-9)[14].

This then I call the Preservation Principle or PP hereafter: the people or culture that has preserved most *ceteris paribus* has moved least. I examine and re-affirm this with some 500 lexical items in my paper 'Coherence & Preservation in Sanskrit' 2007, Vishvesvarananda Vedic Research Institute *Research Bulletin* (Hoshiarpur).

2. The all-inclusiveness of the *RV* in the realm of mythology is also observable in the sphere of poetics. There is hardly a major poetic device in the various IE branches that

---

[14]Elst thinks otherwise (1999:121) and cites the example of Old Icelandic as being Proto-North-Germanic although Iceland was not the urheimat. The example is unfortunate. Old Icelandic moved from Scandinavia in the 9th century CE. From that area, in the 1st century CE (or thereabouts) the Goths moved south-east ending in (what is now) Ukraine c 300 CE. So it would seem that the Old-Norse location was a sort of urheimat and a conservative one until about 700 CE when it began to undergo rapid change as the Vikings began to move in many directions (Lockwood 1972:96-7 & 121-2). This is not quite parallel to the movements of other IE and Gmc (sub-) branches: first, the Norsemen moved to Iceland within a short period in the 9th cent (during the oppressive reign of Harold Haarfagr) and, unlike all other branches, in ships; second, travel in ships is different from that on land with carts and animals; third, the ships met no other cultures on the seas, which subsequently protected Iceland from other influences. In these respects Old Icelandic is quite unique and therefore unsuitable for comparisons.

is not present in the *RV*. A significant aspect, for example, is that in early Greek poetry (epics of Homer and Hesiod, and some epigraphic material) the fairly strict syllabic metre (the hexameter with its dactylic, iambic and other variants) is preponderant with only traces of alliteration; in Germanic poetry alliteration prevails while the syllabic metre is very loose: both are present in the *RV*. The situation becomes very clear in the detailed examination of the large range of material in Watkins 2001. Early Irish poetry (6th century CE) has both metre and alliteration (and rhyme) but this hardly counts since the Irish poets knew these poetic devices "from Vergil and Ovid" (Watkins 2001:121) and, of course, the Romans developed them from the Greek culture. Of the Vedic poetic art Watkins writes: "The language of India from its earliest documentation in the Rigveda has raised the art of the poetic figure to what many would consider its highest form" (Watkins 2001:109).

3. "The language of India from its earliest documentation in the Rigveda": in this sphere too the PP operates most profoundly. Burrow, whose The Sanskrit Language (1973) is still the authority in this field, says: "Vedic is a language which in most respects is more archaic and less altered from original Indo-European than any other member of the family" (34: emphasis added); he also states that root nouns, "very much in decline in the earliest recorded Indo-European languages", are preserved better in Sanskrit, and later adds, "Chiefly owing to its antiquity the Sanskrit language is more readily analysable, and its roots more easily separable from accretionary elements than... any other IE language" (123, 289). Nobody, as far as I know, has even attempted to dispute this and the presence of dialectal variants and innovations or erosions and losses in Vedic (and Sanskrit) does not invalidate Burrow's judgement. Vedic is superior also in respect of its inner organic cohesion: from roots *dhātu* by simple and fairly regular processes are generated primary (*kṛt-*) and secondary (*taddhita-*) derivatives in nominal and verbal forms[15]. This organic cohesion of Sanskrit is another example of the PP, confirming that the IAs moved very little or not at all.

4. Another aspect of the organic cohesion and the PP deserves a look. Consider the word 'son' and its cognates in other IE languages. Apart from S *sūnu*, it appears in Gmc branches with the stem *sun-* (also O Norse *sonr*), Gk νἱός-*huios* (and dialectal variants), Av *hunu*, Slavic syn- (and variants), Toch A *se* and Toch B *soy*, etc. It does not appear in Latin, in the Celtic branches or in Hittite. The stems for 'sow', which are generally accepted on philological grounds as cognates of the forms of 'son', also have widespread incidence; Gmc *sŭ* (*gu*), Gk σῦς, ὗς *sūs*, *hūs*, L *sŭs*, Av *hŭ-* etc. Curiously, in no language do we find other cognates, nouns or verbs, nor an explanation of the relation between 'son' and 'sow': apart from late developments the two words hang isolated. Sanskrit provides both a plausible explanation and several cognates. Skt *sūnu* 'son' is a derivative from root √*sū* > *sūte* 'beget': this is quite a regular formation, as with √*gṛdh* > *gṛdhnu* 'eager, greedy' or √*bhā* > *bhānu* 'shinning-one, sun', etc. The root *sū* gives in S not only a full declension for the verb 'beget' (*sūte*, *sauti*, etc, pr; *asāvit* etc, aor; *suṣāva* etc, prf; *pra-sū* etc) but also a host of nominal

---

[15]Greek, which is supposed to be very close to Sanskrit, lags far behind. No common root emerges from φα ϱέτ ϱα *pharetra* 'quiver', φέϱω *pherō* 'bear', φόϱος#*phoros* 'tribute'; or φθείϱω *ptheir* φθάϱ- 'waste', μα *phtharma* 'corruption', φθε ϱ, φθο ϱά *phther-, phthora* 'ruin'; or πλέω/πλείω/πλώω *pleō/pleiō/plōō* all 'sail', ? πλευσ *pleus-* both verbal and nominal, ? πλόος/πλοῦς *ploos/plous* 'sailing', ? πλοτον *ploion* 'ship', πλωτήϱ *plōtēr* 'sailor'; πέτο-μαι *petomai* 'fly', ποτάο-/ποτέο-, *potao-/poteo-*, contracted verbal/nominal stems? πτα-/πτε-/πτη-/πτο- *-pta-pte-/ptea-/pto-*, and reduplicated ? ηιητω *piptō* 'fall', ? πτω- *ptō-*; δίδωμι *didōmi* 'give', εδο- *edo-*, εδω- *edō*, δέδο- *dedo-* verbal forms, δόσιζ *dosis* 'giving', δωτήϱ *dōtēr* 'giver'. Even where scholars now give hypothetical roots (eg √δο- √do- for διδωμι *didōmi*) the formation of verbal and nominal forms is mostly haphazard, as the examples I give testify (and there are many more). The same applies to all other branches—and worse.

forms: *sū*, *sūti* (fem 'birth, production'), *sūtū* (fem 'pregnancy'), *sava* (m 'instigation'), *savitṛ* (m 'impeller'), *savitrī* (fem 'mother'), *sāvaka* 'generative', etc. In S 'hog' or 'swine' is *sū-kara*, which some interpret as 'making the sound *sū*' while others connect it with √*sū* 'begetting'—and the latter sounds the more probable since hogs/swine make grunts not hisses. Thus, when the nominal *sū* 'begetting, begetter' is taken also into account, Sanskrit furnishes a plausible link between 'son' and 'sow'. The word 'daughter' also is orphaned in English, Gmc *tochter*, Lth *duktē*, Gk θυγάτηρ *thugatēr*, etc; again S *duhitṛ* alone has a root *duh* 'milk' (cf √*jan* 'generate' > *janitṛ*, √ *van* 'win' > *vanitṛ*) and other cognates. Another interesting example is 'mouse'. This too remains isolated in English, Gmc *mūs*, L *mūs*, Gk *μῦς* *mūs*, etc and only S *mūṣ-aka* has a root *musw* 'steal' (cf √*car* 'move' > *caraka*, √ *yāc* 'ask' > *yācaka*) and many cognates which denote theft, plundering and the like (and in Md Gk a thief is still known as a "mouse"). A final example is the 'sun'. In almost all IE languages the solar globe is masculine: Gk ἥλιος *hēlios*, L *sol*, S *svar/sūryā*, etc, but in German it is feminine. Again Vedic alone has also the fem *sūryā* 'sun-maiden', thus covering both genders.

Perhaps philologists better qualified and equipped than myself will turn their attention to this aspect of language as much as to the isoglosses, uncertain loanwords and conjectural PIE asterisk forms. I am well aware that there are cognations in IE branches exclusive of Sanskrit, particularly the common words in the languages of North-West Europe. But (a) many words listed by eg Meillet (1908: ch 1) can be shown to be connected with S stems: Meillet himself mentions some, then rejects them, while with L *vas* (*vadis*) 'pledge' etc may be cognate S √ *vad-* 'speak' and with L *homo* 'man' etc S *ksā/jmā* 'earth'. (b) The examples I give for Sanskrit explain lacunae in other branches and are derivatives of roots having other verbal/nominal cognates within Sanskrit itself.

5. No other IE branch preserves so much of the PIE inheritance as the Vedic tradition; and a cursory glance in Baldi 1983 Szemérenyi 1996 or any other similar study will demonstrate that the Vedic language itself suffered far fewer losses (Kazanas 2007). Retaining the dual to this day, conservative Lithuanian has, even so, lost the neuter gender and the ablative case, reshaped its verbal system and regularized the comparison forms of adjectives. As for Slavonic, which for many centuries occupies one of the most favoured urheimat (the Pontic Steppe or the Urals), though it came here long after the early dispersal, it did not retain the common IE stems for 'horse, dog, town, copper', having instead *kunji* (and variants), *pis-*, *grad-*, *med-* respectively. The difference in the actual preservations in Vedic is far too great to be assigned to chance. No people who had been on the move for many decades, if not centuries, could have preserved so much.

On the basis of the foregone discussion, I think it is as certain as can be in present circumstances that the IAs are indigenous and that the bulk of RV was composed in the 4th millennium, before the rise of the ISC, while some of it may be far older. However, there are several other secondary aspects that seem to present problems. These are mainly archaeological and linguistic and I shall now attempt to offer solutions. Be it noted that these aspects are thought to be problematic only because of the heavy assumptions upon which depends the AIT.

VII. Horse and chariot

1. How do we know what kind of animal denoted the rigvedic word *aśva* (also *atya*, *vājin*, *haya* etc)?... Certainly the Greek, Latin etc cognate words denoted a particular equid, but how can we be sure that the rigvedic animal is the same?... After all, the only description we have is of an equid with 34 ribs in *RV* I, 62, 18 (a late hymn). This may contain a mythological element as Witzel says but since, on the other and real hand, there is a 34-rib horse (Witzel 2001:§ 21, and n 184), why assume that the Rgvedic *aśva* is of necessity the 36-rib horse found in other IE regions. Thus when RS Sharma describes domesticated horse remains at Mehagara dated at 5000 as "an isolated species of a horse distinct from the one inhabiting areas in the USSR, Iran, Afghanistan etc and associated with the Aryans" (1995:17), he has very obviously prejudged the case. Since the rigvedic horse has 34 ribs (I 62, 18), it has not come from distant lands where the horse has 36 ribs: like the IAs the rigvedic horse is indigenous.

Horses were used in racing (*āji*) and (more often mares) for pulling cars. One hymn undoubtedly refers to horses (*atya*, *aśva*) in races (*āji*). Another refers to war. Some hymns refer to horses running but not necessarily in a race (IX, 36, 1; 74, 8). Others refer to races (IV, 35 and VIII 80) but not necessarily horses. Hymn X, 102 is the only one that describes at length a chariot race and here the animals are oxen: this is the Mudgala-Mudgalānī race. Hymn III 53, 17-8 also has oxen, while stanza 5 has *vājin rāsabha* either 'horse' and 'ass' or 'fast ass' for Indra(!). The ass is not unusual since I, 34, 9 also has the yoking of *vājin* ('horse' or 'fast') (and) *rāsabha* ('ass'), here for the *Aśvins*; also I 116, 2 and 162, 21! (Could one speculate further that *vājin* and perhaps *aśva* might at times denote 'ass, onager, hemione'?). In post-rigvedic texts we find more races, often with horses. In the early *Aitareya Br* IV, 7-9, however, in a race among gods, Agni's car is drawn by mules, Usas's by cows, Indra's by horses and the Asvins' by asses. It is a most curious situation that a post-Ṛgvedic text should have all these animals yoked to race chariots while that of the horse-deities themselves (Aśvins) is drawn by asses. But then in the *RV* the Asvins' chariot is often said to be drawn by birds (eagles in I, 118,4; swans in IV, 45, 4; birds unspecified in VI, 36, 6; etc). Pūṣan's car, again, is pulled by goats (VI, 55). Dawn's car is drawn by oxen (I 92; V 80) as often as by steeds (III 61; VII 75).

All this suggests to me that, contrary to widespread belief, horses may not have been plentiful at all periods and in all places. Certain hymns mention, of course, large numbers of horses: VI 63, 10 has 100s and 1000s; VIII 46, 22 has 60000! In VIII 55-3, 400 mares are mentioned in a *dānastuti* "praise of gift". What would anyone want with 400 or even 100 horses let alone thousands, unless they had a large force of cavalry ? Or they drank the mares' milk and ate horse meat. Or have we here hyperboles?.. Other hymns speak of very few horses: IV 32, 17; VI 45, 12; etc. Now, if there were plenty of horses why should a sage like *Vāmadeva* (IV, 32) be praying to Indra for horses (for his whole clan, the Gotamas)?... Perhaps, and I repeat perhaps, the horse was not so common in Saptasindhu as is usually thought. Elst (1999:181) and R. Thapar (1996:21) suggest that the horse was "symbolic of nobility" thus giving social status.

Now, Witzel cites R. Meadow and A.K. Patel to the effect that no **clear** examples of horse-bones have been found in the area before 1700 (2001:59). What we are not told is that this paper by Meadow and Patel (i) seeks to refute S Bakonyi, who actually does accept finds of horse remains at Surkotada, and (ii) was completed in 1994 (published in 1997) and therefore does not cover data presented in late 1994 and after. Be that as it may, BB Lal (1997:285-6) presents sufficient evidence for horse in the ISC. He dismisses as suspect the evidence at Rana Ghundai (p 162) but finds evidence at Lothal, Surkotada and Kalibangan though he states "one would like to have more and more examples" (p 286). Kochhar also, who advocates the AIT, mentions horse remains at different sites of the ISC found in well-established strata before the alleged IA entry (c 1700–1500) from 1800 to 2155 (2000:186, 192). GR Sharma who favours the AIT found ample evidence for wild horse c 18000 and domesticated horse 6570 to 4530 at the Bolan and Son Valleys (1980:110ff; also Kazanas 1999:33-4)[16]; this

[16]The Report was published by Allahabad University. Sharma had as co-workers Dr M Williams and K Royce, members of a team under Prof J Desmond Clark of SOAS, London.

is in the Ganges basin well to the east of Saptasindhu. These bones were reexamined by another non-indigenist Indian, RS Sharma, who confirmed the early date for domesticated horse at 5000 and some c 1000 (1996:17). How many horse-remains would satisfy invasionists?... Of the many millions of dead humans in the ISC (who were cared for often through burial) only a few hundred skeletons have been unearthed, so we should not have excessive demands for horses.

There are now several reports for horse remains from mature ISC.

(i) Allchin and Joshi found "lumbar vertebrae of horse" at Malvan, a Harappan site at Shaurastra (1995:95).

(ii) Dhavalikar (1995:116-117) reports horse bones unearthed at Kuntasi, periods I and II (=2300-2000).

(iii) Thomas *et al* found 9 bones of true horse (0.13% of the total faunal remains) and 9 bones of the onager at Shikarpur from mature Harappan levels, ie c 2300 (1995).

Finally, there are the terracotta horse figurines. Their presence in ISC sites was acknowledged by Thapar and Mughal (1994:254). Then Lal states again that the horse was present in the ISC and presents in addition the photograph of a horse figurine from mature Harappan levels in Rakhigarhi (2002:73ff). Thus I take it that there is now sufficient attestation of the horse in the ISC. (For more evidence, see paper Nine.)

2. As for the chariot, the basic assumption that the rigvedic *ratha* was like the chariots of the NE or Europe in the 2nd millenium may be justifiable under the preconceptions of the AIT but it is not warranted by the testimony of the *Ṛgveda*. Although many references to *ratha* and its aspects in the *RV* are mythological and we cannot be certain that they apply to human physical realities, there are enough others to enable us to form a good picture. The many more realistic details in the later Vedic texts are too far removed in time to be of indubitable relevance. Many interpretations of rigvedic issues suffer from precisely this drawback: because of insufficient information in the *RV* scholars seek help from later texts and even from non-Indic material, always under the spell of the AIT. Such procedures have generated assumptions that are untrue and arguments that are circular (as those noted by Bryant, pp 117, 144, etc). Here I shall use only rigvedic evidence and such references from later texts as do not affect it; I shall ignore historical semantics since most such material comes from IE branches of late attestation.

Witzel refers at length to an Egyptian chariot of the 15th century (now in Florence) with parts of it made of elm, ash, oak and birch, all imported from places like south Russia, and weighing 30 kg (2000:6). He does not say here that this is like the rigvedic chariot but as he states elsewhere that the latter also weighs c 30 kg (2201:n 192), this is what he intends. This may be legitimate but utterly irrelevant and misleading since the rigvedic vehicle is made of *śalmali* (X 85, 20; also *kiṃ-suka*?) or *khadira* and *siṃśapā* (III 53, 19) and its axle of *aratu* (VIII 46, 27)—all these woods being native to India. We have no information at all about its weight.

Most of the evidence is collected in the *Vedic Index* under *Anas* and *Ratha* and all other erudite studies add nothing—except confusion imported from other texts and/or non-Indic material. Under *Anas* it is said that the cart is "sometimes expressly contrasted with the chariot (*ratha*) for war or sport": the reference III 33, 9 is given (but note that the phrase "for war or sport" is not of rigvedic origin but an imported notion that beclouds the matter). This hymn doesn't present any express contrast: it says simply (in stanzas 9 and 10) that Visvāmitra " has come from afar *ánasā rāthena*, ie "by means of *anas/ratha*" which may mean "by cart [and] chariot" or "by cart [which is] chariot" (or vice versa). One must wonder here why a priest of high order, a renowned ṛṣi who displays magical powers in stopping the onrush of the river-waters, would need a chariot "for sport or war". The *VI* corrects its first statement saying (now under *Ratha*) that "this distinction [between *anas* and *ratha*] is not absolute".

Indeed, Uṣas has *ratha* in (late) I 48, 10 and (early) III 61, 2 but *anas* in (early) IV 30, 11 and (late) X 73, 7. Indra, the mighty warrior who is called arranger *ājikṛt* and lord *ājipati* of the race (or battle: VII 53, 6-14), is said to be *anar-viś* (in late I 121, 7) "seated on a cart" not chariot. The references are by no means exhausted but enough has been said to show that, in fact, there is little if any distinction in *anas/ratha*: "of differences in the structure of the two we have no information" (*VI*, *Ratha*).

3. Measurements and dimensions of the chariot are given in the much later Śulba Sūtras, so I shall ignore them. But there is one passage in the *RV* that is helpful (perhaps more). In VI 61, 13 the river Sarasvatī is likened to a chariot: *rátha iva bṛhatī́*: "like a chariot tall/big/stately/bright". So if a large river is compared to a chariot for size (*bṛhat-*), the chariot cannot be a small and narrow contraption of 30 kg (In III 33, 2 a river is again compared or related to a chariot *rathyā+iva* but the size is not explicit here). This hint of large size is reinforced by the references that follow.

These vehicles, *anas* or *ratha*, were drawn by 1, 2, 3 or 4 animals. "Horses were normally used for chariots but the ass (*gardabha*) or mule (*aśvatari*) are also mentioned" (*VI*, *Ratha*) as indeed we saw above. What is surprising is that while in the Upanishads the cars are said to have two wheels, in the *RV* they have one wheel (I 53, 9 & 164, 2; VI 54, 3; VIII 63, 2 where the sun is obviously meant), sometimes 3 wheels (eg that of the Ṛbhus in IV 36, 1), sometimes 7 (II 40, 3) —all obviously mythological. Once the car has 2 wheels and, all-golden, is that of the Aśvins (VIII 5, 29, again mythological) but in 6 other instances this car is said to be 3-wheeled *tricakra*. In X 85, 14 the car is again *tricakra* but in the next stanza *one of the wheels is missing*! It is not clear to me whether the Aśvins had a 4-wheeled car, now left with three, or a 3-wheeled car now left with 2 wheels. These cars have another curious aspect in the *RV*: the *ratha* has normally "seats" or space for two, the driver and another, but often it has space for three. I am not referring only to the Aśvins' car which carries the Sun-maiden too, but also to III 6, 9 and VI 47, 9 where the *ratha* carries three and more on its *váriṣṭhe...* vandhúre: "widest seat/box". Then in (late) X 53, 7 we find a chariot *ratha* that has seating for 8 *aṣṭā́vandhura*.

All these details (plus the fact that, as we saw in § 1, above, the chariot is drawn by an ass or ass and horse) constitute the picture of a vehicle that is not at all like the (war) chariots appearing in the 2nd millenium in the NE. P Raulwing's admirably erudite study on the IE chariots and horses sheds not one ray of light on the rigvedic vehicles. The evidence for the development in the NE of the first light chariots for war (Littauer & Cronwel 1996) as against the Pontic Steppe (Anthony & Vinogradov 1995) seems fairly convincing. But neither the former not the latter tell us anything useful about the *RV*.

Witzel took umbrage (2003) to this view accusing me of using only mythological evidence (which is untrue: see VII, 1 re Mudgala race) but himself used the most obviously mythological references (Aśvins' golden wheels, *RV* 8.5-59; etc and *RV* 10.85.11 which speaks of Suryā's bridal car which has *the sky as its covering* (st 10) and is in fact *manas* 'the mind', but, because he probably used Geldner's German translation, he thought this was *ratha* whereas it is *anas* (st 10, 12!) etc).

4. Further confusion comes from projecting non-Indic material onto the minor aspect of the *rathavā́hana*, in VI, 75, 8. Mentioned by Witzel (2001:n 192) and usually translated as a platform or large vehicle for transporting the supposedly fragile, light (30 kg) chariot, the word occurs also in *AtharvaVeda*, III 17, 3 in a list—"cow, sheep, *prasthāvad rathavāhamam* and a lusty fat girl": all these a plough should dig up (*lāṅgalam ... udvapatu*). This passage with slight variations is found also in some Brāhmaṇas. If we put aside any notions from NE (hypothetical) parallels and modern racing-cars (Witzel ibid), it is very difficult to see how this "chariot-transport that-has-a-support or -a-platform" (surely pleonastic?) fits with the cow, sheep and girl. To my mind the whole phrase seems to be a metaphor for a horse ("chariot-puller that-has-stability") but I wouldn't bet on it and WD Whitney translates "on-going chariot-frame" (note: *not* 'platform'). The word occurs also in the prose texts and there it may have the meaning "platform, conveyor", though in a text like Baudhāyana Śrauta Śrūta XI, 6, 72, 8 it is probably used metaphorically: *athaihi yajamāneti*: *ratha eṣa dakṣiṇe śroṇyante rathavāhana āhito bhavati*: "Come, O sacrificer! he says; this chariot is placed on the platform [which is] the southern hip (śroṇi-) [of the altar]". All such references are much too late. (See Sparreboom 1985 *passim* for the mainstream view) .

The use of the word in *RV* VI 75, 8 can be taken differently. First of all, if the *ratha* was dismantled and placed on the platform, as is generally thought (Sparreboom, p 30), this hymn would have been an ideal place to mention such a fact. But the hymn does not say that wheels and box are separate; in fact the chariot *ratha* is not lauded *per se* as other things are. Here the *rathavāhana* itself is equated with the oblation *havis*, just as in other passages the hymn or thought offered is given in the figure of a chariot (eg V 29, 15). Then since the chariot itself is not lauded (as the warrior is in st 1, the cow in 2, the good charioteer in 6, horses in 7, the whip in 13, the mail or armour 18-9), it seems reasonable that *rathavāhana* is the chariot itself, lauded *per se* in st 8; to use Whitney's translation, it is the "(on-going) chariot-frame". There is no need to assume a chariot-carrying platform[17].

[17]*rathavāhana* could mean "the conveying by chariot" or "the chariot's [function of] conveying" or even "the conveyor that is a chariot". Some might refer to grammar rules and accent and insist that here is an Acc tatpuruṣa "chariot-conveying". I would simply remind that the accent is not invariable (eg ***á****śvam-iṣṭi* "horse-seeking" but *viśvam-inv****á*** "all moving", etc). Then we find *aritra-páraṇa* "going-across with oars" and not "going-across oars" (Macdonell 1916:454-7).

Pāda 8c *tátrā rátham úpa* śagman *sadéma* is translated by WO'Flaherty (1981:237) as "on it [ie the platform] let us place the working chariot". This rendering can hardly be correct since the verb *upa-sad-* means "sit on/by, approach respectfully" and the like (the causative *upasādaya-* alone means "place on"): so the phrase should give "let us revere/ honour the efficient chariot." Furthermore, this very stanza says that upon this vehicle are already laid *nihita* weaponry *āyudha* and mail varma. So O'Flaherty and others say that on this "platform" weapons and mail are first laid and then the chariot itself. Is it likely that practical men would load the chariot (whole or dismantled) afterwards and thus possibly damage the weaponry ? Of course not.

It may be thought that my interpretation of the *rathavāhana* is far-fetched and ignores the traditional meaning given by scholars. This may be so, but the more I read the hymns the more I wonder whether the traditional, generally accepted meanings that I learnt formerly are true. Consider one well-known passage. Every sanskritist knows the *Nāsadīya Sūkta* X 129: pādas c and d read *kím ấvarīvaḥ kúha kásya śármann ámbhaḥ kím āsīd gáhanaṃ-gambhīram*: roughly 'What covered (or was-there covering)? Where? Whose protection? Was it *ambhaḥ* profound unfathomable?' All translations that I know give 'water' for *ambhas* (Geldner: 'Wasser'); even Jeanine Miller, who always approached the hymns with great sensitivity and strove to bring out some spiritual significance, here translated 'water' and connected this with other mythologies (1972: 68). As most mythologies/religions speak of "water" at a very early stage of creation (Judaic, Egyptian, Mesopotamian, etc) it is assumed that *ambhas* (connected with *abhra*, *ambara*, *ambu*, all denoting 'cloud, sky, rain, water') also does the same. But this cannot be justified: it is negated by the first hemistich which states unequivocally "Then there was no existence nor non-existence, nor space (*rajas*) nor the upper heaven". How, when there was no existence of any kind (known to us), could there be "water"? There couldn't. Here the word *ambhas* means 'potency' (Mayrhofer: *Gewalt*). Behind the traditional (Western) thinking is the notion "Why shouldn't the rigvedic mythology be like the other *primitive* mythologies?" And so this preconception will continue to produce translations of "water", ignoring what the text says and what plain logic enjoins. The hymn here is significantly different from other mythologies in advocating a Primal Unity as the First Principle of all creation. Similar preconceptions (and prejudices?) operate and, I think, misinterpret or ignore the data about chariots and many other rigvedic matters.

Final point. Even if some rigvedic vehicles resembled the early one-man, two-wheeled chariot of the NE, this does not mean that the Vedic *ratha* came from there and, still less, from the Urals[18]. The Harappans already had the technology for its construction. For other types of vehicles, of course, there is ample evidence: "a more sophisticated type of vehicle with one or two pairs of wheels ... is known from the Rhine to the Indus by around 3000 BC" (Piggott 1992:18; for more details Kazanas 1999:33). The absence of actual remains does pose a difficulty but is not in itself evidence of absence.

VIII. The river Sarasvatī

1. Many hymns in nine of the ten books of the RV (but not the 4th) extol or mention a divine and very large river named Sarasvatī. This flows mightily "from the mountains to the [Indian] Ocean" *giríbhya ā́ samudrā́t* VII, 95, 2 and gives sustenance to many kings and the five Aryan tribes that were settled along its banks (VI 61: etc) and along the Indus,

---

[18]In yet another misrepresentation Witzel writes: "The spoked chariot wheels that Sethna wants to find on the Indus seals turn out to be in most cases, oblong—resulting in singularly bad transport for Indus merchants". (2001:n 194). However DK Sethna makes it quite explicit (1992:50-1) that these identifications were first made by Parpola and other Finnish scholars; he merely followed! Parpola is an invasionist and co-editor of Witzel's EJVS!

Dṛṣadvatī and the other rivers. In historic times the river appeared to be a minor stream Sarsuti (<Sarasvatī) or Ghaggar or Hakra, which ended in the desert at Bhatnair, far from the ocean so that modern scholars (Roth, Griffiths et al, *VI* vol 2, 434) thought that the poets referred, in fact, to the Indus which alone still flows to the ocean and justifies such references.

Witzel does not think that Sarasvati tells us much about the date of the *RV* and the IA origins; in fact he doubts it is the Indian river at all, writing: "Whether the immigrant Vasistha [i.e. the poet of VII 95 hymn] was from the Iranian area of *Haraxvaiti* (=Sarasvatī Arachosia) or not, he may have echoed the praise of the *ancient* Sarasvatī, that is the local S. Avestan Haraxvaiti ... or he may just have spoken in the hyperbolic style of the *RV*" (2001:66).[19] It would be too time-consuming and tedious to describe all the various notions Witzel has resorted to in the last few years both in publications and on the Internet to explain why the Sarasvatī is not really the Sarasvatī but some other river "having pools" or being in Afghanistan or flowing in the sky as the Milky Way, and so on. I shall deal only with Witzel's point about the river Beas capturing the river Sutlej from Sarasvatī and thus diminishing it: in the end Sarasvatī flows to *samudra* which is not the ocean but only terminal lake(s) (2001:65). This is thought important by Bryant also (2001:168). But before proceeding I should agree that Sarasvatī is also a goddess and had a celestial aspect for the IAs (eg *RV* V 43, 11; VI 61, 11; X 17, 7-9) as the river Nile was also the Milky Way in heaven for the Egyptians (Shafer 1991:108).

[19]It is worth noting that Haraxvaiti is one of the 16 places the Iranians had passed through before settling down. See section III, 3 above. In Indo-Iranian linguistics the sound shift is from *s* to *h* (*V su, soma*/ Av hū̆, *haoma* etc); so *Sarasvatī/Haraxvaiti* would indicate a movement out of Saptasindhu (as also *Haptahendu*) rather than the reverse. This suggests to me a movement of IAs north-westward and eventually into Iran. It could have been a large contingent, and the areas sparsely (or not) populated so that the immigrants could give new names reminiscent of their homeland.

2. Sarasvatī is praised, like no other river, in many hymns and to confine the discussion, as Witzel does, to two hymns III, 33 and VII, 95 ignoring the information contained in others, is not good scholarship. Hymn III 33 indeed says that ṛṣi Viśvāmitra, domestic priest to King Sudās, went to the confluence of the two rivers Beas and Sutlej and there asked the rivers to hold their current so that he (and the accompanying Bharatas) could cross. People, of course, do not usually go to a confluence, where the current is most turgid and vehement to cross over: they either go higher up and cross two rivers or lower down where the flow is smoother. However, since Viśvāmitra was a mighty sage, he could perform miracles, so the rivers complied with his request and stopped flowing. The word *samāraṇa* also suggests a "confluence". But to me it is not as clear as I would like. Then, in the late X 75 the river Beas Vipāś is not mentioned, only Sutlej *Śutudrī* (st 5): this suggests that the latter absorbed the former rather than the other way round! Adding to the confusion, III 53, 9 says that Viśvāmitra induced only one river to hold back (*astabhnāt*) its flow: here it may be a different river, Sindhu itself (*sindhu* = "river in general" and "Indus"), in which case Viśvāmitra made a habit of stopping rivers! The *VI* thinks III 53, 9 to be a (later) reference to the same feat (in III 33): indeed, it is a brief reference in one half-stanza (a & b) and it includes King Sudās (c-d) while the three following stanzas pray that Sudās defeats his foes and wins wealth and the Bharata people be protected. (For what it is worth, Indra too stops with his māyā the overflowing waters of river Vibalī in *RV* IV 30, 12. In V 31, 8 also he stops the rushing waters for Yadu and Turvaśa. Then in VII 18, 5 Indra made "the spreading tumultuous waters shallow and easy for Sudās to cross": this hymn in praise of Indra is by Vasiṣṭha but seems to refer to the same incident as III, 33, which is a hymn in praise of Indra by Viśvāmitra.) The situation as a whole is not at all clear. (*Nirukta* II 23-5 & Bṛhaddevatā II 135-7 add nothing to our understanding.)

Be that as it may, when we turn to the information in other hymns we see that Sarasvatī is a very great river in the later hymns as well, except *perhaps* in X 75. In II 41, 16, Gṛtsamada calls Sarasvatī, *nadītamā*, *ambitamā* and *devitamā* "best river, best mother, best goddess". Following Oldenberg, Witzel considers Bks II-VII to be the oldest ones but also gives several conditons which nearly nullify this (eg "the 'younger form' of a hymn does not always signify its 'younger age'," 1995:309-11). Thus he considers II, 41 and III 33 to be older and therefore describing the river as it was initially and then losing one of its tributaries and so shrinking. But in addition to the later VII 95 (see above), VI 52, 6 also praises Sarasvatī, which is (still) **swollen *pinvamānā* by many rivers *sindhubhiḥ***: so ṛṣi Bharadvāja tells us that this river is still fed by many others! Thus even if Sutlej had been weaned away, there were still enough rivers pouring into Sarasvatī and keeping it swollen and large. Then hymn VI 61, 8-13 lauds the river as endless, swift-moving, roaring, most dear among the sister-currents and, together with her divine aspect, nourishing the 5 tribes. Surely it can't be that the ṛṣi of Book VI also like "immigrant Vasiṣṭha", twice lauds an ancient or non-Indic river. In the definitely later VIII 21, 17-8, the ṛṣi Kāṇva says that king Citra bestows wealth only like Indra or Sarasvatī and that Citra and many lesser kings dwell along Sarasvatī: this does not sound like a diminished river. Then, VII 96, 2 (as well as 95) prays to the rivergoddess for sustenance and good fortune and so does again X 177 while X 64, 9 calls upon Sarasvatī, Sarayu and Indus as "great" and "nourishing". All these poets can't be referring to an ancient river or a shrivelled one (and these 3 hymns are not singled out in Witzel's 1995 paper as early).

3. Witzel writes: "In sum, the middle and later *RV* (books 3, 7 and the late book, 10.75) already depict the *present day* situation with the Sarasvatī having lost most of the water to the Sutlej (and even earlier, much of it also to the Yamuna). It was no longer the large river it *might* have been before the

Ṛgvedic period [ie before 1200]" (2001:66: emphasis in the original; square brackets mine). This statement is of course a gross misrepresentation of the situation since it ignores the facts. These middle and late hymns (VII 95 and 96, VIII 21, X 64 and 177) describe in the present the river's greatness, say that many kings live along its banks and pray for sustenance and good fortune without any hint anywhere (in these or other hymns) that the river has shrunk (as indeed we find in later texts like eg *Manusmṛti* II 21 and scholiasts thereon). If Sarasvatī had shrunk, surely these hymns would be lamenting such a misfortune and praying for the reappearance of ample water—as Vasiṣṭha confesses former sins to Varuṇa and begs for forgiveness in VII 86 and 89 or as the gambler bewails his predicament and begs for release in X 34.

Consider 3 more points on this. **(a)** The terminal "lake(s)" is etymologising on Witzel's part since Sarasvatī is usually rendered 'she who has pools'. The word *saras* certainly came to mean 'pool' and this may refer to the sources of the river being lakes which formed as the ice was melting: considering the name was given when the river was at its grandest (from the mountains to the ocean), it would refer to lakes at the origin and not the teminal point. But there is another aspect here. The root √*sṛ* and all its derivatives imply 'motion, extension, running-on'; *saras* too originally meant most probably (not 'pool' but) 'whirlpool' or 'eddy' in a river's current. Sarasvatī was the river with the mighty current and strong swirls. **(b)** Hymn X, 75 does not give prominence to Sarasvatī but praises *sindhu* which may be the river Indus or the Spirit of Rivers deified; in any case, it is a list of the rivers from east to west and Sarasvatī is in the correct place, after Ganges and Yamuna. **(c)** More important, hymn III 33 speaks of the two rivers Vipāś and Śutudrī (st 1-2) as rising from the mountains (parvata) and flowing down to the ocean *samudra*. Or should we here also take *samudra* to be "a terminal lake", as Witzel would have it (2001:76) for

Sarasvatī in VII 95, 2? In both we have the rise of the rivers from mountains and their flow to *samudra*. But I 71, 7 also says *samudrám ná sravátaḥ saptá yahvī́ḥ* '[sacrificial offerings turn to Agni] like the 7 mighy rivers flowing to the samudra': is this samudra too Sarasvatī's "terminal lake" into which turn/ flow all 7 rivers?... I find it more reasonable to take *samudra* as the 'ocean' and that Sarasvatī also flows there. (For a full discussion see paper on *samudra* herein).

To sum up, Sarasvatī in all of the *RV* is a mighty river that nourishes the 5 Aryan peoples (and many kings) along its banks as is shown by VI 52, VI 61, VII 95 and 96, VIII 21 and X 64 and 177. All these were composed before 1900, when by most accounts the river lost its tributaries and shrank (Rao 1991:77-9; Allchins 1997:117). Consequently the (bulk of the) *RV* must be dated prior to 1900 and since it knows nothing of the ISC[20], as Witzel too admits, it must be even older, ie before 3000.

IX. Some linguistic considerations

I have no desire, and it would take too long, to follow Witzel along all his tortuous twists and turns in the conjectural philology of proto-languages. I shall deal only with four aspects three of which are considered important by Bryant.

---

[20]a)Another revealing point is Witzel's misrepresentation of ruins "(*armaka, vailaṣṭhāna*, cf Falk 1981) in the RV" (2001:§ 22). The implication is that there are references in the RV to ruins, particularly I, 133 (*armaka, vailasthana*) and that H Falk (1981) presents all this evidence. This is very far from the truth. Falk deals with *kapāla* "potsherds" in the later texts (1981:167ff) as one would expect. RV I, 133 does not refer to any ruined cities as Burrow tried to show (1963:159-68): there is no mention at all in this hymn of ruined houses or walls, no stones or bricks (building material of the ISC)—only ghosts and friends (see Kazanas 2000:95 and n 14; also Sethna 1992:130-4).

b) He misrepresents Misra again, writing (2001:34) "Misra's main thesis, emigration from India, has already been refuted on linguistic grounds by Hock (1999)." Hock, on the contrary, admits the possibility of emigration on linguistic grounds and rejects it on quasi-archaeological considerations about horse and war-chariot (1999:13). See § IX 3, below.

1. Witzel admits (2001:§ 18) that the earlier Kassites who conquered Mesopotamia had IA elements but attempts to show that the somewhat later Mitanni language has no such elements and that any similarities derive from a Pre-Vedic Old Indo-Aryan. Fact is that once you start postulating Pre-this-language and Proto-that-language, you can prove almost anything you like in this field. Other philologists are fairly explicit about this matter. Burrow accepts the IA presence in Mitanni and that the elements "are to be connected specifically with the Indo-Aryans ... partly on *linguistic grounds* [my emphasis here] and partly on ... the Aryan gods mentioned ... [who] are specifically Vedic... [and] the word *eika-* which corresponds to Sanskrit *eka* whereas Iranian has *aiva-*" (1975:28-30). Bryant endorses Burrow's view finding "Indo-Aryan prominence in this field" (p 136). SS Misra, Professor of Linguistics at Benares, argues along similar lines (1992:13-4) but he is an indigenist and Witzel feels he can deride him describing his work as "nothing more than a cottage industry exploitation of a new popular trend" (2001: § 12, 1 and § 12, 4-12, 8).

Why Witzel, Professor at Harvard, thinks it fit to insult his colleagues is not very clear.[21] This mode of attack reaches a climax in his article in *Frontline*, a marxist journal, in which he assails some publication which allegedly used fraudulent material (*non vidi*) but goes beyond this to insult all indigenists, Indian and Western alike, non-academics and academics, including Misra (2000:14). Why he should have resorted to a marxist magazine to publish such a critique

[21]G Erdosy, another invasionist, refers to S Talageri, whose publications (1993, 2000) may contain errors and faults but are fairly honest attempts to present the indigenist case (see Bryant 2001:65-6, etc), as one on the "lunatic" fringe (Elst 1999:55). The same scholar makes curious remarks about archaeologists who, he thinks, do not understand "gradual and complex phenomena" consequently "denying the validity of any migrational model" (1995:xiii, xv): here we have an implicit charge that archaeologists are obtuse whereas invasionists are perspicacious and imaginative—which of course is derogatory sophistry (see also n 10c, above).

when India has so many academic journals is not very clear either.

2. More important is the matter of **loanwords**. A number of words in Vedic, not having correspondences in other IE branches and not being capable of resolution into some (hypothetical) PIE form are thought to be borrowings from Dravidian or Munda or "some unknown northeastern language" (Hock 1996:113 citing B Tikkanen). Several scholars advocate this borrowing (Burrow 1973, Mayrhofer 1956-, Kuiper 1991 & 1995, Witzel 2001). This is said to be very important, if not decisive evidence and Bryan states "any discussion of Indo-Aryan origins that neglects the substratum data simply cannot be taken seriously" (107). Excellent! But first let us consider some pertinent points.

To begin with, the disagreement among linguists is startling. A long line of non-indigenist mostly Western scholars, including Emenau (1980), expressed grave doubts about the nature and the extent of this borrowing: P Thieme doubts Burrow's lists, Hock those of Mayrhofer and R Das the list of some 380 words of F Kuiper (Bryant, 84-90); Misra also rejects Kuiper's list (1999:17-8). In the 1980's Ememau rejected the lot, even the unknown tongue "totally lost to the record". More recently Witzel rejected Bryant's suggestions (2001:nn 64, 65, 66). It is worth quoting Das, who is a non-indigenist but on different grounds: "*not a single case* [exists] in which a *communis opinio* has been found confirming the foreign origin of a Ṛgvedic (and probably Vedic in general) word (...) many of the arguments for (or against) such foreign origin are often ... statements of faith" (1995:228, emphasis original). Let one example suffice: Burrow gives *bala* 'strength' as of Dravidian origin (1973:384) but Mayrhofer (under *balam*) connects it with Gk βελ-τίων bel-tion, L *debilis* etc. Such disagreements may not impress philologists themselves since they are habituated to disputes and controversies but to others they indicate that something important is amiss. Just as remarkable is the fact that some scholars reject Dravidian and Munda and postulate an unknown language—as if every word in Vedic must have a correspondance in some other IE branch or the (hypothetical) reconstructed PIE. What is strange here is that scholars discuss this in seriousness not realizing that they are attempting to explain in this complicated science-fiction fashion what needs no explanation, as many of them hint anyway! If, as I maintain (sect VI, above) Vedic is the oldest IE branch preserving many more linguistic and cultural elements than the others, but not without erosions too, then it is just as likely that the other branches lost any trace of these alleged loans. (But see two paragraphs from end of this § 2.) Also, if we postulate one non-IE language, why not have two or more?... Where would this lead us then?... What is the benefit? We are dealing with totally unknown and unhelpful entities. All we can say with realistic certitude is that *there may have been loans from X language* (*s*).

To what extend can we trust the reconstruction of proto-languages?... True, many fine results have been obtained by the detection (or application) of philological laws operating in large areas of a language or of a family of languages, like IE. However, the old but regular correspodence of S *bh* and Gk *ph* as also in the perfect stem *lebhe* and εἴληφα *eilēpha* 'have received' would lead us to expect a Gk present stem*λα**φ**-/λαμ**φ**- **la**ph**-/lam**ph**-*, but in actuality this is λα**β**-/λαμ**β**- *la**b**-/lam**b**-*. Hock (1991) gives many more examples with laryngeals (582), Armenian *erk-* (583), Baltic, Slavic and Germanic (585) and so on (up to p 591). Thus it is equally true that there are areas where the general rules do not apply and we would reach wrong conclusions—but for the documentation. No law, moreover, can account for the variations in the following S and Gk correspondences: *tiṣṭhāmi*/ἵστημι *histēmi* 'stand', *dadāmi*/διδωμι *didōmi* 'give', *dadhāmi*/τιθημι *tithēmi* 'put' *piparmi*/πιμπλημι *pimplēmi* 'fill' (the Gk nasal, an echo of *pṛṇāmi* ?) and *juhomi*/χ**ε**ω *cheō* 'pour' (cf aor pass ἐχνθην, *ech**u**thēn* χύτρα *ch**u**tra* 'pot' etc which suggest a root-stem χν- *chu-*

similar to S√*hu*)). Can we be 100% sure then that the forms we ‘reconstruct’ for protolanguages, (and especially Munda), are actual? I don’t think so; nor would any judge and jury in an impartial court of law. Writing on Kurylowitz’s ‘laws’ of analogy, Hock, one of the most eminent scholars in Comparative Philology, states: “a prediction of when change will or must occur is impossible” (1991:211). And of course, without the necessary analogical information (ie documentation of some kind) we cannot predict *what* the change will be.

Let me give some examples. In Greek the guttural plosive γ (=g) is now pronounced as a fricative, sometimes like y in ‘you’ and sometimes like *w* in ‘wolf’—and this in both initial and medial positions. It is a general law without any exceptions. However there are many words in Md Gk that did not originally have an initial γ but developed it from different vowels and in some cases through loss of vowels: eg γεράχι <ἱέραξ *geraki* *<hierax* ‘hawk’, γερός <ὑγιηρός *geros* *<hugiēros* ‘healthy’ (but cf γέρ /-ων/-ον- *ger/-ōn/-on* ‘old’), γιαλ-/γυαλ- <ὑαλ- gial-/gual-/<hual- ‘bright’ (Md Gk ‘glass’), γιαλος <αἰγιαλος *gialos* < *aigialos* ‘shore’, etc. Without the documentation we would be ‘reconstructing’ some very absurd unreal forms. Without documentation no law could possibly lead back to the originals (second in each of the pairs): δενω/δεω *denō/deō* (and διδημι *didēmi*) ‘bind’ (cf μενω/μενω *menō/menō* ‘abide’: no change), λυνω/λυω *lunō/luō* ‘loosen’, χυνω/χεω *chunō/cheō* ‘pour’; γλειφω/λειχω *gleiphō/leichō* ‘lick’, (cf ἀλειφω/ἀλειφω *aleiphō/aleiphō* ‘besmear’: no change). Then take the group—αδραχνω *adrachnō* (fut -δραξ- *drax-*) ‘grasp’, δειχνω *deichnō* (fut δειξ- *deix-*) ‘show’ and σπρωχνω *sprōchnō* (fut σπρωξ- *sprōx-*) ‘push’. With the help of S *diś-āmi* (fut *dekṣ-*) and L (*in-*)*dic-are* both ‘show’, an original *δεχ-/διχ- **dek-/dik-* may be postulated; encouraged we may now take S *sprś* (fut *sprakṣ-*) ‘touch’ or, perhaps, *spṛh* ‘be eager’ (and L *sparg- ere* ‘strew, hurl’) as cognate with σπρώχνω *sprōchnō*, and S *dṛś* (*darś-* fut *draks-*) 'see' with -δϱάχ-νω *drach-nō*; then we postulate a law that original χ>χ *k>ch* with an intrusive -ν- *-n-* or an original -χν- *-kn-* with loss of -ν- *-n-* in Sanskrit and Latin. This 'law' is then applied to other similar verbs and we have original *ϱιχνω* *rhiknō* for ϱιχνω *richnō* 'throw', *διωχνω **diōknō* for διωχνω *diōch-nō* 'drive away'. Unfortunately, all this apparently 'scientific' approach is sheer fantasy and only διωκ-ω *diōk-ō* (without the -ν- *n*) would be correct: for the rest the originals are δειχνυμι *deiknumi*, (α-)δϱασσω (*a-*)*drassō* (or δϱαπτω *drattō*), for ϱιχνω *rhichnō* ϱιπτω *rhiptō* and for σπϱωχνω *sprōchnō*, after several incredible changes, (εισ-?) πϱοωθεω (*eis*?) *proōtheō* ! Without documentation analogous fantasies will, of course, be generated by the following: θλιβω *thlibō* 'press/pinch', νιβω *nibō* 'wash', σχυβω *skubō* (pronounced *skivo*) 'bend', τ ϱβω *stribō* 'turn/twist', τϱιβω *tribō* 'rub', etc which come from θλιβω *thlivō* (no change), νι**πτ**ω *niptō*, χυ**πτ**ω *kuptō* στϱεφω *strephō* and τϱιβω *tribō* (no change). I trust I am forgiven for not having any confidence at all in comparisons and reconstructions of this type (without documentation).

E Pulgram discussed caustically the same dangers with regard to Latin and the Romance languages (1958:147). He also dismissed 'linguistic palaeontology' with very good reasons—as many others have done before and after him (see also Bryant, ch 6). As S Zimmer put it (1990): "The long dispute about the reliability of this 'linguistic palaeontology' is not yet finished, but approaching its inevitable end—with a negative result, of course". Indeed, some few scholars still resort to it judiciously (Elst 1999:130-3; Witzel 2001:42-6) to prove their (opposite) view.

Now, if so many important changes in a language occur, despite literacy, outside the influence of any recognizable regular law within only a few centuries, then the changes in a language without literacy (unless it has a strong hieratic oral tradition like that of the Indoaryans) in a period of over a millennium can hardly be calculable. "The hypothesis of an unknown substratum... is methodologically dubious (...) The enormous difference between the Indo-Aryan [*alleged*!] arrival ... and the first attestation of the northwestern languages places formidable obstacles" (Hock 1996:79-80, my square brackets). Surely then, when reconstructions of protolanguages, and consequently phenomena arising from them, cannot really be trusted, and when eminent linguists cannot agree among themselves about the nature and extent of the subject under discussion (in this case loanwords), how could we and why should we take this sort of 'evidence' seriously?...

However, I do accept the possibility of the presence of other non-Sanskritic languages in the larger area and of loanwords in Vedic. After all some denote important items, like *khala* 'threshing-floor', *bila* 'hole' and *lāṅgala* 'plough' and occur frequently. Nonetheless, even if all these loanwords and other similar linguistic elements are taken to be valid, this does not indicate an IndoAryan intrusion, even if such elements are present only in Vedic and in no other IE language. As I pointed out on the Internet (2001a:n 8) we can envisage such non-IE influences coming from south and east of Saptasindhu and affecting all adjacent dialects but not those further north-west (which in fact emigrated—before, during or after the arrival of the foreign elements).[22]

Not surprisingly, Bryant himself arrives at a similar conclusion: "As far as I can determine, there is very little that is decisive that can be brought forward to deny the possibility that Dravidian or Munda speakers intruded upon an Indo-Aryan speaking area and not vice versa" (105); here again there is, in fact, *nothing* decisive beyond the AIT itself.

[22]Elst suggested (1993), when D McAlpin's Elamo-Dravidian affinities and Dravidian migrations were fashionable (see also Mallory 1989:55-6 and Renfrew 1991:13-4), that the Elamo-Dravidians moved along the Gujarat coast and down into south India without intruding into the ISC (127-9). Without new firm evidence all such proposals are conjectural and of little value.

In support of this Bryant cites Witzel who provided data that "Dravidian influence is not visible in the earliest layers of the Ṛg but only in subsequent layers" (102). And he concludes: "In short, while certainly suggestive, it is difficult to see how the 'evidence' of a linguistic substratum in Indo-Aryan, in and of itself, can be used as a final arbitrator in the debate over Indo-Aryan origins" (107). Bryant should have added that there is nothing else.

3. *The 'Out of India' theory* (=*OIT*). Even more important is Hock's article which discusses the possibility of Old IndoAryan being the PIE language and the possibility of IEs emigrating out of India (1999).

Hock rightly rejects the notion that PIE was Vedic, but he is wrong in ascribing this view to Misra, who makes no such claim as far as I know. Misra exhibits some sentiment, perhaps because of patriotism and religious feelings, but he is careful throughout his study (1992) to keep Sanskrit quite distinct from PIE: "the Sanskrit language has also suffered linguistic changes and the original Indo-European proto-speech was not the same as Sanskrit" (p 2); also, Sanskrit "is the oldest Indo-European" and the "nearest language to original Indo-European" (p 84).

Then Hock, unaware of J Nichols's evidence which requires a locus of dispersal at Bactria—Sogdiana (unlike his own vague "vast area from East central Europe to Eastern Russia", p 17), nonetheless indicates that there are no substantial linguistic arguments against the proposition that IE branches moved out of India. He states that apart from the gypsy emigration, there are "three more IA languages moving out of India: Gandhari Prakrit (in medieval Khotam and farther east), and Parya (in modern Uzbekistan)... and Dunaki (close to present-day Shina)... to the outer northwestern edge of south Asia" (also in Hock 1996:82). He states also that the PIE could "a priori" have been "originally spoken in India" (p 11) and rejects the idea *not on linguistic* but archaeological(!) grounds (p 13) of the kind usually employed by invasionists (horse and chariot). This, as we saw (sect VII) is no real difficulty. On p 14 we find Fig 1, the genetic table of the IE branches which is generally accepted. On p 15 is Fig 2, the isoglosses which, despite uncertainties about archaisms and innovations, again present no difficulties (see next § 4). On p 16 we read that if the model in Fig1 is accepted, then the OIT would be "relatively easy to maintain". He then invokes the "principle of simplicity" as an additional difficulty (p 16): one migration into India as against many out of it. But he ignores the fundamental fact that there is plenty of evidence of IE branches invading the areas they occupy but there is none for India: this makes considerable difference, surely. What is more, this "simplicity" applies equally to all proposed homelands. Now, if the difficulties are insuperable or grave, then a view is *not* "relatively easy to maintain"; if it is so, then there are no serious difficulties. (And "relatively" to what?... There is only the (opposite) view, the AIT.)

Just as important is Johanna Nichols's view (1997, 1998) stating (in her Introduction) that "the locus accounting for the distribution of loanwords, internal innovation and genetic diversity within IE could only have lain well to the east of the Caspian Sea" (1997:123). As my article has gone well out of the limits originally envisaged, I won't reproduce her detailed analysis of the evidence (see Bryant for good summaries and implications—pp 124-6, 151-4). All the different aspects of the data point to a location "far out in the eastern hinterlands... a locus in western Central Asia", which, in her 'further implications' she specifies with precision: "the locus of the IE spread was ... somewhere in the vicinity of ancient Bactria-Sogdiana" (ib 137). Examining arcaeological data too, B Sargent also finds that Bactria is the urheimat and outlines a movement from there to the Russian Steppes

[23]"Archaeologists have not in fact succeeded in locating the Indo-Europeans... [but] are generally agreed that the so-called Kurgan peoples... spoke an Indo-European language... [and] some time around the middle of the fifth millennium... expanded from the steppe zone north of the Black Sea into the Balkans and adjacent areas." (Watkins 2000:xxxiv)

which generated the Kurgan culture (1997)[23]. Sargent sends the Indo-Iranians also from there to their historical habitats. However, Nichols's evidence shows "westward trajectories of language" (p 135) but there is no mention of any south or southeastern trajectory to account for Indo-Aryan. Bactria is not far from Saptansindhu and could be a first concentration point for out-of-India travellers and subsequent dispersals.

4. *Isoglosses and palatalization.* I am not sure that I agree with everything that experts say about the isoglosses, and particularly what archaisms are and what innovations. I note that Hock in his 1999 paper mentions no obstacle or difficulty presented by the isoglosses with regard to the out-of-India scenario. Indeed, to the best of my knowlegde no invasionist has used this as an argument against the OIT, except indirectly, with attempts to prove the Russian Steppe as the original homeland. There is moreorless general agreement, whatever other disputes may exist, that according to the isoglosses the IE branches form two distinct groups: (A) Hittite, Tocharian, Italic, Celtic, Germanic, Baltic and Slavonic; (B) Indoaryan, Iranian, Thraco-Phrygian (Armenian) and Greek (or Hellenic). This group B has certain isoglosses in common: the augment in past tenses; the formation of the perfect; the prohibitive mã (I-Ir)/μη *mē* (Gk)/*mi* (Armenian); etc. No major isogloss cuts across the line between the two groups except palatalization which is now generally thought to be a "late phenomenon" occuring in "a post PIE era" when the original unity had broken down after "most of the dialect groups had dispersed" (Winn 1995:324). (Incidentally, the r-isogloss whereby the passive of verbs is formed and is shared by group A (Hittite etc) is sometimes ascribed to Phrygian, but this is rather speculative.)

SMM Winn uses palatalization to establish the urheimat. It is a late phenomenon, as was said, so he writes: "Looking at the geographical distribution of this isogloss, we may note its absence from the peripheral languages: Germanic (at the northwest limit...); Celtic (western limit); Italic, Greek and

Hittite (southern limit); and Tocharian (eastern limit). It is the languages at the center that have changed... [Palatalization] never reached far enough to have any effect on the outlying languages" (1995:326). Winn accepts the Pontic Steppe as the urheimat taking as central languages naturally Baltic, Slavonic,Iranian and Indoaryan. We observe also that Iranian and Indoaryan are not placed in their historical habitats, unlike all other branches including Greek.

Here we have two difficulties. One, Slavonic is a comparatively recent (c 450 CE) intruder into the area of the Pontic steppes (though this situation could have been true at a very early period, the Balto-Slavs moving northwest and the Slavs returning much later). Two, the IA branch is not put at its historical habitat as it would then have formed the southeast limit and this would have spoiled the balanced picture of the developing centre and the outlying periphery where palatalization could not reach (as with Greek in the South and Tocharian in the East): so IndoIranian is made to stay in the central region. But here is the second difficulty. Greek belongs to group B (with Phrygian, Iranian and Indoaryan). If it had left before palatalization, then it is difficult to envisage the situation whereby it developed the isoglosses it has in common with IndoIranian to the exclusion of BaltoSlavonic (which, despite palatalization, belong to group A). The whole concept is self-contradictory.

Let us now transpose all Winn's conditions to Saptasindhu. Here again palatalization began after the various branches moved to their historical habitats (allow for some variation in the order): Hittite leaving first westward, then Tocharian to the east, then Germanic and Balto-Slavonic to the west and north-west, Celtic and Italic to the west and south-west, and finally Thraco-Phrygian and Greek (with the distinctive isoglosses they shared with the Indo-Iranians). Here too we have the difficulty of the position of the Balto-Slavs, but, as was said, perhaps in the early period (in the 6th millennium?) they were close enough to the IndoIranians. Thus palatalization spread from the Indo-Iranian "core regions" to the adjacent Slavo-Balts but not to the extreme limits of the "periphery" (particularly as many non-IE cultures intervened between the Indo-Iranians and the Hittites, Phrygians and Greeks).[24] Bryant discusses other possible OIT scenarios (146-9).

This scenario with Saptasindhu as the urheimat seems much more reasonable. Or so it would be, if I accepted the theories about protolanguages and isoglosses. I don't—and this has little to do with C Melchert's arguing (1987) that Anatolian Luvian is neither *centum* nor *satem* (where palatals have become affricates *z* and sibilants *s*; see also Hock 1991:13-5), or with the Himalayan proto-Bangani (perhaps) being *centum* (Elst 1999:122-3; Bryant, 142). We know, or rather surmise, that there was a PIE language but *we don't know what it was*, nor when, where and how it changed: we merely conjecture and theorize about these phenomena—and writing pseudoscientific texts just perpetuates the illusory knowledge, which becomes deception. Thus, again, without documentation we would not know that English 'help-helped' or 'starve-starved' were strong verbs in OE 'helpan-healp—geholpen' and 'steorfan—stearf-gestorfen'. Nor would we know that in Celtic alone of all branches the original IE *p* was dropped but retained in altered forms (eg *-pt* = *-cht*) and that many words with *p* are loans from other languages (eg Welsh *pysq* '*fish*' from L *piscis*). Nor, again, that S ***g*** would correspond in Gk sometimes to **b** (*gauṇ-/bous* 'ox'), sometimes **g** (*gir/gērus* 'voice') and sometimes **k** (*gṛha/korthis* 'house/heap') and in Latin, similarly, sometimes **b** (*gauḥ-/bos*) and sometimes **g** (*guru/gravis* 'heavy').

When Bryant states "Archaeologists, whether western or Indian, cannot simply dismiss or ignore linguistic reality", he is making a sweeping and confused statement. Even more

[24]Here I accept for argument's sake that the group-B isoglosses are innovations. But in the IIO scenario these could just as easily be archaisms lost by group-A branches.

than linguists' interpretations of facts, linguistic conjectures, which posit hypothetical, non-existent factors x and y and then take them as *facts*, **are not realities**. Consequently I have irremovable doubts about any linguistic phenomenon one step away from facts like correspondences that are generally accepted because of phonological and semantic correlations. Nobody should dismiss or ignore linguistic realities but everybody should avoid fantasies. For a comparative study of Sanskrit and PIE, see the paper 'Sanskrit and Proto-Indo-European': Kazanas 2005 in *Indian Linguistics*.

X. Conclusion

The Aryan Invasion Theory, despite its 150-year-long life, has no real support anywhere except continued prejudice. It has now been substituted, in a similar shameless frame of mind, by "migration" of an alleged complex and to the archaeologist or anthropologist incomprehensible nature; this is a deception, since the aryanisation of North India on so enormous a scale could not possibly have been effected without conquest and coercion—for which there is no testimony of any sort. Why this preposterous proposition should have acquired the status of historical fact among serious indologists is for me a mystery. There may have been racist prejudice as many writers aver (Shaffer 1984; Leach 1990; Frawley 1991, 1994; Feuerstein 1995; Trautmann 1997; Bryant chs 1-2, 13; many Indian writers like Talageri 2000 and Indian-American Kak 2000); this was perpetuated by mechanical repetition rather than logical consideration. Renfrew too was right perhaps in seeing nothing in the *RV* demonstrating that the Indoaryans "were intrusive to the area: this comes rather from a historical assumption about the 'coming' of the Indoeuropeans" (1989:182): this also is a kind of prejudice—illustrated by Hitze's "*Like nearly all the peoples* of Indo-European origin, both the Iranians and Indians first came as immigrants into the lands which they later inhabited" (1998:139, my emphasis: and note that most IE peoples appeared not as "immigrants" but invaders).

In sharp contrast, all the primary materials of a historian agree in showing no evidence at all for any entry. On the contrary, such testimony as has been preserved, early historical documentation and later traditions testify that Indoaryans are indigenous to Saptasindhu. These traditions (corroborated by foreign writers of the 4th cent BC) affirm that the IAs have been in Saptasindhu since at least the 4th millenium; this is now fully supported by Archaeoastronomy which places the great Bhaarata war at 3067, a Brāhmaṇa text c 3000–2900 and the Vedāṇga *Jyotiṣa* c 1800. Given that archaeologists, anthropologists et al, specialising in the prehistory of that area, affirm unequivocally since 1980 that the local culture has an uninterrupted continuity since c 7000 (except for the break in the skeletal record c 4500), we can say that the IAs have been in North India since that time. There is also the fact that the *RV* knows nothing of elements in the ISC whereas the later texts have these elements; moreover even in very late hymns the Sarasvatī is a large river supporting the Aryans on its banks: therefore the *RV* must belong to a period before 3000.

On the reasoning so far, the PIE language or forms of it were spoken in that area and therefrom arose Vedic with its own dialects which later developed into Sanskrit. People may have emigrated in northwestern directions at different times early in the 4th millenium and before; or there was a common language and culture continuum from North India to the Caspian Sea which gradually lost its unity so that different cultures developed at different locations. Evidence from the *RV* suggests the former. Linguistic evidence suggests that there was no unitary PIE language, that we can reach. "In fact, detailed comparison makes it clear", states Burrow, "that the IndoEuropean that we can reach by this means [of comparison] was already deeply split into...varying dialects" (1973:11, my brackets). Most probably there were also spoken non-IE languages in the region. Unless fresh evidence comes into the light of day, I doubt whether we can get any closer—remaining within the rational bounds of realism.

Quite rightly some scholars expect that one should demonstrate how various linguistic developements and archaeological data harmonize in the movement(s) away from the urheimat (Mallory 1997). With the available evidence this expectation will face grave difficulties. As was pointed out above, the PIE was as full of dialectical variants as Old English, Italic, Germanic or Greek: no protolanguage can be reconstructed in reality. In fact, it is just as likely that different dialects or branches of Greek (or Germanic or whatever) developed independently of one another from separate but close dialects or branches of PIE with the influence of substrata: we simply don't know.[25] Then again, with the available archaeological evidence the difficulties are probably insuperable since tools, weapons and other finds do not provide clear patterns of diffusion and certainly cannot furnish linguistic facts. Mallory is sufficient realist to acknowledge all these difficulties (1997:117). On this, I Pejros too mentions various difficulties (1997:156-7).

We are left with some clear realities and possibilities. All IE branches other than the Indoaryans have demonstrably moved to their historical habitats from some homeland: there is evidence of this of one kind or another. There is no evidence of any kind that the Indoaryans moved into their historical habitat at c 1500 as the AIT maintains. New

---

[25]See V Pisani's view (1971:XXXII): le varie lingue ie non sono la continuazione di un tipo linguistico completamente uguale per tutte: bensi esse representano lo sviluppo di antichi dialetti o gruppi di dialetti i quali tutti erano tenuti assieme da un certo numero d' isoglosse: 'The various IE languages are not the continuation of one linguistic type, entirely uniform for all; but they represent the development of ancient dialects or groups of dialects which were all held together by a certain number of isoglosses' and so on. I consider this just as possible as any monogenetic evolution. We simply don't have all the facts.

evidence may emerge showing beyond doubt that the Indoaryans were intruders, but this seems at present extremely unlikely. The linguistic exodus from Saptasindhu is, to use Hock's words, "relatively easy to maintain". How exactly the various branches moved westward to the extremities of Europe, I do not know. I could offer several variations of elite dominance, trading and artisan movements or even cultural missions, but they would all be conjectural. Personally I prefer to leave it to others to create their own scenarios[26] while I remain with "not-knowing"; after all, there are so many other important things in life I don't know—the beginning of language and of man, birth and death. It may happen that competent archaeologist/indologists will re-examine the accumulated evidence without the prejudices of the past and discover, perhaps, clear patterns of diffusion from Saptasindhu—as was very nearly done by B Sargent (above, IX, 3).

That most mainstream philologists will react unfavourably to this thesis I take for granted. I know well in myself the force of habit and of attachment to deep-rooted notions that reacts more through emotional outbursts than cool rationality. I repeat that the issue of origins, of *when* and *how*, is one not for philologists but for archaeologists and experts in related fields. We owe it, other than to the peoples of India who, I think, have long been wronged (by their own faults no less than foreign influences), to truth itself, which is the primary concern of all of us, to consider this thesis without prejudice.

---

[26]Kak suggests several modes of dispersal (1996). So does Ṭalageri who, further, identifies some peoples in the West with Vedic tribes and clans: Phrygians/Bhṛgus, Hellenes/Alinas and so on (2000:204-5; 258-66); but some of the cognations here are implausible.

Two: **Vedic Religio-philosophical Thought**

Introductory

1. Civilization in Ancient India, or *Bhārata-Varṣa*, is much older than the first extant written materials or the earliest Harappan culture. In this article I am concerned with the religio-philosophical thought that developed in the North-Western part of the Indian Subcontinent and what is today Pakistan, which formed a unitary culture in the fourth millennium BC. The Harappan culture is only one of its material phases and is wrongly termed 'Indus Valley Civilization'; it will be called hereafter ISC (=Indus-Sarasvatī Civilization) since the river Sarasvatī just as much as, if not more than, the Indus formed roughly its axis (McIntosh 2002: 24, 28). As archaeological investigations continue both in Pakistan and the land of the Bhāratas, new finds may necessitate modifications of the picture we now have of the (proto-)history of that region. We may have to revise even some of our notions about the earliest phase of the Vedic Tradition itself as expressed in that remarkable document, the *Ṛgveda*, and the texts *Atharvaveda*, the other *Saṃhitās*, the *Brāhmaṇas* and the Upaniṣads. As far as is known it was an oral tradition, (unrivalled in the history of mankind), and it was sustained even as recently as the 20th century of the Common Era by brahmin families devoted to its sacred lore.

The *RV* (=*Ṛgveda*) is remarkable not only in containing at once religion, science, poetry, ritual, history and legend but also in being an absolutely primary text and perhaps the oldest known document of mankind revealing the beginnings of the Indoaryan civilization. It is now generally assumed that "civilization" implies urban structures, tools, weapons and other material artefacts. This is essential for archaeologists and (proto-)historians since it is the presence of such artefacts that enables them to know anything about non-literate communities of the past. However, even in Rome the word *civis* 'city dweller' (from which the word 'civilization' comes) and its cognates implied the idea of law, constant and well-defined, as opposed to rapacity and lawlessness implicit in barbarism. Plato's first ideal society is a community with simple agriculture, animal-husbandry, essential crafts and trade (exchange), feeding on barley-bread and bulbs, drinking wine in moderation and singing hymns to the gods (*Republic* 370Cff). This sounds remarkably like the way of life we find in the *RV*. R Rudgley cites a modern scholar, Prof. Yoshinory Yasuda who found "a marvellous principle" for civilization which is "a respect for and co-existence with nature" and wrote further: "Civilization begins to appear when a workable system for living, that is a proper relationship between man and nature, is established in accord with the features of a given region": Yasuda wrote this in regard to the Jōmon culture in Japan beginning c 11000 BC (Rudgley 1998:31-33). This too is apparent in the RV in Saptasindhu, the-land-of-the-seven-rivers, the axis of which was mighty Sarasvatī, "flowing pure from the mountains to the ocean" (*RV* VII, 95, 2). This implies a fair knowledge of the processes and rhythms of Nature in the seasonal changes, the weather, the behaviour of animals, plants and minerals—in other words "scientific knowledge". And this the ancient Indoaryans had since they had agriculture, animal husbandry, building, metallurgy and the tools necessary for these arts and crafts—as the *RV* testifies. Their religion with its many deities, who are said to be manifestations of One Primal Cause, constitutes their attempt to penetrate the mysteries of Nature and life and death and know the unseen causes behind the observable phenomena—again as the *RV* testifies. Moreover, as another author writes on Ancient Egypt, "In a civilization, men are concerned with the quality of the *inner* life rather than with the *conditions* of day-to-day existence ... a concern ... to master greed, ambition, envy" (West 1993:6-7)—a concern clearly expressed in the Vedic texts. Their simple mode of life (and aspirations) did not require advanced technology, oppressive urbanization and enormous buildings, though it was not entirely free of pressure, anxiety and conflict—as shown by the prayer to Agni to avert poverty and neglect (*RV* III, 19, 25-6) or to Varuṇa for forgiveness of sins (VII, 89) or the gambler's lament (X, 34). Those ancient Āryas ('noble, civilized' people, as distinct from the *anārya* 'irreligious, uncivilized') left no monuments like the ziggurats of Mesopotamia, the pyramids of Egypt or the megalithic structures of Malta, but they left the *RV* which is a monument of language[1].

The Ṛgveda

2. Being an absolutely primary text, the *RV* can be, and has been, interpreted in many different ways. More often than not, because the uniqueness of the *RV* was not given its due importance and because much material in the hymns is elliptic and/or enigmatic, material from post-rigvedic (and even other Indo-European) texts was used. Sāyana's tradition saw it mainly as a text for ritual and this view coloured heavily the approach of the European scholars in the

---

[1]Throughout this study the dates are BCE except where stated as CE. The date after the name of an author in brackets denotes a modern date, of course. Eg (McInstosh 2002:24, 28)—where 2002 is the year of the publication and the other numbers denote pages in that publication.

I take it for granted that the ancient Indoaryans are indigenous from at least the early 5th millennium BC and that the (bulk of the) *RV* was, as the native tradition has it, compiled just before 3102, which marked the onset of the Kali-yuga (papers One and Nine) although there may have been (Witzel 1995) later redactions, insertions and other modifications of the original text.

19th cent CE; moreover these scholars imported, often unconsciously, the political, ethnic and religious notions, prevalent in that period—colonialism, European supremacy, the Christian missionary zeal, the theory of evolution, anthropological views formed from the study of 'primitive' peoples, materialism and the like[2]. Thus one reads of polytheism, fetishism, the evolution of religious ideas and forms, deities and demons representing forces of nature, theriomorphism and anthropomorphism or "arrested anthropomorphism" or "opportunist monotheism" (Hiriyanna 33, 39) and so on. Most of these views are mentioned by AB Keith in the first seven chapters of his classic study (1925). In the 20th century new views appeared on the rigvedic gods: psychosomatic or spiritual forces within man (Shri Aurobindo, 1956; Coomaraswamy 1942; Frawley 1991); forces of fertility and sexuality (O'Flaherty 1980a, etc); even forces of Thermonuclear Physics (Rajaram 1999)[3]. Although I have consulted all these and many more studies, I shall ignore their conclusions. Post-rigvedic texts and other IndoEuropean traditions can, and sometimes do, shed light on some rigvedic issues, but since the *RV* is an absolutely primary document it must be interpreted chiefly by its own terms.

3. The One-and-the-Many is an important theme in the *RV*: all deities are expressions or appearances of the One Source which is prior to all manifestation and beyond description. With this is connected the theme of man's

---

[2]From the many publications I select few Western ones which expose these prejudices: Shaffer 1984; Leach 1990; Feuerstein et al 1995; Trautmann 1997; Bryant 2001.

[3]Alone K Warner's 1989 article adheres to the rigvedic material; also to a degree, D Frawley (1991) and Jeanine Miller (1974, 1985). I do not know translations of the *RV* in modern Hindi or other Indian vernaculars. English, French and German (Geldner 1951-7) are very inadequate.

I suspect that for a good rendering the translator would need, apart from a good knowledge of Vedic, the very state of consciousness of the ancient ṛṣis themselves.

"divinization" (ie the actualization of inherent divine powers) or Self-realization in the later tradition. This is missing from mainstream academic studies because of the bias mentioned in § 2 expressed in such terms as 'primitive, pre-philosophic, pre-scientific' and the like, and because the term 'philosophy' is used in post-Aristotelian senses and not as it was understood by the Socratic circle in the late 5th and early 4th centuries in Greece, where it was first used extensively, especially by Plato, in a specific sense[4]. In the Socratic-Platonic teaching *philosophia* (>philosophy) meant 'love of wisdom' which entailed daily living according to ethical precepts and the exercise of virtue or excellence *aretē* (cognate with Vedic *ārya*), the pursuit of self-knowledge through reasoning and "dialectic", the contemplation of the highest causes, and the practice of some form of meditation, all of which lead to divinization. On the face of it, all this sounds far removed from the *RV* and akin to the Upaniṣads, but it is also very much a pre-occupation of many rigvedic hymns. In any case, there is no reliable information on the reasons and criteria used for the compilation of the ten Maṇḍalas as we have them.

In fact, philosophy in Ancient India does not start with the schools or systems Nyāya, Mīmāṃsā etc, with their epistemological, ontological and similar problems, nor with the Upaniṣads, but with the *RV*. Calling the hymn "the most famous Rigvedic speculative symposium", W Johnson examined at length the questions posed in the *brahmodya* of *RV* I, 164: 'Who witnessed Agni, the first-born?' (4a); 'Who created space and hence all phenomenal manifestation?' (6c); 'what really is the source of everything, that mysterious one?' (6d); and so on. He wrote, not without a note of condescention (a common feature in many other writings), "Despite their archaic age, these questions should not be dismissed". (Who dismisses them?) Then he added, "As the

[4]See *GEL* under φιλοσοφεω philosopheō and φιλοσοφος.

first formulations of serious pre-philosophical inquiry, these questions present remarkably sophisticated concepts even while using images and mythological themes, as Plato did, for their articulation" (1980:106-9). Such questions are not pre-philosophical formulations since they enquire after the first or highest causes; they present indeed remarkably sophisticated concepts. Stanza 21 ('the mighty herdsman of the whole universe, he the wise one has entered into me') and 35 ('this holy-brahma-power is Vāk's highest heaven') indicate that they are closely linked with Plato, one of the greatest philosophers of the West. Johnson did not examine stanzas 21 and 35 and their implications. Before we do so, we should deal with some general concepts of the rigvedic Cosmos.

4. The *RV* contains no well defined system of cosmogony or metaphysics. It is a collection of some 1000 hymns to deities mostly, that are considered 'sacred revelation' *śruti*, apprehended by 'seers' *riṣi* in an extra-ordinary state of consciousness. The linguistic variations indicate clearly that they were composed at different places and periods of indeterminate date[5]. It is not surprising, then, that we find inconsistencies and incomplete information on many subjects in the hymns.

This state of affairs has caused some major misinterpretations of the Vedic religion by many scholars. For F Kuiper for instance "the fight of Indra with the dragon (*vṛtrá/Vṛtrá*) is a creation myth" (1967:98) but secondary to

---

[5]Eg the common ending in the dual nominative **-ā** gives way to -**au** (masc; different in fems and neuts) in later hymns; so also neuter nom pl **-ā** to **-āni**; and so on. Besides, several hymns mention ancient and modern ṛṣis or hymns: eg I, 1, 2; I, 48, 14; IV, 50, 1; V, 42, 6; VII, 53, 1; etc, etc. It is known that of the 10 Maṇḍalas the 10th is the latest while the six family ones (2nd to 7th) are early, but no dates can be assigned: the difference between them may be many centuries, given the conservatism of old traditions. Moreover, linguistic variants may also have been used concurrently in different geographical areas and this may have applied to some/many hymns/ passages of the AV, which on the whole seems to be linguistically younger (§ 16). The whole issue requires a new systematic study in depth.

the cosmogonic myth of the waters even though, as he admits, "clear references to the primeval waters ... are found in the last and most recent book of the *Rig-Veda*" (p 99). But because other cultures have cosmogonic waters Kuiper finds it quite reasonable that this applies to Rigvedic thought as well (p 100). He thinks the same of the dragon/snake, found in NE legends (p 108). He gives only a passing reference to That One (in *RV* X 129, 3) but does not mention (p 132) that all gods and all phenomena are expressions of That One. W. Norman Brown, again, said much the same as Kuiper (1978:21-33) and found a basic dualism in 'real' *sat* and 'unreal' *asat*, *RV* VII, 104, 8-12 and X, 129 (1978:14-19).There is of course, no such simplistic duality in the *RV*. On the contrary as will be demonstrated below (§§ 7-8), what stands out in the *RV* for the careful reader is that the great multiplicity (of gods and other phenomena) is product of triplicity, that is of the three major levels within the cosmos, and this in its turn is an expression of a primal Unity: 'It being One became variously all this.' *ékaṃ vā idám ví babhuva* sárvam (*RV* VIII, 58, 2).

5. The picture of the Cosmos that emerges in a general broad outline is a primary one of two levels, sky and earth (=the dual deity *Dyāvāpṛhivī*, often called *rodasī* and presented as two bowls *dhiṣaṇē* 'full of intelligence(?)' I, 160, 1, or *camvā* III, 55, 20); but also a commoner tripartite one of sky, midspace *antarikṣa*, and earth. The three are said to have three levels each, giving a total of nine. (The numbers 3, 9 and 7 have mystical and magical significance.) Air fills the region above the earth while the extended earth is likened to a wheel or disc (X, 89, 4) having risen out of and floating on water (*AV* XII, 1, 8). There are streams in the sky (*RV* I, 32, 12; VII, 101, 4) and Sarasvatī is both a terrestrial and a celestial river (V, 43, 11; VI, 61, 11; etc). The sun and the moon are known and worshipped as deities but there seems to be no worship of any other celestial body. The planets may have been known, but certainty comes with later texts. Time has day and night marked by the rising and setting of the sun; there is a 10-month gestation year and a solar year of 360 days, while a thirteenth supplementary month is mentioned (eg I, 25, 8)[6].

The Cosmos is characterized and maintained by *ṛta* 'order, course-of-Nature'. This force is not deified but it is very powerful. Everything flows from the Seat of ṛta (I, 164, 47: *sádanād ṛtásya*)[7] and the year is its wheel with 12 spokes (st 11). Generated out of tapas (X, 190) it may never be infringed. Uṣas never deviates from *ṛta* (I, 123, 9); Varuṇa and Mitra have their great powers through ṛta, which they uphold and promote (I, 2, 8; V, 63, 7); Agni is repeatedly called *ṛtāvan* 'observer of, true to, ṛta'; and so on: in fact, all 'the gods have ever followed the laws vratāḥ of *ṛta* (I, 65, 2). The term has religious significance as the order-of-sacrifice 'rite, ritual' (II, 24, 8; X, 16, 4) and also a moral connotation 'right, truth, reality' and *anṛtā* the opposite; the latter acquires prominence in later texts.

6. The gods in the *RV* are supposed to be 33 (I, 34, 11), though, certainly, several more appear. There are 8 Vasus, 11 Rudras and 12 Ādityas but the first two differ in number in the lists of (later) texts; there are also the Vasus associated with Indra (and later Agni). Although the gods abide in heaven (as do the Fathers *pitṛ*, the 7 ṛṣis and heroes, in stellar form, in X, 68, 11, in 107, 2 and 154, 2), they are connected,

---

[6]Much more precise information appears in the later Vedic texts: see *VI* under *graha* and *māsa* ; see also Kak 2001 and 2003 with more and updated information.

[7]This follows directly st 46 which states that to the One the wise-poets give many names—Indra, Mitra etc; st 47 itself starts with *kṛṣṇám niyánam* 'dark is the descent': so the Seat of ṛta may be that One and ṛta itself may be Its expression as cosmic order or course-of-Nature. The idea of monism is quite pronounced in the *RV*, as we shall see, and here we have an instance of it.

in three groups of 11, with the three regions of earth, midspace and heaven[8]. *RV* X, 158, 1 prays "May Sūrya protect *pātu* us from heaven *div-*, Vāta from midspace *antarikṣa* and Agni from earth-regions *pārthiva-*", where Vāta (=Vāyu) may stand for Indra also, as is evident in later texts[9]. Indra has a special affinity with Vāyu and, in any case, apart from being the Wargod *par excellence*, he is also solar and aerial (filling the midspace in IV, 18, 3-5).

Apart from the Sungod *Sūrya/Savitṛ*, celestial gods are Varuṇa, Mitra and Aryaman (all three of the moral order, law, regulation, harmony), Dyaus 'Skygod' (but only a name, really), Bhaga 'the bountiful provider' (again, only a name), Viṣṇu 'the active/expansive one' of the three strides, whose abode is highest heaven (VIII, 52, 2; X, 1, 3); here too are Pūṣan and Vivasvant (aspects of the Sun), Uṣas the Dawngoddess (to whom are addressed some of the loveliest hymns: I, 48; 92; IV, 52; etc) and the Aśvins 'twin horse-deities' who succour and cure; also the Moon, Candramās or Soma, connected with the mind (X, 90, 13).

In midspace, apart from mighty Indra 'of the bolt' *vajrin*, who slays the dragon Vṛtra and releases the waters and cows (I, 32-33; IV, 18; VIII, 16; etc, etc: a major theme of rigvedic mythology), and *Vāta/Vāyu* the Windgod, we find Mātariśvan, related to Agni (III, 29, 11) yet bringing Fire to men (I, 60, 1; III, 2, 13; X, 46, 9); Apāṃ Nápāt 'Offspring-of-Waters', a form of Agni in the atmospheric waters (eg II, 35); Āpaḥ, the atmospheric Waters, providing an abode for Varuṇa (VII, 49, 3) and Agni (III, 1, 12; X, 91, 6); the Maruts 'Stormgods' who aid Indra and gleam with lightning (I, 88, 1;

[8]This triple division is adopted by Yāska (Nir VII, 5): it is largely correct but has inconsistencies, as expected. For more details about the deities see Macdonell 1898, Keith 1925 and E Ghosh 1933/1983. The first two have misinterpretations due to the prejudices of their age. The last one has some misinformation due to bad translations and typographical errors. Otherwise all three are very useful.

Hereafter Keith will be given with page number only.

[9]*Maitrāyaṇī Samhitā* IV, 2, 12. For a full discussion see Keith, 86-7.

V, 54; etc); "fierce" Rudra, father of the Maruts (I, 114, 6; II, 33, 1) with some destructive traits (I, 147, 7; II, 33, 11); Parjanya the rain-giver, god of fertility—in cows, mares and women (VII 102, 2) and father of Soma (IX, 82, 3); the old but subordinate and rather obscurer deities, Ahi Budhnya 'Serpent of the Deep', Aja Ekapād 'the Unborn One-footed',[10] which in *AV* XIII, 1, 6 makes firm the two worlds (cf *aja* in *RV* VIII, 41, 10; also X, 65, 13); Trita Āptya of the secret abode (IX, 102, 2) who prepares Soma (II, 11, 20; IX, 34, 4).

Agni is terrestrial but he is the most repeatedly invoked god after Indra and, being a personification of the sacrificial fire and a messenger between gods and men, appears in all three regions, is identified with some 15 gods and goddesses (including Aditi, Bharatī and Iḷā: *RV* II, 1), comprehends all deities (V, 3, 1) and knows all (*viśvavid, viśvaveda-* and, of course *jātavedas* VI, 15, 13). Other terrestrials are *Pṛthīvī* 'Earth', quickening the soil (V, 84); the Rivers with Sarasvatī as the "best mother, best river, best goddess" (*ámbitamā nadītamā devitamā*: II, 41, 16). Then Soma is the plant and drink, coming third in importance after Indra and Agni; it has its origin on the mountains in its physical aspect and in heaven in its divine one, brought down by an eagle (IV, 26; 27). Bṛhaspati or Brahmaṇaspati 'lord-of-prayer' (I, 190, 2) is the divine priest, closely linked (I, 33, 13; etc) to Agni *purohita* 'domestic priest' (I, 1, 1), but also allied to Indra in destroying demons and goblins with fire (II, 23, 14; X, 68, 4-8) or with his roar (IV, 50, 5; X, 68, 8).[11]

---

[10]Often translated as 'One-footed Goat' (Keith, 137). A goat could be conceived of as divine, like a cow or a horse, but how could 'one-footed' convey any significance? Even lightning (ibid and Macdonell 1898:73) could hardly suggest 'one-footed goat'! Some have plausibly suggested 'mushroom' (Wasson 1971; see also § 12.)

[11]Many of (the names of) these rigvedic deities are found in the ancient religion of other Indo-European peoples: *Dyaus*—Gk Ζευς/+ια-, Roman Ju[s]piter, Hittite [D]Siu, Germanic *Tiwaz*; *Parjanya*—Slavic *Perun*, Baltic *Perkunas*, Nordic *Fjörgyn*; *Uṣas*—Gk *Ēos*, Roman *Aurora*, Germanic *Eostre*; etc. For a full presentation see paper Three.

Echoing a long line of scholars, Th. McEvilley writes of "two types of gods... *devas* and their adversaries ...*asuras*"; he adds that "*māyā*, magical illusion, is used in connection with [asuras]" (2002:257-8): the former are Aryan the latter native non-Aryan, in the normal frame of the AIT (=Aryan Invasion/Immigration Theory). Given to easy generalizations, this scholar does not bother to tell his readers that this *deva-asura* contrast appears only in few late hymns of the *RV* and in post-rigvedic texts. If he had examined the hymns he would have found that deva and asura are interchangeable terms in the early and middle strata describing thoroughbred IndoEuropean gods like Mitra, Varuṇa and others, including Rudra. See, eg V, 42, 11 *namóbhir devā́ṃ ásuram duvasya* 'do adore with salutations the deva asura [Rudra]'; VIII, 25, 4 *mahā́ntā mitrā́varuṇā/samrā́jā devā́-ásurā* '2-great Mitra-and-Varuṇa, 2-imperial-lords, 2-devas [and] 2-asuras'; etc, etc. These deva/asura deities fight demonic forces (§ 9, end), not one another. The asura is *ahura* 'god' and the deva is *daeva* 'demon' in the Iranian Avesta. Nor does McEvilley know that māyā ('power through knowledge' <√*mā māne*; also Mayerhofer under *māyā*) is wielded by these *deva/asura-s* and the demons equally. I shall mention him often because he purports in a 700-page study to delineate *The Shape of Ancient Thought*, concluding, with much similar misinformation and rather superficial judgments, that Mesopotamia and Egypt were the sources of most of the ancient cultures. While it is true that the two great civilizations influenced other cultures in the Near East and the Eastern Mediterranean, including Greece, he ignores the Proto-Indo-European heritage (which goes back to c 7th millennium) and dismisses the antiquity of the Veda.

An equally curious view is given by MJ Shendge, the leftist historian who adheres to the AIT (2001). She applies "a new methodology consisting of criteria of rationality and realism" (p 146) and finds that "The Asuras and others were really the human clans who inhabited the Indus Valley" and "opposed the advance of the Āryas" (p 148). In an incredible outburst of "rationality and realism" she tells us that the *RV* was composed in Akkadian "by the Asura poets", ie by the Indus Valley natives who actually spoke Akkadian, and that the *RV* was adopted by the Aryan conquerors (p 153). This extraordinary theory is put forward despite the fact that all (Western invasionist) vedicists from Max Müller to Keith and to Witzel (2001) agree that the *RV* was composed in Vedic by the Indoaryans in Saptasindhu. (See also n 85, end, for Shendge's linguistics.) At least, Shendge does not ignore that the terms *asura* and *deva* are interchangeable.

We should note finally that the deities are said to obtain immortality (X, 53, 10) by the grace of Savitṛ, the sungod (IV, 54, 2), or through Agni's mind-powers *kratubhiḥ* (VI, 7, 4) or by drinking Soma (IX, 106, 8).

7. Such a polytheism appeared also in Mesopotamia, Egypt, Greece and other areas of the ancient world. But there are some important differences. Obviously, the gods in all those ancient religions represented natural phenomena: the Sungod was the sun in the sky; the Firegod was the fire in a hearth, a burning forest or lightning; the Raingod was the rain that filled rivers and lakes and fertilized the soil invigorating plants and animals; the Nightgoddess was the night that absorbed the sun, bringing darkness and dangers but also rest to creatures; and so on. In this they all agreed. Some of them also agreed that the deities were the numinous forces, the spirit within the natural phenomenon that made it behave as it did. In this, they recognised a numinous or causal realm that was imperceptible to the senses but apprehensible by the mind and responsible for the manifestation and sequence of natural events in the physical world. This divine realm could be approached and to a degree influenced by men (mainly ṛṣis), or special functionaries like priests, through various modes of worship, ritual, prayer, meditation, offerings and thanksgiving, so as to yield desired results out of the normal order of things.

However the rigvedic gods differed in some very important respects. First, it is very obvious that there was no king of gods the way Anu initially and later Marduk was in the Mesopotamian pantheon[12], or Zeus on Olympus. In the Vedic pantheon the gods have extraordinary fluidity. Thus, to take the example of Agni, this god, without losing his character or chief function of 'blazing', is said to be or have the attributes of Wargod Indra and of the Law-and-Order Varuṇa; he knows the doings of men and gods (VII, 46, 2) and, like the Aśvins, has healing remedies (II, 33, 7). This is due to the fact—and this is another and the most important difference—that all these deities are appearances/expressions of That One (*tadékam*: X, 129), an otherwise unnamed Being (which I shall call Godhead), the source of all divine and mundane manifestations[13]: as VIII 58, 2 says, *ékaṃ vā́ idāṃ ví babhuva sárvaṃ* 'It being One has variously become this All [and Everything]'. This aspect we shall examine below together with the third, equally important difference that these divinities are also functions within man's total organism, ie mind and body, constituting an underlying doctrine of Unity of Being that fused together cosmic and human powers.

[12]In this article, 'Mesopotamian' denotes the totality of Sumerian, Akkadian, Babylonian and Assyrian cultures, which, despite differences, have a clear continuity. I follow specialist-assyriologist Stephanie Dalley's example where she collects the translation of many texts from these cultures under the title *Myths from Mesopotamia* (1991).

[13]I do not know what Indian authors have written on this issue, except Shri Aurobindo. But mainstream scholars in the West do not give due emphasis to, or do not mention at all, this subject (eg Macdonell 1898; Keith 1925; Johnson 1980; etc). Notable exceptions are Miller (1972, 1974, 1985) and K Werner (1989). I find this omission remarkable since there are several explicit statements and many more implicit ones, but it is understandable in view of the prejudices mentioned in § 2.

Keith notes this rigvedic "assertion of the unity of the gods and the world" and comments that the *RV* "asserts [this unity] as a fact but which it does not justify or explain in detail" (p 434). This is partly true since the hymns are not explanatory treatises. Detailed explanations are found in other texts. But there are enough details in the *RV* to show that this unity was known well enough both intellectually and emotionally as an underlying system at least in some circles (see next § 8).

8. *RV* X, 114 again says explicitly that sages have traced the One Cause of everything abiding in distant and mysterious chambers (st 2) and that wise poets describe in many different figures that which is One in nature (st 5). Just as explicit is the statement in I, 164, 46, "the sages give many names to what is One—Indra, Mitra, Varuṇa, Agni", etc (here the One may be the sun); stanza 6 again refers to the One Unborn that has established firmly the world's six regions/dimensions: the presence of the "One as the Absolute' in this hymn is acknowledged even by WO' Flaherty (1981:73). These passages may be said to belong to the late (Maṇḍalas VIII and X) and middle (Maṇḍala I) strata of the *RV*. But III, 54, 8 is decidedly early (the Viśvāmitra family-book): "The All which is One *víśvam ékam governs patyate* what moves and what is at rest, what walks and what flies, this multifarious manifest creation *viṣuṇaṃ vi jātám*".

Then, the 22 stanzas of III, 55 (same Bk III) have as refrain *mahád devā́nām asuratvám ékam* 'great and single is the lordly-power of the gods'—which implies that gods are gods by participating in that single great power existing independently of every one of them. And in this simple phrase, in one of the early Books, long before the philosophical schools Nyāya etc, we find the kind of reasoning that Socrates will employ in fifth century Athens to arrive at definitions of essential ideas, as is shown in the early Platonic Dialogues and as Aristotle notes in his *Metaphysics* (978b1 and 1078b3-5): and this, 3000 years earlier than the Greek philosopher. The refrain has also implications about appearance and reality, the phenomenal and the numinous. The hymn refers to many deities—Agni, Indra, the Dawns, Heaven and Earth, Mitra and Varuṇa, the Cow-of-plenty, Bhaga, Tvaṣṭṛ, and others. Now, to take one example, within every form or manifestation of fire is the *deva* Agni, the numinous force responsible for the particular appearance: consider I, 59, 1 *vayā́ íd agne agnáyas te anyé* '*Agni*, other fires are your own branches/energies (vayā[ḥ])'.

This force is before, beyond and after, as well as within, every particular phenomenon of fire—in the hearth, on the altar, in a blazing forest, etc. Hence, the collocation *sahasaḥ putra/sūnu* 'son of strength/force', the strength/force being the cause of every appearance of fire. Similarly, Indra is 'son of might' or 'of truth' (*RV* IV, 24, 1; VIII, 58, 4) and, as Macdonell notes, all divinities are termed 'offspring of immortality' or 'of skill/creativity' (1898:12). Similarly, then, the *devas/asuras* as a class are manifestations of *asuratva* 'godhood/lordship', the One Power which is within every one of them, before, beyond and after them all. Just as every fiery phenomenon is a transient manifestation of the one permanent *deva* Agni, so every *deva* is an expression of the One Godhood. Thus, implicit in this simple statement, iterated 22 times, is the idea that not only mundane phenomena but the divinities themselves are transient and therefore unreal in relation to the permanent One Godhood. This very concept is articulated in I, 68, 2/4 '*bhájanta viśve devatvám nā́ma* 'all enjoy/share godhood, indeed' and in II, 33, 9 where Rudra's *asuryá* is said not to leave him and to make him ruler of this world: rudra is *īśāna* thanks to this *asurya*. (We may note also Indra's *indriyá* 'Indra-power', which is "uttered-forth" in I, 55, 4, etc.) This idea will find, of course, full articulation in the Upaniṣads (§ 26).

Thus we have the simultaneous presence of many deities and the One Godhead from which they have all issued and which any individual deity can represent, as indeed Agni, Indra, Sūrya, Varuṇa and others obviously do at times. K Werner put it nicely saying that the older "evolutionary view of religion did not apply to Vedism", adding: "In place of a linear notion of evolution of the Vedic religion from lower to higher stages, we shall then have a structural notion of synchronicity, of simultaneous co-existence of multiple stages and layers" (1989:13), or, in other words, Monism and Polytheism at once. He also dismissed the notion that the

Vedic deities were deifications of natural phenomena or "abstractions of action" and adopted R Otto's "hidden power of the numinous" (p 21). Naturally, "the ādhyātmika understanding and apprehension of reality was then, as in all other times, limited to a minority[;] far more interest was directed towards the diverse lower forces ...[than] the one power" (p 23). And this interest in lower forces is amply exhibited in the spells, exorcisms and curses of the *AV* (=*Atharvaveda*), examples of which are found in the *RV* too.

In fact, we can go one step further and state that almost all known cults are mentioned in the *RV*, mostly in small, sometimes in large. McEvilley writes that the Aryans seem to have opposed initially some "sexual cults" which "they partially accepted in the Middle Vedic period" (=*RV* Book X and *AV*) and then directed them into "a process of mentalization, a conversion to an antimaterialistic and antisensual idealism which arose in part in reaction to the body practices of the ancient cults" (2002:276-7). This is not only a confused statement but also thoroughly misinformed. Alone hymn I, 179, which belongs to an earlier rigvedic period, and describes the sexual act between sage Agastya and his wife Lopāmudrā (with all the complex nuances of that situation), should suffice to show that the rigvedic seers were not squeamish about sex and understood fully its part in life. In *BU* VI, 4, 1ff (and *CU* V, 7 and 8), the sexual act is again described in full in its physical details, not as a "mentalization", but with its spiritual dimension, as befits the human being, who has mind and spirit in addition to the gross body. If in his vague generalization McEvilley refers to incest, harlotry and homosexuality (practised fairly freely in Mesopotamia), these certainly are not condoned in the *RV* nor any post-rigvedic texts. While fertility (Parjanya) and sexuality are acceptable, incest is rejected in the well-known hymn X, 10, where Yama repulses his sister Yamī's sexual approaches—in contrast to the Iranian twins Yima and Yimeh who do unite and produce offspring (Macdonell 1898:173).

Some instances of incest among gods occur in the hymns. But this is easily comprehensible. At one level, as was said, rigvedic deities represent natural forces or phenomena; these mingle to generate new phenomena and often some of the former mingle again with the latter to produce yet newer phenomena (as heat and air give winds, then with moisture clouds, then rains or storms which cause growth of plants, fruit and so on): thus at this level, incest is understandable. But it is not acceptable in the human society. This rigvedic morality must go back to the Proto-Indo-European period (at least c 6000) since incest etc are not endorsed by any other IndoEuropean tradition—Greek, Roman, Germanic etc. McEvilley does not seem to know well enough the *RV* and the IndoEuropean cultures and many important issues escape him. Thus he mentions (pp 258, 264) in connexion with shamans the Muni or *keśin* of *RV* X, 136 "with his claimed ability to travel throughout the universe at will" (280) but not seer Viśvāmitra who stops the river(s) in the early Bk III, 33; he mentions the *brahmodya* (§§ 3, 22) in *ŚB* XIII, 5, 2, 11 calling it a "Vedic ritual... within the greater Vedic sacrifice" (408) but is unaware of its presence in I, 164 where the sacrifice is mentioned in different forms of riddles (stanzas 15, 35, 50) but none is taking place. He is also unaware of the deities' aspect as functions within the human organism, physical and mental.

9. The powers of the numinous are also in man. The poet of I, 164, 21 explicitly declares that the Godhead is within him: "Where ceaselessly the fine-feathered birds sing out in light their share of immortality with knowledge, there the mighty Herdsman of the whole universe, *sá mā́ dhī́raḥ pā́kam ātrā́ viveśa*—he, the wise one, has settled in me, the simple one". We may be uncertain of the exact location where the birds sing, but there is absolute certainty that the Godhead, in the figure of the world's Herdsman, is within him; and, naturally, He would function again as the Herdsman or regulator of all other phenomena within the man. Then, Agni the god who encompasses all gods (V, 3, 1:13, 6) and knows all (III, 1, 17; VI, 15, 13), and thus appears as an apt manifestation of the Godhead, is the light and source of all inspiration *kratu* in man's heart *hṛd́aya ā́hita-* (VI, 9, 6) and is perceived through mind *manasā nicāy-* (III, 26, 1; cf also I, 67, 2; IV, 1, 20)[14]. Indra too is internalized in IV, 26, 1 by identifying himself with Sūrya but also the sages Manu, Kakṣivān and Uśanās; moreover, VIII, 70, 3, says that Indra, or his state, may be attained by men (though not by deeds or sacrificial rites). Certain qualities, recognizable in man, are presented as deities, like *devī́ prámati-* 'goddess foresight' (I, 53, 5) or *devī́ táviṣī* 'goddess strength/vigour' (I, 56, 4). The 'holy-power' *bráhman*, inherent in prayer and ritual, is often the means whereby the great seers performed their miraculous deeds: Vasiṣṭha helped king Sudās defeat the confederation of the 10 hostile kings (VII 33, 3); Atri rehabilitated the sun with the fourth level of *brahman* (V, 40, 6), which J. Puhvel called "silent meditation as opposed to varieties of articulated speech" (1989:153). This fourth *brahman*, says I, 164, 35, *brahmāyám vācáḥ paramáṃ vyòma* 'this brahma-power is Vāk's highest heaven'. This Vāk 'goddess of Speech' or brahman is obviously innate in man, otherwise he would be unable to pray, speak or sing: 'may we be conspicuous with our horse[-skill] or with our bráhma-power' (II, 2, 10). And VI, 75, 19 states *bráhma várma mamā́ntaram* 'the brahma-power is my inmost

[14]Without adducing any evidence from the hymns, WO' Flaherty sees Agni as "the sun within your umbilicus" (1981:46) but J Gonda (1963), Miller (1974) and Johnson (1980) see him as the unitary force of consciousness that vivifies and watches over all the functions of man leading finally to immortality. VI, 9, 4 *idáṃ jyótir ámṛtaṃ martyeṣu* is taken as not 'this immortal light *in* men' but '*among* men' by O' Flaherty (1981:116) and KF Geldner (vol 2, 101: *unter den sterblichen*); this must be rejected since st 5 calls Agni "swiftest thought" and "mental energy" *kratu* (so also O' Flaherty and Geldner) and st 6 has him as "light placed in the heart".

armour': *antara* 'inner' cannot refer to anything gross and external. Even Keith conceded that in many passages *brahman* "must be taken rather as holy power than as prayer or holy rite" (p 446). All these are aspects of what I termed earlier (§ 7, end) the doctrine of the Unity of Being.

The interiority of the deities becomes quite obvious in the *AV*. For instance, here, Vāta/Vāyu is the life-force *prāṇa* (V, 9, 7) in general; this is universal *prāṇa* and *apāna* in the supreme god *Skambha* 'support' (X, 7, 34) but also in individual plants and men as in- and out-breath (XI, 4, 13-14). Man *puruṣa* is the *pur* 'stronghold' of gods with eight cakras (inner centres of cognition or experience) and nine openings (ie two ears, two eyes etc: X, 2, 31). Man is the *brahman* and in him reside all the deities as cattle in a pen (X, 8, 32). S. Kak explores this theme in his *Gods Within* (2002c).

It follows that in many cases the demons and fiends (Cumuri, Namuci, Śambara, etc), whom gods like Indra, Agni and Soma destroy together with their 'defences' *pur-*, are also internal. Thus there is an inner conflict between the forces of light (knowledge and piety) and those of darkness (ignorance and arrogance).[15] The supernatural battles between gods and demons also symbolize the battles between good and bad impulses within man's mind.

10. Cosmogony and theogony. Different hymns ascribe the genesis of the world, or parts of it, to different gods. The six regions, earth and heaven are measured out by Indra (VI, 47, 3-4) or Varuṇa (V, 85, 5) or the Sages (III, 38, 3) or Viṣṇu (I, 154, 1). Other gods make earth, midspace or heaven fast with various supports (I, 56, 5; IV, 50, 1; VII, 99, 3; etc). While Varuṇa measures out the earth with the sun as his rod, the Sun Savitṛ fixes the earth with bands (X, 149, 1). In I, 115, 1, Sūrya (allonym for Savitṛ) is "the

[15]In many cases too the foes are other human beings, designated by the collective terms *dasyu* and *dāsa* (I, 51, 8; II, 13, 9; X, 86, 19) or *paṇi* (II, 24, 6; IX, III, 2): see also *VI* and Mayrhofer. For *pur* see paper Four.

spirit/soul/self (*ātmā*)[16] of what moves and what is at rest"; in IV, 53, 2 Savitṛ has the epithet *prajāpati* 'lord-of-creatures'. In X, 121 *Hiraṇyagarbha*, who may be the sun (=*sūra*, st 6), is the creator god and is called *Prajāpati* in the last stanza.

A different concept, clearly pantheistic, appears in the *Puruṣa Sūkta* X, 90. Puruṣa is the cosmic being/man who manifests the world with only a quarter of himself becoming all beings, while the other three are immortality in heaven. From his sacrificial dismemberment by the primal gods arose all else: the holy chants and formulas, animals, men and celestial bodies; from his mind the Moon, from his eye the Sun, from his mouth Indra and Agni, from his breath Vāyu, from his head Sky; his mouth became the Brahmin caste, his two arms the warrior (*rājaṇya* = *kṣatriya*), his thighs the Vaiśya and his feet the Śūdra. McEvilley calls this hymn "macranthropic" and sees in it "a major element of late Mesopotamian influence" (p 26). He finds antecedents for it in the Egyptian Memphite Theology where various deities are described as parts of god Ptāḥ and the great *Hymn to Amun-Re* in which, again, other deities are parts of him, and ignores the fact that the first is not earlier than 1200 and the second c 1500. He finds antecedents also in Mesopotamian hymns to deities like Inanna/Ishtar and Marduk—again ignoring that these are not earlier than 1500 at best (pp 24-7). But what he also misses here is the important aspect that the Cosmic Puruṣa is *sacrificed* and his different members become parts of the universe: it is (not a "macranthropic" but) a cosmogonic hymn. Moeover the Puruṣa sacrifice is IE since we find a similar cosmogonic motif with a divine being's dismemberment like Skygod Ouranos in Hesiod's *Theogony* (185ff) and Scandinavian Ymir (*Edda*, p 10ff). Hymns closer

---

[16]This may be one of the first uses of *ātma-* in the sense 'self' that will become common in post-rigvedic texts. See also IX, 2, 10 where Indra is "the primeval self/soul (*ātmā́*) of the sacrifice"; also IX, 6, 8.

to the Marduk one, in which this god is identified with other deities and appropriates their functions becoming king of gods, would be *RV* II, 1 and V, 3 where Agni is identified with some deities (but in no way becomes King of gods). However, McEvilley thinks these two hymns present Agni, ie the element 'fire', as "the underlying world-substance' (p 302), which is utterly fallacious. With an evident panache for finding parallels and influences where they don't exist, and missing them where they do exist, he disregards the cosmogonic/theogonic import of the *Puruṣa Sūkta*.

In this X, 90 Sūkta we have also an explicit theogony. In other hymns different gods engender others. Often Dyaus and Pṛthivī are the parents of the gods (I, 159, 2; etc) even though they sprang from Puruṣa's head and feet and Indra is elsewhere said to have generated them (V, 30, 5; VIII, 36, 4; etc). Brahmaṇaspati is the gods' father (II, 26, 3) and he also fashioned the world like a smith (X, 72, 6). Soma also is said to be the gods' father (IX, 87, 2). Uṣas is said to be the gods' mother in I, 113, 19. Here she is called Aditi who elsewhere is a separate goddess and the mother of the Ādityas (X, 72) and of *mārtāṇḍa* 'dead-egg', who is the sun being born and dying again and again (X, 72, 8-9). There are others.

Behind this apparent confusion lies, presumably, the idea that it does not matter what deity is given priority or superiority at any one instance since every one is the expression of the Godhead and could therefore take on this role: to quote Kak, "the various gods are, in turn, the disguises of the same [R]eality" (2001:18). This is a form of henotheism which, while admitting polytheism and in this case also monism, yet ascribes importance/supremacy *hic et nunc* to only one god.

11. All these aspects of cosmogony and theogony (and anthropogony) are woven together in the remarkable *Creation Hymn* X, 129. Here, in the beginning, before creation, before existence and non-existence, immortality and death, there was only 'That One' *tâd ékam* breathing (*an-*) of its own power *svadháyā*—absolutely nothing else existed (st 1-2).[17] It was unfathomable Potency *ambhas*

---

[17]Here, three words deserve attention. In 1d is *ambhas* (only once, here, in the *RV*), invariably translated as 'water/ocean' (Macdonell 1917; Geldner 1951-6 *Wasser* 'water'; Miller 1972, 1985; O' Flaherty 1981; etc, etc): this is unwarranted and unjustified since "nought else existed", including 'water'. The meaning must be 'potency/potential' (*Gewalt* 'power' and *Wucht* 'force' in Mayrhofer; also *MSD*). So 1d—'Was there Potency, profound and unfathomable?"

In 3b *is salila*, again translated as 'water'. This is also unwarranted. At this stage, still nothing has been manifested or created. Only *tamas* 'darkness/inertia' and *tuchya* 'void/emptiness' are mentioned, both being non-material, whereas 'water' is material and does not ontologically belong here. So *salila* must be the 'fluctuating energy' of the 'breathing' of 'That One' which was 'Potency'. Given the alternation of *ṛ/ḷ* and *r/l* in Vedic, *sal-* probably<*sar*<√*sṛ gatau* in the *Dhātupāṭha* 'movement'; Mayrhofer 'extending'. See also *salila* in X 72, 6 wherein the gods stand closely-clasped and from them, as from dancers, *reṇu* 'dust, germinating pollen (?)' was produced and from this ocean *samudre* (st 7) the worlds and the sun; it is very difficult to see how dust/pollen could arise from water.

In 3d is *tapas*, translated as 'heat'. Undoubtedly it means 'heat, fervour' and 'penance, austerity' and the like. But need this be the only meaning(s)? The *Dhātupāṭha* certainly has √*tap-a santāpe*, covering all meanings of 'heat, conflagration'. But it also gives *aiśvarye* 'supreme dominion/power'. Here in 3d it must mean the 'power-of-transformation' which generates laws but can also modify or annul them. So *ābhu* 'that-which-becomes (something or other)' arises with the inherent power of transformation in That One, from *salila* through energy, heat, light, vibration.

There is nothing physical in this description. Even mental forces must be excluded since mind does not appear until later (st 4). Consequently, here we have causal power(s) of a very fine and high level. Mental forces and the gods appear at a lower stage (st 4-5), all within mind. Thus the gods are within man. See Kazanas 2005a, § 5 .... Like many others, mistranslating "an undistinguished ocean", McEvilley sees here Near Eastern influences, Egyptian and Akkadian (p 29), then misinforms his readers that "the Vedic creation myth is also clearly based on Near Eastern antecedents" (p 112), when there is absolutely no creation doctrine/myth in Mesopotamia or Egypt remotely resembling *RV* X, 129. Although he claims to be undogmatic, he very obviously follows the hard-line view that the Aryans came to India c 1500 and the *RV* was composed c 1200-1000. He even cites—not disapprovingly (p 664)—R Drews (1993) who has the Aryans invading India in the 16th cent not accross the Hindu Kush but by sailing in ships accross the Persian Gulf. Unless the invaders were no more than ...

enveloped in darkness *tamas*, yet having 'fluctuating energy' *salila* without any distinct form *apraketa* (st 3). From that, by the power of transformation *tapas*, arose *ābhu* 'that-which-becomes', still enveloped by the void *tuchya*. Desire or 'love' *kāma* evolved upon that—desire which is the 'first seed of mind' *mánaso rétaḥ prathamám* (st 4). After that came other powers and energies (st 5), the whole creation and the gods (st 6). But whence and how exactly it all comes about, is not known—not even by the 'Overseer in highest heaven' (st 7)! Nonetheless, the sages seeking with discrimination/wisdom *manīṣā* in their heart *hṛdi* find the bond bandhu of 'what-is' *sat* in 'what-is-not' *asat* (=*ābhu* 'becoming').

This hymn, *Nāsadīya Sūkta*, is most astonishing. Much can be and has been said about it. I mention three points. **a)** It is remarkable in that in seven stanzas it outlines the evolution of the creation, the macrocosm and the microcosm, the universe and man, and suggests that this can be discovered within one's heart or mind. **b)** The poet displays unusual humility in admitting that the absolute beginning of creation, the transformation of *ābhu*, is not really known or, at least, cannot be described. **c)** Men can discover in the ever-changing *asat* or *ābhu* the bond of true being *sat* within their heart/mind with discrimination.

A fourth aspect concerns the triple manifestation of the One in *kāma*, *manas* (and *hṛd*) and, implicit but not stated, *śarīra* 'physical body'. Desire/love, *kāma*, the force regulating *ābhu*, here represents what later schools call *kāraṇa* 'causal, spiritual'; this is the Supreme Will which the

... 200-300 (how could so few conquer and aryanize the vast expanse of the ISC?), the fleet required to carry warriors, horses and chariots must have been enormous! Yet neither Persian nor Mesopotamian sources mention such an event. The views of Drew are not followed by other indo-europeanists and, clearly, McEvilley does not bother to weigh hypotheses against facts and probabilities.

Māṇḍukya Upaniṣad will term *prajñānaghana* 'mass of consciousness', *sarveśvara* 'lord of all' and *antaryāmin* 'inner regulator'. Then there is *manas* and *hṛd* corresponding to the later *sūkṣma* 'subtle' or *antaḥkaraṇa* 'the inner organ of mind' being in between the causal and the material and linking them (the *taijasa* 'brilliant one' of the *Māṇḍukya*). Finally all this is embodied in the material body, the *sthūla-śarīra*. K Werner (1978) showed that this triplicity is found in different passages in the hymns but not in any systematic way; he identified *aja* 'the Unborn' with the highest body, the true Self of man or *ātman*. However, it is possible to find among the scattered references in the hymns three bodies apart from aja, ie physical, subtle and causal, which correspond to the terms given here in X 129. But, I repeat, there is no such systematic exposition in the *RV* hymns.

12. The discovery of 'true being' in oneself is in fact no different from the 'divinization' of oneself (§ 3) since all powers, or substances, or levels of being, are within oneself (§ 9). In the *RV* this divinization is accomplished through inner purification by means of *yajña* 'sacrifice' which entails the intervention of a higher power, also within oneself[18].

In the *RV* ***yajña*** is both external and internal. The word means, as many writers show, 'worship, offer-of-praise, offer of material things' and the like.[19] For *yaja-ti/-te* Mayrhofer gives *verhert*, *huldigt*, *opfert*, *weiht* 'worships, does-homage, offers, hallows'. These senses reflect largely the definition in the *Dhātupāṭha yaj-a = deva-pūjā-saṅgati-karaṇa-dāneṣu* which I take as relating four terms to *deva* 'god(s)'. Thus *pūjā* is 'worship/reverence/homage' to gods; *saṅgati* is 'meeting/uniting with' the gods; *dāna-* is 'offering, gift'. The term *karaṇa* 'instrument, making' is

[18]For a full discussion of this process in the *RV* see Kazanas 2002b. Here only a brief outline will be given.

[19]For details and bibliography see Kazanas 2002b.

more difficult[20]: it could mean 'being an instrument for the gods' or doing something for them, or 'making (oneself? something else?) a god.' I take the option *deva-karaṇa* 'making oneself a god'. Besides, this is implicit in many hymns, and Keith noted some such transformation in *yajña* where the performer "is filled with a sacred spirit" (p 276). The external ritual and its mechanics, seeking to propitiate the gods with prayers and offerings and to obtain benefits like offspring or wealth, has been studied and described frequently and in detail. Here I concentrate on the inner process of purification and illumination that is divinization.

We have seen that Agni is an immortal light in man's heart, the source of inspiration (§ 9). He also purifies by destroying darkness (I, 94, 5; VIII, 43, 32), demons (III, 15, 1; X, 87, 1) and guilt (IV, 12, 4; VII, 93, 7), protects with his magical *purs* (VI, 48, 8; VII, 3, 7) and confers immortality on men (I, 31, 7) and, through his *kratubhiḥ* 'mind-forces', on gods (VI, 7, 4). This light is invoked to find a path for the holy power of prayer (*brahmaṇe*:VII, 13, 3). Agni is entreated to purify *punīhi* "our prayer *brahman*" with his cleansing glow, together with Soma and Savitṛ (IX, 67, 19-26). This purification of prayer refers obviously to that fourth state of brahma-power which is most silent and potent, *Vāk*'s highest heaven (§ 9): this fourth holy brahma-power (V, 40, 6) the *ácittaṃ bráhma* 'the *brahman* beyond thought/conception' (I, 152, 5), is known only to Brahmins who have comprehension (I, 164, 45). It is the process which *Viśvāmitra* describes in a hymn to Indra: "They [=the sages] rested seeking with mind *manasā*, making with hymns the way to immortality *amṛtatva*" (III, 31, 9). Elsewhere it is described differently: 'the wise poets harness their mind and reflections' *yuñjáte mána utá yuñjáte dhíyo víprāḥ* (V, 81,

[20]Some suggest a tatpuruṣa compound *saṅgati-karaṇa* 'making a meeting/union with' but I don't agree because *saṅgati* 'union-with' is self-sufficient and does not need *karaṇa*; the definitions are always brief and want every term to count and denote something distinct.

1); or, 'they found the spacious light as they were reflecting' *urú jyótir vividur dídhyānāḥ* (VII, 90, 4). Harnessing their mental powers and refining them the sages reach realization in light. Thus, contrary to most scholars' belief (eg Mahoney 1998:120) that in later texts there is a gradual interiorization until the process becomes meditation in the Upaniṣads, this is already present in the *RV*. When later texts will say that the *yajña* is within man (§ 22, end), they will be restating what is in the *RV*.

The one ritual repeatedly mentioned in the *RV* is that of Soma—the pressing, the pouring, the filtering, the drinking. This too has its inner aspect, explicitly mentioned. The purifying filter (normally outside) is said to be in the heart: 'three filters has he set within the heart' *hridý-antár ādadhe* (IX, 73, 8). And the Soma flows forth with right word *ṛtavākena* (or 'word' [harmonized] with ṛta), truth *satyena*, faith *śraddhayā* and transforming power *tapasā* (IX, 113, 2). Soma too has four states corresponding to its four stages of preparation (IX, 96, 16-20); but the adjectives used here (*ṛṣimanās* 'with the visionary mind of a seer', *ṛṣikṛt* 'making a seer', *svarṣāḥ* 'disclosing heavenly light') and elsewhere (eg *pátir dhiyáḥ* 'lord of insight/vision' IX, 75, 2; *ásamaṣṭakāvyaḥ* 'of infinite wisdom' IX, 76, 4), again suggest an internal process. Ordinary people do not know of the higher states: "Nobody tastes of the Soma the brahmins know," says X, 85, 3, adding "As you stand listening to the singers, O Soma, no earthly person tastes of you." The seers themselves declare: "We have drunk Soma: we have become immortal; we have gone to the light and found the gods" (VIII, 48, 3). Some non-indologist scholars identified *soma* with the liquid extracted from the mushroom Amanita muscaria or 'fly-agaric' (Wason 1971, 1986). This seems to be the only reasonable identification as DH Ingalls was the first to acknowledge (1971).

Clearly there are wise men who have knowledge and others, the multitude, who have not. In the enigmatic hymn

I 164, the poet says (st 6): "As one who has no realization *acikitvān*, I ask those sages here who have realization *cikituśaḥ... kavīn*, I who know not for the sake of wisdom *vidmane*: what is the One who in the form of the Unborn *aja* has established apart these six regions/dimensions *rajāṃsi*?" Now the rest of this long hymn shows that its author, Dīrghatamas Ancathya, knows more about Reality than most, yet he is honest and humble enough to call himself *pāka*, a simpleton, and to admit that he is *ácikitvān* or *ná vidvā́n*, ie lacking full realization with regard to the Unborn One which having no prior cause is Itself the First Cause. He knows that the mighty Herdsman of the universe abides within him (st 22) and that *Vāk* has four divisions (st 45) yet says "What I am really I don't know being all tied up in my mind... I have obtained only a portion of *Vāk*" (st 37). Similar humility is displayed by seer Gṛtsamada in II, 27, 11, where he says he does not know much and prays for guidance to the Ādityas. This aspect of knowing yet not having full realization is also stressed in the Upaniṣads, especially in *Kena* II: "If you think you know well the Brahman then you know only its small form in yourself or in the gods." There are, then, the wise who have realized and the learned but unwise who do not really know but go through the mechanical motions as if they know. This distinction is made very clearly in X 71, the hymn dedicated to *jñāna*: those who look but do not see and listen but do not hear (st 4) are not real brahmins and are left far behind by the others who have realized (st 8). No doubt there are gradations of attainment but another clear distinction is made in X 85, 3-4: the Soma true brahmins know is not tasted by others who are enmeshed in earthly concerns. The Soma here must be the wisdom and power that comes with the full realization of the unborn and immutable Godhead.

Thus "they found what lay secretly high above, the supreme domain of *yajña*... They found through mind while reflecting (*mánasā dídyānāḥ*) the first path to the gods" (X, 181, 2-3). However, we must not ignore in all this that the seers attained the supreme state by the aid or intercession of a higher power (=deity: Agni, Indra, Soma, Vāk, etc) to which they directed their meditative prayers.

Another important aspect is that this divinization is obtained by humans before death. Some scholars try to connect this Vedic idea with Egyptian notions of immortality but ignore the fundamental difference that the Egyptian doctrine is found only in *funerary texts* (*Pyramid texts, Coffin Texts, Book of the Dead*: see paper Eight); but nowhere as a possibility in this life with the obvious implication that immortality will be achieved in the Afterlife! (For such misconceptions and false parallels see McEvilley 2002: *passim* and, for this case, 135-9.) This is evidenced very clearly in seer Kaṇva's second birth, when he states in VIII, 6, 10: "Having received from my father the essential-knowledge (*medhā-*) of the Cosmic Order (*ṛta*) I was born even like the sungod Sūrya". Here we should note also, apart from the brilliance that this knowledge produced, the tradition whereby the father transmits the sacred knowledge to his son—a feature continuing even in much later periods. (In *RV* IV 4, 11 Vāmadeva has acquired from his father Gotama his power to destroy mighty enemies through speech *vácobhis*.)

13. On the whole the *RV* has a joyful, optimistic outlook on life—and death. While *Viśvāmitra* complains that in his time people see only the gods' lower abodes (=*avamā́ sádāṃsi*: here, the stars? usual states of being and consciousness?) and there are not many who can declare the path leading to them in their remote regions (III, 54, 4-5), nonetheless the ṛṣis still communicate and meet with the deities—as Vasiṣṭha does with Varuṇa in the god's boat (VII, 88) or when gods and mortals come together in VIII, 48, 1. (See also close relation between Atharvan and Varuṇa in *AV* V, 11, 1-3.) We find humorous and even satirical touches in some hymns towards the sacred—as in the frog hymn VII, 103 or regarding Indra in X, 119. There is none of the pessimism we find in Mesopotamia (see paper Seven) or the gloom of

Hades in Greece. There is an "abysmal region" for evil and false people (IV, 5, 5), and all kinds of evil-doers, including sorcerers, may be cast into an abyss of botomless darkness (VII, 104). But generally the concern is with the joy and light of heaven: "O Soma Purifying, put me in that imperishable deathless realm where shines light everlasting... Make me immortal in the third sphere of inmost heaven where there is movement according to will... where there is joy and bliss" (IX 113, 7-11).

Virtues bringing reward are piety and worship, faith, adherence to ṛta and truthfulness—already mentioned. To these should be added *tapas*, an element in sacrifice and purification, bravery (X, 154, 2) and liberality (I, 125, 5; X, 154, 3), liberality having a hymn to itself, advocating the giving of wealth and food: *kévalagho bhavati kevalādī́* 'who eats alone is all-sin' (X, 117, 6).

Immortality is not automatically conferred on the dead, even if they have led a virtuous life; otherwise, the prayer cited just above, or V, 55, 4 "Lead us to immortality", would serve no purpose. In fact the dead go to different places—in the realm of celestial light (=Sun, stars?), of Yama, of inmost heaven, of the Moon and of bliss *ānanda* (IX, 113, 7-11), of the Sun (X, 107, 2; 154, 5). Immortality itself is attained by those who have reached divinization (§ 12).

14. Is there **transmigration** in the *RV* ?... Most scholars think not, but some few do find evidence for it (Miller 1974: 184; Werner 1978:286ff).

To begin with, the phenomenon for repetition/recurrence is common in Nature. Every day light breaks at dawn and the sun rises; after sunset, night comes and then a new day. The moon too waxes and wanes in measured cycles. Then, men sleep and wake up and sleep and wake up. Of course, no day (or night) is exactly like the previous one, but the recurrence is a fact. So, not surprisingly, the rigvedic poets wrote that Dawn, though ancient, is born again and again *púnaḥ punar jā́yamanā purāṇī́* (I, 92, 10; cf also III, 61, 3) and thus gives fresh life (VII, 80, 2); then, in I, 6, 4 the Dawns (or the Maruts, according to others) "again have obtained the embryo-state (*garbhatvâm*)". Associated with Dawn, the Moon also is born anew anew *nâvo navo bhavati jā́yamana... candrā́mās* X, 85, 19).[21] Then, the Sun *mārtāṇḍa* was again (*punar*) brought forth by Aditi for life and death (X, 72, 9); and in the form of Mitra, the Sun "orders the seasons and is born again" (X, 85, 18).

By themselves such references may be taken to be simple metaphors and so prove nothing—although metaphors relate to what the poet considers real-life phenomena compared and conflated in any one metaphor. A stronger indication is the rebirth/reincarnation implicit in Indra's or Vāmadeva's declaration that he was formerly Manu and Sūrya (IV, 26, 1). A different indication appears in seer Pratikṣatra's statement that he has knowingly yoked himself to the 'pole' *dhur* and carries that-which-gives-help and conveys-accross but he seeks no release and no turning back again *nā́vr̥̄taṃ púnaḥ* (V, 46, 1).

Much clearer indications appear elsewhere. HD Griswold cited in full X, 16, 3 and X, 58 (1923:313-4): a) "May your eye go to the sun, your spirit/breath (*ātmā*) to air; go to heaven and to earth according to your *dharma* 'nature/ merit'; or go to waters if there be your lot (*hitam*); with bodies stay within plants"; b) Your *manas* 'mind/spirit' that went to Yama... to heaven and earth... to the four directions... to the flooding sea... to rays of light... to waters and plants" and so on (X, 58, 1-7). Surely, all these references suggest transmigration. The same holds for X, 14, 8: *hitvā́yāvadyám púnar ástam éhi/ sáṃ gachasva tanvā suvárchāḥ* 'leaving evil come again home; in full brilliance, move with your subtle-form (*tanu-*)'. Of similar import is I, 164, 30: *jīvó mr̥tásya carati svadhā́bhir ámartyo mártyenā sáyoniḥ*

[21]S Radhakrishnan (1953:44) and Werner who follows him (1978:286) assign this to Mitra, which should in fact, be the previous stanza 18.

'according to its own nature/habits, the life-element of mortal-man moves on—the deathless brother of the mortal'; and st 38, *ā́paṅ prā́ṅ eti svadháyā gṛbhit* [*ó*] *'marty* [*aḥ*] 'the immortal [element] comes and goes gripped by its own nature/habit'.[22]

Passage IV, 54, 2 is much clearer, (despite the mistranslation of Macdonell and Geldner): *savitar vý-ūrṇuṣe 'nūcīnā́ jívitā́ mā́nuṣebhyaḥ* 'O Savitar, you unfold/open-out successive lives for humans'.

This statement is as plain as it can be[23]. True, there is

---

[22]Keith dismisses these examples either as similar to aboriginal beliefs (1925:571 and n 12) or as not being explicitly part of the ethical system of merit and demerit expounded in the Upanishads. He is doubtless a great vedicist but not free of the prejudices of his time. The argument about the ethical system is sound but misapplied. First, words like *dharma*, *hitam* and *svadhā* imply an ethical system (also *devāyu* 'devoted to god(s)' I, 154, 5) as do the different locations where the soul/spirit goes—heaven, earth, water etc. Second, as is obvious, the hymns do not constitute a mythology manual nor a theological/religious tractate to give expositions of (to us incomprehensible) ideas. Even simple tales like that of the Eagle breaking free or bringing Soma and that of Bhujyu being rescued by the Aśvins remain unexplained in detail by the later texts. But the authors and audience of the hymns obviously connected with these allusions and had no problem. This aspect too shows that the *RV* is much much earlier than other Vedic texts. We should not expect every idea to be explained so that **we** can be satisfied. We must use our reason and make the best we can out of such fragments and allusions. The beliefs of aborigines discovered in the 19th and early 20th centuries are irrelevant to the *RV*.

On the ethical argument, it is noteworthy that 55 years later similar statements are repeated: "When we examine the eschatology of the Ṛg Veda we are confronted with an unethicized religion" (Obeyesekere 1980:156).

[23]For translations similar to mine—RT Griffith, Miller (1974:184) and Werner (1978:287). Werner cites with approval H Grassman's free translation *Leben, das auf Leben folgt* 'life which succeeds/follows-upon life'.

McEvilley first writes that the *RV* "does not teach reincarnation" and assigns *RV* IV, 26, 1, "I was formerly Manu and Sūrya...", one of the early hymns in a Family Bk, to the Middle Vedic period c 1000 which includes Bk 10 as well (!p 112 and n 42, p 146). He has a Late Vedic period also with Brāhmaṇas and Upaniṣads, but I found nothing about an Early period. ...

no explicit exposition of the upanishadic doctrine of reincarnation in the *RV* but the passages cited are quite adequate to show that the *RV* knew some form of this doctrine. After all, the Celts up in Gaul had reincarnation, according to Caesar (*De Bello Gallico* VI, 14); this indicates that reincarnation was IndoEuropean and an inherited element in the Greek Orphic and Pythagorean traditions also.

15. Closely linked to reincarnation is the idea of the twofold path—*pitṛyāṇa* 'the Fathers' way' and *devayāna* 'the gods' way'. This too can be traced in the *RV*. Again, there

---

... He cites X, 16 "May your eye go to the sun, your spirit/breath to air..." and finds in it "the theme of cosmicization" of the dead soul which is "strongly reminiscent of Egyptian afterlife myth, where also the dead soul expands throughout the universe"—BUT he cites no Egyptian parallel wherein the eye goes to the sun, the breath to air etc, since there is none. It is again a case of non-existent parallels. Then he cites *AV* XIV, 2, 24, "which may reflect additional Egyptian input" from the Book of the Dead, but does not cite *AV* VI, 53, 2 (§ 19, below). To cap it all, he misinforms us that "the Aryan establishment admitted tribal influences from Munda and Dravidian peoples along with renewed Near Eastern influences" at the time just before the Upaniṣads and that "the primitive forms of the doctrine of reincarnation may go back to indigenist animists [?!] of the Ganges Valley or even earlier to the pre-Indus culture of "Austric proto-Australoids'" (pp 112-3). I find much confusion in all this and sloppy scholarship. Reincarnation appears clearly in Egypt and the Near East only after 300 BC under Greek and, perhaps, Indic influences.

McEvilley slips into sloppiness again when he refers to *RV* I, 164, 46 translating "That which is One the seers speak of in various terms: they call it [among other things] Fire" (p 38; square brackets original); thus the *RV*, he states, "teaches the ultimacy of fire as a symbol of the One'. Of course the *RV* does nothing of the sort: the cited stanza says "They call it Indra, Mitra, Varuna, Agni"—a very different proposition from "ultimacy of fire". Intent on *proving* the "ultimacy of fire' in the Veda and to connect it with the Heraclitean fire in Greece, McEvilley cites *Muṇḍaka Upaniṣad* II, 1, 1, finding that here "fire is seen as the source and goal of all things" (p 38). But he does not see that the *MU* passage is a simile, an analogy, denoted by the correlatives *yathā... tathā* 'as from a fire... so from the Imperishable'. We meet several similar egregious misreadings and misrepresentations in this author.

are the natural phenomena of the sun's and the moon's courses in the sky. In the rigvedic circumstances, the Sungod's course would more appropriately be connected with the way to immortality. The sun-course itself has its upward and downward movement (I, 35, 3). Then, Reṇu Vaisvāmitra says: "I have heard of two ways *srutī* for fathers, gods and mortals: all that moves travels on these two between father[-heaven] and mother[-earth]" (X, 88, 15).[24]

Here I stop. I have been long on the *RV* because most major religiophilosophical ideas of the Vedic tradition and many elements of what later is collectively called 'Hinduism' are present in the hymns. Hereafter I shall adumbrate briefly the important developments in the *AV*, the Brāhmaṇas and the Upaniṣads.

Atharva Veda

16. Magical spells, apotropaic, purificatory or therapeutic, charms, exorcisms, curses, and the like, constitute the bulk of the *Atharva Veda*—though some examples are found in the *RV* too. Book XX and about one seventh of the rest of the *AV* is taken from the *RV*. This Saṃhitā is also known as *Atharvāṇgirasaḥ* 'the Atharvans and Aṅgirasas'. Bk X is wholly, and Bk XVI mostly, composed in prose while prose passages are found in other Books as well. In addition to the magical incantations and cultic formulas which seek to influence the divine or supernatural world, the *AV* contains hymns with new cosmogonies and new divine figures of henotheism and a developed philosophical terminology that takes us to the upanishadic doctrines. Linguistically the *AV* hymns are generally younger, and although some may be as old as those of the late or even the middle strata of the *RV*

---

[24]It is difficult to see how Keith finds here "a reference merely to day and night" (195:571). Griffith translates according to the traditional view of the two paths; so does Werner 1978. I found not one allusion to reincarnation in the *RV*, not even a dismissive one, in O' Flaherty 1980b.

and most scholars believe that they contain older primitive material,nothing in fact can be determined with certainty and such scholarly beliefs are merely conjectural.[25] There is not the slightest proof that the Vedic religion started with such spells. The *AV* merely records this level of religio-magical practices (see § 8). For, although I concur with the general view that the *AV* on the whole is later than the *RV*, it is very likely that portions of it are contemporaneous with the late and even early strata of the *RV* but the task of identifying such passages/hymns and assigning dates even approximately would require a separate and lengthy study. Nor can we have absolute certainty.

17. Here are given some examples of these magical spells from different areas of experience. Agni has displaced Indra in the general preference and is mentioned about 650 times while Indra 450 (Singh 1997:31, 45). Agni is invoked in charms of all kinds, since some ritual with fire (and often water and/or some plant) was involved. Thus I, 25 is against *takman* 'yellow fever', son of Varuṇa (also V, 22, VI, 20; etc). Agni is often invoked (and other gods) against sorcerers and demons (I, 7 & 8; V, 14 & 31, etc); against *piśacas* as disease-demons (VI, 36) and disease generally (III, 31, 6) or against disease and death (V, 30, 11-14); in III, 12 Agni is to provide longevity (also VII, 53). He also cures madness and wards off rakṣasas (VI, III, 1-3). In VI, 85 and X, 6 Agni is associated with the *varaṇa*-tree (against disease) and the amulet of *khadira-wood* (for faith, strength, abundance, superiority, etc). In Hymns II, 1 and 2 Agni burns up enemies' schemes and deprives them of hands. There are charms for merchants' gain (III, 15) and success at dice (VII, 50, 3). With II, 36 a suitor is obtained for a maiden while

[25]See Winternitz 1981, vol 1; 116-7. Scholars who have failed to discuss fully such ideas of the rigvedic religion as the Many-out-of-the-One, the esoteric side of yajña, the aspect of divinization, and their wider implications, are hardly in a position to evaluate correctly the Vedic religion and its beginnings.

VI, 130 rouses a man's passion for a woman (also 131, 1-3; cf III, 25; etc). With VI, 106 Agni himself is to avert fire. Then we find charms for expiation of sin (VI, 45) and good fortune (VI, 110). In II, 10 Agni is to remove hereditary disease, curses of relatives, hatred from others, Varuṇa's fetters and guilt. Many other spells could be cited invoking other gods or using amulets, plants, water etc for various purposes, but enough has been said to indicate the range of these magical-ritual practices.

18. From the point of view of this study, more significant is the emergence of new deities into prominence while others recede in importance. (This could be due to geographical differences in henotheism, but any such speculations do not seem to be susceptible to proof). Thus, Soma, one of the more important rigvedic deities (120 hymns and numerous other passages in all 10 Maṇḍalas) is mentioned 280 times but while it is the best of plants (VI, 3, 2) and is used in sacrifice (also magical and medicinal practices), as a god he is now identified with the Moon (*candramās*:: VI, 81; XI, 6, 7). Uṣas is mentioned in several *AV* hymns and invoked with other deities in various charms (III, 7, 7; IV, 4, 2; XI, 6, 7; XVI, 6, 5; etc) but is also cosmic god Vrātya's *puṃścalī* 'harlot' (XV, 2, 13: a rather vulgar expression here).

Book XIII is devoted to the cosmic deity *Rohita* (and his consort *Rohiṇī*). He is evidently a solar deity, omnipresent and omniscient, like other deities (Skambha, Kāla, Prajāpati). In fact all gods, the past and the future, death and immortality are united in him (XIII, 4, 21-5). *Kāla* 'Time' is another such deity, celebrated in two hymns, XIX 53 and 54: existing in many forms, the lord of all, and father of Prajāpati, he is the highest god, ever moving on. But I can't help wondering whether 'time' is a correct rendering of kāla (the root being √kal *śabdasāṅkhyāna-yoḥ* 'sound and measure'). More significant is the rise of Prajāpati. The name started as an epithet of Savitṛ (*RV* IV, 53, 2) and Soma (*RV* IX, 5, 9) but was given to a cosmic deity in *RV* X, 85, 43, in 169, 4 and 184, 1; in the *AV* he acquires greater importance, generating the creatures (VII, 9, 1) and all worlds from the sacrificial rice (XI, 3, 52), identified with *Brahmacārin* (XI, 5, 16: in this hymn, cosmic deity), Rohita (XIII, 2, 39) and Vrātya (XV, 1, 2), and will be the chief god in the Brāhmaṇas.[26] Here we certainly observe the development of a motif.

---

[26]We may note here, also, that Rudra is given the epithet *paśupati* (XI, 2, 5, etc) which will remain in later texts with god Śiva; however, already in *RV* I, 43, 6, Rudra grants health to horses, rams and ewes and cattle (without the use of the epithet *paśupati*). Note also that *Bhūmi* 'Earth', originally herself water, has the quality *gandha* 'fragrance' found in people too, and here may be the beginning of the doctrine of the distinctive quality of each of the five elements (earth-scent, water-taste, fire-light/form, air-texture/touch, ether-sound).

McEvilley thinks that the *AV* "represents the *asura* view as against the *deva- oriented Ṛg Veda*" (p 257). He thinks that "magic and witchcraft" enter into the Vedic Tradition at the time of the *AV* as well as the hymns to *Kāla*, the Cosmic Person (=Puruṣa Sūkta in *RV*:p 258), the Vrātyas and the like (thanks to shamanic, Dravidian and Near Eastern influences). Again, he displays confusion and ignorance. Magical practices are found also in hymns of the earlier strata in the *RV* (I, 23, 21-2 and 133, 3; V, 12, 2; VII, 104; VIII, 23, 14-5; etc). There is no Egyptian hymn like the two of Kāla in the *AV*- and Ancient Egyptian has no word for 'time' (Assman 2001:79). There is nothing asuric about Kāla, Prajāpati, Rohita, Skambha. McEvilley says also that Akkadian words *apsu*, *tiamat* (*abzū* and *ti'āmat*, in fact) and *ummal umā* came into Vedic. If he searched a little further, he would have found that the common Vedic apsú 'in waters' is a locative plural of *ap* (*ap+su*) with strong-stem nominative plural *ā́paḥ*; *ap* is a common IE stem found in Iranian *ap/āf-*, Old Prussian *ap-e* and Lithuanian *up-e* all meaning 'water' or 'river'. It is hardly possible that Mesopotamian *āp-əm/Abū*'freshwater' reached the North-European languages as well! The *taimāta* (*AV* V, 13, 6) 'brown/black water-snake(?)' is thought by Mayerhofer to be cognate with *tim- a/i* 'large fish' (and √*tim* 'become wet') and so could hardly be borrowed from *Akkadian Ti' āmat*, the sea-water goddess whom Marduk killed. As for Vedic Umā (*Kena U* III, 12), later consort of Śiva, her name has the homonym umā 'flax', also thought by Mayrhofer to be IE (perhaps from √*ve* 'weave'). Thus, with the removal of the AIT blinkers, we can reasonably claim that Akkadian borrows from Vedic. This is another example of McEvilley's hasty and superficial judgments. Although in instances like that of '*Umā*' or *Skambha* we may have innovations/ developments from native elements, other cultural elements in the *AV* seem to me to stress or expand unobtrusive rigvedic ones (or, again, be cultic occurences in geograpical areas where the main rigvedic deities were less popular).

19. In the *AV* the two paths of gods and fathers *devayāna* and *pitṛyāna* are mentioned explicitly in VI, 117, 3 (also VIII, 10, 29:*devayāna*). The dead go to *antarikṣa*, from there to heaven and then beyond heaven's vault *nāka* to celestial light (IV, 14, 3). They ascend to heaven apparently retaining their male/female sex and capable of enjoying pleasures similar to earthly ones (IV, 34, 2; XII, 3, 40). But they can also assume varied forms (eg charioteer or bird) and move beyond (IV, 34, 4)—whatever that means. In XII, 4, 36, occurs the phrase *naraka loka* which thereafter designates 'hell', the place where evil female sorceresses (and, later, murderers and other sinners) go, a place of blackest darkness (II, 14, 3; V, 30, 11; etc). Moreover, the idea of reincarnation is found in *punaḥ prāṇaḥ punar ātmā na etu* 'may the life-force, may spirit come to us again' (VI, 53, 2).

The holy power *brahman* becomes in the *AV* yet another cosmic deity but also the conscious First Cause of all creation. Being everywhere and full of knowledge, it has manifested the bond of everything and articulates all the births of gods (IV, 1, 3). The Brahmacārin (XI, 5) is in every sense the *brahman* since this is what he practises and bears (*bibharti*: XI, 5, 24)—the Power permeating all creation. Skambha too is identified with *jyeṣṭha-brahma* 'the highest/eldest *brahman*' (X, 1, 34)—entering into, supporting and containing everything (X, 7, 10ff). The *brahman* has settled in the *kośa* 'case/sheath' or *pur* 'stronghold' of man (X, 2, 32-3). Man's *prāṇa* 'life-force' continues only by virtue of *brahman* (XI, 4, 23). Therefore the sage who knows this *puruṣa* knows him to be *brahman* (XI, 4, 23). Brahman as Spirit *yakṣa* is described as *ātmanvat* (X, 2, 32); *ātman* is desireless *akama*, wise *dhīra*, immortal *amṛta* and so on: whoever knows him thus does not fear death (X, 8, 43-4). These passages foreshadow the upanishadic formula *ayam ātmā brahma* 'this Self is Spirit Absolute'.

Sacrificial Ritual

20. Generally speaking a sacrificial rite required four types of priest. Even the *RV* has sacrifices other than that of Soma as the two hymns to the Horse (I, 162 and 163) attest for the *aśvamedha*. All four types are attested in the *RV*. The hotṛ 'invoker' recites the *ṛcas* 'verses' praising and inviting the gods. The *udgātṛ* 'singer' accompanies with chants the whole performance.The *adhvaryu* is the practical priest who carries out the liturgical acts muttering the sacrificial formulas *yajus*. The *brahmán* 'highpriest' supervises the whole performance and corrects any errors with the appropriate sacred words. With these functions are connected the three Vedas: the *Rgveda* with the *hotṛ*; the *Sāmaveda* with the *udgātṛ*; the *Yajurveda* with the *adhvaryu*.

21. The **Sāmaveda** consists of verses found in the *RV*. Only 75 verses do not occur there but are found in other Samhitās or works on ritual. As such, the Sāmaveda is of no interest to our study.

22. The **Yajurveda** has come down to us in six recensions four of which belong to the kṛṣṇa 'Black' school and two to the *śukla* 'White'.[27] The best-known of the four recensions of the Black Yajurveda is the *Taittirīya Saṃhitā*. The White school is represented by the *Vājasaneyī Saṃhitā*. The difference between the two is that the *VS* contains only *mantras*, ie prayers and incantations, while the *TS* has also a description of the rites. The rites include the *agnihotra* 'fire-offerings' (morning and evening), the *rājasūya* 'coronation', *aśvamedha* 'horse-sacrifice', funeral ceremonies, etc. The prayers are dedications and petitions.

---

[27]These are the *Kāthaka*, the *Kapisthala-Kaṭha*, the *Maitrāyanī* and the *Taittirīya* Saṃhitās of the Black school and the *Kāṇva* and *Mādhyandina* Saṃhitās of the White school: the last two differ only in minor respects.

A simple dedication formula mentions the offering and the deity: "this (or, you) for Agni (or Indra, or whoever)". A simple petition formula is: "You Agni, are protector of bodies: protect my body! You Agni, are giver of life: give me life!" (*VS* III, 17). During some ceremonies are used riddles, known as *brahmodya* (found also in the *RV* and *AV*). Eg in the *aśvamedha* is found the following: "Who wanders lonely on his way?/ Who is born always anew?/ What is the cure for cold?/ What is the great container?// The sun wanders lonely on his way./ The moon is always born anew./ Fire is the cure for cold./ The earth is the great corn-container.//" (*VS* XXIII, 45ff).

Several more points need mention. One is the Śatarudrīya the enumeration of the 'hundred names of Rudra' in *VS* XVII. This practice will develop in later religious texts into the 1000 names of Śiva and the 1000 names of Viṣṇu: their recitation was (is still) considered a highly meritorious act of worship. Secondly, we find some sacrificial invocations like *svāhā* 'hail!' and *vaṣaṭ* 'hail/amen'. Here is found also the sacred syllable *OM* which in the language of the gods signifies what is denoted by *tathā* 'thus, so it may be' among men (*AB* VII, 18) or which expresses consent 'yes, so be it, amen' (*CU* I, 1, 8).

Thus although concern with the ritual is preeminent, devotional or philosophical passages are not lacking, though almost invariably subordinated to the sacrifice. Eg "May life accord with the sacrifice; may expiration... inspiration... the eye... the ear... mind... body accord with the sacrifice;" and the text adds the theme of divinization: "We have come to heaven, to the gods; we have become immortal; we have become the offspring of Prajāpati" (TS I, 7, 9). In these texts Prajāpati rises to supremacy: "All the gods are Prajāpati ... From his body Prajāpati fash ioned the bull and the cow" (*TS* II, 1, 4). Here also, in connection with Prajāpati as creator-god, appears the formula, "Prajāpati desired 'May I create offspring'; he did *tapas* and created..." (*TS* III, 1, 1). Nor is the esoteric aspect of the sacrifice forgotten; it is in fact stressed in several passages: the sacrificer calls forth the Waters "with mind" (*TS* I, 6, 8); "Prajāpati performed the sacrifice with mind" and the sacrificer "remains silent to support the sacrifice" (ibid; also II, 5, 11, 3); "When the hotṛ invokes Iḍā, the sacrificer... should in mind reflect on Vāyu" (I, 7, 1); etc.[28]

23. All these elements are developed *in extenso* in the prose texts known as ***Brāhmaṇa***, which treat in greater detail, and often (for us) tediously, the various sacrifices already mentioned. The best known are the *Aitareya* and *Kauṣītakī*, both attached to the *RV*, and the *Śatapatha*, belonging to the White Yajurveda. Another and older name for *brāhmaṇa* was *bandhu* 'connexion', indicating that the purpose of these texts was also to explicate connexions between the rituals and prayers or other religio-philosohical ideas. Thus Manu tells one of his sons, "the Aṅgirasas are

---

[28]JC Heesterman (1993) is well aware of the esoteric aspect and cites Baudhāyana Śrauta Sūtra XXIV, 2: "Where then is the sacrifice?... It is in man" (p 5); or, "both hotṛ and sacrificer are said to be the self (*ātman*) [in *Kauṣitakī* Br IX, 9; *ŚBr* IX, 5, 2, 16] (p 144). Yet, he chooses to resort to traditions and cults later than the Vedic Tradition (Iranian, Greek, Judaic, Christian) and to stress the anthropological and sociological elements related to the ritual, like "the domestication of fire" (p 6), "the solemnization of food and its distribution at a communal meal" (p 10), conquering "the world of the wild... through fire" (p 30), the emergence of "an exclusive specialized priesthood" (142-3), etc. All these observations are partly true, of course. But this (predominantly structuralist) approach leads to some very strange conclusions. Thus, "at the heart of the sacrifice there is the threat of catastrophe overthrowing all order" (p 27)—as if such a threat does not exist with most phenomena in this world of change; or, the fire-cult "gave rise to the concept of the *ātman*" (p 217)—as if any (normal) man does not first have awareness of his own self and does not relate all his perceptions and everything else to this self; and "it was ritualism that achieved the decisive break and so led to the Upanishadic *ātman-brahman* doctrine" (p 220)—when this is already implicit in the imagery of the *RV* (§§ 9-13) and explicit in the *AV* (§ 19, end).

performing a *sattra* [=sacrificial session] but they cannot discern the heavenly world; you declare this *brāhmaṇa* to them" (*TS* III, 1, 9). But *bandhu* also indicates the connexion of sacrifice between man, god and the cosmos[29].

While all Brāhmaṇas describe the sacrifice, those of the *RV* stress the Hotṛ's duties, those of the *Sāmaveda* the Udgātṛ's part, and those of the *Yajurveda* the Adhvaryu's function. Apart from technical matters like the construction of the fire-altar *agnicayana* (eg *ŚB bks VI-IX*) and descriptions of rituals like the *aśvamedha* 'horse-sacrifice (*ŚB* XIII), there are legends developed from hints contained in the *RV*, like the story of Naciketas, the boy given by his father to Yama (*TB* III, 11 from *RV* X, 79, 5) or of *Śunaḥśepa*, another boy who was given as a sacrificial offering in the place of a king by his avaricious father (*AB* VII, 13ff from *RV* V, 2, 7 and I, 24-30) and the love-story of king Purūravas and nymph Urvaśī (*ŚB* X, 5, 1 from *RV* X, 95); another tale is that of the Flood wherein Manu was saved by a fish (*ŚB* I, 8, 1). These may be fuller versions than the elliptic ones in the *RV* or attempts at filling the gaps in the rigvedic references. Since the rigvedic brief allusions imply the presence of full legends, religious myths and historical events well known at that time, and since the Vedic transmission has proved to have enormous mnemonic power, I would incline towards the first alternative—for there are allusions, like the story of Bhujyu, who is saved by the Aśvins, that were not later given in fuller versions with the implication that they went out of the memory of the Tradition.

---

[29]Many views have been published about yajña from F Kittel (1872) to Keith (1925:chs 18-22) and later. Dandekar saw in it "profound cosmic significance... a representation in miniature of the cosmic order... the rhythmic course of nature" (1967:70). More recently, S Kak thinks that the sacrifice "posits an identity of the sacrificer and the universe... [and] the knowledge central to the sacrifice... becomes the vehicle of the transformation of the participants" (2002a:5). See also Keith, 442 and n 1.

24. Many and varied are the cosmogonic accounts in the Brāhmaṇas. In one account a golden egg appears on the primeval ocean and after a year Prajāpati broke out of it and proceeded to create through monosyllabic utterances (*ŚB* XI, 1, 6). In another one Prajṇpati creates man from his own mind, various animals from his vital airs and others from his different organs; in as much as he created man from his mind "man has all animals"(*ŚB* VII, 5, 2, 6). In yet another account Brahman created the gods and then the worlds for their abodes—earth to Agni, midspace to Vāyu and sky to Sūrya; then it descended into these worlds through name and form (*ŚB* XI, 2, 3; also *TB* II, 8, 9, 3-7). In a fourth one, *brahman* springs to life as mind and then Prajāpati into whom *brahman* enters so that he may become a progenitor (*TB* II, 2, 9; also *Jaiminīya Upaniṣad Brāhmaṇa* III, 38, 1). In a longer account (*AB* V, 32) after the genesis of the gods and the Vedas, Prajāpati took three sounds, **a**, **u** and **m** and brought them together into **OM**, the Praṇava (which will be the subject of the *Māṇḍukya Upaniṣad*).

However, of much importance is also the continuation of the theme of the absolute brahman and of the elements of the Macrocosm being in man, the Microcosm. One passage says that gods and other creatures are in various parts of man: *ātman* is the *ātman* in his heart, Indra is his strength, Parjanya in his head, and so on, and what is immortal is in *brahman* (*TB* III, 10, 8). In the *Kauṣītaki Br* "the holy power *brahman* born first in the east is yonder" (VIII, 4) while the last section of the *AB* gives the cycle of life and death of the holy power *brahmaṇaḥ parimara* where everything arises and dissolves on that cycle (VIII, 28). More important, the *brahman* and the *ātman* are identified and knowledge of the *ātman* as the self frees the man from the pollution of action (*TB* III, 12, 9); the same idea is found in ŚB X, 6, 3, 1-2, where one meditates on *satyaṃ brahma* and *ātman*, identified with the puruṣa.

All these threads continue in the Āraṇyakas and the Upaniṣads.

The Upanishads[30]

25. The central teaching of the Upaniṣads declares: **a)** *sarvaṃ khalv-idaṃ brahma* 'truly all this [universe] is Spirit Absolute' (*CU* III, 14, 1); **b)** *ayam ātmā brahman* 'this Self [in man] is Spirit Absolute [=the Self of All]' (*BU* II, 5, 19); and so *ahaṃ brahma-asmi* 'I myself am Spirit Absolute' (*BU* I, 4, 10). This I called the doctrine of the Unity of Being and, as we have seen (§ 9), this can be traced in the *RV*, in mythological and poetic images and symbols, in the *AV*, in the other Saṃhitās and in the *Brāhmaṇas*. The Upaniṣads present this most ancient doctrine in greater detail. And the theme of 'divinization' is now termed 'self-knowledge' *ātmajñāna* or 'knowledge of brahman' *brahmavidyā*. The doctrine of reincarnation is also presented more explicitly and fully in that good conduct will result in a good birth and foul conduct in birth in lower forms (*BU* III, 2, 13; IV, 4, 6; *CU* V, 10, 7; *KU* II, 2, 7). The two paths devayāna and pitṛyāna are also given (*BU* VI, 2, 2 and 2, 9-16; *CU* IV, 15, 5 and V, 3, 2; etc).

The Upaniṣads were composed and/or compiled by different sages who lived in different periods and places. Even the *Bṛhadāraṇyaka* is not a unitary work but a collection of at least three separate pieces since adhyāyas II, IV and VI have a teachers' *vaṃśa* at the end; the names of the teachers (60 to 65) are different except for few that are common to the first and second: thus we must assume

---

[30]Here I am thinking primarily of the ten early ones: *Bṛhadāraṇyaka*, *Chāndogya*, *Aitareya*, *Taittirīya*, *Īśa*, *Kena*, *Kaṭha*, *Praśna*, *Muṇḍaka* and *Māṇḍūkya*. Obviously, the *Śvetāśvatara* and *Maitrī*, contain useful material and, later, for Śaṅkara's view one needs *Kauṣītakī*, *Subāla*, *Jābala*, *Paiṅgala*, *Kaivalya* and *Vajrasūcikā*. I omit the *Āraṇyakas* since they fade imperceptibly into the Upaniṣads.

For detailed analysis of variant doctrines in the Upaniṣads one should consult Keith 1925.

different schools or traditions[31]. It is understandable, therefore, that there should be differences and even contradictions in some of their doctrines. The main doctrine being man's salvation/liberation *mokṣa* through Selfrealization, the variations are largely due to the different approaches presented for the achievement of this aim. Another reason would be the varied experiences obtained by the sages in higher states of consciousness, their varied perceptions and insights into aspects of the nature of the world and man, the significance they assigned to these experiences and, of course, their judgment or predilection as to what they should include in their teaching in response to the needs of their students. When scholars write of "advance" and "evolution" of thought, they mean I suspect, a movement towards a clearer, common and constant terminology.[32]

[31]The upanishadic traditions go back many centuries. Taking an average period of 20 years for each of the 60 teachers we obtain 1200 years. These traditions do not present a clean break from the texts on rituals or the older hymns. Eg *BU* I, 1 presents the sacrificial horse in its mystical cosmic aspect and section III, 9, 1ff examines the number and nature of the gods, while CU II, 1ff deals with details of the morning litany and the three pressings (cf also IV, 16, 1ff) and *Kena* III, 1ff brings in Agni, Vāyu and Indra (but subordinate to *brahman*). On the other hand, *MU* I, 2, 7-10, rejects rites altogether as futile activities in ignorance. I see no real contradiction here because many people may well find rites more amenable being in no condition to follow the ascetic's way of life and concentration on the *ātman-brahman* identity. Nor is there any real contradiction between "pantheism" and a God immanent in the world or a transcendent Absolute. Such "problems" exist not in the Upaniṣads themselves but in the fixity of the later Systems (or Schools) and in modern scholars' minds, which, in any event, like to indulge in casuistry, not realizing fully that supposedly "scientific" definitions have no end since every term in every new definition requires further definition ad *nauseam*.

[32]Historians of Philosophy write at length about "the evolution of thought", and, no doubt, there are many instances of such an "evolution". Personally, I find little doctrinal change in the Vedic texts, only differences in the mode of presentation of ideas and in emphasis of detail. One scholar sees "advance" and "evolution", eg in the doctrine of the elements (earth, water, etc): there is only water in the *RV*, then earth, water and fire in the *Chāndogya* (VI, 2, 2-4) and all five of them in the *Taittirīya* (Hiriyanna, ...

I shall ignore the apparent differences and the various interpretations that gave rise to the later Schools (Mīmāṃsā, Vedānta, Sāṇkhya etc) and focus on the essential teaching.

26. However, before examining this essential teaching we must mention parenthetically and briefly the theme of the 'real-unreal' which becomes a major issue in the discussions of the later Schools. Implicit throughout the Upaniṣads, and sometimes overtly stated, is the doctrine that Brahman alone is real while the world and its mutable multiplicity is unreal. Thus, for example, *BU* II, 1, 20 describes, with the analogy of threads issuing from a spider and sparks from a fire, how all vital forces *prāṇāḥ*, gods, etc, emanate forth from the *ātman* and concludes by stating that the One Self is *satyasya satyam* 'the true/real of the true/real', because, although these forces are regarded as real, yet the reality behind them is truly the *ātman*; their own reality is only relative. This idea is implicit in the *RV* and was held at least by the elit of the ṛṣis who understood that the Many are expressions of the One (§§ 7-8). This reality is denoted by *sat* 'being, existen-t/-ce', though in the case of the Brahman strictly nothing can be predicated. In *CU* IV, 19, 1, we meet an apparent problem since it is said that "In the beginning this [world] was 'non-being' *asat*; the same view occurs in *TU* II, 7. (This goes back to *RV* X 72, 2-3 where sat is said to have issued from *asat*.) But here *asat* obviously does not mean 'absolute non-

... 1994:64). Such statements ignore that all five elements, including air and ether, are mentioned in *CU* V, 14, 16 and VII, 4, 2 and are presented as divinities in the *RV* (ether being denoted by *div-* or *rajas* and similar words); the absence in earlier texts of the *Taittirīya* formulation does not indicate that the elements were not known.

Another issue often emphasized is the (apparent) rise of kṣatriyas who teach brahmins—seen as a conflict between castes. That there were conflicts cannot be doubted: there have always been good and bad kṣatriyas, wise and foolish brahmins. But while there were kṣatriyas who attained wisdom with study and practice and could therefore teach brahmins who had not, we cannot ignore the simple fact that *Yājñavalkya* (*BU* III, 1, 1ff) and Aruṇa (*CU* VI, 1, 1ff), two great teachers, are both brahmins.

being' or *nihil* but only 'unmanifest' or 'non-existence in perceptible form and name'. The notion that absolute non-being is the origin of All is refuted in the *CU* itself, in VI, 2, 1: *katham asataḥ saj-jayeta* 'how could being (or the real) manifest from non-being (or the unreal)?' Thus this is no problem. The doctrine that Brahman alone is real is found, among other places, in *BU* I, 3, 28 in the prayer "From the unreal/non-being *asataḥ* lead me to the real/being *sat*". It could be any humble ascetic/yogin/seeker praying to a Higher Power or any student requesting his master. The 'real/being' is the Supreme Self expressed in the *ātman-brahman* identity: It is imperceptible, inconceivable, indescribable, ungenerated, undying and unchanging, its only allowable predication being *prajñānaṃ brahma* 'the Absolute is pure Consciousness/Intelligence' (*AU* III, 3) and taught in 'Thou [man] art that' (*CU* VI, 8, 7). It is real because it does not depend on anything and does not change at all, unaffected by whatever changes seem to us to occur in its substance. The world is 'unreal' because it is, as a creation/emanation, dependent on the Brahman and changes constantly since all its constituent phenomena have beginning and end. Terms like 'monism, idealism' and the like which we use for this teaching seem inadequate (and irrelevant) since those ancient sages seem to speak from experience and not mere abstract intellection, an uncontrolled habit for disputation. The real test for us would be not in ratiocination, to read, talk and write about this, but to follow their practical instructions and see for ourselves in actual experience—as it is implied in the proverbial proof of eating the pudding...

27. As sparks fly from a fire so all beings issue from the Imperishable: gods, other celestials, humans, animals, birds and plants, mountains and oceans issue forth and return (*MU* II, 1, 1-9). How is the return effected? All beings issue forth and return according to the natural movement of the "breathing", to put it synoptically, of That One (*RV* X, 129):

the out-breathing is generation and the in-breathing is the absorption. But man has the possibility of accelerating for himself this process and, moreover, of rising above, or escaping from, this cycle of generation, withdrawal and reissuing into the creation, and thus attaining absolute freedom in uniting with the Primal Cause. This now is the meaning of Self-realization or liberation. And how is this effected? Through education, training, preparation. There is lower knowledge and higher knowledge (*MU* I, 1, 4-5; *CU* VI, 1, 1-4). Lower knowledge concerns the world and higher knowledge the *brahman*. Ignoring *brahman*, the Immutable One Reality, whence they emanate, and which is in them as their Self (eg *CU* II, 6; *AU* I, 3, 12), the vast majority of people follow their desires for the things of the world and get enmeshed in the widespread nets of death (*KU* II, 1, 2). *Maitrī* III, 2 gives a good description of man in ignorance—"affected by the *guṇas* of material nature... no longer sees Himself, the bountiful Lord... defiled, unstable, cut off, full of desires, scattered, he falls into arrogant identification (*abhimanitva*) 'I am so-and-so, this is mine'...". This is not unnatural but it entails delusion (*moha*) and suffering (*śoka*, *duḥkha*). Only the realization in one's being of the *ātman-brahman* identity brings liberation (*mokṣa*) and real happiness (*ānanda*). Education in ethics is indispensable. A man can remain in the world and enjoy life, as *Īśā* 1 says, but with renunciation (*tyaktena*), not coveting anyone else's goods (*mā gṛdhaḥ*): restraint of desire is stressed repeatedly. The prudent follow the good (*śreyas*), the foolish the pleasant (*preyas*:*KU* I, 2, 1-2). The moral virtues are not different from those in the *RV* (§ 13), *tapas* 'austerity', *dāna* 'liberality', *ārjava* 'straightness/integrity', *ahiṃsā* 'non-harming', *satyavacana* 'truthfulness' (*CU* III, 17, 4); to these should be added compassion (*dayā*) and self-control (*dama*) (*BU* V, 2, 3). *TU* I, 9 adds 'hospitality' and duties to other men and one's wife and progeny but also *svādhyāya* 'self-study' and *pravacana* 'recitation/speaking-forth'[33]. The 'self-study' (or 'study of the Scriptures', as most take it) entails seeing and hearing the Self in oneself and others, and thinking and reflecting on the Self, and so coming to know the Self: *ātmā... draṣṭavyaḥ śrotavyo mantavyo nididhyasitavyaḥ* (*BU* II, 4, 5, end). All this requires quietude and tranquillity of mind (*BU* IV, 4, 23; *CU* III, 14, 1; *KU* II, 3, 10).

In the end, however, no matter how pious and virtuous, no matter how self-restrained and tranquil one is, Selfrealization will come only by the intercession of grace from the *ātman* himself. The Self cannot be reached by senses, by learning or even great intelligence (*MU* III, 2, 4; *KU* II, 3, 12) but only by revealing Himself to the man He chooses (MU III, 2, 3).

One process is through purification of the mind to bring senses and lower mind under the control of the *buddhi* (higher, discriminating intellect), merging speech into mind, this into intellect and this into the greater aspect of spirit (*KU* I, 3, 8-15; II, 3, 6-10). Another is to detach by stages oneself from the material sheath of food (*annamayakośa*), from that of life-energy (*prāṇa-*), from that of mental activity (*manas-*), from that of discriminating intellect (*vijñāna-*), reach that of bliss (*ānanda-*) and be Oneself (*TU* II, 1-8). A third one is, again by stages, to realize and transcend the Self as Viśva in the waking state, as Taijasa of the dreaming

[33]In view of all these statements which Keith also cites, it is astonishing that he ascribes to the brahmins "lack of ethical sense" (p 586). That there were immoral brahmins is surely not worse than immoral priests and Popes in the Christian Church. Equally astonishing is Keith's (wrong) judgment that the ideal seeking of truth is in asceticism "by turning away from the things of this world and concentrating unnaturally the mind on the object" (!!ibid:587). Surely Yājñavalkya with his two wives, his ashram and his cattle, no less than King Aśvapati Kaikeya (*CU* V, 11, 3tt), and so many other sages with families, were not ascetics except in that they were *inwardly detached* from the world. YK Menon, again, wrote that the 'virtue' of the ancient Greeks' "justice" is omitted or is secondary (1976:93). But surely *dharma* 'duty, attribute, law', which he mentions often, means also "justice".

state and as Prājña, the Inner Controller (*antaryamin*), of deep sleep which is "undifferentiated mass of consciousness" (*ekībhūtaḥ prajñānaghana*) and attain Turīya, the non-dual and otherwise indescribable Fourth hypostasis, which is the Self (*Māṇḍukya Upaniṣad*). There are other approaches. In each case the theory can be described briefly and easily; the realization requires a lifetime of application involving many practices, such as remembering that one is not what one is observing (sensations, thoughts, feelings, desires, etc), attending to whatever one is doing, setting aside the various notions one usually has about Oneself (*...neti...neti...*) and the like. When Selfrealization is attained, when the man "knows thus 'I am *brahman*' he becomes all this [universe]; even the gods cannot prevent this, for he becomes their very Self" (*BU* I, 4, 10). Indeed, he sees all creatures in himself and himself in all creatures (*Īśa*, 6-7).

One final point. The *Bṛhadāraṇyaka* opens with a homology where the sacrificial horse is presented as an embodiment of the different parts of the Cosmos: it may be a suggestion that one should view all creatures in a similar way. The final section of the Upaniṣad deals with the human sexual act which is so essential to the perpetuation of the species. This too is a kind of homology where, as the couple embrace, the man corresponds to father-sky and the woman to mother-earth (*BU* VI, 4, 21). Thus this common and crucial act is shown to have, beyond any other ordinary aspect, a cosmic dimension and spiritual significance. (See also *CU* V, 7 and 8.)

28. In Conclusion, we have followed religio-philosophical motifs and themes from the *RV* to the Upaniṣads holding fast onto the thread of the Unity of Being, presented in myth, cult, ritual and philosophical enquiry. In some texts myth and symbol preponderate, in others the sacrificial ritual and in the Upaniṣads plain descriptions of Selfrealization. Later will follow other Schools and sub-branches with their own terminology placing emphasis on different aspects of the Unity of Being. But at all times the Vedic Tradition retained its broad, unitary character. Perhaps one day, with less arrogant casuistry and more of the ethical and meditative practices of the upanishadic sages or the rigvedic seers, it will reemerge in its non-assertive splendour.

Three: **Diffusion of Indo-European Theonyms: what they show us**

1. Argument. In presenting this collection of Vedic and Indo-European theonyms I discuss the derivation of some and argue that, since the *Ṛgveda* alone contains all these names, the *RV*[1] must be older than other IE[1] texts and more clearly indicative of the Proto-Indo-European culture, while Vedic is both older and closer to PIE than any other branch. Moreover, since the *RV* is richer in cultural and linguistic elements than other early IE traditions (Kazanas 2005, 2007) we can conclude that the Vedic speakers moved very little or not at all from the PIE homeland. These ideas have been published elsewhere and attracted some criticism mainly from JP Mallory; this is now being refuted.

2. In presenting his overview of G Dumézil's work on IE comparative mythology, CS Littleton wrote that in

---

[1]**Abbreviations:** AIT = Aryan Invasion/Immigration Theory; Alb = Albanian; Arm = Armenian; Av = Avestan; *Av* = *Avesta*; *AV* = *Atharvaveda*; B = Baltic (=Lth, Ltt, OPr); *Br* = Brāhmaṇa(s); C = Celtic (=OIr, Gallic, Welsh, etc); cf = compare; cogn = cognate(s); cpd = compound; dial = dialect; E = English; exc = except; f = feminine; gen = genitive; Gk = Greek; Gmc = Germanic (=Gth, OE, OHG etc); Gth = Gothic; HG = High German; Ht = Hittite; IA = Indo-Aryan; IE = Indoeuropean; IEL = IE Linguistics; Ir = Irish; Ks = Kassite; L = Latin; Lth = Lithuanian; Ltt = Lettish (=Latvian); m = masculine; M = Middle; Mcn = Mycenaean; Md = Modern; Mt = Mitanni; N = Norse; O = Old (before other designations, like OIr = Old Irish); PIE = Proto-Indoeuropean; R = Roman; Rs = Russian; *RV* = *Ṛgveda*; S = Sanskrit (and Vedic); Sc = Scandinavian; Sl = Slavic (=O Bulgarian, Serbo-Croatian, Russian, etc); T = Tocharian A or B, or both; V = Vedic.

Dumézil's view Roman religion can be understood only in relation to other IE religious systems and that "*the* most fruitful source of comparative materials is the ancient Indic literature" (1973:118). This paper confirms this view but in a context much broader than just Roman religion. The Table of IE deities that follows was presented (but not so full) in various papers from 1999 onward. The most recent one was my 'Indigenous Indo-Aryans and the *Rigveda*' (Kazanas 2002). In the present version I have made several corrections and additions.

In the Table I put the 20 Vedic names on the left and the others on the right for the simple and almost incredible reason that while the Vedic Tradition has all these names and cognates with one or other IE branches, **no two other traditions have a common theonym to the exclusion of the *RV***. The only exception is the highly dubious one of the Roman goddess 'Iuventas' and the Irish 'Oeagus' (according to Dumézil from PIE* *yuwn̥ko*: Littleton 1973:61, 93)[2]. On the right, on the top line are the cognate names. On the line(s) below are cogn nouns in branches that do not have the corresponding deity. This shows that the particular branch(es) suffered a loss in their religion. Eg the IE theonym for a Horse-deity (S *Aśvin*, Mcn *Iqe-ja*, C *Epo-na*) does not appear in most branches yet these do have the IE stem for 'horse': Gk *hippo/ikko-*, L *equus*, C *eoh*, Gmc *ech*, B *ešva* (and Sl *kon-ji* which is not IE but, though unrelated, does indicate a further loss).

[2]This is so tenuous that I do not include it. Beyond the dubious reconstruction (one can prove many things with untestable reconstructions) it must be noted that the supposed cognates occur in Italic and Celtic only, which are generally thought to have had a common Italo-Celtic past so that cognations limited only to these two prove nothing. Precisely because IEL thinks there was a common Indo-Iranian period I have disregarded common Indo-Iranian names. Long ago, L Bloomfield showed that correspondences in closely contiguous languages like Italic-Celtic or Celtic-Germanic, etc, may well be intra-familial borrowings, no more (1933:350-60).

With the theonyms I follow the English alphabetic sequence since this is common. Only Apāṃ Napāt is placed in apparently wrong place, but only because the cognates are in connexion with *Napāt* not *Apāṃ*. The S *ṛ* is given as E *r*. With the branches themselves, I start with India and move westward: S, Ht, Ks, Mt, Gk, L, Sl, B, Gmc, C Tocharian, Arm and Alb contain negligible material.

The Table

Agni	Ht *Agnis*; Sl Ogon. L *ignis*, Lth ugnis, Ltt *uguns* (Note: even the Iranians who had Fire-worship did not preserve this name, not even as a demon like Indra, Sauru etc, though the stem appears in the name *daštaγni*). Ht 'fire' *paḫḫur*.
Aryaman	Mcn *Are-mene*; Gk *A rẽ-s*; C *Ariomanus* (Gaul)/*Eremon* (Ir); Sc *Irmin*. The ar-stem in most IE languages 'move, rise, stir'.
Aśvin	Mcn *Iqeja* (horse-deity); C *Epona* (Gaul); Gk *hippos*, (Mcn *iqo*, dialect *ikkos*), L *equus*, OE and Ir *eoh*, B *ešva*, all 'horse'.
Bhaga	Ks *Bugas*; Phrygian *Bagaios* (Zeus, Gk); Gk *Phoibos*; Sl *Bogu*.
Bṛhaddivā	C *Briganti* (a), later *St Brighid* (Ir).
Dyaus	Hittite ^{D}*Siu-s*; Gk *Zeus/Dia-*; L *Ju[s]piter*; Gmc *Tˇiwaz*; Rs *Divu*(?). Lth *dievas* (usually 'god' cognate with S *deva*, *dīv*).
Indra	Ht *Inar* (a); Mt *Indara*; Ks *Indaš*; C *Andrasta*, *Andarta*. Gk *anēr/andr-*; Av *indra* (a demon).
Marut-as	Ks *Maruttaš*; L *Mars*; C *Morrighan* (Ir). The stem *mar/mor/mer-* 'shine' etc is common in all IE branches.

Manu	Gmc *Mannus* (in Tacitus *Germania* 2), father of the Gmc people, like the V semi-divine figure who was regarded as the father of mankind.
Mitra	Av *Miθra*; Mt *Mitrasil*.
	Gk *mitra* 'band for chest or, mainly, hair' (>E *mitre* 'bishop's pointed head-gear').
Apāṃ-Napāt	Roman *Neptunus*; C *Nech-tan* (Ir); Gmc (ON) *sævar niðr* 'kin of water (=fire)'! Gk *a nep-sios*, L- *nep-*; OHG *nevo*, OE *nefa*, OLth *nep-* etc 'nephew, cousin'.
Parjanya	Sl *Perunv̆*; B *Perkunas* (and variants); Sc *Fjörgyn* (-n, Thor's mother).
	L *spargo* 'throw about, besprinkle', C *eira* 'snow'.
Ṛbhu	Gk Orpheus; Gmc *Elf* (and variants).
	Gth arb-*aiþs*; Sl *rabŭ*, Rs *rabota* 'work'; L *orbu* (S *arbha*, Gk ὀρφανός) 'deprived' etc.
Saraṇyu	Mcn & Gk Erinus, *Helenē*.
	L *salio* 'leap', *salax* 'fond of leaping'; TB *salate* 'leaps'.
Sūrya	Ks *Śuriaś*; Gk *Hēlios*; L *Sol*; B *Saule*.
	Gth *savil*, ON *sol*, W *haul*, Sl *slunice*, Rs *solnce*.
Tvaṣṭṛ	Gmc *Twisto* (Sc).
Uṣas	Gk *Ēōs*; L *Au[s]rora*; Gmc *Eostre*.
	Lth *auśra*, Ltt *ausma*, C *gwawr*, etc.
Varuṇa	Mt *Uruwna*; Gk *Ouranos*; B *Vēlinas* (-and cf *jur-*=sea). L *kūrina*, ON *ver* (=sea).
Vāstoṣ-pati	Gk *Hestia*; L *Vesta*.
	Gth *wisan* 'to stay'; OHG *wist* 'inhabiting'; T A/B *waṣt/ost* 'house'.
Yama	Sc *Ymir*.
	L *gemi-nus* 'twin'; Gk *zēmia* 'damage', Av *yam*, *Yima*.

3. Now follows a brief description of the deities. For more details and full references see Kazanas 2001. Note that all Vedic deities come from the *RV*.

Agni is the Firegod born of Sky and Earth (or the Greatergod Tvaṣṭṛ and the Waters)—though at times he is the progenitor of all gods. God of inspiration and consciousness in man (*RV* II, 9, 4; VIII, 91, 8; etc) he has three births and abodes in heaven, midspace and earth and thus can mediate between the terrestrial world (and man) and the celestials; he is a major divinity in the Vedic Tradition. Among the Hittites only the name *Agnis* survives without any significant mythologems beyond the Fire-cult. Among the Slavs *Ogon/ Ogŭn* is the god of fire and heat, known as *Svarogich*, ie the son of high god *Svarog* (see under **Sūrya** below); he helps his brother *Dazhbogŭ* 'who grants plenty', an aspect of the Sungod, to win Lada, the Ocean's daughter but little else remains about him except his fire-cult.

Aryaman in the *RV* is the third member of the triad with Mitra and Varuṇa, a god of harmony and reconciliation (marriage-hymn , X, 85, 23 & 36; V, 3, 2) and of the unbroken course/path. We don't know anything much of the Mcn and C deities—except that Eremon (Ir) was a warrior-king. In the *Av Airyaman* is connected with wedding and healing (I, 228-235). In Scandinavia there was reverence of Irmin's *Sūl* the cultic 'World-pillar', and talk of Irmin's *theod* 'people' (=mankind). In classical Greece, *Ares* is taken as the Wargod, but, in fact, no mythologem supports this and he never wins a battle. He is vanquished by his sister Athena (who never loses a battle); he is imprisoned by some giants and Hermes rescues him; he is derided and scolded by his father Zeus as being utterly incompetent (in the *Iliad*). The Gk name is obviously a relic of Mcn *Are-mene* (=S *Aryaman*).

The **Aśvins** were twins, Horse-gods, called also *Nāsatya-*. They were physicians and rescued people from storms or fires etc; they may have been separate originally, but in the VT they are born as twins of *Saraṇyū* (see the name and *RV*

X, 17, 2)—but elsewhere Heaven is their father (I, 182, 1 etc) and the Oceanwaters their mother (I, 184, 4). They escorted the Sun's daughter Sūryā to her wedding. The Mcn *Iqeja* is only a name. The Greeks later had the demigod twins, Kastor and Poludeukes (=L *Pollux*), the *Dioskouroi* 'lads of Zeus', brothers of beautiful Helen (of Sparta and Troy); like the V gods, they rescued ships, escorted once their sister to safety and were expert horse-men. The Balts too had similar heroes (more than two), *Dievo Sūnelai* 'god's lads' (Lth) who saved the Sunmaiden *Saules Dukteryus* from drowning. The C *Epona* is also only a name. Cognate with V *Nāsatya-* is the Av *Nānhaiþya* and the Mt *Našatia(nna)*—absent in all other branches.

Bhaga is the Bountiful Provider, brother of *Uṣas*, the Dawn-goddess (*RV* I, 123, 5); he is invoked in the wedding ceremony (X, 85) but also increase of progeny (*AV* XIV, 2, 13) and deepening the plough (*AV* III, 12, 4). In later times appears the adj *bhagava(n)t* the blessed one'. The name becomes the generic name for 'god' in the Iranian and Slavonic branches. In Phrygia in Anatolia (modern Turkey), the stem appears as adj *bagaios* for Zeus. The Gk *phoibos* (S *bh* = Gk *ph* and S *g* often = Gk *b*), is another name for the Sungod.

Bāhaddivā is the name of one of the divine mothers in the *RV* (eg II, 31,4, etc) but nothing else is said of her. The stem *bṛha(n)t(ī)* appears as C *Brigantia* (in Britain), who was Sulevia in Gaul and then *St Brighid* in (Christian) Ireland.

Dyaus is, as a m stem, the bright Skygod and Father invariably coupled with mother *Pṛthivī* 'Earth'. As a f stem *dyaus* is the Sky as matrix, the source of manifest phenomena. The Av *daeva* and Sl *divu* denote devils, not gods and are cognates with S *deva* rather than *dyaus* though both ultimately come from *div/dyu-*. The Hittites venerated ^{D}*Siu* while in two sub-branches we find the Sun as *Tiwat* (Luwian) and *Tivaz* (Palaic). In Greece, this appears as *Zeus/Dia*, the Thunderer, King of gods on Olympus. The Romans had Jūpiter (<*Jus-/Jup-pitar* = Gk *Zeus-patēr*). Among the Gmc people the Skyfather appeared early as *Tiwaz* much as in Luwian and Palaic. See that Lth *dievas* is usually 'god' and only in some Ltt songs means 'skygod'. The name appears as *Divŭ* among the south-eastern Russians, a watching, protecting god.

Indra is the beloved god of the IAS—the Thunderer vajrin, 'who holds the bolt' victorious in battles, generous *maghava(n)t*, the Soma-drinker, performer of many miracles and *vṛtrahan* the slayer of *Vṛtra*, whereby he released the waters. In the *Avesta* he is a demon *daeva*. But among the Mitannis he is *Indara* and among the Kassites *Indaš*. The name may appear as goddess *Inar-a* in the Ht tale where she helps vanquish the dragon Illuyanka. (Some translate *Inar-a* as m: Ht has no masculine and feminine, only animate and inanimate. But as Inara has an affair with a man, it is most likely that the name denotes a goddess.) The Iceni tribe of the Celts in Britain had a Wargoddess *Andra-sta* (=*Andar-ta* in Gaul). This stem *andra/andar* and, of course, *indra* sound very much like the Gk stem for 'vigorous man' *andr-* (< in oblique cases of Gk *a-nēr* = S *nṛ/nar-*).

Manu is the revered "Father" (*RV*, II, 33, 13) and survivor of the Flood (*Śatapatha Br* I, 8, 1, 1ff) who generates a new race of men through sacrifice. In post Vedic texts he is the lawgiver, the guardian of a *kalpa*, etc. He was the son of *Vivasvat* (=sungod) and *Saraṇyū*, daughter of Creator-god *Tvaṣṭṛ*. The Roman historian Tacitus reports (*Germania*, ch 2) that the Gmc people worshipped *Mannus*, the son of earth-born god *Twisto*. Mannus had three (or more) sons from whose names are known the tribes of the Germans (=mankind).

Marut-as are storm- and war-gods assisting Indra (*RV* VIII 8, 24): they are said to be as many as 7×7 (V, 52, 7) and more. Riding on their golden cars with bright javelins and arrows and a golden axe they disperse darkness (I, 37, 9) and dispatch demonic foes (VII, 57, etc). The plural name appears in the singular *Maruttaš* in the Kassite list of gods. The stem appears as *Mārs* in Rome—the husband of Rhea Silvia and father of Romulus and Remus, founders of Rome; apart from his martial aspect he must have had a fertility side too as he was called *silvanus* 'of-forest'. The Celts had many war-deities and the Irish *Mor-righan* contains the stem *mar-*: she was known as the 'war/phantom queen'.

Mitra, men's 'Friend', has only one hymn to himself (*RV* III, 59) elsewhere being in company with Varuṇa and sometimes Aryaman. He is a great *āditya* 'deity of light and freedom'—like *Bhāga*, *Sūrya* the Sungod, and others—and brings men together; later he is associated with day and Varuṇa with night (AV IX, 3, 18; XIII, 3, 13). In Iran he is *Miþra*, the guardian of fidelity and high god *Ahura Mazda*'s power of light; later *Miþra* becomes a Sungod whose cult spreads in the Near East and the Roman Empire. In the Ks/Mt documents we find only the name *Mitra-sil*.

Apāṃ Napāt is the bright 'Offspring of Waters', an aspect of fire, a "swift horsed" self-luminous spirit among the Water-divinities (*RV* II 35; I, 65; X, 51). In the *Avesta* Apām Napāt is again 'swift-horsed... the shining lord ... of females [ie Waters]', and the 'luminous glory' of kings *X^Varənah*, the most desired object in the struggle between Good and Evil. Lying at the bottom of the ocean or rivers, it can be approached only by the most worthy. A Gk early tale has Theseus dive into the sea to retrieve a golden ring, thereby proving he is the worthy son of Poseidon, and there meets "a brilliance shining like fire [from the Nereids = semi-divine Water-nymphs]"; but here the cogn name is missing. This appears in the name of the Roman sea-god *Nept-unus*. It also appears in the Irish name *Necht-an*, the lord of the Tuatha De Dannan, who has a secret well; only he and his three cup-bearers could approach it with impunity because of the powerful luminous energy residing in its depths. The Offspring of Waters appears in Nordic lore too as *Szevar Niðr*, again an aspect of fire.

Parjanya is the god of rain and storm—a quickener of vegetation, father of Soma (*RV* IX, 82, 3) and producer of fertility in cows, mares and women (VII, 102, 2); he is connected with Indra (VIII, 6, 1, etc). He appears as *Perenu/ Perun* among the Slavs, the great War-god, Lord of the World and regulator of wind and rain, thunder and lightning etc; like Indra and Zeus he too slew a serpent and released waters and cattle. In the Baltic tradition appears *Perkunas* (and variants) but little else is known about him, except that a perpetual fire burnt before him, attended by Vestal females (see under **Vāstos-pati**). In the Scandinavian tradition we find Fjorgyn (m) and Fjorgynn (f: Thor's mother) but nothing beyond the names: mighty Thor overshadows them.

The **Ṛbhus** are three brothers, skilled artificers, poet-artists (*RV* 1, 161, 6). Their deeds were performed through unusual power of mind (I, 20, 2; IV, 33, 2; etc) providing not only material artefacts but also prosperity, vision, longevity, fame, and the like. They attained immortality and divinity in the Mansion of the Sungod having served as priests there. The name appears as *Orpheus* in Greece, a poet and musician, who descended into Hades to bring out his wife Eurudikē but didn't quite succeed. He too had served as a priest of the Sungod Apollo neglecting his worship of Dionusos—and so the MÊnad-Bassarids tore him apart; but his severed head floated down to the sea, still singing, and became a well-guarded oracle in Ionia. The same stem appears as *Elf* (and variants) in the Germanic branch. There were dark elves living underground but also fair ones in Alfheim: associated with the sun, they could heal, but otherwise played no important role.

Saraṇyū, 'the Nimble One', is a mysterious lady. Daughter of Tvaṣṭṛ she gets wedded to (the Sungod) Vivasva(n)t and bears twins but then disappears leaving in her place her Double or Shadow *Savarṇā* (RVX, 17, 1-2). In Yāska's *Nirukta* (XII, 10) Vivasvat finds Saraṇyū in the form of a mare, becomes a stallion and from their union are born the Aśvins. This links with a Gk tale (Pausanias VII, 25, 3-7) where, in Arcadia, goddess Demeter *erinus* (=V *saraṇyū*) was found as a mare by Poseidon, god of the sea; he became a stallion and from their union were born a splendid horse Areion, and a girl, *Despoina* 'Lady-mistress'. The same name *erinus* was that of a deity earlier in Mycenaean times. (In Homer and Hesiod the name appears in the plural as 'avenging powers').

Sūrya is the theonym par excellence of the Sungod. Both this (and *svar*) and the allonym *Savitṛ* derive from √*sū* 'begetting, enlivening'. Sūrya like Bhaga and others, is an *āditya* (*RV* I, 35, 1; etc). In Old Iranian the sun is *Hvare* (=V *svar*): he has swift horses like Sūrya and is the eye of Ahura Mazda (*Av* I, 225; II 85ff) as Sūrya is the eye of Varuṇa (*RV* VII, 63, 1). The Ks list includes god *šuriaš* (=V *sūrya*). In Greece he is *Hēlios*: at first he is quite distinct from Apollo *phoibos*, but later both appear as one deity. As Sol he was worshipped also in Rome; the Romans then borrowed Apollo (like many other deities and elements) from the Greeks. But the name appears also among the Slavs as *Svarog* (and variants) being probably a conflation of two IE cognates, like S *svar* 'sun' and *svarga* 'heaven'; he was the Skygod. The Balts have tales only of the sun's daughter *Saules dukteryus* (Lth) who is wooed and rescued by the [Sky-] god's lads (see **Aśvins** above).

Tvaṣṭṛ is a minor creator god who is responsible for the birth of men (*RV* X, 10, 5) and "begets mankind in varied manner" (III, 55, 19). He is Saraṇyū's father and, therefore, grandfather of Manu, borne of *Saraṇyu's* Double (and called *sāvarṇa*). Among the Germans he seems to appear as *Twisto*, a chthonic god, who begets Mannus whose sons are the progenitors of the Teutonic Tribes.

Uṣas is the Dawn-goddess who never infringes ṛta, the cosmic order. The hymns addressed to her are among the loveliest in the *RV*. She is connected with the Sungod and the Aśvins. In Greece the cogn name is *Ēōs*, the rosy-fingered

Dawn (of Homer). The Romans worshipped her as *Au[s]rora* and, among the Germans and the Anglo-Saxons as *Eōstre* (>Easter), the goddess of spring. Among the Balts, the Lettonians had the worship of the sun in the spring as *ushing* (=V *uṣās*).

Yama is a curious figure. He and his twin-sister Yamī were the first pair born of Saraṇyū and Vivasvat. Yamī wanted to have sex with her brother but he strongly refused (*RV* X, 10) showing that incest was not permissible. Yama's birth was unattended by death (X, 83, 5) and he looks after the abode of the dead in heaven (IX, 113, 7; X, 18, 13): all go to him by the same path (X, 14, 1; see also *AV* XV, iii, 3, 13). The Irn *Yima* is also son of Vivanhant (Av I, 10ff; II, 59ff), has in later literature a sister Yimeh and does copulate with her. With high god Ahura's guidance he gathers creatures together in an underground shelter against an oncoming severe winter that ends all life outside. In the Sc myth *Ymir* (=V *Yama*) rose out of the melting ice in the form of a giant and was nourished by the milk of the primeval cow Audhumla. Gods Odin, Vili and Ve slew Ymir and from different parts of his body were created different parts of the world: the sky from his skull; mountains from his bones; the sea from his blood, etc. (Here we see affinities with the *Puruṣa sūkta*, *RV* X, 90, where again the different parts of the world, including the gods, come from Puruṣa's being).

Varuṇa is the great ethical god in the *RV* who strangely recedes into the background later as a minor deity of waters. He is the High King (*samrāj-*) Skygod who encompasses all (√*vr.>vṛṇotī/vṛṇūte*), lays down laws *dhāman* and creates and rules through māyā unfathomable 'power of knowledge of measure'. He watches everything and has spies (*spaśa*) everywhere; he binds the sinner with fetters *pāśa*, but can also accept repentance. He is frequently lauded with Mitra and sometimes with Aryaman forming a triad. The name appears as *varəna* in the *Avesta* denoting the sky and the mythical region where Thraetona smote the dragon Aži

Dahāka. Both V *Varuṇa* and Av *varəna* are described as 'four-cornered'. The stem appears also as the Mt *uru-wna-asil* preserved in the list of gods, where appear also *Mitra-sil* (=V Mitra) and *Nasvatiya* (=V *Nāsatyā* = 2 *Aśvinau*). In Greece too, early on *Ouranos* is a major deity married to Earth but soon gets castrated and pushed out of the pantheon by Kronos (and Kronos by Zeus). The Balts also had a deity *Velnias*, whose name is now a term for 'demon/devil'. Its ancient form was *Vēlenas/Vēlinas*. This god granted magical powers and was associated even until the 20th cent with waters. (Given the S/Lth corresponse *ṛ/il* and *r/l* as in *v**ṛ**ka/ v**il**ka* 'wolf' and sū**r**ya/*sau**l**e* 'sun', the *Varuṇa/Vēlinas* identity is certain).

Finally, **Vāstos-pati**, the divine spirit of dwellings. This deity has one whole hymn, *RV* VII, 55 but no deeds like those of Indra or Varuṇa. In Greece this appears as *Hestia* the virgin goddess of (house and) hearth, which, when lit, in those days gathered round it the family. The stem appears in Rome as *Vesta*, also a female deity, served in her temples by (Vestal) virgins.

4. In 2002 I presented this material encapsulated in a Table of Theonyms and used it as one of several arguments to show that the IAs were by 1700-1500 indigenous to Saptasindhu (and India generally). Prof Mallory, editor of the *Journal of Indo-European Studies* thought this unscientific and, in the same issue 2002, presented various counter-arguments serious and facetious. I dealt with some of them in a paper published by the *JIES* in 2003. As we had some friendly exchanges subsequently and he reproduced his (counter-) arguments without taking stock of what I had actually said in every case, I shall deal with them afresh.

JP Mallory's criticism

5. It is astonishing that the *RV* alone from the whole of Indic literature contains so many theonyms that have correspondences in one or other IE tradition. Thus V has all

20 names; Gk has 9; Gmc 8; L and C 6; Mcn, B and Sl 3; Ht 2. (I do not count the Kassites and Mitannis because apart from names, they have little else).

Just as astonishing is the absence of a name common to any two IE branches to the exclusion of the *RV*. Some branches, like the Celtic, the Germanic and the Baltic certainly borrow from the Romans (or Greeks) deities like Mars, Mercury, etc, but no two have in common a truly inherited name.[3]

I called this phenomenon the P(reservation) P(rinciple) and used it as a major argument for the antiquity of the *RV*, for its close proximity to the PIE culture and for the probability not only that the IAs are indigenous by 1700 BC but also that the Saptasindhu and its larger neighbourhood was the homeland of the IEs—without excluding the possibility that the homeland extended loosely from Saptasindhu to the eastern Pontic Steppe (2002). Mallory criticised this as 'unscientific'. He argued that this is only a partial view, that some of the other branches do not have the rich Indic literature, that with the years they suffered cultural and linguistic impoverishment, intensified by the advent of Christianity and that some of the theonyms like those of the Firegod or the Horse-deity are not inherited but were created *ad hoc* by, say the Hittites or the Celts, because these people naturally felt that they should have the respective deities (2002).

6. I replied to some of these charges (2003). Here I shall briefly recapitulate and start by asking , what is 'scientific'? Everybody loves to use the term. But what does it really mean? Telepathy is a well established phenomenon that occurs frequently between twins and sometimes between a mother and her child(ren) or, less so, between other persons. Yet, at present, there are no 'scientific' means to verify it, other than ordinary observation and common sense.

A modern scientist, JM Schwartz, an American neurophysiologist at UCLA, wrote of "the cult of scientism" as

[3]See again § 2 and n 2.

"the fallacy of believing that the method of science must be used on all forms of experience and, given time, will settle every issue" (2002:6). Five decades earlier another American scientist had written: "expressions such as 'scientific truth' should only be taken in a very limited sense... There is no scientific truth in the absolute sense. The phrase *Ad veritatem per scientiam* [='To truth by means of science'] is an absurdity" (Du Noüy 1949:23).

But if we regard extant theonyms (or vocabulary) in every IE branch as partial or fragmentary evidence and therefore not scientific, what should we say about the archaeological statements regarding very fragmentary evidences of past cultures? What is so "scientific" about these? How can we be certain of dates and identifications with this or that people? Nobody knows what language(s) the people of the so-called Kurgan culture spoke and, in his voluminous work examining all anthropological evidence on the subject of the IE dispersal, J Dean expresses grave doubts about this putative locus of original dispersal saying "the ancient cranioskeletal evidence in Europe for expansions by the Kurgan groups is surprisingly meagre in places" (2001:317). Thus adherents of the AIT, including Mallory, have one standard (apparently loose and 'unscientific') for their own theories yet demand high exactitude in other areas which is, in any case, impossible.

In any event, the 'scientific' method, like every successful method in any human investigation or, indeed, any activity, requires three ingredients: passionate interest, clear observation and bright reasoning. Passionate interest directs attention to the particular field and keeps it there against all difficulties until the work is completed. Observation, setting aside wishful thinking and all bias, collects data related to the enquiry. Reasoning discriminates between relevant and irrelevant, accurate and inaccurate data and also premises and so arrives at (correct) conclusion(s). All this holds for every discipline in the sciences (Beveridge 1968) but also for the humanities. The fact that a science like biochemistry uses much highly complex technology does not alter the need for the three basic aspects that are common to all human endeavour. Because of faulty reasoning and/or inadequate observation scientists make as many and big mistakes despite their technical instruments as researchers in any other field (ibid, p 115ff). Furthermore, insight or inspiration and lucky circumstances, all of which are out of one's control, play important part in the sciences no less than in other areas (ibid, p 27ff).

Finally, Thomas Kuhn angered many when he stressed with much evidence that a personal factor intervenes (bias, prejucide, self-interest) so that many scientists promote the mainstream paradigm within which they operate and ignore, dismiss or cover up anomalous data that don't fit in (1970). A classic example is, of course, the violent reaction of scholars in the late 16th and early 17th centuries to the new heliocentric model of our solar system, presented first by Copernicus, then advanced by Brache, Kepler and Galileo, despite official prohibition and persecution (Koestler 1964). Prof CB Pert of Georgetown University medical Center, Washington, gives several recent examples in the biochemical sciences (2002:19; 161-2; 223).

So we can bypass this and move on.

Early and large literatures

7. It is simply not true that the *RV* is larger than the early literatures of the other branches, even Celtic, Germanic and Slavic, all having mostly but not exclusively the *New Testament* and other ecclesiastical texts, but not Baltic which is non-existent until late times. Otherwise, the *RV* is very much shorter and highly repetitive!

Now Hittite extant literature is both early (c 1600) and quite voluminous yet poorer in IE theonyms than the 'poor relatives', C, B, and Sl. To write (as Mallory wrote to me: 2004) that "Anatolian [=Ht] documents are so riddled with Sumerian, Akkadian, Hurrian and Hattic forms that it is reasonably obvious that it is not comparable" does not explain anything. The statement describes the situation; it does not explain it. The question is: Why do the Hittites, despite their early and rich literature and their dominance in all the neighbouring area, have so few elements of PIE? Why are their documents "so riddled" with non-IE material—to the extent that they have none of the 8 IE stems denoting the closest relations (husband-wife, father-mother, son-daughter, brother-sister) almost all common to all other branches?

The Hittites are mentioned in documents of the Near East by 1900 BC. So they had come to Anatolia earlier and soon established a kingdom which by 1600 expanded to form an Empire that would threaten other peoples, including the Egyptians, and would last down to the 12th century.[4] Obviously, they had not been coerced into abandoning their IE heritage and absorbing the cultural features of their neighbours. They did this because they found the new cultures just as good as, if not better than, the one they had brought. They were too far from their homeland, obviously, and not numerous enough to influence culturally the local peoples. I would add that probably they brought no families (ie women and children) or not many, with them and so adopted the corresponding words of the local languages. They adopted also the gods (and their names) that prevailed in that region.

Very obviously, here literacy played no part whatever in preservation because the loss of inherited cultural elements had happened much earlier. But if early literacy and substantial literature did not help preserve inherited PIE elements in this case, then the two may well prove irrelevant in other cases too, while losses are due to causes other than late literacy and a small volume of literature.

---

[4]See Bryce 2002; Dunstan 1998; Puhvel 1994. For the view that they are indigenous and that Anatolia is the IE urheimat, see Renfrew 1999.

8. Greek has 9 names—perhaps due to its voluminous literature. But note some facts. The theonym 'Ouranos' does not appear in Homer, where *ouranós* denotes only the sky-vault; it appears in Hesiod's *Theogony*, first as the son of Earth (l 127) then as her consort (l 133). 'Orpheus' again does not appear in Homer nor Hesiod, but first in some fragments of Ibycus (6th cent BC) then Pindar (5th cent BC) and in some iconographic material (relief and pottery) from c 580. 'Hestia' too is not in Homer but is in Hesiod (l 454), in two Hymns to Hestia (White:448, 454) and one hymn to Aphrodite (White: lines 406-9). 'Demeter Erinus' is also unknown to Homer and Hesiod. Goddess Demeter is, of course attested; so are the *Erinues* (pl), Fate's avenging spirits (f). The first mention of Demeter Erinus of Arcadia (south Greece) is in Callimachos, 3rd cent BC—but only a name. The story itself which links this deity with Vedic Saraṇyū is found only in Pausanias, 2nd cent CE! Thus if we took Homer and Hesiod only as Gk sources we would not have Orpheus (and perhaps would not make the connection with V Saraṇyū). And if we took only Homer, then we would miss Ouranos and Hestia too. Thus the 9 retentions would decrease to 6—which is less than Gmc and only as many as L and C. So, Gk seems, indeed, to be saved by its large literature, starting early and spreading over several centuries.

But there is another side to this issue. Homer writes in Ionia, ie the isles and shores of eastern Aegean. Hesiod writes in Boeotia, which falls west of Athens and Attica. Arcadia is in the Peloponnese, well to the south of Attica. Orpheus, again, came down from north Greece. Thus we have, simplifying matters considerably, five areas with partly different traditions. Ouranos as a god is unknown in early Ionia and Orpheus, whose cult came from the north, seems to be unknown in the early period in all the other regions. Now, to take an obvious example, the name *Erinues* (pl) was known to Homer, Hesiod and others; Hesiod has them arise from the blood-drops that fell on earth after the castration of

Ouranos by Kronos (*Theogony* 185). But the tale of Demeter Erinus was preserved only in Arcadia in, presumably, an unbroken oral tradition, as the cult of Orpheus was similarly preserved in northern Greece. On the other hand, in Homer and Hesiod, who recorded the oral traditions in Ionia and Boeotia respectively, we find many theonyms of non-IE provenance: Aphrodite, Apollo, Artemis, Demeter, Dionusos, Hephaistos, Kronos, Persephone, Pluto, Poseidon, etc. Not one of these names has cognates in other IE traditions. Even earlier, in Mycenaean times, we find many non-IE theonyms like *Drimios*, son of Zeus, *Emaa*, *Ipemedeja*, *Manasa*[5], etc.

We must therefore conclude that the different Greek tribes adopted alien deities even as they forgot, or threw off, many that belonged to their inherited religion. It is possible they disliked the cults of the IE Firegod, or Wargod or Raingod and did not even take them along when they left the homeland. Thus the names, say for convenience's sake, corresponding to Agni, Indra and Parjanya were jettisoned quite early (including the cogn stems in other lexical forms, except perhaps *andr-*) and new deities were adopted instead. Surely it can't be insignificant that there is no trace in Gk of the IE stem *agni/igni/ogni-*, of manu, nor of *parjan/perun/perkun-* etc. If the Greeks (in Arcadia) could preserve for all these centuries the name *Dēmētra Erinus* and the tale of

[5]C Davaras conjectures that this is cognate with Hindu snake goddess Manasā (devī) who is "possibly originating in Harappan times" (2005:138). This may be so but it is a very long shot. Davaras follows S Bhattacharji (1993:4ff) who deals only with medieval Bengali poems. Manasā is the name of a snake in *Mahābhārata* 1 52.5 and later is the sister of Vāsuki, lord of snakes. In later texts other legends are told about her (see Dimock & Ramanujan 1964). There is no evidence whatever that the Harappans had a snakegoddess called Manasā since their writing has not been deciphered, nor that the Mycenean *manasa* was a snakegoddess since nothing else is said about this theonym. There are several more similar unclear cases (eg S *śrī* L *ceres*; S *budhna* Gk *puthon*; etc) but they require a separate study.

her union with Poseidon (both in horse-form: see § 3, under **Saraṇyū**), surely they (in any region) could have preserved these IE theonyms as well; but, instead, they preserved the non-IE ones like Aphrodite, Apollo, etc. Thus the decays and losses the Greeks suffered with their theonyms had little to do with literacy and literature: as with the Hittites (§ 7), these occurred despite early literacy and voluminous literature because they occurred long before these two phenomena. The Greeks either disliked some cults or their oral tradition was not effective enough to maintain those cults, or both. And their system of oral transmission was ineffective because they were on the move for a fairly long period far from homeland.

9. A similar situation prevailed in the other branches—and **Christianity** played no part.

A striking fact is that although L has an early and large written literature, it has only as many IE theonyms as C and less than Gmc, which acquired a literature many centuries later. (Thus, here again early literacy and a large literature do not play a significant part in preservation—as we noted in § 7, above, though they may help at times, as with Gk in § 8.)

Then, L has many theonyms that have no cognates in the other branches—Angerona, goddess of coming spring, Bacchus (=Gk Dionusos), Dis (=Gk god of Hades), Janus, 'god of passages', Mercury (=Gk Hermes), Minerva (=Gk Athena), Quirinus, patron of producers, Saturnus (=Gk Kronos), etc. All these names can hardly be of PIE origin since they are not found in the other IE branches. The name of *Jūno*, consort of Jupiter, is thought to come from the stem found in S *yuvan/yun-* 'young'; of *Venus*, goddess of beauty and love, from the root in S √*van* > *vanas* 'desiring, obtaining': both names are innovations, not found anywhere else as theonyms. The old Italic people lost much of their heritage and acquired much non-IE material (some borrowed directly from the Greeks—Apollo, Hercules, Proserpina etc) long before literacy.

Neither did the "poorer" branches lose the IE theonyms because they had no early literacy or because they were christianized. They lost them long before Christianity and perhaps before they settled in their historical seats. This is well demonstrated by the references to Celtic, Germanic, Baltic and Slavic deities found in epigraphic material and in Roman and Byzantine records and, particularly for the Balts, in Latin, German and Russian chronicles (Puhvel 1989:passim). We find very few IE theonyms in all these documents but many from the Graeco-Roman culture and many more from unknown sources in Celtic:—eg C Dea Artio, Belenos, Cernunnos, (A-)Esus, Lugus (cf *Lugu-dunum* =Lyons, in France), Maponas, *Ogm-alius* (=Gk Hercules), Taranis, Teu/Tou/Tu-tates, etc (in Gaul) and Mother Danu (cf S *dān-ulavas*) and her brother *Dagda* 'the Good God', the *Ollathair* 'Allfather', death-god Donn, etc (Ir); also Gmc Aegīr, Idmun, Loki, Nerthus, Njord, Skadi, Thor, Ullr, etc; then B Andaj, Autrimpus 'sea god', Diviriks, Occopirmus 'Very-first (=sky-god)', Potrimpus 'rivergod', Puschkaytus 'earthgod', Suaixtix 'sungod',Teljavel 'divine smith', etc; finally, Sl *Dažībogŭ* 'Sungod', Khursu (< Persian *Xoršīd* 'sun'), goddess *Mokošī* an allonym for Mati Syra *Zemlja* (=S *kṣam-*) 'Mother Earth', Simaroghŭ, Stribogŭ, Svantovit 'god of light', Svjatogar 'mountain-god', Triglav 'god of darkness' (?), Vele/Volŏ-sŭ 'god of cattle, riches', etc. Note that not one of all these names has a correspondence in another IE branch or link with Christianity; so they must be pre-Christian. (For Celtic and Germanic names MacCulloch 1949; for Balitc, Blažek 2001; for Slavic, Simonov 1997; for all Puhvel 1989.)

Undoubtedly late literacy and Christianity are responsible for many losses in all these branches. But, as the names above testify, there is no dearth of pre-Christian theonyms. Except Vedic, every other branch has only few IE theonyms but many non-IE names. What is lacking is information about them and, more important, **IE theonyms** which were replaced by others much much earlier. These "others" have no cognates in the IE branches, so they must have come from the cultures that prevailed in Europe before the arrival of the IE-speaking peoples.

These people lost their IE gods (at least these that are identified as such by their incidence in Vedic and one or other branch) because they could not maintain them in an oral tradition that had weakened through long, constant movement, because they did not care for them and because, far from the homeland, they found the deities in other cultures just as good. It must be realised that the IE deities had dropped out of all these oral traditions before Christianity had even began—because the people had moved away from home. That people on the move tend to lose more cultural elements than sedentary folk is stated by several comparative linguists (Hock 1991:467-9; Burrow 1973:10; Lockwood 1969:43).

The Firegod

10. The case of the Firegod is quite instructive in many ways. AA Macdonell, an eminent Sanskritist at the turn of the 19th to the 20th cent, wrote: "Though *agni* is an Indo-European word (Lat *ignis*, Slavonic *ogni*), the worship of fire under this name is purely Indian. In the Indo-Iranian period the sacrificial fire is already found at the centre of a developed ritual" (1898:99)[6]. This is a typical invasionist statement, but Macdonell can be excused since in his days

---

[6]See also other similar comments of his, eg on Aryaman: "The name goes back to the Indo-Iranian period, as it occurs in the Avesta" (p 45). But he should have known that it occurred in Gaul as *Arionamus*, in Ireland as *Eremon* and in Scandinavia as *Irmin*. So the name is not Indo-Iranian but PIE. This is confirmed, of course, by the Mcn deity *Areimene* found in the Mcn documents which were deciphered in mid-twentieth century (Ventris & Chadwick 1973). But Macdonell and others at the time were thoroughly enthralled by this "common Indo-Iranian period", which is entirely hypothetical and not supported by any solid evidence (other than conjectural linguistic reconstructions). See further § 17 and n 7.

many data (eg knowledge of Hittite) were missing and the AIT was gaining strength. Yet even in those days it should have been known that among the Slavs there had been *Ogon/ Ogŭn*, the Firedeity, son of Skygod *Svarogŭ*. So the worship of Agni was not a purely Indian affair. Even among the Balts there was a strong fire-cult connected with god Perkunas (see under **Parjanya**) and the word for 'fire' was *ugnis/uguns*, cogn with *Agni*. We know now that the Hittites too worshipped firegod *Agnis* and so we are sure that **there was a PIE cult of Agni.** It was not just Indian or Indo-Iranian! (For the IE nature of this deity see also Polomé 1991:74.)

The Greeks, Romans, Celts, Germans and Balts used fire in some of their rituals but there was no specific fire-cult. At least the Romans and Balts (and Slavs) retained some IE stem for fire. The other languages (Gk, C, Gmc) lost that as well as the theonym. The Iranians did not preserve the cognate of Agni, despite their intense worship of fire (Av *atar*); the stem survived in the name *Dašt-aγni* nonetheless. What is the explanation?

In the case of the Iranians, Zarathustra's religious reform must have been responsible for the loss of the theonym, cogn of *Agni*, but it would not as a matter of course expunge the ordinary stem for fire also. The loss of the ordinary noun must have had other causes. Elsewhere we must assume that the different peoples moved for long away from the homeland and could not, or did not want to, maintain the fire-cult finding it perhaps difficult or bothersome as they moved on. The Balts retained it but transferred it to Perkunas and lost the fire-theonym. The Slavs and the Hittites retained something of it together with the theonym, but none of the rich lore that we find in the *RV*.

Firedeity and Horsedeity

11. It is possible, of course, that in their dispersal some IE tribes decided that it would be nice to have a Firegode or Horsegod or whatever. And (as per Mallory, 2002) they did so. Indeed, it would be quite natural that, say, the Slavs and the Hittites before them would have created a Firegod while the Celts set up a Horse god. But I can't help wondering why other peoples did not feel a similar need, people like the Greeks, close to the Hittites, or the Balts, Germans and Celts, close to the Slavs: all these did not have a specific fire-cult. Then, again, apart from the ancient Mycenaeans in Greece and the Celts in Gaul, the others did not feel the need for a specific Horse-deity.

The Slavs had the IE stem for fire in *ogni* so it is not strange that they should call their Firegod 'Ogon' (and variants). But the Hittite stem for 'fire' was *paḫḫur* (cogn with Gk *pur*, Gmc *fȳr*, etc). So if they had created independently a Firegod they would have given him a name related to this and not the name *Agnis* which has no other cognates in the Ht language, but rather miraculously coincides with the S and Sl theonyms. So we must conclude that Ht *Agnis* and Sl *Ogun* are names cognate with the PIE inherited name for the Firegod. So these Firegods are inherited not invented.

Similarly, the Mycenaeans had the IE stem for 'horse', *iqo/iqe-*. Their Horsedeity was accordingly named *Iqeja*. But the Celts had, in their different dialects, different names for 'horse': *capall*, *cullach*, *ech*, *marc(h)*, etc. Of these *ech* (OIr) is IE (cf Gmc *eoh*, S aśva, L *equus* etc). So we would expect the name of their Horsedeity to be related to one of these names—even *ech*-whatever. But the name is *Epo-na* and the deity is female. I should add that both ancient Greece and Ireland have a very rich mythology related to the horse and also various kinds of horse-sacrifice (Anderson 1999). So 'Epona' is inherited, not a chancy innovation.

The inevitable conclusion from this discussion is that the names of these deities are inherited, not independently invented, and therefore form valid evidence for the Preservation Principle, showing that Vedic has many more retentions than any other IE branch.

Writing in India

12. There is also the vexed issue of literacy and oral tradition. During some exchanges, in a message to me, Nov 2004, in the context of general lexical retentions, Mallory wrote that Italic "was not seriously attested for about 1000 years later (or more by your [ie Kazanas] reckoning) than Vedic." This number of years is very curious. My own reckoning for the *RV* date is the 4th millennium BC. The AIT reckoning is 1200 BC. Now Italic (Latin, Oscan, Umbrian) is "seriously" attested in epigraphies by 500 BC and more "seriously" c 300. Greek again appears epigraphicallly from c 700 and more "seriously", say, 550 BC, when Peisistratos arranged the "edition" of the Homeric poems. (Some classicists now hold that Homer himself might have made use of writing in the 8th cent, after the development of the Gk alphabet from the Phoenician one: Lesky 1971:73ff.)

But what are we talking about actually? In Italy we have ample writing after 300 while in Greece we have after, say, 550 a strong literary tradition. In India the first serious testimony for writing is Aśoka's Rock Edicts, 260-250 BC. So no arithmetic will give us 1000 years. It is from this fact that AIT-adherents (with Max Müller at the head) worked out backwards the other dates for Vedic literature. But, in any event, the Edicts are written in Prākṛta vernacular, not Sanskrit let alone Vedic. Now, however, there is evidence of IA Prākṛta Brāhanī script in Shri Laṅka from the sixth cent BCE (Deraniyagala and Abeyratne 1997). This again gives no 1000 years.

However, here we must distinguish between the Vedic sacred texts on the one hand and on the other secular writings—legal, literacy and commercial. There is no evidence of any kind for writing down the Vedas. On the contrary, since their study was prohibited for certain low castes in most severe terms and since the brahmins would want to keep to themselves this knowledge in order to preserve its purity and to maintain the power it gave them, I can think of no reason why the families transmitting it would infringe their sacred tradition and put the Vedas into writing. Otherwise, manuscripts (palm-leaves and strips of birch-bark) and perhaps collections of them of secular texts may have appeared "seriously" from the 6th cent CE onward. The writer Bāṇa c 620 maintained his own reader, but this can be interpreted in many ways and certainly does not mean that Bāṇa had manuscripts of the Vedas. Very few pieces survive now from before the 14th cent. Inscriptions in few wooden planks have been found near Khotan (west of the desert Takla-Makan) dating from the 4th cent and on copper and silver (one golden) discs going back to the 1st cent CE. Nonetheless the Chinese visitor I-Tsing mentions **in the 7th cent CE** that **the Vedas were being transmitted orally** (Winterwitz 1981:31). And it is a well established fact that they were transmitted orally even in the 20th century.

The first known commentary on the *RV* is that of Sāyana in the 14th cent CE. This is the only evidence for the possible writing down of the *RV*. By this time, the strict tradition may have loosened up. Since all the Indic theonyms are from the *RV* it is this text alone that we consider.

Thus on the Greek side we know that Homer and Hesiod (and others) were put into writing by 500 BC. On the Indic side we know that the *RV* was passed on orally and a commentary on it was composed in the 14th cent. So, I should think that, regarding written texts, **the advantage lies with Italic and Greek and it is about 1800 years.**

Oral tradition, literacy and Christianity

13. An oral tradition existed in all IE branches for millennia before the advent of literacy, else we would not have any information about them and their language and culture. Oral transmission was used in Greece for centuries after the Mycenean collapse into illiteracy (c 1100 BC) and even after the renaissance of literacy c 800 onward, well into Roman times, particularly by esoteric movements like the Orphics and Pythagoreans (Kingsley 1995:322ff; Murray 1993:100). Obviously, the other branches had some sort of an oral tradition that preserved various elements of their inherited culture. We have Caesar's testimony in the first cent BC that the Celts used writing borrowed from Greeks for secular purposes but the Druid-schools in Gaul would not commit to writing their sacred texts which they transmitted to students over a period of 20 years of apprenticeship (*De Bello Gallico*, VI, 14). Thus the Celts had writing early on (at least 100 BC and probably much earlier), but they used a system of oral transmission for their sacred lore. This sounds very similar to the Indic tradition where it was the sacred duty of certain Brahmin families to pass on their knowledge with a complex but very safe system of transmission from generation to generation (Winterwitz 29-32, 51-2).

Writing in Ireland, in what is known as the Ogam script, appears on inscriptions in the 4th cent CE and manuscripts survive from the 7th cent—but, as was said, writing was certainly used in the 1st century BC in Gaul and probably much earlier, borrowed from the Greeks. Patrick died in 461, so Ireland was christianized in the 5th cent CE. The Italic people themselves had writing from at least the 6th cent BC and did not distinguish between secular and sacred. The Visigoths of the Germanic branch had literacy from the 4th cent CE at least, when Bishop Wulfila translated large portions of the Christian *New* and some parts of the *Old Testament*; other sub-branches like OE and OHG evince writing c 700; but the Scandinavian group has inscriptions in the Runic alphabet from c 300; in fact there are few scattered inscriptions from the century before Christ. The Scandinavians were christianized in the 11th cent CE. Although very little is known about it, an oral tradition must have been in existence among the Slavs too, since writing and Christianity came to them rather late, in mid-ninth cent CE, from Byzantium: the earliest recorded writing is Old Church Slavonic (=Old Bulgarian) and consists of ecclesiastical texts; be it noted that Md Bulgarian began to produce its own literature only in the 18th cent. Old Russian is documented from the 11th cent. Other Slavic languages are attested from the 13th cent and afterwards. Baltic is attested only in the 14th cent CE, even though the Balts are thought to have settled in their historical habitat by c 2000 BC. The first Christians there are recorded from the 13th cent CE. Thus, as noted in § 9, Christianity had little to do with the loss of IE theonyms.

14. The Baltic culture presents something of a paradox, as appears at first sight. It has preserved only 3 of the theonyms examined above, but, on the other hand, Lithuanian (and, to a lesser degree, Lettish) is one of the most conservative of IE languages. As a comparativist puts it, "Lithuanian is generally held to be the most archaic living Indo-European language... [and] some demonstrably older forms are often referred to as Old Lithuanian" (Baldi 1983:97). This conservatism is not evident in the Lth pre-Christian religion. In this case, we must accept that Christianity may have played a significant part in the loss of IE theonyms and their cult. On the other hand the three names are the only ones that were in use long before Christianity. One would have expected that the preservation of IE theonyms would have been comparable to that of the general linguistic features.

But the case seems to be that people on the move far from the homeland, will, more easily than people settled at home, lose much of their religion and many social customs long before they lose linguistic features. If they have literacy, as the Greeks that set up colonies on the shores of the Black Sea, at South Italy and Sicily and on the north-western shores of the Mediterranean, or the Jews in Diaspora after their dispersal in the second cent CE, then they retain their religion and many social customs, so long as these do not create problems with the indigenous population or so long as the immigrants are not coerced. But when, as was the case with the IE peoples, they are non-literate, then it is difficult, when trekking with carts and horses or (more likely) bulls and donkeys, to maintain an effective oral tradition that will preserve most of their inherited culture, other than the part of language which is a daily necessity. In these circumstances, even the language will suffer break-downs and losses accordingly, as some old customs and cultural features fall into desuetude. And as the people come into contact with alien cultures and acquire new customs, even new deities, some or much of their language will change (see § 9, end). The changes will be even more precipitous and pervasive if the indigenous population have literacy and a rich culture with long history.

15. It is certain that the Balts and the West and Scandinavian Germans did not come into such a cultured environment. But the Hittites did in the Near East—and were swamped. So, also the Mitannis and the Kassites—who retained some theonyms only and only very few IE stems of Indic provenance. But we see clearly similar cases with the Viking invasions. One contingent under Accold, an officer of chief Riurick, conquered Kiev in the Ukraine in 860 CE setting up their own kingdom, but within two or three generations they got absorbed by the natives and were christianized under Igor (912-45). Under Rollon, another contingent invaded Normandy (N-W France) in 911 and set up a mighty kingdom that was respected by the French kings. But in 2 or 3 generations, they too were absorbed by the French culture that surrounded them. The same story with the Norsemen was repeated in Scotland and eastern Yorkshire (Britain) and in the Dublin area (Ireland).

16. If the IAs had immigrated into Saptasindhu in (small) waves c 1700-1500 and met there the natives who had literacy and a civilization going back many centuries, as the AIT claims, they too would have been subsumed by the indigenous culture. Instead we find that the natives learnt the difficult language of the immigrants and, all of a sudden, the names of mountains, rivers etc became Indoaryan! This might happen in a fairy tale only, not in hard history. It could have happened only if there had been a thorough and fierce conquest. This was believed to be true until the 1960s, but thereafter it was shown that there had been not even the mildest conquest, and so the "invasion" became "immigration". But the new term still begs the question: How did the Aryanization of so vast an area (today's Punjab, Gujarat and Haryana in N-W India) was effected so completely? There is no answer, so the AIT must be discarded.

Conclusions

17. The Indic branch differs considerably. As their own preservation of the numerous theonyms indicates, and as is corroborated by the absence of a common inherited theonym in any two IE branches to the exclusion of the *RV*, the IAs do not appear to have suffered any comparable losses. Losses they too must have suffered since some of the names like Indra or Parjanya do not have obvious cognates in Vedic/ Sanskrit. Moereover, many tales in the *RV* are sketchy or elliptical like the rescue of Bhujyu by the Aśvins, which is not given in a fuller version in later literature, or the affair of Yama and Yamī, or Indra's fight with the Sun, etc. But such decays and losses come naturally in the ordinary history of all non-literate peoples until they acquire literacy or they establish clearly the body of their sacred lore (eg the *RV*) and then create a systematic oral tradition for its effective transmission. Even then decays and losses happen gradually, imperceptibly over the centuries.

Here we should note some absurd peculiarities in the AIT. This theory claims that the IAs and the Iranians were originally one people—after leaving the homeland in the Steppes—and they went through the common "Indo-Iranian period" (see § 10). Linguists of this persuasion (ie all mainstream comparativists) have even reconstructed this original common 'Indo-Iranian' language. The AIT says that this people passed from the Urals and stayed in the area long enough to have linguistic exchanges with the Finno-Ugrians who lived there. However there are some problems. The Finno-Ugrian loanwords are all thought to be of Indo-Iranian descent (Burrow 1973:25), yet they can also be explained as derivatives of plain Indoaryan (eg: S *śata* '100', FU *sata/śado/śāt/cuotte* etc; S *udhar* 'udder', FU *utar/odar/vodar*; etc). Then, if the Indo-Iranians moved on and eventually the Iranians settled in Iran while the IAs moved onto Saptasindhu, a word like *chāga* 'he-goat' which is supposed to have come into Sanskrit from Finno-Ugrian should be present also in Avestan; but Av has *būza-* instead and no other word for goat (like S *aja* or *eḍa*—cogn of course with Gk *aix*, Lts *ozys* and Arm *aic*, and also Av *iz-aēna* 'leathery'); also *kūpa* 'hole, well' is in Av *xān-/čat-* (and in any case S *kūpa* is cogn with Gk *kupē* 'hole', L *cūpa* 'cask', Gmc *hūf*-r '(ship's) hull')[7]. Then the IAs entered Saptasindhu but found that the natives were moving eastward because of the drying up of the river Sarasvatī and the general desiccation of the region. Naturally they too moved eastward to the Gangetic basin; for it is not likely that they would have remained behind in the desiccated area and compose hymns that say nothing about any immigration (so recent in their experience), mention constantly "seven rivers" and their own settlement there of old and praise the river Sarasvatī ("running pure from the mountains to the ocean": *RV* VII 95.2) as a goddess and source of nourishment but do not refer to any desiccation or cities with deserted and ruined buildings made of bricks, as then were the towns of the Indus-Sarasvati Civilization.

18. Obviously the IAs did not develop their incomparable oral tradition before arriving at Saptasindhu, otherwise they

[7]It is possible that the Iranians were together with the Indoaryans for a period sharing a common language and culture. But this happened in Saptasindhu and it is from there that the Iranians moved to their historical seat as I argue elsewhere. This movement can account for all facts and those that appear as anomalies in the AIT.

would have preserved memories of the long journey and the adventures therein[8]. Nor did they develop it after they moved east of Saptasindhu; for it is universally agreed from the times of AB Keith (1923:79) to even M Witzel (2001:§ 3) that the *RV* hymns were composed in Saptasindhu or, more precisely, an area which had as its axis the river Sarasvatī. So they developed their system in the short time they stayed in Saptasindhu before moving eastward.

But if so, if they had no elaborate system of oral transmission, how did the IAs preserve during their trekking so much of the PIE heritage evidenced in the theonyms discussed?... Then, we know that there are many different chronological strata in the *RV*: we can see this both in the changes of linguistic idiom, grammar and orthography and in the references in early hymns to "ancient ṛṣis" who composed invocations—IV.50.1; V.42.6; VI.21.1-5 and 22.2; VII.29.4 and 53.1 and 76.4. The implication of many generations, long out of memory (especially IV, 50, 1; VI, 22, 2; VII, 29, 4), could not possibly fit within the short time that the IAs stayed in Saptasindhu before moving on.

The only reasonable conclusion is that the IAs did not move from Saptasindhu, or not much. The corollary to this is that the other branches moved away from Saptasindhu; the Iranians certainly seem to have done so since they say in the

---

[8]Mallory mentioned the Jews who, he claims, developed an oral tradition even as they moved . This is most unlikely (see § 9, end). When the Jews first surface in historical times in 11th cent BC, they are literate (Dunstan 1998). They had literacy in Moses' time (hence the 10 commandments on tablets!) and they came from Mesopotamian Ur (c 1800 BC) where there had been literacy more than 1000 years earlier. In any case, if we accept all their tradition (and many do not), they mention their journeys, the places and the peoples they met. In the early Vedic documents there is no mention of travels through other places and of encounters with other people on the way. A more suitable example would be the Gypsies who left India in the early centuries CE and, through Iran, dispersed into the Near East and as far as Britain (Fraser 1995): wandering through many lands over many centuries, they retained very little of their original language and culture.

Avesta that they had lived in the 'Land of the Seven rivers' *Haptahəndu* (§ 17, n 7). It may be counter-argued (and Mallory did so in 2002: see § 5) that people closer to the putative urheimat should have more preservations. For instance since, say, the Hittites are closer to Saptasindhu than the Celts or the Scandinavians the former should have more retentions, which is manifestly not true: in other words, "more distance from the putative urheimat, fewer preservations". This would be too simplistic because after moving away, a people may have many and various experiences which have little to do with distance travelled: one branch may start with a dislike of their native culture and abandon it easily; another may encounter a more developed culture with literacy and succumb to it; a third may be subjugated by a stronger people; a fourth may wander here and there absorbing different elements from alien cultures; and so on. The formula "more distance, fewer preservations" won't do.

However, another alternative is that there was a continuum of IE-speaking peoples extending from Saptasindhu up to the Pontic Steppes and from here the different branches moved off to their historical habitats. In any event, the preservation in Vedic of so many IE elements of religion and language shows that the IAs had an incomparably secure and effective system of oral transmission, which means that the IAs moved very little or not at all.

Finally, Sanskrit proves to be much closer to PIE than any other branch—since it preserves so many more theonyms than any other branch and in several cases bridges gaps and links items which otherwise might have remained unconnected.

Four: **Rigvedic *Pur***

The word *pur* occurs in the *RV* (=*Ṛgveda*) more than 70 times, when compounds *pūrbhid* and *puraṃdará* are put aside. Mayrhofer (1956-) rightly questions a relation with *piparti*[(1)] 'füllt, fills' but surprisingly makes no connection with *piparti*[(2)] 'rettet, schütz/saves, protects'; the ancient *Dhātupāṭha* gives √*pṝ pālanapūraṇayoh* 'in the sense of protecting and filling', where obviously the first meaning connects with *pur*.

The word is recognized as cognate with Greek *polis*, Lithuanian *pilis* and Lettish *pils*, all three meaning 'town, fort'. However, a careful examination of the use of *pur* in the *RV* (with the aid of A Lubotsky's *Concordance...* and the *Vedic Index*) shows that it has only the meaning of defence or protection. Take the example of Śuṣṇa's 'mobile' *cariṣṇu pur*, VIII 1, 28. None of the structures mentioned above can fit here: no such structure in the Rigvedic material world is mobile and, in any case, this *pur* belongs to the demon of drought, a supernatural figure. (It was once suggested that *pur* might be a chariot, but *pur* is a defensive structure and not offensive like the chariot.) K Geldner translates *wandelnde Burg* 'mobile/mutable town/fort' and adds in a note (28a) *die Zauberburg* 'the magical Burg' which seems correct (1951-7). He helps further by giving two references: (a) I 121, 10 is ambiguous because it speaks of light and darkness, of Śuṣṇa's *ojas* 'might' and of his *phaliga* which has uncertain meaning but has been thought to be 'cloud' or 'cave'; (b) V 31, 7 is unambiguous in that it lauds Indra's strength shown in killing the serpent Ahi, in arresting Śuṣṇa's *māyā* 'magic, occult power' and in driving away the Dasyus. Māyā will be discussed later on but we can note here that it is not unconnected with pur. Then, ṛṣi Agastya prays (I 166, 8) to the Maruts (regarded as Storm-gods) to protect (*rakṣ-*) from evil (*agha*) and injury (*abhihruti*) the man they favour (*av-*) "with hundred-fold purs *śatâbhujibhiḥ pūrbhiḥ*": here too no physical structures with hundred walls or folds could possibly protect a man from evil (sin or impurity) and injury; no such many-walled structure existed (allowing for a hyperbole) and, in any case, the Maruts are not builders. Here, however, Geldner gives (1951-7) *Mit hundertfachen Burgen* 'with 100fold Burgs (=towns/forts)'—which means nothing. Of course it could be argued that the use here is metaphorical, but we shall find that in all instances the use is "metaphorical" and that *pur* rarely denotes unambiguously a material fortification and nowhere a town. Most frequently it denotes a supernatural, occult or magical protective force or field.

In a reply to Prof M Witzel D Frawley thinks that the *RV* is connected with a "semi-urban culture like the Harappan" (2002:13). He states: "the term *pur* for city (a term that obviously means city in Greek thought, ie Pura = Polis) is common throughout the text [of the *RV*]". The Greek and Baltic cognates being far too distant cannot furnish acceptable evidence for rigvedic usage any more than the later use of *pur/pura/purī*; so all this must be disregarded in respect of the *RV*. However, as was indicated earlier, a metaphorical use of a material defensive means should not be ruled out. Starting with a simple protective bulwark (even a hump on the ground or a fissure) this developed into an elaborate defensive wall protecting a human settlement; this in turn extended to the human settlement, ie a town/ city fortified. This is well reflected in the Greek *akro-polis*, usually the fort a little above the urban area, or in the later Indic *-pura* 'a (fortified) town', as in Hastinā-pura, Jai-pur(a), etc. But in the RV *pur* has no such significance.

Frawley continues, "Both the Vedic people and their enemies have a hundred, ie several [purs] (*śatapura* eg Rigveda 6.48.8; *RV* 2.4.6; *RV* 4.27.1)".

a) The first reference 6.48.8 is a prayer to god Agni to protect (*pāhi*) from anxiety (*aṃhas*) the one—who-kindles-the-fire with *śatáṃ pūrbhiḥ* "a hundred purs"—whatever *pur* might be. Here the text *does not* say there are 100 'cities' but that a specific type of person should be protected with 100 *purs*; obviously, as above, a fire-kindler can't be protected from anxiety with 100 forts or cities!

b) The second reference (2.4.6) is to Indra crushing the 100 purs of Śambara, a much repeated motif in the *RV*. If Śambara is not a native aboriginal king against whom the Aryans are fighting but is a fiend or demonic figure in a magical, *non-material* dimension of the world we know, then his 100 (or 99) *purs*, prove nothing about the existence of actual Aryan cities.

c) The third reference is again to 100 *purs* but these are *āyasī*, ie of metal (copper, bronze?), and surely the Vedic people had no metal-made cities. What is more, these 100 metallic *purs* are said to guard/confine/conceal (*rakṣ*) the celestial Eagle (or some such divine figure). There is no conceivable sense in which 100 cities could possibly do such a thing; here Geldner translates *hundert eherne Burgen* '100 bronze Burgs' but connects them with demons (*Dämonen*, n 1c). (Further down, in note 2, he considers the possibility that these purs are within the womb *garbhe*.) Consequently all three references (and one could quote several more just as inapt) do not indicate that there were cities in the ordinary world of the *RV*.

d) However, in a fourth reference Frawley cites *pur* as 'wide, broad and extensive" (in *RV* I 189, 2). But in this hymn also the poet prays to Agni to lead him and his clan or people afresh and with prosperity (*svastibhiḥ*) beyond all difficulties and become (*bhávā*) a *pur* "wide, broad and extensive" for them and their offspring (*tokā́ya tánayāya*). It is again inconceivable that Agni would become a "city". Here, surely Agni will become divine protection—something quite unknown to us and to material considerations.[1]

RS Bisht, the eminent archaeologist, excavator at Banawali, also takes *pur* to be 'city/town'; this is one of his main points of convergence between the RV and the Harappan or Indus-Sarasvatī Civilization (1999/2000). He gives a long list of references assuming *pur* to mean 'town' but does not apply philology to analyse contextually any one of them: the mere repetition that pur indicates a town/fort proves nothing. What is worse, there are mistranslations of some passages in the RV where the indeclinable pur*á*s 'before, in front' (with uddāta on the termination) is (inadvertently?) taken as the nom/acc pl p***ú***ras 'towns' (with accent on the stem: p 410-411 and n 190). Also, he should know there is no evidence of Harappan 'hundred-buttress forts' and metallic ones (*āyasī pur* in RV) nor of towns destroyed by human violence (eg fire). The RV is definitely pre-Harappan on two very significant counts (and others, less important). First, it knows not rice *vrīhi*, so essential to later rituals, cotton *karpāsa*, silver *rajata-*, brick *iṣṭakā* and fixed hearths/altars (amply attested in the Brāhmaṇas and/or Sūtras)—all of them important items of the Harappan culture. Second, the Sarasvatī river dried up almost completely by c 1900 BC, and RV VII, 95, 2 says that the river flows "from the mountains to the ocean". So the RV is earlier than 1900 BC. However, G Possehl, another expert on the ISC, examined (1998) all the palaeoenvironmental and geological data relevant to the Sarasvatī and concluded that the river could have flowed down to the ocean only before 3200 *at the very latest*, preferring a date closer to c 3800! PH Francfort had arrived at a similar conclusion six years

[1]If one thinks the rigvedic people lived in towns and had forts, one should look for other kinds of evidence—though I think there is no indication of urban structures in the *RV*.

earlier (1992). Between, say, 3200 and 1900 the river stopped flowing into the ocean and went through further stages of dessication. So, on this evidence, the RV is pre-Harappan; it is the Brāhmaṇas that converge with early Harappan phases. The towns of the Harappan mature or late phases are a far cry from the Rigvedic settlements—which are more accurately reflected in Plato's early ideal community, leading a simple agricultural life, eating barley-bread, drinking wine in moderation and singing hymns to the gods (Republic 372E). The word *pur* provides no evidence at all for the existence of towns or forts (as in historical times) in the Rigvedic world, as is shown in this study,[1] though some crude material defences were used at times.

G Erdosy too rejected any equation of the rigvedic purs with Harappan urbanizations (1994:224) and advocated that their "primary aim was to guard against spiritual ills and magical practices". With this I concur fully and disagree with Erdosy when he ascribes them "to the realm of mythology" (1994:232). Neither Frawley, nor Witzel, nor others have read Erdosy's paper, unfortunately. I shall not tire the reader with other writings which claim that *pur* denotes 'city/fort' or any of the meanings listed above (see particularly W Rau 1976, Mayrhofer 1996, and Sharma R.S. 2004). I shall only advert briefly to the *Vedic Index* (I, 538-9), which also refers to I 189, 2 with its *prithvī́ bahulā́ na urvī́ pur*, stating that this "fortification" must have been "of considerable size": I dealt with this in an earlier paragraph. This valuable work notes that "a fort 'made of stone' (*aśmanmayī*) is mentioned", also "strongholds of iron (*āyasī*) ... but these are probably only metaphorical". It refers to the "Autumnal (*śāradī*) forts" which "apparently" belong to *Dāsas*, perhaps "against Aryan attacks or against inundations in that season," and to forts "with a hundred walls (*śatabhunjī*)". It concludes by mentioning the "siege of forts" in post-rigvedic Saṃhitās and Brāhmaṇas and that fire was used in these sieges according to *RV* VII 5, 3.

This is a good brief summary but the comments in the *Vedic Index* are misleading since they are based on the Aryan Invasion Theory. Starting with the last point—the use of fire during sieges is imaginary. It is well established now that no Harappan towns had been sacked by allegedly invading Aryans. *RV* VII 5, 3 says merely that the 'dark tribes' (*víśa ásiknīḥ*) fled in disarray for fear of Agni Vaiśvānara, the god (not ordinary fire, surely) who shone glowing while 'rending' (*darayan*, not 'burning down') their purs. The 'dark tribes' could be fiends or fears active at night and/or evil, demonic forces.

The references to later texts concern conflicts between *asuras* 'demons' and *devas* 'gods'. In fact, in *Aitareya Brāhmaṇa* I 23 the Asuras made the earth a copper/bronze (*ayasmayī*) *pur*, the Midspace (*antarikṣā*) a silver (*rajatā*) *pur* and the sky a golden (*hariṇī*) one. Obviously these *purs* have nothing to do with any kind of human towns or citadels. The same Brāhmaṇa, a little further on, II 11, says that the gods, in order to protect their sacrifice from the Asuras, placed around the sacrificial post three *purs agnimayī* 'made of Agni'. Surely it would be absurd to suppose that Agni built three 'fortifications' of stone or metal or mud or wood round the post. In fact this same passage explains that the repulsing of the Asuras is done by taking the holy fire round the place thrice (*paryagni kurvanti ... tripuraṃ- paryasante*)! Here surely we have a kind of ritual magic. And the same is found in *Taittirīya Saṃhitā* II 5, 3 where if a man comes under attack of witchcraft (*abhicaryamāṇa*), he should perform the ten-night-ritual and thereby surround himself with the protection of a *devapur* 'divine *pur*'! In the same Saṃhitā VI 2, 3 the Asuras had three purs, the lowest being of copper, the next of silver and the highest of gold: Rudra cleft them with an arrow made up of the powers of Agni, Soma and Viṣṇu.

The *pur* of stone (*aśmanmayī*) occurs only once in *RV* IV 30, 20, where Indra overthrew 100 of them for the benefit of his protegé Divodāsa, a liberal offerer. On the face of it these stone-forts would seem to belong to human enemies of Divodāsa. But from other references to this incident (I 51, 6; 112, 14, the Aśvins help here; 130, 7; etc, but especially II 14, 6 and 19, 6) these *purs* belong to the drought-demon Śambara. So even these cannot be said to be in any way ordinary human forts (or cities) built of stone. I submit that the *aśmanmayī pur* no less than the *āyasī* 'metallic' one is metaphorical denoting a degree of hardness and colour or some such quality (like the silver and golden ones in *Aitareya Brāhmaṇa* and other post-rigvedic texts).

The references to metallic *purs* are many. One at least says that Indra with the bolt in his arms killed the Dasyus and brought down (*nitārīt*) [their] metallic *purs* (II 20, 8). Here we might think the Dasyus are local aborigines destroyed by the invading Aryans, but they had no metal-forts, surely. We can say that this is a metaphor and refers to hardness and/or colour also. But I don't see why the poet should describe an ordinary fortification of stone+mud+wood as "metallic". Stone is just as shiny and hard as the metal *ayas* and mud or wood or both can hardly be shiny or hard like metal. (We don't really know what is involved exactly since the construction and constitution of the purs are nowhere given in the *RV*.) Moreover it is Indra, a super-natural force, that destroys them—not men's weapons. Let us see the other references. We have already examined the 100 metal-forts that guarded the Eagle (IV 27, 1): here these forts are in the womb *garbhe* (or under the charge of demons).[2] Then three

[2]Here Geldner and others think that demons hold imprisoned the Eagle in these metal forts. This is possible, of course. Truth is that this myth with its various interconnections is lost to us. There is not enough information in the *RV* to enable us to reconstruct it even approximately. Post-rigvedic sources with their fragmented references already indicate that they no longer have it complete or understand it fully. For references, see *Vedic Index* under 'Vāmadeva'. I find most interesting the re-occurrence of the verse *RV* IV 27, 1 in *Aitareya* Upanishad II 1, 5 and its interpretation there. The Upanishad suggests that here the spirit of seer Vāmadeva is confined and breaks free.

references (I 58, 8; VIII 3, 7 and 15, 14) are prayers to Agni to protect the poet (and his people) from various calamities including anxiety *aṃhas* (I 58, 8) with *purs* of metal. Another one, X 101, 8, is a prayer to the Viśvedevās to "fashion (*kṛṇudhvam*) inviolable metal *purs*" in connection with the pouring of the soma-drink; since only demons interfere with the sacrifice, the required purs would be of such substance as to stop those other-worldly forces. Another one (VIII 95, 1) calls the river Sarasvatī "a metal *pur*" which is a secure support/defence (*dharuṇa*). In yet another one (VIII 100, 8) the Eagle (*suparṇa* here) pierced the metal *pur* with the speed of mind, flew to heaven and fetched soma to the Boltbearer. All are non-material *purs* including those of the Dasyus in II 20, 8. The three of Agni and the one of the Viśvedevās are certainly magical or super-natural in some way.

However, the reference to the seven purs of the enemies of king Sudās in VII 18, 13 seems to be different. This hymn refers to the fighting of Sudās and the confederation of the ten kings, an internecine war which Sudās won with Indra's help. In this hymn Indra destroyed all their 'fixed/firm defences' (*dṛṃhitāṇi*) and their 7 purs, which here probably describe some kind of material structure. But even here some aspects are ambiguous. It is not as though Sudās attacked the 10 kings on their own native ground. This battle took place by the river Puruṣṇī where Sudās and his army was hard pressed, surrounded on all sides by the more numerous forces of the 10 kings (*RV* VII, 83, 6-8). What exactly were the *dṛṃhitāṇi* and purs destroyed by Indra? Surely the confederate foes could have had no forts/citadels, unless they were 'secure defensive positions'. But I am again inclined to think that the reference is to non-material protective means. The incident is most probably historical, but the number 7 has mystical associations and occurs in other cases.

Interesting are some references to 'autumnal' *śāradī purs* but not many. In I 131, 4 Indra overpowered unspecified "autumnal *purs*" known in former times. In I 174, 2 he broke down the seven autumnal *purs*, shelter of tribes "with abusive speech *mṛdhrâvāc*". Here these tribes could be human beings. In VI 20, 10 Indra again destroys seven autumnal *purs*, shelter of Dāsas. Here too the Dāsas may be said to be human beings. These may be instances where the *purs* could belong to humans. However, the recurring mystical number 7 and the destruction by a god introduce strong elements of doubt and suggest again the supernatural. Moreover, I wonder if we are entitled to translate this adjective *śārada-* as 'autumnal'. It would be more correct, perhaps, in these cases to translate as 'ancient/old/enduring', or 'annual' in the sense of being renewed every year. These are ancient or annual (and to us) supernatural means of protection.

In connection with the supernatural aspect, most interesting is the curious reference to Śuṣṇa's 'mobile' *cariṣṇu pur*, VII 1, 28, which Indra crushed with blows of his bolt. Clearly, a mobile *pur*, as shown earlier, is beyond all concepts of forts, cities, ramparts or whatever, in the physical world of the Vedic people. (Quite rightly Geldner connected it with magic.) Only a concept within what is usually regarded as the "mythological" super-natural sphere can make sense of Śuṣṇa's *cariṣṇu pur*. This at once illumines and suggests a similar sense for Agni's metallic *purs* and particularly the one which is *śatâbhujī*, VII 15, 14: obviously this fiery field with 100 folds or encirclements can only be magical or occult. One may argue that it is ordinary physical fire that destroys the *purs* of enemies but it is difficult to see how such a fire (or many fires) could repulse inimical armies. (Surely the enemies also could use fire as a weapon.) Fire would dispel the darkness of night or creatures of darkness like ghosts and fiends—or wild animals. Then, there are the prayers that Agni should guard people against distress and anxiety with his *purs* (I 58, 8; VI 48, 8), which would involve an esoteric psychological or spiritual type of protective means. The śatábhujī *pur* of the Maruts, I 166, 8, is not very different, as was indicated earlier.

Just as interesting is the reference to *āmā́su pūrṣú paráḥ* wherein is protected the Offspring-of-Waters *Apāṃ Napāt* II 35. WO' Flaherty translates this as "far away in fortresses of unbaked bricks" (1981:105) and one can't help but wonder where she found the "bricks", since the *RV* mentions them nowhere! I can only assume she follows Geldner who translates *In den rohen Burgen* 'in raw towns/forts', which means nothing, and who, to cover up the deficiency, adds in a note (6c) *nicht wie die gewönlichen Burgen aus gebrannten Ziegelsteinen gemacht* 'not like the usual Burgs made from baked bricks' (!) without telling us where in the *RV* we find 'usual Burgs made from baked bricks' (1951-7)—since there are no such constructions! Then O' Flaherty in an explanatory note mentions Agni, "safe... among enemies who do not control fire and so do not fire their bricks, or who (as the sun) is safe from his enemies... in his own 'natural' citadels not made of baked bricks, ie the clouds". The confusion here is almost unbelievable. Why and how exactly would Agni feel safe in such conditions and who are these "enemies"? Fire's biggest enemy is water; so fire dives and dwells in the waters protected within fortresses of unbaked bricks! Is this at all sensible? I don't think so. As for the sun, are not the clouds themselves his only traditional enemies? Neither unbaked-brick-fortresses (in water?!) nor physical enemies are involved here. *āma-* here (and perhaps elsewhere) should mean 'non-artificial, natural'. Thus Apā́m- Napā́t in his own non-artificial, natural, divine condition with his own occult, defensive powers (*pūrṣu*) is protected against any malignity or niggardliness (*arāti*) and falsehood or unrighteousness (*anṛta*). If we had even one description of material forts/towers elsewhere in the *RV*, we could take *pūrṣu* here as being metaphorical towers (billows, perhaps).

Another interesting case is the *gómati púr* in *RV* VIII, 6, 2. The phrase at first sight presents a difficulty since the adjective is usually translated as 'having kine'. But *go-* can mean 'wealth' by extension and certainly 'star, light'. So the phrase can just as plausibly be translated as 'protective-fold rich in light'. So this is ambiguous: it could be a pen with cows also but hardly a city.

There are many more instances of *pur* without any other distinctive feature: I 33, 13; II 19, 6; IV 16,4 and 26, 3; VI 20, 3; VII 19, 5; etc. All the non-divine *purs* are destroyed by Indra mainly, to a much lesser extent by Agni (VI 16, 39; VII 5, 3; X 46, 5) and even less by Soma (IX 48, 2). In one case Indra is said to have shattered (*vṛṇak*) the *purs* of Cumuri, Dhuni, Pipru, Śambara and Śuṣṇa—all demonic figures. Elsewhere he destroys other demons' *purs*, Vala's (VI 18, 5) and Namuci's and Vaṅgṛda's (I 53, 7-8). Often he uses his bolt (eg I 33, 13) which is said to be his bull (I 131, 3) but in other cases he uses simply his *ojas* 'might/strength' (eg I 53, 7) or his *māyā* 'magical power' (I 51, 5). He uses this māyā in other exploits also as when he stops the overflowing waters of a river or puts to sleep 30.000 Dasas (IV 30, 12 and 21). This occult power is of course an attribute of other gods as well, chiefly of (Mitra and) Varuṇa; it is by means of this that Varuṇa, the chief *māyin* 'wielder of māyā', creates and regulates various phenomena in the world.

The power *māyā* is also an attribute of *asuras*, in the later sense of 'demons'. As we saw, in V 31, 7 Śuṣṇa is said to have *māyā*. Then, in X 138, 3 Indra destroys the firm works (*dṛḷha*, here but elsewhere *pur*) of demon Pipru who is described as *māyin*; in I 117, 3 the Aśvins offset the *māyā* of "the malignant Dasyu" and free Atri. I think that *māyā* and *purs* are connected in that the *purs* are created by gods and asuras with this power. Nowhere in the *RV* do we find one single statement that any *pur* (or *dṛḷha*) was destroyed by human beings just as we find no statement that any *pur* was constructed by human beings (though VI 45, 9 does refer to men's *dṛḷhāni*, which however are created by *māyā*, and asks Indra to destroy them). In VI 75, 19 the poet says 'the holy power (or prayer) is my inmost armour' *bráhma várma mamā́ntaram*. The divine *pur* is like this inner *varma* which is *brahma*.

In *Atharvaveda* V 8, 6 we find the interesting verse "when [the enemies] attacked the divine strongholds (*-pur-*), the holy-power (*brahma*) made protective armours (*varmāṇi*)" (or "[Indra] made the brahma-power into armours"):[3] here we have all three elements. From this point of view the hymns refer perhaps to an age we have long forgotten and ceased to believe in, the age when divine beings mingled with human beings and helped them with divine *purs* against demonic beings and their *purs*. I say "perhaps" because it is difficult for us to accept such a situation as real, yet it does not seem impossible.

In that far distant age some men too are said to have used *māyā* or a manifestation of it as mental power, speech, knowledge, or the holy brahma-power. This spiritual power is used by Vasiṣṭha to help king Sudās defeat his enemies (*brahmaṇā* instr VII 33, 3); by the same *brahmaṇā* Atri disclosed the sun (V 40, 6). Vīśvāmitra stopped the flow of the rivers by the force of his speech *vacas* (III 33, 8 and 10). The Ṛbhus, again, used 'power-of-mind' *manas* (IV 33, 9) and 'true holy-spells' *satyamantra* (I 20, 2-4) or *dhī* and *dhīti* 'thought, visionary power' (I 110, 4; IV 36, 2 and 4) to perform their miraculous deeds, like the rejuvenation of the Parents (IV 33, 3) and so on; consequently they were given immortality in the mansion of the Sungod (I 110, 2-4). For almost 2000 years Christians, most learned people and scientists as well as uneducated folk, have accepted as true the miracles performed by the prophets of the Old Testament (Moses crossing the Red Sea, etc) and by the apostles and saints (rescuing and healing people). Yet when they meet similar miraculous works by the ṛṣis (=prophets and saints) in

[3]For similar uses of *brahma* being *varma* see also AV VII 100, 1; VIII 2, 10; IX 2, 16; XVII 1, 27-28: all noted in Geldner (vol 34, p 178, n 19d).

the Vedic hymns, they call them "mythology", as if divine powers are restricted only to Christianity. Moreover, the ṛṣis' attainment of a divine condition or immortality is, surely, no more "mythological" (unreal or incredible) than the prophets' and saints' attainment of a celestial or paradisal state basking in God's radiance. Most modern scholars think to solve the problem of this discrepancy by rejecting all miracles, religion and spirituality—which seems to be a much more general attitude now. But surely the miracle of life, birth and death, and the spirituality of mind, word and action will never cease, however materialist and drab or hedonistic ordinary life becomes.

Indeed, Dr J Mack, a psychiatrist at Harvard University, writes: "It appears ever more likely that we exist in a multidimensional cosmos or multiverse... The cosmos ... far from being an empty place of dead matter and energy appears to be filled with beings, creatures, spirits, intelligences, gods ... that have through millennia been intimately involved with human existence" (1999:169). Thus, there is no reason not to interpret *pur* as a supernatural defence.

Five: **Samudra in the Ṛgveda**

Introduction

The Hindu printed in several issues (18th, 25th June, etc, 2002) letters from Dr D Frawley and Prof M Witzel amounting to a controversy whether the rigvedic people had towns/forts and knew the ocean; also whether the river Sarasvatī flowed down to the ocean. I sent a letter to that newspaper in mid-September 2002 giving my own views, but for unknown reasons my letter was not published. I have since revised the whole piece. Here I show that *samudra* does denote the ocean/sea and that Sarasvatī did flow to the ocean prior to 3200 BC.[1]

With regard to *samudra* Frawley presented some very good evidence (I 71, 7; V 55, 5; IX 84, 4 etc) and some very dubious examples (I 130, 5; I 190, 7; VII 33, 8 etc: July 16, pp 4-6, 20-3). Witzel ignored all the sound evidence and digressed on some weak points and obvious generalities, such as—"Varuṇa is not just a god of *samudra* but ... of Rta ..." (as if Frawley didn't know this).

The important point here is whether the rigvedic people knew the ocean/sea (in our modern sense of the words) or not. If they did, then obviously *samudra* can mean ocean/sea. If they did not, then *samudra* cannot mean ocean/sea. How do we find out?

---

[1]All ancient dates hereafter are BCE. Some abbreviations used: AIT = Aryan Invasion/Immigration Theory. Gk = Greek. Goth = Gothic. OE = Old English. PIE = ProtoIndoEuropean. *RV* = *Ṛgveda*.

To say that *samudra* means 'ocean' and that therefore the *RV* knows the ocean (so Frawley) is circuitous and really begs the question. Similarly, to say that in one verse it means 'a terminal lake', in another 'heavenly waters', in a third 'confluence' etc, and that therefore the *RV* does not know the ocean (so Witzel), is no better.

Since the *RV* is an absolutely primary text, *philology can be of limited help to settle this issue.* When Witzel claims that philology is necessary (true of course in many ways) and dizzyingly refers to various sources (all distant from, and some later than, the *RV*), to recent scholarly authorities (often irrelevant), protolanguages (all conjectural and hardly admissible in a court of law) and so on, and when Frawley falls into the trap and argues against all this, they both labour under a fallacy. The word *samudra* means literally 'all-together' *sam* and 'water' *udrá* (cf *anudrá* = waterless). That *udr-a* is connected to the hypothetical Proto-Indo-European **udn-*, (found nowhere except modern books!), to Gr *hudor*, Latin *unda*, Goth *watō* etc, etc, does not help us in the slightest any more than Gr *polis* and Baltic *pilis*, *pils* and later uses of *pur-* in India help with rigvedic *pur*.[2] And this, because we don't and can't know if the original PIE word(s) had one meaning in all places, all tribes and all classes of the communities, and because the use of the cognates in many cases developed differently in the separate traditions according to different conditions of place and time. (Eg: Vedic *arṇa-/va* 'surging, wave, flood' is connected to Hittite *aruna* 'sea' and Gr *ernos* 'branch, shoot' and Norwegian *run(n)e* 'branch': thus, if the cognates are correct—and who can be certain?—we have two distinct lines of semantic development. Cf also √*nu*> *navate/nauti* 'sound/praise' and 'go' but Gr *nevō* 'nod/wink' and Latin *ad-*

[2]*pur* in the *RV* never means 'fort' or 'town' but a magical, esoteric defence. Merely citing verses in the *RV* but not analysing and exploring their meaning is not very sound scholarship. See chapter 4 on '*Ṛgvedic pur*'.

nuo 'make a sign'; then √*man*>*manyate* 'think' but Gk *maino-mai* 'be furious', OE *mænan* '*signify*' (also *mūnan* 'remember') and Goth *munan* 'think'; also *manas* 'mind' but Gk *menos* 'force/spirit'; again, *sar-ít* 'stream' or *sár-as* 'lake, pond' and Gr *hals*- 'salt, sea' or *helos* 'swamp', Latin *sal-/inus* 'salt-/y', Goth *sal-sus* 'salt'. In all these examples the semantic development diverges considerably.) To say then that in *RV* VII 95, 2 *ā́ samudrā́t* the word means 'a terminal lake' in which the river Sarasvatī ends (Witzel 2001:76) is not philology at all: it is a mere and arbitrary interpretation with the use of some reasoning or logical process which, however, here is defective because it is conditioned heavily by the AIT (=Aryan Invasion/Immigration Theory). That it is based on erudite studies of the past (eg K Klaus, et al) is not at all helpful since they too are arbitrary interpretations heavily conditioned by the AIT: moreover they have no more information about *samudra* than I have or Geldner or the *Vedic Index*, since the *RV* is an absolutely primary text.

So how do we find out? Any mass of water more than one drop could be *sam-udra*: water in a jar, a small pool, a large lake or the sea. When we say it is a confluence or a river, we have introduced the element of movement—moving, not stationary water. Now, such is also water-from-a-spring, a cataract or heavy torrential rain. Perhaps *sam-udra* denotes these moving water-masses also?... Let us try a different approach—a common sense one.

For the sake of the argument, I assume that the AIT is correct. So at about 1500 BC the Aryans come from Afghanistan, they do manage to climb up the north-western mountains with their carts (*anas*-, *vāhana*-) and their *rathavāhana*- upon which rest the war-chariots (*ratha*-), then roll down into the valleys of Saptasindhu and with peaceful and/or violent means eventually take control of the natives. I also assume that the Sarasvatī does not flow into the Indian/Arabian ocean; only the Indus does so. Meanwhile the Harappan culture is collapsing and many natives move to the east and south followed by the newcomers. The Aryans come from a landlocked place and know nothing of the ocean—only lakes, rivers and confluences. Then they begin to compose their religious hymns and a few hundred years later they arrange and produce, say c 1200-1000, the *RV* collection—in which there is no knowledge of the ocean. This has been the mainstream AIT scenario with minor variations.

With regard to the knowledge of the ocean, this scenario contains a fatal flaw. At their arrival the Aryans may (in this scenario) have known no ocean, but is it at all likely that they continued to be ignorant of it in the next 300 or even 3 years? Of course not. *They would have learnt about it from the natives, at least.*

To begin with, it is well established that the Harappans knew the ocean and had maritime trade with Mesopotamia since the late third millennium if not earlier (Saggs 1989:130; Crawford 1994:148; Lal 1997:182-8). They had large ports like Lothal and perhaps Dholavira (on an island) and Dvaraka (later) and obviously large ocean-faring ships and smaller craft, sailing up and down the Indus, the "terminal lakes" and the other rivers. Surely it is not likely in all those decades and centuries that the Aryans never heard from the natives about the expanse of the ocean in the south and the former trade. Then, the Aryans themselves were intrepid adventurers who had trekked 100s of miles over rough and dangerous regions and had conquered the Saptasindhu. Surely it is not likely that nobody thought of travelling by chariot to the south, or by boat down the Indus (see example 5, below) and so gain first-hand knowledge of the ocean. And if a few did this, then more would follow and, in any case, knowledge of the ocean would spread among the Indoaryans, including some of the composers of the hymns.

Thus common sense compels us to accept that the Indoaryans had knowledge of the ocean/sea even in the AIT scenario. With its customary caution the *Vedic Index*, which does not at all promote indigenism or an early Ṛgveda, but adheres to the AIT, states "knowledge of the ocean ... was almost inevitable to people who knew the Indus" (vol 2, 432). Why modern scholars abandon common sense in favour of a mis-applied "philology" is a mystery.

Consequently we must accept that there may well be references to the ocean in the *RV*. Common sense again dictates that out of the many words that denote 'water-mass/ flood' a very likely one is the frequent *samudra* because this is so used commonly and consistently in post-rigvedic literature.

Are there such instances in the *RV*? Yes, many.

We should first note that the recent claims about *samudra* denoting various water-masses other than the ocean are not new nor more "scientific". The *Vedic Index* (1912) mentions some scholars who rejected totally the meaning 'ocean', others who accepted it in few and others in many cases. It cites Zimmer who thought *samudra* "denotes the river Indus when it receives all its Panjab tributaries" and gives numerous references (see example no 10, end). But it adds "even Zimmer who is inclined to restrict [the Vedic Indians'] knowledge of the sea as far as possible admits it in one passage of the Rigveda and of course later" (*Vedic Index* II 431). Zimmer's one exception is VII 95, 2, (*Vedic Index* II 432), Sarasvatī flowing *gíríbhya ā́ samudrā́t* 'from the mountains to the ocean' (which Witzel takes as 'terminal lake')! K Klaus (1989:365) also in his study agrees with Zimmer and accepts that in this passage *samudra* may denote *Meer* 'sea'. On the other hand, in some instances *samudra* can denote 'confluence' (*RV* III 33, 2) and in others primeval celestial 'ocean' (X 190, 1-2), while in yet others earthly 'ocean/sea'. Let us now pass to some examples in the *RV*. And I start with one of Frawley's examples.

1) I 116, 4: For three nights and three days (*tisráḥ kṣápas trír áha-*), o Aśvins, you carried Bhujyu ... *samudrásya dhánvan ārdrásya pāré* 'to the distant dry-shore of the watery ocean'. Here the key is the 3 nights and days. Obviously, no lake or river is so wide that the Aśvins would need so long to ferry Bhujyu across. Even an ordinary (rowing) boat would cross in a few hours! Only an ocean will do here. Klaus refers only to the aspect of moisture (*feucht*) ignoring all else (1989:366, n 12)—and I can't help wondering at such superficial scholarship.

That the tale may be pure myth does not invalidate the duration of the Aśvins' flight to the dry *dhanva-* 'sandbank' (Mayrhofer KEWA vol 2) and the expanse of the *samudra*. Even if it is a hyperbole, it is used presumably to emphasize the expanse of waters. Consequently, in the many other references to the rescue of Bhujyu by the *Aśvins samudra* denotes ocean: eg I 118, 6; VI 62, 6; VII 69, 7; VIII 5, 22; etc. Perhaps it is not out of place here to note that this motif of the Aśvins as rescuers may be PIE since it appears in Greece where the two Dioskouroi 'the bright Skygod's sons' deliver men and ships from tempestuous seas (long *Hymn to Dioskouroi* 6-8, in White 1935) and in the Baltic countries where the Dievo Sunelai 'the [sky-]god's lads' save the Sunmaiden from the sea (Ward 1968).

2) V 55, 5 *úd īrayathā marutaḥ samudrató yūyám vṛṣṭiṃ varṣayathā* 'O Maruts, you raise up rain from the samudra [and] cause-to-rain'. Here there is plainly an upward (ud) movement of water/moisture/vapour and then rain caused by the Stormgods. The upward movement excludes an atmospheric or heavenly water-mass since the waters would not go even higher before they fall as rain; so it must be a water-mass on earth. The *samudra* here is singular. So it cannot be one river or confluence since there are many of these; moreover, these are in motion and even the rigvedic people would know that vapour would rise more easily from stationary waters. Nor can it be one "terminal lake" since there are other small and large lakes. Consequently *samudra* must here denote either the sum-total of waters, stationary and moving, or a single very large watermass which is the ocean/sea. Again, the rigvedic people must have known that evaporation occurs more in hot conditions rather than in cold; so they would not refer to *all* waters. They must also have known that it is hotter further south of Saptasindhu. Now, even in the AIT scenario, as we saw, they must have known that, further south where it is hotter, there is a very large, almost limitless watermass and that most evaporation would take place there. So here *samudra* must refer to the ocean/sea. Klaus (1989:370) takes this as a possible reference to the Indus, but this ignores the facts given here.

The next example mentions an upper but also a lower *samudra*. I trust I shall be excused hereafter if I don't indulge in such ludicrously detailed analyses to demonstrate the obvious.

3) VII 6, 7: Agni Vaiśvānara received treasures in the rising of the sun *ā́ samudrā́d ā́varād ā́ parasmād... divā́ ā́ pṛthiviā́ḥ* 'from the *samudra* lower and upper, from sky/heaven and earth'. Here we have a lower and an upper ocean and sky and earth: so we take the lower ocean to be earthly and the upper one atmospheric or heavenly. Or we may also have a chiasmus figure (ad-bc: *avara-samudra* with *pṛthivī* and *para-samudra* with *dyu-*) which amounts to the same. But here the lower water-mass cannot be the heavenly one as well, nor a terminal lake nor a confluence of two rivers. Nor could the poet have in mind the sun rising from a lake or river, however wide: there was no large watermass in the east of Saptasindhu to account for such a phenomenon. So *samudra* must be 'sea/ocean' here. Or, Agni received treasures from those four places.

We find another differentiation and contrast in a hymn to the Maruts who knew the ocean.

4) VIII 20, 25: Whatever medicinal balm is in the Indus and Asiknī rivers... *samudréṣu... párvateṣu* 'in the oceans... on the mountains'. Here now we have (two) rivers and their drinkable waters, then oceans/seas with salt-water and mountains—a totally earthly area. Thus we can exclude the heavenly ocean, lakes (with sweet water) and confluences (also sweet water). I do not preclude the possibility of the meaning 'lake' but medicinal balms were found in the ocean too.

5) I 56, 2: To [Indra] go praises... *samudrám nā saṃcárane saniṣyávaḥ* 'as to the *samudra* [go] in company those desiring gain'. *saṃcaraṇa* and the plural *saniṣyavaḥ* imply more than two going together. Yes, it could be to a lake or a large river, the only one according to the AIT being the Indus (for fish, shells, commerce?). But if they have a large enough boat to take 3 or more persons and merchandise, surely it could reach the ocean in the south. However, to me (and to the *Vedic Index* I, 461-2, under **nau**) this suggests the ocean/sea.

6) I 32, 1-2: Indra killed the dragon, opened outlets for the waters splitting the breasts of mountains (1cd) then ... *syándamānā áñjaḥ samudrám áva jagmur ā́paḥ* (2cd) 'flowing directly to the ocean down rushed the waters'. Here the "mountains" may be a metaphor for clouds but even so the rainwaters would not end up in one terminal lake, or one river or one confluence (*samudra* is singular), but in the ocean. Only strong prejudice under the AIT would insist otherwise. Geldner who is obviously aware of the earlier dispute about *samudra* here translates: *eilend liefen die Gewässer stracks zum Meere*, the only difference from mine being *Meer* 'the sea'. I' ll settle for "the sea" quite happily.

In fact Geldner uses in his translation *Meer* 'sea' and *Ozean* 'ocean' very frequently—and even in places where I would hesitate. Here are some examples.

7) V 78, 8: *yáthā vā́to yáthā vánaṃ yáthā samudrá éjati.* Geldner renders: *Wie die Wind, wie der Wald, wie das Meer bewegt* 'as the wind, as the wood, as the **sea** stirs'. Here samudra *could* well be a lake, but Geldner is unhesitant.

8) II 35, 3: *sām anyā́ yanty úpa yanty anyā́ ḥ, samānám ūrvám nadíaḥ pṛṇ anti*: literally 'while some flow together, others flow towards; the rivers fill the common receptacle'.

In Mayrhofer (KEWA vol 1) *ūrva* = 'dungeon', but also Meer 'sea'. 'Flow together' probably means flow one into the other. Geldner gives much the same but also makes an insertion in the first part: ... *münden andere* (*ins Meer*) 'others flow (into the sea)'. And the last part he renders freely as *den gemeinsamen Ozean* 'the common ocean'.

9) III 33, 2: Impelled by Indra ... you-two [rivers] *samudrám̐ rathýeva yāthaḥ* 'like chariot-horses go to the sea'. Geldner gives the same—*geht ihr zum Meere*. Here we could perhaps have 'you go to your confluence' since the two rivers are thought to join together; yet, even here, the simile of the chariot-horses (or, loosely 'chariots') would seem most inapt since a confluence for them would be a disastrous collision. Nor can it be said that here is meant the confluence with the Indus because this would come later, after the two rivers have joined. So we have an unclear situation. Confluence is possible.

Now Geldner not only is aware of the disputes regarding ambiguous words, phrases or passages, but also has translated all *RV* and so should know the text better than most. His numerous references to parallel passages in other Vedic texts shows that he knows the entire spectrum of the Vedic literature. This does not mean that he is free of errors, but these are due mostly to the limitations of the AIT which he also held but with far better reasons in his time than modern vedicists.

Allow me here to open a parenthesis on (mis-)translations and misconceptions under the influence of this wretched AIT. In this very hymn III 33, Viśvāmitra asks the rivers Vīpāś and Śutudrī to stop flowing so that he and the Bharatas can cross; the rivers comply. Now in stanza 11 we find *gavyán grā́maḥ* and in 12 *bharatā́ gavyávaḥ*. In both cases Geldner translates the words *gav-* with *Rinder*(*beute*) *ausziehend-* 'extracting/removing (ie stealing?) cattle' (KEWA vol 1). C Watkins translates (2001:86-88) with the compound 'cattle-raiding' ('host' in 11 and 'Bharatas' in 12). It is possible that cattle-raids did occur in rigvedic times, as we find similar practices later in Greek and Irish texts also. But in this hymn there is no mention of any raid or cattle-stealing. The adjective *gavyu* means 'desirous-of-cattle' according to the MSD (also 'delighting-in-cattle') and Mayrhofer (*Rinder begehrend* 'desiring cattle'). The MSD gives the same meaning for *gavyat*. These meanings are not quite the same as cattle-rustling, which comes from AIT notions. *gavya(n)t-* is found in several hymn-prayers to Indra together with *aśvaya(n)t-* 'desirous-of/delighting-in horses': eg in IV 17, 6; VII 32, 23; etc. *gavyu* again is used also for Soma (eg VIII 46, 10; IX 97, 15) where the desire is presumably for the cows' milk. Surely a group of people on the move guided by a great seer need not be cattle-rustlers just because they are described as 'desirous-of/delighting-in cattle'. I would like to know if there is any clear reference to cattle-raiding in the *RV*. SA Dange examined in detail many passages about the alleged "battle for the gain of cows" (*gaviṣṭi/go-iṣṭhi*) but found no evidence at all for cattle-raids and the like (1967: 78-108); it is a pity this study has not become (better) known. End of parenthesis.

I do agree with the *Vedic Index* and Zimmer (therein) that in some verses *samudra* may denote the confluence of certain rivers/streams with the Indus. Eg, III 36, 7 *...samudréṇa índhavo yādamanāḥ* '... streams uniting with the river' (*not surely uniting with 'confluence'*); *VI 36, 3, ...samudrám ná sindhavaḥ* 'like streams/rivers to their confluence'; etc: here, yes, *samudra* could be a river or confluence. Another ambiguous passage follows.

10) I 71, 7: All offerings go to Agni *samudrám ná sravátaḥ saptá yahvíḥ* 'like the seven swift-ones flowing to the ocean'. Here, since the Indus itself is one of the 7 rivers and flows down to the ocean, *samudra* must denote 'ocean', terrestrial and nothing else. It can be argued here that *yahvī* means 'daughter' or 'she-young-one' (which is one of the two meanings given in MSD and Mayrhofer) and that the 7 rivers are "young" (ie smaller) tributaries flowing into the "elder" (ie larger) Indus. However, first, we don't know if the Indus was larger than the tributaries before it received them. Second, and more important, only a very confused mind would speak of tributaries as "young daughters". No daughters in any sense at all flow into an elder person (their mother?) the way tributaries stream into another river. Nor can it be said that several youngsters together grow into a single elder being. When Agni is described as *sáhaso yahúḥ* (IX 60, 13; or *sáhasaḥ putrá-* in V 11, 6) 'son of might', might is conceived as the pre-existing parent from whom emerges the offspring, and no poet would suggest that the tributaries emerge from the river they feed. Consequently, such thinking is as worthless as Mayrhofer says is the attempted connection of *yahu* with *Jehovah*. Thus the 7 restless rivers flow with the Indus to the ocean.

Although from this we can see that the Vedic people probably had the wider (and not difficult, surely) concept of all streams/rivers eventually flowing into the ocean/sea in the south—and this is their only "terminal lake"—this is not explicit. Indeed, here *samudra* could also denote the confluence with the Indus, as we see in example 9 and other cases mentioned by Klaus (1989).

Another and final example where the word means ocean/sea:

11) X 66 11 *samudráḥ síndhū rájo antárikṣam ajá ékapāt tanayitnúr arṇaváḥ*: 'the *samudra*, the river Indus, the region/space, the midair/sky, the deity Aja Ekapād (=the one-footed Unborn or Goat), the thunder, the flood (should listen)'. In this sequence the midair/sky, Aja Ekapād and the thunder are definitely non-earthly but atmospheric or celestial phenomena; so "the flood" is most probably the atmospheric non-earthly ocean. Consequently *samudra* cannot refer to this domain but must be a terrestrial watermass, as is the river Indus; and *rajas* is the general earthly vicinity or space. This seems to follow naturally from the preceding stanza 10c which says that waters and plants should speed the songs forward. There is absolutely nothing before or after to suggest 'confluence' for *samudra* and a pond/lake would be much too specific for this context since there are more than one of them. It cannot be 'a terminal lake' since the Indus flowed to the ocean. So *samudra* must be the normal earthly ocean. The sequence moves from the ocean/sea to the river Indus, then upward to the atmosphere/sky and its phenomena.

Now, if one examines carefully Klaus's paper on *samudra* (1989), one will agree with some of his findings (as in the *Vedic Index*) but will also notice three methodological faults: a) he jumbles together *RV* and post-*RV* passages as if they are all of the same value; b) he refers to numerous *RV* passages and theorizes in generalities but analyses in detail very few; c) he omits several passages like those I use, eg examples 2 (VII 6, 7 yet cites VII 33, 8 etc), 3 (VIII 20, 5 yet he cites many others from Bk VIII), 6 (I 56, 2 yet cites I 52 and 55), 9 (II 35, 3 yet cites others) and 11 (X 66, 11 yet cites others). However, these latter examples show that *samudra* denotes 'ocean/sea'. As for Klaus's objection that the saltness (*Salzigkeit*) of sea-water is not mentioned, it is not serious, because there are contrasts between sweet-water streams and the ocean; no context demands anything else, nor is it anywhere stated that the river-water is drinkable. TY Elizarenkova (1996:21) contributed to this misunderstanding (and misrepresentation) when she wrote "it is a problem whether the Rigvedic Aryans really knew of the sea or the ocean"; in her article, which was about words denoting 'water', she did not examine any contexts for *samudra*, opted (blindly) for the meanings 'confluence, pond, spring, etc' (but not 'ocean/sea') and ignored Mayrhofer's lemma in EWA (or the KEWA Supplements) which does give 'sea' (but cited EWA for other cases). Surely, neither Geldner nor Mayrhofer are authorities to be ignored on this matter, even if one disagrees with them. Take a final example.

12) X 98.5 *sá úttarasmād ádharaṃ samudrám apó divyā́ asṛjad* 'from the upper to the lower Samudra he [the ṛṣi Devāpi] released the celestial waters'. Here clearly the celestial waters were released from the heavenly ocean not to a river, a confluence or a lake since there are many of them, but to the lower corresponding one ocean. We need say no more.

I think the evidence given above should be quite adequate. Mayrhofer in his EWA Dictionary (1996) admits now the meaning 'a large river formed by the confluence/combination (*Vereinigung*) of two or more rivers'; but he also gives (and for the *RV*) *Flut* 'flood' and *Meer* 'sea' (but no "terminal lake"), as he had done earlier in his KEWA (vol 3, 1980). I'll settle for "sea" happily. So the Indoaryans knew quite well the earthly ocean/sea. By extension they had ocean-going ships *nāváḥ samudríyaḥ*: I 25, 7. This deserves a note. In this hymn, *RV* I, 25, Varuṇa, the god of *ṛta* 'natural order' and of the moral code, knows the paths of birds and winds, the changes of the moon, the dwellers on high, all kinds of marvels, the past and future—in stanzas 7-11; he knows also samudra-going ships. Now is it likely that the seer of the hymn puts in this last detail referring only to canoes floating on nearby, well-known streams, lakes and confluences(?!) ? Is it not more likely that he has in mind ships travelling far and, like the other details, well out of the ordinary ken of the people? I think the latter and this means very distant sojourns. Evidently the seers of the hymns were more concerned with devotion and esoteric journeys than travel abroad, so they give no details about the latter.

The Sarasvatī topic is discussed in chapters One and Nine.

Six: **Anatolian bull and Vedic horse in the Indo-European diffusion**

1. Argument. In this paper I examine the presence of bull and horse in the various IE branches. It is notheworthy that the IE stem for 'horse' is absent in Hittite while all other major branches have it. The horse has no place at all in the religion, ritual or mythology; the horse's function is taken over by the bull. This alone suffices to show that the Hittites are not indigenous in Anatolia as some scholars claim and that therefore, Anatolia is not the original PIE homeland. Other types of evidence are used from mythology and linguistics to support this conclusion. The myth of the Weather god killing the dragon, which is a common IE theme (India, Greece, Scandinavia etc), is quite swamped by Near-eastern material. The Hittite language itself has some IE relics but is otherwise flooded with Mesopotamian, Hurrian and Assyrian elements.

Some scholars (mainly Lord Renfrew, 1991 and after) claim that Anatolia (what is today central and south-eastern Turkey) is the cradle from which the IEs (=Indo-Europeans) dispersed to their historical habitats. This view presupposes that the Hittites, and other peoples who spoke related languages (Luvian, Pallaic) are autochthonous. Renfrew claims precisely this on vague and dubious linguistic conjectures, an area in which, he admits, he is no expert (1999). Incidentally, Renfrew's theories, connecting the spread of language with spread of wheat and rice, are now meeting much greater resistance from other scholars. As one of them puts it: "New archaeobotanical evidence suggests the spread of wheat and rice cannot explain language change in India and Southeast Asia" (Shouse 2001:989). Historians, archaeologists and expert hittitologists disagree with Renfrew and regard the Hittites intrusive to Anatolia (Gurney 1990; Puhvel 1991 and 1994; Roux 1992; Dunstan 1998) while most main-stream scholars prefer the Pontic Steppes and some few others regard Saptasindhu as the original homeland of the IEs (Friedrich 2004; *Paper 1*; Feuerstein et al 1995; Sethna 1992; et al). However, apart from archaeological/historical considerations, there are other factors indicating that the Anatolians were intrusive. One such factor is the horse-sacrifice which is, in one form or another, present in most major IE traditions, from Vedic in the east to Celtic and Scandinavian in the west *but totally absent in Anatolia*. Significantly, the IE stem for 'horse' (S *aśva*, L *equus*, Celtic *ech* etc) is also absent, the Hittite word being *anśukurra* of Sumerian origin.

The horse was not unknown in Anatolia in the early 2nd millennium (all ancient dates are BCE) unlike Egypt. This animal was introduced into Mesopotamia from Iran late in the 3rd millennium but came into common use only in the 2nd millennium a little before it reached Egypt at c 1600 (Saggs 1989:213-4). According to P Raulwing, some scholars "presuppose the introduction of the domesticated horse (*Equus ferus f caballus*) into Anatolia... as early as the 4th/3rd millennia BC" (2000:33), in other words c 3000, the same time as Iran. But Raulwing points out that the existence of domesticated horses in Anatolia cannot be proved before the Hittite period (p 34), that is not before 1700, at the earliest, when the Hittites are known to begin to form their kingdom. Indeed, he lists several scholars stating it is the Hittites or Indoaryans, ie Mitannis c 1600, who bring domesticated horses to Anatolia and northern Syria (p 34).

Be that as it may, the Hittites show an exclusive preference for the bull in their religion. The horse is certainly known to them when they emerge in historical times and steadily forge an empire c 1600 that lasted almost 5 centuries. Nonetheless, the horse does not figure in any way in the Hittite cults (Gurney 1990:109-140; Bryce 2002:156, 192). No deity is associated with a horse and there is no horse-sacrifice or horse-mythologem of any kind. In Anatolia the sacred animal is the bull and it is associated with the principal deity, the Weathergod Tarhunnan/Taru/Teshub. In the Anatolian iconography the god is depicted driving "a primitive kind of chariot drawn by bulls... The bull is his sacred animal and may stand alone on an altar as his cult-symbol" (Gurney, p 111, also 123; Bryce 2002:156, 192). In another instance two bulls are standing by the legs of the Weathergod and his consort and wear "the conical hat of divinity" (Guerney p 117; plate 16, facing p 83, shows the king and the queen worshiping the bull). During the funeral rites for a king or a queen, writes Gurney, two oxen are sacrificed and eighteen sheep (pp 137-8).

But the bull-cult has additional aspects. ER Anderson mentions a practice similar to the Vedic *aśvamedha*, during which the chief queen *mahiṣī* is said to practise copulation, simulated or actual, with the dying/dead horse, whereas the Hittite practice is a bull-sacrifice (1999:386). C Watkins (whom Anderson cites) describes in detail the well-preserved iconography of this ritual where the king and the queen have sex during a bull-sacrifice (2001:266-7 with references).

Some form of bull-cult is not unknown among several of the other IE peoples but what preponderates markedly is the horse-cult and the horse-mythology. Among the Iranians, the bull "appears as one of the incarnations of Verethraghna", the Avestan equivalent of Indra (Macdonell 1995:150); there is also the myth of the first man Gayomart and the first bull Gosh, which may have been the source of the Mithraic sacrificial bull in Iran and subsequently other countries. In Greece, Zeus becomes a bull and carries off Europa, Dionysos is described as a "bull-god" (Kerényi 1982:109),

Talos the Sun is also called Taũpos *Taurus* 'the bull' (*GM* 92, 7), while Achilles sacrifices several oxen during the cremation of his friend Patroclos's corpse (*Iliad* 24, 165-7); the significance of the bull in Greece probably derives in large part from Minoan times when bull-rites were common. Writing of the "great bull" in Ulster (Ireland), A and B Rees cite G Dumézil to the effect that the animal "symbolizes the warrior function both in Rome and India" (1995:124). In India too, apart from the glorious bulls depicted on Harappan seals, we find that Manu had a miraculous bull who could kill demons and foes with his mere snorting; he was sacrificed and his power passed eventually into the sacrificial ritual itself (*Śatapatha Brāhmaṇa* I, 1, 4, 14). In the same text (II 5, 3, 18) the bull is said to be Indra's form; earlier, in the *RV* (=*Ṛgveda*) Indra is repeatedly called a bull *vṛṣabha* (I 54, 2; II 12, 12; etc) and less frequently other gods (Agni I 31, 5, etc; Rudra II 33, 4; etc etc). Nonetheless, in all IE branches it is the horse that has strong religious significance as we see with the two Aśvins in India, *Iqeja* in Mycenaean Greece, Epona in Gaul (all denoting 'horse-deity') and the myths and rituals involving horses and horse-sacrifices from Ireland and Scandinavia right through to ancient Saptasindhu in India—*everywhere except Anatolia*. The Balto-Slavs have retained no important horse-mythology (see the white horse of pre-Christian Svantovit and the later flying horse of Ilya-Muromyets) but, on the other hand, the bull is totally absent (except for Svantovit's bull-horn filled with wine annually and serving as an omen).

The horse-sacrifice in one form or another, as already stated, is a fairly common feature of all the major IE traditions. One frequent myth is that of a god taking on the form of a horse for various reasons. For example, in Vedic mythology Saraṇyū, the daughter of god Tvaṣṭṛ, marries Vivasvant, the Sungod, then disappears and takes the form of a mare; her husband becomes a stallion, mates with her and as a result the Aśvins are born (*RV* X, 17, 1-2; *Bṛhaddevatā* VI, 162ff).

We find a similar tale in Greece when goddess Demeter became a mare to avoid the harassment of Poseidon, god of the sea; he became a stallion and mated with her in the plains of Arcadia: as a result were born Areion, a noble horse with black mane, and a girl, and Demeter came to be worshipped in Arcadia as Demeter 'Epivũs *Erinus* (=*saraṇyū*?) The story is in Pausanias VIII 25, 5). A different myth appears among the Scandinavians when Loki, the god of tricks and transformations, becomes a mare to attract from work the giant-mason's stallion Svadilfari; as a result is born Sleipnir, a horse with eight legs, the swiftest animal in the world, which is given to Odin, king of the gods (*Edda* p 35-6; Crossley-Holland 1993:11-14). But the horse serves also as an offering in sacrifices in Greece, Rome etc. In the Vedic tradition this becomes a highly elaborate royal ritual known as *aśvamedha* (described at length in the White Yajur Veda, *Vājasaneyi Saṃhitā* XXII-XXV, the Black Yajur Veda, *Taittirīya Saṃhitā* IV 6, 6; V 4, 12, VII, 4, 12ff and in *Śatapatha Brāhmaṇa* XIII, etc). Here, at some stage of the rite, a splendid stallion is killed and the chief queen spends the night and is supposed to copulate with the animal, as was said earlier. Variants of this are found among the Celts (king with mare), Scandinavians and Romans (Anderson 1999; Puhvel 1989:269-276).

The Hittites have their own variation which, as was said above, involves a bull-ritual. This is most significant.

If we accept that the IE peoples branched out and away from Anatolia (Greeks, Romans and Celts to the west, Germans and Balto-Slavs to the north and north-west, Indo-Iranians to the east), then we must suppose that, while the Hittites preserved the pristine tradition of the bull-rite unadulterated, the others in some miraculous manner adopted the horse-sacrifice, all giving it primary importance over and above any bull-rites they retained, and this despite the fact that they travelled away in carts drawn by oxen, as the Hittite iconography indicates, at a time long before the horse came into common use. It is clearly absurd to suppose that all these peoples separated by thousands of miles adopted not only the horse-sacrifice in place of the bull-rites but also developed almost identical myths about their deities and horses. The absurdity becomes even greater when we take into account the fact that in all these distant locations (Saptasindhu, Greece, Gaul) the bull was present in abundance.

It is far more reasonable to suppose that the Hittites came to Anatolia from another and distant land. Their texts mention no migration, but when the texts appear first in writing c 1620, the Hittites must have been living in Anatolia for 600 years and more, mentioned in foreign documents as early as 2200 (Gurney, pp 141); so memories died out. They came (say c 2500) bringing both the horse- and the bull-rites. In the Near East as well as Crete and the eastern Mediterannean, as is well known, the bull (not the horse) had from early times acquired religious significance. It would be natural for the Hittites who came perhaps as a small band of warriors (an elite dominance group) to abandon and forget the horse-sacrifices and maintain in common with the local population only bull-rites. C Watkins gives details not only of one of these rites, amply documented in iconography, but also mentions that the extant Hittite Law Code condemns with punishment of death all forms of bestiality with cattle, sheep etc, but *not with horses and mules*; in the latter case the only punishment is that the offender could not become a priest (2001:266; also Puhvel 1989:276 and 1991:64). This suggests that the Anatolians preserved the memory of a practice that was considered lawful, or at any rate was not unknown, among the warrior class or the royalty; for, indeed, one form of horse-sacrifice included, as we saw, sexual contact between the queen and the stallion (in Ireland the king and a mare).

The evidence from these rites and laws indicates thus that the Hittites were not autochthons but intruders into the area.

This conclusion is reinforced by an additional consideration. The closest and commonest relationships among humans are those of parents and children—denoted by the words 'brother, daughter, father, mother, sister, son'. These words, exactly as they are in English and all Germanic languages, have cognates in almost all other IE branches. Thus Sanskrit has *bhrātṛ, duhitṛ, pitṛ, mātṛ, svāsṛ, sūnu*; similarly Greek has *phratēr*, *thugatēr*, *patēr*, *mātēr* and so on. To these we should add 'husband' and 'wife': S *pati*, Baltic *pats*, etc, and 'wife' S *patnī*, Gk *potnia*, Baltic *patī*, etc. All IE languages have two, three, four and some all of these words (including Tocharian). *Hittite has none*. We find many absences also in words denoting parts of the body which are quite constant with people despite any other changes. Hittite has some IE words like those for eye (=*akessar*, S *akṣi*, L *oculus*, etc), beard (=*zamangur*, S *śmaśru*, Baltic *smakra* etc), bone (*hastai*, S *asthi*, Gk *osteon*, etc), foot (=pata, S *pad-*, Gk *pous/pod-os* etc). But it has no IE stem for arm (S *bāhu*, Gk *pēchus*, Tocharian *poke* etc), ear (Gk *ous*, Latin *auris* or S *śrotra*, Celtic *clyst* Gmc *hlyst*); flesh (S *māṃsa*, Gmc *mimz*, Toch *misa* etc); nail (S *nakha*, Gk *onux* etc); nose (S *nas-*, L *naris*, Gmc *nasa* etc); and so on. The incidence of these stems (and many more) in most IE branches brings out the fact that they were quite common; yet they are absent from Hittite. As it is inconceivable that all other branches innovated with identical words in this respect, we must conclude that the words existed in the original Proto-Indo-European dialect(s) and Hittite lost them in course of time. This could only come about by reason of long travel far from the original homeland and of mingling with alien, non-IE, cultures. Also, the immigrant warriors brought no women and children with them, or very few, and so the PIE stems for those most intimate family relations were lost.

We observe similar (heavier) losses in the Hittite mythology (=religion). Apart from some minor elements (see Puhvel 1991:62ff), only the myth of the Stormgod slaying the dragon Illuyanka who had offended him has something of an IE character. But even this has a most un-IE frame. There are two versions of this myth (analysed in Watkins 2001: chs 30, 33 and especially 45, 46; the alleged parallel with the Irish saga of Fergus in ch 45 seems to me utterly irrelevant). In the first version the goddess Inara invites the gods and the dragon with his brood to a feast, where the dragons get overfed and can't enter their hole. Meanwhile she has, with a prepayment in sexual intercourse, secured the assistance of a human, Hupasiyas, who now proceeds to bind the dragon, whereupon the Stormgod comes and slays Illuyanka. (Inara then installed Hupasiyas in a house telling him not to look out of the window; but he did, saw his wife and children and weeping prayed to go home. Here the text breaks off. It is obvious that, even if the tale is wholly Near Eastern, Hupasiyas is unnecessary to the main action of the slaying of the dragon and belongs to a different legend which is fused with the god-dragon fight.) In the second version, the plot is even less IE. The dragon at first overcame the Stormgod and took his heart and eyes; the god married a poor man's daughter and had a son who married the dragon's daughter and went to live in her home; at his father's request, he then returned the heart and eyes, whereupon, with his former powers restored, the Stormgod went into the sea and killed both the dragon and his own son, at the latter's request: here again we seem to have the fusion of the motif 'god-slays-dragon' with another tale. Very different is the simple plot of the IE tales in which the god, or human hero, alone or with companions, kills the oppressive serpent/dragon: Vedic Indra, Iranian Thraetaona, Greek Zeus (*Theogony*) and Apollo (*Hymn*), Scandinavian Thor (himself being killed even as he slays the Midgard serpent) and Russian Perun.

One wonders if the two Hittite tales (and they *are* distinct) are at all IE. With the killing of the dragon, the IE myth provides, apart from anything else, release from oppression or threat of some kind. Even in the Mesopotamian tale

The Epic of Creation, the killing by Marduk of the dragonness Tiamat (goddess of an older generation) brings about release, while her dismemberment has cosmogonic results (Dalley 1991:254-5). This aspect of release is totally lacking in the two Hittite tales. Citing other scholars Watkins sees the dragon as a symbol of chaos and stagnation and his death as the return of Cosmic Truth and Order (p 299) and thus links the tales with the IE legends. This symbolism however is only what the scholiasts have imported into the tales. In the IE myth the symbolism holds because, in the Vedic legend, for example, the dragon Vṛtra is said to block the waters, while in the Greek legends the dragons actually threaten gods and mortals. In the extant Hittite texts the dragon blocks nothing and threatens nobody.

If in these two tales the very barest and basic element of the Stormgod killing the dragon is of IE origin, then it is fused with Near Eastern material. Watkins criticizes F Vian, S Littleton and J Puhvel for speculating about this fusion (449-50) and asserts that even the second version with the temporary discomfiture of the Stormgod is IE: he thinks we should be guided in our judgment by the diction of the texts "and hug the formulaic ground closely" (450). For this he adduces the verb *taraḫuta* 'overcame' in the Hittite second tale and the Avestan cognate verb *titaraṯ* (in a passage that is not strictly parallel, since here Good Thinking and Fire overcome the hostilities of Angra Manyu but don't slay him), and some more examples in chs 34, 35. This I find inadequate, to say the least. If I speak a language which has words that are phonetically and semantically cognate with words in another language, then I shall of necessity use these words in ways similar to those in the other language, whether the context is liturgical or not; the resemblance and connection or not of my speech with a passage in the other language will be determined not by one or two cognate words but by the subject-matter, theme, structure and other similarities. Walkins does not provide such similarities. Then,

Watkins forces a similarity that is not there in the Avestan passage: the Evil Spirit Angra Manyu is about to overwhelm the creation but in fact does not because it is overcome by Fire and Wisdom (Watkins, 355, 450). A far closer parallel is found in the Mesopotamian legend of Ninurta, god of war and agricultural fertility, who hunts Anzu, the lion-headed Eagle, on the mountains but suffers a setback when the monster, (with the power of the Tablet of Destinies he had stolen) makes the arrows of the god turn back against him (Dalley, 214).

Nonetheless, despite my disagreement with Watkins on these issues, I do think that even the Hittite second tale contains some IE material as well as Near Eastern on four counts, some of which escaped Watkins.

a) 'God slays dragon' *is* an IE theme.

b) The name *Inara* may well be cognate with *Indra* (Kazanas 2001).

c) In *RV* II 11, 5 (also V 30, 5) Indra fights and kills Vṛtra within the waters *apsu* (and so has exclusively the epithet *apsujit* 'victorious-in-waters') just as the Stormgod in the Hittite second tale slays the dragon in the sea.

d) In two *RV* hymns Vṛtra is overcome at first but fights on again and then is killed by Indra (I 32, 5-7; V32, 4-8); this motif could have been reversed in the Hittite second version producing a temporary defeat of the god. Then in *RV* I, 32, 12 there is a hint that Vṛtra struck back at Indra and in IV 18, 9 the god is struck to the ground by demon Vyaṃsa and has his jaw broken; so there *is* a parallel of the god being discomfited also. Now, in all these Vedic contexts the verb used in *han-* but the other similarities are sufficient to suggest possible kinship between the Hittite and the Vedic situations. The presence of two cognate verbs alone would not have been adequate.

Be that as it may, I have indulged in this digression only to stress the paucity of blue-blooded IE material in Hittite mythology (also Puhvel 1991:61) and to let Watkins describe the situation: "The Hittites were from the earliest times exposed to the influence of other languages each of which had literary tradition... [They] were profoundly influenced by Mesopotamian culture as mediated through the Peripheral Akkadian... and by the contact with the Assyrian merchant colonies of the 19th and 18th centuries... The major cultural influence, at least in religion and cult came from Hurrian ... [resulting in] the Hurrianization of the Hittite pantheon" (2001:52-3). T Bryce also traces influences from Mesopotamian and other cultures (2002: ch 12).

It is again inconceivable that the Hittites stayed in the homeland (while the others left), proved strong enough not to be conquered by their non-IE neighbours and proceeded themselves to conquer others and build an empire, yet mysteriously lost the words for the most basic of relationships, lost the religious significance of the horse and their I-E pantheon and absorbed heavy doses of vocabulary and prodigious amounts of cultural features from their neighbours. Such losses could not occur to the culture of an indigenous, conquering, dominant people. We cannot but assume that the Hittites came from a distant land and initially were not numerous or powerful enough to impose their own culture but found it easier to adopt cultural elements from the local indigenous peoples: this is the view also of the historians mentioned in the first paragraph above—Dunstan, Guernay, Puhvel and Roux. Thus we conclude that Anatolia was not the IE homeland. Puhvel thought the same and wrote: "As for the Anatolians, it is equally clear [ie as the Germanic peoples] that they were not autochthons of Asia Minor but had migrated to that habitat in a less than immemorial past" (1994:253). Watkins expresses a similar view (p 53). As for the Russian scholars, TV Gamkrelidze and VV Ivanov, who also argued for the IE urheimat in north-eastern Anatolia, EC Polomé wrote: "The shorter version of these linguists' views published some years ago in *the Journal of Indo-European Studies* ha[s] given rise to a number of critical comments, to say nothing of their *Urheimat* and migration theory. Most vulnerable are, indeed, their views on the road taken by the Indo-European tribes leaving their alleged Anatolian homeland to reach Europe and spread over their western territories" (1994:300). Polomé should have included the entry into Saptasindhu in the east which is even more problematic since there is no evidence for it of any kind.

In the title of this essay the epithet 'Vedic' and not 'IndoEuropean' is used deliberately, because another proposed cradle of the IEs is the Saptasindhu—as has been argued in several other studies (Friedrich 2004; Kazanas 2001a & 1999; Feuerstein, et al 1995; Sethna 1992; Frawley 1991, 2001; et al). There is ample evidence, textual and/or archaeological, for the migration of the Celts, Scandinavians, Romans and Greeks, Balts and Slavs and even Iranians. There is no archaeological or literary evidence at all for any Indoaryan immigration into Saptasindhu from at least 4500 to c 600, since there is a change in the skeletal record in that area c 6000-4500 only; no other mass entry can be detected until the Persian encroaches after 600 BC. Moreover, it is well-established that the Gypsies left India through Persia in the early centuries CE (Fraser 1995; Hock 1996) and spread to the Near East and western Europe. Groups of Indoaryans could have left at earlier periods, also. So Saptasindhu has just as serious a claim to be the IE homeland. And this mythological/cultic matter of the horse- and bull-rite reinforces this claim.

However, one must take into account JP Mallory's objections about the Out of India Theory (2002). This indo-europeanist sets up various models and demolishes them in an attempt to demonstrate the grave difficulties entailed in the Out of India migrations (ibid). He had done a similar exercise with other proposed homelands like Central Europe, Pontic Steppe in South Russia, etc, and showed that each one was beset with difficulties; in the end he chose the Pontic Steppe as "the least bad' solution (1997:115). But the entire framework, set up under the light of the wretched Aryan Invasion/Immigration Theory, is erected on tiers of conjectures and prejudices. Nobody really knows that the alleged migrations from the Steppe involve IE-speakers. Such are the prejudices of the received paradigm, that JV Day accepts the Steppe even though his own voluminous cranioskeletal research shows evidence, "*surprisingly* meagre in places" only as far as "Hungary and the northern Balkans and perhaps Greece" (2001:317, 326 my emphasis, to indicate the writer's expectations). Another alternative is that there was an Indo-European continuum spreading from Saptasindhu to the Pontic Steppe and that "there were movements of people, some quite indeterminate, within it and in and out of it" (Kazanas 2001a). The evidence in its present state allows no other firm conclusion.

This in no way affects my earlier conclusions that the Indoaryans are by 1500 indigenous in Saptasindhu and that the large bulk of the *RV* originates in the 4th millennium BC (Kazanas 2001a). Quite independently, in a recent study comparing Vedic and Mesopotamian religious developments Dr S Levitt concluded that most of the *RV* belongs to the 3rd millennium but the early hymns may well be of the late 4th millennium (2003).

Seven: **Vedic & Mesopotamian cross influences**

Introductory

1. Here I examine systematically affinities between the Vedic and Mesopotamian cultures and possible cross influences. There are many similar elements, themes and motifs in the religious texts of both. Some are found in other cultures the world over: eg the worship of Sun, Moon, Wind, Fire, etc; search for immortality; god/hero kills dragon/monster/serpent; tree of life; and so on. Such universal motifs will be ignored. But if the Sungod travels in a boat, as happens here, rather than on a horse-drawn carriage, as we find in Greece and elsewhere, then the motif deserves comment. Other common themes are the separation of heaven and earth by a god of wind (and light); the cosmic cow of plenty; the virile bull; the divine bird which is a messenger of, or symbolizes, a deity; the horse-sacrifice; creation through the dismemberment of a divine being; the Flood; the turtle/tortoise; etc.

2. Until now it has been generally assumed (eg Dalley 1998; Bottéro et al 2000; McEvilley 2002) that the Vedic Tradition is the borrower in all cases (brick-building, certain rituals, astronomy and mathematics, writing, mythological motifs, etc). The assumption has been based on the widespread belief that the Fertile Crescent in the Near East is the cradle of all civilization and, with regard to India, on the AIT (=Aryan Invasion/Immigration Theory), which should have been dismissed as soon as the ISC (=Indus-Sarasvatī

Civilization) came into the light of day in the 1920s. I shall show that, apart from the anteriority of the Vedic texts (the bulk of the *Ṛgveda* being dated at c 3200 BC and before), which may be doubted, the internal evidence in the documents and other types of evidence indicate that India is not the borrower; if anything, Mesopotamia (and Egypt) probably borrow from Saptasindhu, the land of the seven rivers in N-W India and Pakistan. I do not hide the fact that I am in a way prejudiced. I am now convinced, as I have argued elsewhere (Kazanas 1999, 2002, etc) that the Indoaryans are by 1500 BC fully indigenous having come to Saptasindhu at the very latest in the early 5th millennium and that much of the *RV* was composed before 3100[1].

Th. McEvilley claims to be undogmatic but, in fact, is no less prejudiced in favour of Egypt and Mesopotamia[2]. Many

---

[1]Throughout this study the dates are BCE except where stated as CE. The date after the name of an author in brackets denotes a modern date, of course. Eg (McInstosh 2002:24, 28)—where 2002 is the year of the publication and the other numbers denote pages in that publication. I take it for granted that the ancient Indoaryans are indigenous from at least the early 5th millennium BC and that the (bulk of the) *RV* was, as the native tradition has it, compiled just before 3102, which marked the onset of the Kali-yuga (Kazanas 2002 and 2003b) although there may have been (Witzel 1995) later redactions, insertions and other modifications of the original text. See other papers in this volume: esp One and Nine.

[2]He writes: "Indian religion and thought were in a state of meltdown... The Aryan establishment admitted tribal influences from Munda and Dravidian peoples along with renewed Near Eastern influences" (p 112). This is dogmatic and entirely hypothetical. "The transition from Jain missionaries to proto-Orphics [in Greece], such as, perhaps, Pherecydes, is still largely invisible (except for glimpses such as Democedes returning to Croton [in South Italy, from the Persian Court]), though it must have occurred" (p 204; but see *GPA* § 29). This too is dogmatic. A final example is on "the revisionist Indian view" which seeks to reconstruct ancient Indian history: "This whole pan-Indian or Indocentric construction may be viewed as a postcolonial reversal ... if those hands seem willful in their handling of the evidence, the reversal will only tend to reinforce the colonists' self-righteous sense that there was real need for them to take charge in the first place" (p 660). No further comment—except that McEvilley himself rather displays repeatedly willfulness in (mis-)representing and (mis-)handling of the evidence.

of his parallels and correlations are highly dubious and many of the things he presents as facts are downright wrong. He devotes many pages to prove that some Mesopotamian iconographic material was related to *kuṇḍalinī* yoga and therefore influenced the development of this tradition in India (and Greece). He gives many reproductions (pp 216-9, 246-273) some of which have similarities. On p 246, a seal impression shows a "Gilgamesh figure holding two lions" (and p 274: "the Nude Hero... like the Gilgamesh icon grasping lions in a conquered position")[3] but while he gives the well-known Mohenjodaro seal of the Nude figure holding off two tigers (p 249), this being similar to the Mesopotamian "Gilgamesh figure", he does not give the rock painting of the Nude hero from India c 4000 or before (Kak 2001b), which shows that the Mohenjodaro seal belongs to the Indic native tradition. On p 247, a Sumerian seal shows three pairs of caparisoned goat-like animals with enormous horns; the two pairs are leaping from above down to a tree on a mound while the central and larger pair flank the mound with the tree and step on the lower part with their front hooves. This is supposed to be similar to (and perhaps the inspiration for) a Mohenjo-Daro seal showing three human figures with different objects and on the left, under a big tree, two goats with upraised forelegs against what could be another goat-like figure or something else, but certainly not a tree. Other seals from the two cultures are decidedly dissimilar or irrelevant. On p 255 a photo shows three Mesopotamian human bearded figurines: all three have their hands crossed and resting on their chest; one of them wears a headpiece with two horns and has hooves but no tail. This "bull-man", again, is supposed to be similar (and perhaps the inspiration for) the figure of a "bull-man" in two different ISC plaques

---

[3]There are other figures also on this: a scorpion, a bearded man holding a staff, a boat with three human figures and fish beneath it—illustrating perhaps the Flood motif.

where the figure in each has two horns, also a long tail, possible hooves in one, feet in the other, and one arm hanging down and the other upraised: except for the horns, the figures are utterly dissimilar. In any case, all these comparisons do not really mean very much since they are unaccompanied by a text that would explain their true significance. We can assume that the Harappans borrowed these designs. People borrow designs, even ugly ones, all the time. But there is no bull-man myth (like the Greek minotaur) in Mesopotamia, nor Gilgamesh-like hero subduing two lions in the Vedic texts: thus these icons, dissimilar as they are in many cases, do not mean much. Unless we know the function of, and the import of the writing on, the ISC seals there is very little that can be usefully said (though much can be and is being conjectured to no useful purpose). McEvilley goes further and makes much out of the Ishtar-rosette and the ISC eight-petalled rosette linking them with the lotus-flower (pp 253-4); but, in this case too, unlike Egypt and Saptasindhu, Mesopotamia has no myth for a lotus-born one. Besides, since India had several eight-petalled flowers and the lotus, why should the natives copy such a design from Sumer and not make it themselves?... Thus all this iconography is almost valueless.

Just as valueless are two more comparisons—the motif of the seductive female and that of the underworld. A Panaino (following others) linked the Indic tale of Ṛśyaśṛṅga 'he who had the horn of a doe' and his seduction by a whore (*MB* III 110-113) and that of Enkidu who also was seduced by a whore in *Gilgamesh* (MM 52-61). The tales may be connected but apart from the seductive female, which is a worldwide motif, there is no other similarity. In the *RV* Yamī tries unsuccessfully to seduce her brother Yama (X, 10) and Lopāmudrā succeeds in seducing an old and unwilling husband (I, 79). Then, Enkidu lost his innocence and died tragically while Ṛśyaśṛṅga reached maturity and happiness through the intervention of higher wisdom in the form of his father Kaśyapa. As for the underworld/hell, some scholars linked the Homeric Hades and the Vedic 'dark pit' (Bodewitz 1999:107-8). But the Greek Hades is a concept more similar to Mesopotamian *kurnugi* where, in both cases, all mortals go. The *RV* has a pit/abyss of no return but only for sorcerers and sinners (VII, 104, 3 and 17), while any devout Aryan can, with spiritual knowledge and good conduct, go to heaven. The concepts and systems of thought are different.

All such cases are ignored.

3. One yardstick in the comparisons that follow is the IE (=IndoEuropean) nature of some of the motifs examined. If a motif in the Veda is also IE, ie it is found in the ancient culture of Greek, Roman, Slavonic, Baltic, Germanic or Celtic peoples, then we must take it that it is inherited in (or native to) India and not borrowed from the Near East. In the absence of the definite IE character of a motif, a second criterion will be the inner constitution of the motif: if this comprises native traditional elements and has no exclusively NE (=Near Eastern) elements, then it must be native to India and not borrowed. The IE criterion is fairly sound and secure. It is certain that there were no contacts between India and Greece, Gaul and Germania before the 6th century. McEvilley (following others) claims that there were channels of transmission from India to Greece through the Persian court in the 6th cent (see his ch 1). This is highly improbable because the philosophical or mythological ideas that are supposed to have travelled via this route (monism, reincarnation, the 5 elements, the Orpheus figure, etc) are not found in Persian or other NE texts. Therefore if a legend or a mythological motif is found in the Veda and in any of the IE traditions in the West (Greek, Celtic, Germanic, etc) then this item is PIE (=Proto-Indo-European) and belongs to the early 5th millennium at the very latest; and I take this period as the lower limit because it is the latest date by which the

Aryans might have entered Saptasindhu, if that. All such themes and motifs in the Veda are inherited, not created and developed under foreign influences. In all such cases, if we insist on postulating influences, the influence would run from Saptasindhu westward to the NE.

However, although a ritual like the horse-sacrifice is, I shall demonstrate, most probably a loan by Mesopotamia from Saptasindhu, I do not disregard the very real possibility that there was, c 6000 or much earlier, a culture with many common features among the peoples of the eastern European plains, the Balkans, the Pontic steppes, Anatolia, the Near East, Iran and Saptasindhu. I have elsewhere accepted the possibility that the IE homeland was a continuum spreading from Saptasindhu to the Pontic steppes. Even if we assume that in the beginning of the 6th millennium or earlier, the IE and NE cultures were substantially different in language, religion and social customs, it is not impossible that they shared some motifs and themes, inherited from an earlier culture we can no longer reconstruct fully but can detect in elements found here and there in different later cultures.

Comparisons

4. The horse-sacrifice is our first test-case. In Mesopotamia a horse-sacrifice is documented in a liturgical text repeatedly mentioning god Marduk and belonging to the Babylonian ritual related to gods Shamash and Adad (Albright & Dupont 1934). One interesting detail of this ritual is that the priest whispers an incantation "into the left ear of the horse" before its immolation. Another one is the presence of seven spots like the Pleiades, on the forefront of the sacrificial animal (ibid 119-120). The lowest terminus for this text is c800 and the upper c 2000 (ibid 117-8). Indeed, the horse came to Mesopotamia from Iran a little before 2000 but was put to common use c 1600 (Saggs 1989:213-4). Before this, the Mesopotamians used asses for their carts and the text mentions the ass as well[4].

The corresponding Vedic ritual *aśvamedha* is abundantly documented and much commented upon by ancient scholiasts and modern scholars. C Watkins wrote "We may legitimately look upon the Aśvamedha as the principal Indo-European kingship ritual" (2001:265). One of the minor features in the Vedic horse-sacrifice is the whispering by the priest to the horse's right ear. Here too, the horse must have the seven spots/stars on its foreneck (*Śatapatha Br* XIII, 4, 2, 1-4). Full if varied descriptions of this lengthy and complex rite are found in the *ŚB* Book XIII, in the *VS* Bks XXII-XXV, in the *TS* spread through Bks IV to VII, and in other texts[5]. Evidence for a simpler, perhaps, ritual is found in *RV* I 162 and 163, two hymns praising the horse, and in III 53, 11 in which king Sudās's horses are to be let loose to wander and thus win wealth for him. (Part of this ritual was to let a royal stallion wander freely for a year in neighbouring countries; the king and a band of 400 warriors followed it, claimed the regions through which the horse passed, and if challenged gave battle.)

Unlike the NE cultures, a rich horse mythology is attested in almost all the IE traditions (except the Hittites) and some form of horse-sacrifice was performed among the Greek, Roman, Celtic and Nordic peoples (Anderson 1999). One frequent myth, among others, is that of a god taking on the form of a horse for various reasons. For example, in Vedic mythology Saraṇyū, the daughter of god Tvaṣṭṛ, marries

---

[4]Albright and Dupont (116-7). They cite also Sir Flinders Petrie who found horses buried with humans in Giza, Egypt, from the 16th cent (pp 113-4). The horse came to Egypt in the 17th cent; the Egyptians had no horse mythology of any kind. Thus, obviously, such finds can hardly count as horse-sacrifices in the sense discussed here.

[5]Abbreviations. *AB* = *Aitareya Brāhmaṇa*; *AV* = *Atharvaveda*; *MB* = *Mahābhārata*; PIE Proto-Indo-European; *ŚB* = *Śatapatha Brāhmaṇa*; *TS* = *Taittirīya Saṃhitā* ; *V* = Vedic; *VS* = *Vājasaneyī Saṃhitā*.

Vivasvant, the Sungod, then disappears and takes the form of a mare; her husband becomes a stallion, mates with her and as a result the Aśvins are born (*RV* X, 17, 1-2; *Bṛhaddevatā* VI, 162ff). We find a similar tale in Greece when goddess Demeter became a mare to avoid the harassment of Poseidon, god of the sea, but he became a stallion and mated with her on the plains of Arcadia; as a result were born Areion, a noble horse with black mane, and a girl, and Demeter came to be worshipped in Arcadia as Demeter *'Ερινύς Erinus* (=*saraṇyū*! The story is in Pausanias VIII 25, 5). A slightly different myth appears among the Scandinavians when Loki, the god of tricks and transformations, becomes a mare to attract from work the giant-mason's stallion Svadilfari; as a result is born Sleipnir, a horse with eight legs, the swiftest animal in the world, which is given to Odin, king of the gods (*Edda* p 35-6; Crossley-Holland 1993:11-14). Surely, it would be absurd to claim that the horse-sacrifice spread from Mesopotamia to all these IE-speaking regions and that, then, each one of them developed almost identical horse-mythologems.

In India, the wild horse is present from c 17000 and there is evidence for its domestication in the Ganges basin c 5000 and in the ISC c 2400 (Chakrabarti 1999; Sharma 1980). Consequently there is no question of the Veda being indebted to Babylon. Nor can it be claimed that this rite descended from a remote common cultural background since the horse did not come to Mesopotamia much before 2000. All that can be said is that it was instituted in Babylon c 2000-1600 after the importation of the horse and Marduk's rise to preeminence c 1800-1600; the Babylonians decided to add this noble creature to the animals they had been using for sacrifice and so enhance the nobility of their own (new) chief god(s). Albright and Dupont mention several Indo-Mesopotamian affinities but, above all, the whispering to the horse's ear and the seven spots/stars on its front are details strongly suggestive of borrowing by the Mesopotamians.

Now let us turn to mythological test-cases.

5. The-eagle-flies-to-heaven is our second test-case.

In Mesopotamia we find a legend with main theme the removal from heaven of some valuable material. It is about a shepherd-king, Etana, who saves an eagle from death, then with the bird's aid ascends to heaven to take 'the plant of birth" so as to obtain a son. It is translated from its Old Babylonian (and later) version in Dalley's *MM* 189-202 and 203-227. There is no Sumerian version. Only some Akkadian seals show the ascent of a man on an eagle's back from c 2390-2249 (*MM* 189; McCall 1992:63); whether these depict Etana's adventure is not known. If so, the legend makes its first demonstrable appearance c 2400. Although the Anzu myth has some relevance since it has been thought that the Tablet of Destinies, stolen by the demonic figure of Anzu, may originally have been plants, as surmised by H Cornford (cited by Knipe 1967:344 & n 77), the tale is more of a panegyric for god Ninurta (who overcame Anzu) and belongs rather to the short-epic genre "god-vanquishes-monster" and will not be examined.

The Etana legend is complex in that it begins with the friendship of the eagle living on the branches of a tree and a serpent having its nest at the roots. Although the two have a compact to help each other sharing their catch, one day the eagle eats up the serpent's young ones. The grief-stricken serpent invokes Shamash, the Sungod, for retribution and he gives good advice on how the serpent might take revenge. Indeed, the serpent captures the eagle, cuts off its wings and casts it into a pit. The eagle now prays to Shamash for help; he relents and sends Etana (who wants "the plant of birth" so that his wife can have a child) to aid the moribund bird. Etana nurses the eagle back to health and then the bird carries him up to the gates of heaven in three stages. There are variants including a fall and a second ascent but the text breaks off. It is assumed that, since in the King list Etana is succeeded by a son, he and the eagle obtained the fertility plant.

Of some significance are the three stages of the ascent. Scholars find much symbolism in this legend: the Tree of Life, the serpent/earth/darkness and the eagle/sky/light and so on, all related to IE motifs and all noted by DM Knipe (1967 passim). However, as all this is imported by modern scholars I shall ignore it. To me it seems that the legend is made up of two discrete tales fused together[6]. I see no organic connection between the serpent and the Etana ascent: the eagle eats the serpent's young ones out of wickedness, so it is no angelic creature. But the third stage of the ascent has close affinity with the third heaven or the third summit where the soma-plant is in the corresponding Vedic myth.

6. In the Indian epic *Rāmāyaṇa* Bk III ch 35, the chief of birds, Garuḍa, destroys the *niṣādas*, taken by Knipe to be serpents (p 348) then flies up to heaven for *amṛta*, the elixir of life. If the *niṣādas* are serpents (something by no means certain) then Knipe is right in seeing here a parallel with the Etana legend even though Garuḍa carries no man to heaven. This brief episode is not strictly related to the main plot, so it may be an old legend that has been grafted onto the epic like so many others.

An older version appears in the Saṃhitās and Brāhmaṇas (*ŚB* III 2, 4 and 6, 2; *AB* III 25-6) with Kadrū and Suparṇī (a female eagle). *TS* VI 1, 6 says that Kadrū and Suparṇī had a dispute about each other's form, Kadrū won and obliged Suparṇī to go to heaven and fetch Soma saying "For this parents rear children: in the third heaven from here is the Soma; fetch it, and by it buy your release". The Jagatī metre first, then the Tṛṣṭubh (here presented as offspring of Suparṇī) fly up but fail to obtain the Soma; finally the Gāyatrī succeeds[7]. *AB* III 26 contains additional information. Here, as

[6]McCall is of the same opinion and cites the short Sumerian story of Gilgamesh and the Halub tree on which live an eagle and a snake (p 63).

[7]For abbreviations see note 4. Having surveyed all the secondary literature about this tale and its variants in the IE traditions, Knipe saw here "a quite transparent form of the seasonal light-darkness-conflict with Kadrū, the ...

in the *ŚB* passages, the gods desire the Soma and send successively the three metres to fetch it, but unlike the *ŚB* text, there is no mention of Kadrū and Suparṇī, who begets the metres. In any case, the Gāyatrī metre succeeds and having terrified the guardians takes the Soma; but on her return flight, Kṛśānu, one of the guardians, hits her with an arrow and cuts off the nail of her left foot. This incident links up clearly with the yet older but fragmentary version in the *RV*.

RV IX 86, 27 says that Soma is 'on the third ridge in the bright realm of the sky". It is there presumably that the falcon/eagle flies to fetch the Soma in *RV* hymns IV 26 and 27. I shall not indulge here in needless speculation about who speaks what lines in these hymns (see Knipe 329-337 for various opinions) because this would not help significantly our discussion. Some scholars translate hymn 27 as though stanzas 3 and 4 say that the bird bore aloft Indra as well (Knipe 331; O' Flaherty 1981:12-130). Here neither R.Griffith (1889) nor K.Geldner (1951-7) translate in this manner, and rightly so, since the text does not warrant it. The bird śyena 'falcon/eagle' or suparṇa 'of fine feathers' or 'of strong-wings" returns with the soma but Kṛśānu shoots an arrow and the bird loses a feather. And this is all we have in the *RV*. The subsequent tales (Kadrū and Suparṇī, etc) may not be the original legend but elaborations; but they may be original and the *RV* version omitted these details.

7. The affinities with the Etana legend are obvious. But the Vedic legend has parallels in the other IE branches. Knipe gives many references for Avestan, Greek, Scandinavian and

---

... earth, the serpent of darkness ... and ... the falcon of light, the heaven, Suparṇī" (345). He may be right, but the text says only *iyam* 'this one' for Kadrū and *asau* 'that one' for Suparṇī. In *ŚB* III 6, 2, 2 Kadrū is again said to be *iyam* but Suparṇī is identified with *Vāc* 'Speech'. It is moreover difficult to see how Suparṇī would fetch the soma from heaven if she herself is heaven. However, there is mention of Arbuda Kādraveya, a serpent-seer and mantra-maker (*AB* VI 1; *KB* XXIX 1; *ŚB* XIII 4, 3, 9) so Kadrū may have been connected with serpents.

Celtic myths. In Iran the *saēna* bird (=V *śyena*) descends from heaven bringing the *haoma* (=V soma). In Greece Zeus is connected with the eagle, who bears nectar, and he himself, in the guise of an eagle, abducts young Ganymedes and takes him to Olympus to become the gods' cupbearer. In Scandinavia Odin, again in the guise of an eagle, steals giant Suttung's mead (= V *madhu* 'sweet, intoxicating drink'), here not from heaven but from within a rocky mountain; be it noted that in Scandinavia the Guardian Tree (*the axis mundi* or Tree of Life) is a wholly separate motif having a dragon gnawing at its root and an eagle at its top (Crossley-Holland 1993:xxiii-xxiv). In Ireland, Lleu is killed by a javelin, ascends in the sky as an eagle and is eventually restored to life; he is the "bright hero", probably derived from the older Britannic god of light, Lugh (Green 1996:34-5)[8].

Now, apart from the antiquity of the Vedic literature, we have the presence of the same motif in all these IE traditions in all these different areas from Asia to northwestern Europe. We must assume therefore that this legend belongs to the PIE period. The oldest version in the *RV* is a simple one: it does not involve (or even hint at) any tree nor enmity between the śyena and a serpent; unlike the Mesopotamian eagle, the śyena is not a wicked but a most noble creature; a tree with two birds on its branches appears quite separately (as in the Scandinavian tradition) in *RV* I, 164, 20-22. Consequently the Vedic tradition did not borrow this myth from Mesopotamia. It may be that the Mesopotamians borrowed the myth from India and combined it with their own legend(s).

8. The 7 Sages is a third case[9].

Stephanie Dalley, the well-known assyriologist, states (1998) that the Mesopotamian tradition of the 7 Sages which

[8]Knipe cites also the theft of the sacred apples in Scandinavian and Irish legends; in both is involved the flight of an eagle/hawk (338-9). In Greece Hercules steals the apples of the Hesperides, but here no bird is involved. These legends also may be variants of the same theme.

[9]A full examination of this subject of 7 Sages in Indic texts will be found in Mitchener (1982). Here I shall be selective.

is linked to the Flood has "no foreign elements" and "there is no reason to doubt that it is indigenous" (p 16). She examines similar traditions in Egypt (where the 7 sages appear in the very late period and could have come from anywhere) and other NE cultures and concludes that this "essential concept", that is "civilization brought by sages, was diffused from Mesopotamia" (ibid). She says nothing about the tradition in India so we don't know if she considers this also to be similarly diffused. She mentions the trade and contacts generally between the ISC (or Indus Valley, as she calls it) and Mesopotamia, then makes this statement: "These were the means, whether by land or sea, by which Mesopotamian culture, notably the idea of writing, sealing and monumental brick architecture, became known to the populous regions of western Pakistan, and seem to have influenced the rise of urban civilization in the Indus Valley, where writing appears in archaeological remains around 2000 BC" (1998:14). Here we find two errors. First, the ISC was, even in 1996 when Dalley was probably writing her study, known to be not confined to "western Pakistan" but to cover much of Punjab and Gujarat in India. Second, even in 1996 it was known that writing in the ISC had began by the mature phase c 2600! A third error comes a little later when she states that the study of grammar and syntax in Mesopotamia had started some 1500 years before Pāṇini himself who "was once thought to be the earliest grammarian in the world" (p 18). Now many people may have thought this but only through ignorance of the fact that Pāṇini himself mentions at least 10 grammarians (Gārgya, Śākalya et al) who preceded him. Thus he could not be the "earliest grammarian". Besides, Pāṇini may have belonged to an era much earlier than the one given by the AIT chronologies.

Apart from such factual slips, it is obvious that Dalley, whose work in her field I respect and consult constantly, accepts fully the AIT and the chronologies linked with it in the hitherto mainstream view of academic Indology. As indicated in n 1 above, this view should no longer be tenable. With regard to Mesopotamian—Vedic relations we should take into account at least two simple but very instructive facts. First, when in the 24th century king Sargon of Agade refers to the ships in his harbour (Saggs 1995:40, 68) the ships are those from other countries, that is Dilmun, Magan and Meluhha (ie, the ISC: Dalley 1998:14). *If Sargon had a mighty ocean-going fleet to trade with other countries he would have been boasting of Mesopotamian ships reaching, or returning from, foreign harbours*. Second, in the Mesopotamian text Enmerkar and the Lord of Aratta (Kramer 1952) it is king Enmerkar of Uruk who sends a messenger and merchants (by land) to distant Aratta (a country north-west of Punjab: see § 33, below) to obtain goods (not the other way round). So I would think that strength and influence lay as much at least (if not more) with the ISC as with Mesopotamia.

9. The 7 Seers (ṛṣis, priests, fathers), are amply attested in the *RV* (I, 164, 34; III, 31, 5; IV, 2, 15 and 42, 8; VI, 22, 2; X, 63, 7; etc). No hymn says who they are or why they are singled out from among the many other ṛṣis. In IV, 42, 8 they are *asmā́kam pitáras* 'our fathers'; in X, 81, 4 and 82, 2-4 the *saptaṛṣi-* assist Viśvakarman 'the All-creator' to fashion the worlds through sacrifice. In X, 109, 4 they again act in concert with the gods and practise *tapas* and in X, 130, 5-7 they rise to the divine condition *daivya* through knowledge of measure and ritual.

Their names we find in *ŚB* XIV 5, 2, 6 and in *Bṛhadāraṇyaka* Up II 2, 6: Gotama, Bharadvāja, Viśvāmitra, Jamadagni, Vasiṣṭha, Kaśyapa and Atri. In the same *ŚB* (II 1, 2, 4) they are said to be the 7 stars in the nakśatra of the Great Bear—and with them will (later) be their, or Vasiṣṭha's, wife Arundhatī. Since the later Vedic texts find it necessary to name them (unlike the *RV*), we must suppose that the legend of the 7 ṛṣis was no longer widely known and this implies a lapse of a very long period. So the legend must be very very old. (Lists with different names are given in Mitchener 1982.)

Apart from the concerted group-action of the Seven, each ṛṣi performs miraculous deeds on his own, too. Thus Viśvāmitra stops the flow of two rivers in RV III 33 and 53. Vasiṣṭha calls upon Indra to aid king Sudās defeat his numerous foes (VII 18) and travels with Varuṇa in the god's boat (VII 88). Atri with his "fourth sacred-utterance *bráhman*" discovered the sun and abolished demon Svarbhānu's black arts (V 40). Kaśyapa engenders all creatures in *ŚB* (VII 5, 1, 1). Agastya, again, who is also one of the Seven (or eight) in other accounts, makes the Vindhya mountains lower themselves (Mitchener 1982:127) and inspires the Vedic culture in South India (Frawley 1991:134, 285; Mitchener, 183-4) being one of the Sages, of the first Assembly for promoting knowledge (Hancock 2002:248-9).

The 7 Sages are found also in some other IE traditions. The Greeks had their 7 *sophoi* or *sophistai* 'wise men' (Herodotos I, 29; Isocrates 15, 235). These became actual historical figures like Thales, the philosopher of Miletus, Chilon of Sparta, Solon of Athens and so on[10]. The Slavic tradition has 7 judges attending the Sungod as he traverses the sky and as judges they watch and assess men's deeds (Simonov 1997:14)[11].

The Greeks had also the tradition of the 7 Argive Kings who perhaps in pre-Iliad times attacked Thebes and that of the 7 Sleeping men of Ephesos (Cox 1882:98, 225). This persistence on 7 wise men or warriors indicates that the tradition is rooted back in the PIE culture. The legend's presence in the PIE period confirms thus its great antiquity, in the Vedic Tradition.

---

[10]Plato's *Protagoras* 343A has a list, but other writers give different lists including Pythagoras or Cretan Epimenides and excluding others. The total comes to 17 of them, as Diogenes Laertius records, (I, 40-2.)

[11]I ignore the Roman tradition with its *septem-viri epulones* (Dio Cassius 48, 32; et al): they were a college of 7 priests conducting sacrificial banquets. But at an early period these were 3 in number and at later periods they were as many as 10. So this sounds like an independent development.

10. In the Mesopotamian mythology the Seven Seers appear as the 7 Craftsmen *ummiānu* or Counsellors *muntalkū* or the divine sages *apkallu*. According to the myth *in Erra and Ishum* (*MM* 286) they were born of King Skygod Anu and Earth. The god of freshwaters and wisdom, Ea (Sumerian Enki), sent them among the people (in the form of *purādu* 'fish, carp?') to teach them the arts and crafts. Each one was sent separately during the reign of an antediluvian king. However, they angered Ea and he dispatched them back to the underworld of freshwaters Apsu for ever. We must note here that some texts mention the 7 *Sebitti* and "their sister Narundi", like the 7 ṛṣis and Arundhatī (De Santillana 1977:301, n 37). Note that just as Vedic lore has 7 demons (*RV* VIII 96, 16), so the Mesopotamian texts have the 7 demonic forces, sometimes described as gods (eg *Erra* and *Ishum*); these latter are connected with the 7 Pleiades (*MM* 327 "Sebitti", offspring of Anu and Earth).

The first one to embark on his civilising mission was Adapa, known also as Uan. This last name appears later as "Oannes" in the *Babylonian History* written in Greek by the Chaldean scholar Berossos c 300 BC (Bottéro 1992:246ff). According to Berossos, Oannes was "an extraordinary monster": its whole body was "that of a fish and under the head was a second one and also feet similar to those of a man"; he taught them writing, science, law, geometry and the building of temples and cities. (For more details see Verbrugghe & Wickersham 1999.) Quite a different tale is told about 1000 years earlier c 1400 in the poem *Adapa* (*MM* 182-8). Adapa/Uan was a priest of Ea in Eridu, traditionally the earliest Mesopotamian city and the first one to receive kingship from the gods. He was created "extra-wise" *atrahasis* (also the name of the survivor of the flood) by Ea "as a protecting spirit (?) among mankind" but not immortal (*MM* 185). He was a fisherman as well and one day, when out at sea, he broke the wing of the South Wind and had to go to heaven to Anu, King of the gods. Ea advised him not to eat or drink anything there because it would mean death. Adapa indeed refused the bread and water that Anu offered but as they were the bread and water of eternal life, Adapa lost the opportunity to become immortal and was sent back to earth (and later presumably back to the underground freshwaters Apsu). The fish-like men are quite evident in Assyrian iconography (Black & Green, 35; Hancock, 1995:86).

Unlike the Vedic seers who rose to divinity and immortality and functioned in harmony with gods, Adapa seems to be at odds with the gods; even the god he serves, Ea, apparently tricks him and makes him lose immortality. The extant text has nothing to show how Adapa was a "protecting spirit" or how he civilized mankind. Perhaps there were other stories, now lost to us, and one of them reached Berossos. Here, in Berossos's narrative, it is interesting that Oannes (=Uan-Adapa) comes out of the sea in a combined fish-man form and brings writing and the other arts of civilisation. This for me has two significant aspects: (a) The Mesopotamians obviously believed, in one of their traditions at least, that writing, geometry and so on came from abroad by a sea-route: this is one significance of the fish-monster Oannes rising out of the sea. (b) The fish-side of Oannes is probably connected with the fish that pulled and saved Manu's boat/ark in the flood (see next § 11)

It is possible that the 7 Sages formed a native Mesopotamian theme. But the plain fact is that apart from Adapa/Uan, we don't hear much about any of the others anywhere in the texts—unless Atrahasis himself, appearing also as Utnapishtim, is one of them as well. Either there was legendry that was lost or the Mesopotamians borrowed the theme from elsewhere but did not develop it further. In any event, the rich lore of the Vedic 7 Seers owes nothing to Mesopotamia.

11. The legend of the Flood is closely linked with the 7 Sages and forms a fourth test-case.

The Vedic legend of the deluge is first related in *ŚB* I 8, 1, 1-10 (or *Kāṇva*-text II 7, 3, 1-8). A small fish sought Manu's protection, then warned him of the impending flood *augha* and later actually pulled his boat to safety; afterwards Manu made a sacrificial oblation from which arose Iḷā and through her he engendered the new generation of men. The spot on the mountain where Manu got off is called "Manu's descent" *manor-avasarpaṇam*. The legend itself is not found in the *RV* but some related elements can be traced there. One *Atharvaveda* hymn mentions "the spot where the boat glided down, on the peak of the Himalayas" (*AV* XX 39, 8). In the *RV* several hymns call Manu "our father" (I 80, 16; II 33, 13; etc) and regard him as the prototype of sacrificers: eg "like Manu we shall establish the sacrificial fire" I 44, 11; "as with priestly Manu's oblations" I 76, 5; also V 21, 1; etc. In X 63, 7 Manu with 7 priests is said to offer the very first oblation. All these elements, except Iḷā, are drawn together (even the horn of the fish) in the *MB* Bk III 185, 1-54: this is still a simple, brief narrative with the additional information that the fish-saviour was god Brahmā, that it pulled the boat through the flood for many years, that Manu was saved together with the Seven Seers and that he carried on the boat "the seeds of all creatures" so that he could create the worlds anew. (The legend is found of course in the Purāṇas also, the fish being Viṣṇu's first *avatāra* 'incarnation in this world'.)

All this suggests a simple and very old legend which at some stage divided into two and appeared with small variations: one version with Iḷā in the ŚB, the other with the 7 Seers and the seeds in the *MB*. There may well have been floods of varied magnitude in India and other places with the melting of the ice after c 16000 which produced heavy rainfall, swollen rivers and rise of the sea-level. But it is most improbable that these floods, however severe, caused the total annihilation of mankind and other creatures as is said in the legend. Consequently we must take it that the legend comes from a much earlier era or at least refers to a much earlier cataclysm that indeed destroyed mankind completely and a new start had to be made. While not denying the fact that real floods may have occurred in the past, some writers stress a different aspect, namely that the legend is symbolic of the collapse of ancient cultures or civilizations and of their regeneration (eg Ouspensky 1953: 56-7). Several others discuss different facets of Flood myths in A Dundes (ed) 1988[12].

---

[12]G Hancock discusses (2002) in detail the probability of floods inundating and submerging large coastal areas in the Mediterranean, the Persian Gulf, the Gulf of Cambay (southwest Gujarat, northwest of Mumbay) and the eastern part of Tamil Nadu, Japan and elsewhere, at c 13000, c 9000 and c 6000. Inundations occurred earlier too, after the end of the Last Glacial Maximum c 15000, but these were mild, as were also those that arose with the Flandrian transgression c 3500. During the devastating deluges of c 13000, 9000 and 6000, cities and regions with an older civilization of megalithic structures, knowledge of agriculture, astronomy and even oceanic navigation, sunk under the abruptly rising sea-level. But wise men managed to save (some of) the arts and sciences and started afresh at other safe locations with their preserved store of knowledge. Hancock thinks the culture that started at Mehrgarh c 7000 with a ready knowledge of agriculture, animal-domestication and building (but not ceramics) is such a case—from an earlier Vedic civilization now sunk in the gulf of Cambay (2002:169-197). D Frawley sketched a similar idea in his own study 2001:30-1. Hancock provides an enormous amount of scientific detail in support of his thesis utilizing the studies of many experts in oceanography, palaeoclimatology, geology etc: eg Emiliani (2000), Oppenheimer (1998), Straus (et al 1996), Vitaliano (1977), Wilson (et al 2000) and many others, and the good services of Dr Glenn Milne and his team at Durham University's Dept of Geology where with a computer-programme they can calculate sea-level changes at different periods (2002:22, 150, 263 etc). Indeed, in recent years ruins and artefacts have been found on the seafloor in the Gulf of Cambay.

I agree with the general idea both in Frawley and Hancock: it is likely that many Flood legends in different parts of the world arose from the inundations mentioned above and chiefly, of course, the last one c 6000. But I suspect that the meagre material on Manu, the 7 ṛṣis and the Flood in Vedic texts is very much older than these two (and other) authors think. The *ŚB* and *MB* texts agree in that all creatures are destroyed except Manu (and the 7 Seers in *MB*). Such a universal destruction occurs not at the end of one yuga but of a mahāyuga (or a manvantara or a kalpa). Now tradition says that the Kaliyuga begins at 3102. If we take the number of years given in *Manusmrti* I, 68ff (not the Puranic hundreds of thousands) we have for Kṛtayuga 4800, for Tretā 3600 and Dvāpara 2400, ie a total of 10800. This plus 3100 make 13900 for the end of the previous cycle and the beginning of the new. This corresponds approximately to the first date computed by Hancock, ie c 13000. But the other two floods were just as big and ...

12. When we turn to the Near East we find two very similar yet very different legends. One is the story of Noah in the Judaic *Old Testament* (*Genesis* 6-8). The other is that of Atrahasīs in the Old Babylonian version of c 1700 (*MM* 3ff) and that of Utnapishtim (or Uta-naish-tim = Atrahasis) in the epic *Gilgamesh* of about the same period (*MM* 109-114: Tablet XI, i-iv): the two Mesopotamian stories are but for some minor variants quite similar. The Vedic and the NE legends differ in several respects. One important difference is that in the Vedic tale the deluge comes in the natural order of things as one big cycle of world-history ends and another begins, while in the NE ones the cataclysm is a means deliberately chosen by God(s) to punish bothersome/ iniquitous mankind.

13. Of the two Mesopotamian accounts the one in *Gilgamesh* is much the shorter. The flood-story is related by Utnapishtim himself to Gilgamesh ostensibly to explain how he had been made immortal by the gods after his survival and how difficult it would be now to gain immortality. The gods decide to send the deluge to destroy criminals and sinners (this is revealed at the end of the tale in Ea's words in Tablet iv) but Ea manages to pass a message to his servant Utnapishtim advising him to build a large ark and deceive his fellow citizens through double-talk about impending gifts/calamities; in this ark, which should have harmonious proportions, he should put "the seed of all living things". The construction of the boat and its dimensions are given at

... destructive at 9000 and 6000. All this does not seem very sensible. I suspect that the years in Manu are *divya* 'divine' and therefore correspond with the Puranic yugas (Kali 432000, etc), and that we are at present very much in the dawn of this Kaliyuga. Seeing the atrocities committed by the Nazis and other vicious regimes in the 20th century and the prevalent corruption which increases year by year, we can't possibly think that the Kaliyuga ended c 1900 (3100-1200) and that we are now in a new Kṛtayuga that will end c 2900 CE (4800-1900)! Obviously this issue needs more detailed examination. Whatever be the case, my discussion of the Vedic Mesopotamian relations c 3000 and after is not really affected.

length, then Utnapisthim loads silver and gold, all the seed of living things, his kith and kin, cattle and wild beasts and "all kinds of craftsmen".

Here we must pause and note that the narrator is actually expanding and elaborating. The initial "seed of all things" (in i) now becomes in addition (in ii) silver and gold, kindred, domestic and wild animals and all kinds of craftsmen. Similarly the initial proportionate and harmonious dimensions become (in ii) actual measurements, 110 poles all round, 6 decks, various quantities of pitch, etc. *The narration seems to be trying to become a "realistic", entertaining and convincing story (and perhaps history)*—not aware that it would be impossible in those days to construct a ship (with 6 decks!) that could contain *all* those people and *all* those domesticated and wild animals. *If they had the seeds of all things, animals would have been unnecessary.*

Then came the deluge: as we read of darkness descending, winds howling, storms and torrents we must assume there was heavy rain as well as swollen rivers and seas, the cataclysm lasting 7 days and nights. The ark arrived at a mountain top and three birds were released in succession to ascertain whether the waters receded. Then Utnapishtim came out and made a sacrifice with "(essence of?) reeds, pine and myrtle" (*MM* 114). The gods smelt the fragrance and gathered there; they conferred immortality on him and his wife and sent them to dwell far off at the mouth of the rivers. Here ends the actual tale of the flood and we must suppose that the kith and kin and the various craftsmen continued to live as before with the transported silver and gold and animals.

Most of these details are found in *Atrahasīs* too which is a much longer narrative with many more elements and events. It begins at a time before man's appearance when the gods did all the work and the lesser ones rebelled against the higher ones and mainly against Enlil. So the gods decided to create mankind to "bear the load of the gods" (*MM* 14-5).

Men increased in number and clamour and the troubled gods sent disease and drought to contain them. This was repeated in 3 or 4 cycles of several centuries and every time Atrahasis, unaffected by all these centuries and diseases and death, interceded to his god Enki on behalf of humanity. Eventually (Tablet III in the Old Babylonian Version: *MM* 29-35), we have the tale of the deluge which does not seem to differ substantially from the one in *Gilgamesh*. There may have been differences but as many lines are damaged and unreadable while large gaps of 30 or 50 lines appear here and there, it is difficult to know precisely. Berossos writes that Xisuthros (=Atrahasis), his wife, daughter and pilot disappeared (went to heaven) but the other passengers heard a voice from the sky telling them to go to Babylon, then rescue the writings with the arts and sciences hidden in Sippar (=the Eternal City) and disseminate them to the world.

Internal correlations and chronology

14. The Judaic legend has many similarities with that of Mesopotamia, the most striking one being the fact that they are stories of a unique event, never to recur. The Judaic story differs from the Mesopotamian mainly in being narrated in a monotheistic tradition (*Gen* 6-8). God sees that man is very wicked and the earth filled with violence and corruption, so He wishes to destroy it through a deluge. But Noah is just and "walk[s] with God", so he is advised to make an ark 300×50×30 cubits and 3 decks. Before the heavy rains come, Noah places into the ark his own wife, his three sons and their wives and one pair of every living creature—animals, birds and serpents, clean and not clean. Here it is interesting to note that there is mention of the "seed" as well in the phrase "to keep seed alive upon the face of all the earth" (ch 7, 3). Another difference is the emphasis given on the duration of the rains (40 days and nights) while the flood receded after 150 days. Noah too sacrifices (clean beast and fowl in contrast with the herbs of Atrahasis) and God smells the sweet fragrance and decides not to destroy the earth and the living creatures on it again. It is most interesting that in the next chapter God prohibits the eating of all flesh telling Noah he may eat only "green herbs" (Gen 9, 3-5).[13]

The Judaic story in *Genesis* may well derive from one or other version of the Mesopotamian legend. The Judaic tradition tells us in definite terms that Abraham and his tribe/ clan left Ur of the Chaldees and came into the land of Canaan (*Genesis* 11, 31 and 12, 5-6). So the Hebrews could have brought with them (some of) the lore from Ur which was in South Mesopotamia, including the legend of the deluge, current perhaps before 1700 or even 2000. Egyptian sources refer to the Israelites c 1200 dwelling in Palestine (Dunstan 1998:193). Chapters 3 to 6 of *Genesis* and 9 and following, have no repetitions, at least no more than the succession of generations requires in chapters 5, 10 and 11. But chapters 7 and 8 contain several repetitions, even from ch 6, as regards the pairs of animals and the flood of waters: this repetition is characteristic of the Mesopotamian texts. Dalley thinks it possible, moreover, that an abbreviation of (Utnapishtim=) (*Uta-*)*naish*(*tim*) might have been pronounced 'Noah' in Palestine (*MM* 2). Thus we can assume that the Judaic legend is a derivative. But it could also derive

---

[13]EA Wallis Budge thinks that the Judaic legend of the Flood is derived from an Egyptian original (1988:40) and indeed gives a summary of the Theban recension of the *Book of the Dead* which contains the legend. Thoth, or Djehuti, here being "the tongue of the Great God", says: "I am going to blot out everything which I have made. This earth shall enter into (ie be absorbed in) the watery abyss of NU (or NUNU) by means of a raging flood, and will become even as it was in primeval times I myself shall remain with OSIRIS, but I shall transform myself into a small serpent which can neither be apprehended nor seen" (ibid, 198). A "flood" is mentioned briefly in Spell 176 of the *Book of the Dead*.

It is possible that the Jews borrowed their legend from the Egyptians as Budge says, but the similarities are scanty. The Judaic account is much closer to the Mesopotamian legend. But when Budge was writing, c 1930 CE, the Mesopotamian literature was not fully known.

directly from a Vedic version. It has not the fish and the 7 Seers and does have the elaborate ark, the wives and kinsmen and the animals, which are all Mesopotamian elements; it also has the waters above the firmament and those under it (*Gen* 1, 6-10), like the Mesopotamian two kinds of waters. But it has monotheism too which is definitely not Mesopotamian, or NE at all. The Jews in Ur may have had direct contact with visiting Indoaryans: their monotheism may derive (with adjustments) from the One supreme Power, which is the creative Cause of All, recognised in the Veda and expressed superbly in the Creation Hymn, *RV* X 129. It may be, as some scholars believe (eg Frawley 1991:268), that NE and Hebrew *El* and *Elohim* (plural) 'God(s)' derive from or are cognates with Vedic *iḍ/iḷ* and *Ilā* 'sacred food/speech' and 'offering' or 'creation' (see § 34). The Veda also knows of two kinds of waters, the celestial and the terrestrial. So the evidence is mixed and ambivalent. Then, creation proceeding from the divine Word is common both to the Veda and *Genesis* but unknown in Mesopotamian texts. Perhaps the Judaic tradition is an amalgam of elements from both cultures.

What of the Mesopotamian one? Scholars have now shown that Ziusidra (=Sumerian for Atrahasis) was a ruler of Shuruppak, as was his father Ubara-Tutu or Shuruppak (=the ancestor of the citizens in that city-kindgom), in the early 3rd millennium. Gilgamesh himself and his father, Kings of Uruk, are assigned to the period 2800-2500. This does not mean that a cataclysm actually took place c 2900-2800 or that its legend was first established at that period. Both the event and the legend may in fact be of a much earlier era. On the other hand, *the legend as we have it in Atrahasīs and Gilgamesh may be not much earlier than the texts, ie c 1700.*

15. What of the Indic legend? The Flood itself is not mentioned in the *RV* and it is not absolutely clear that the reference to the boat on the Himavant-peak in *AV* XX 39, 8 is to Manu's boat. Our earliest explicit reference is that of the

ŚB. In our new chronologies (paper One, Kazanas 1999; Frawley 2001:308) the composition of the *RV* must be placed at 3500 and before, though its present arrangement is traditionally said to be c 3100. The early Brāhmaṇas, ie *Śatapatha* and *Aitareya* should be placed c 3200-2900. So the legend of the Flood in *ŚB* is attested c 3000. The start or the core of the *MB* belongs to at least 3067 according to many astronomical references contained therein (paper One). Are we entitled to assume that the Flood-tale in *MB* III 185 is as early as that? Most probably not as it stands but quite possibly yes in a less ornate version.

Here we must open a parenthesis and examine an aspect of Indic literature that seems most paradoxical. Peoples with an early literature have, apart from religious texts, also tales of battles, heroic deeds, animal adventures and the like. The Greek epics for example contain all these types of tales. Some of the earlier Mesopotamian texts from the 3rd millennium are popular songs of courtship (Jacobsen 27ff). India should be no exception. The fact that the earliest extant texts are religious does not mean that there were no tales about heroic kings and battles, fairy tales or animal fables in circulation at the time. On the contrary, (grand-)parents must have told stories to their (grand-)children from the very earliest times. I suspect that even heroic tales about Indra or the Aśvins and other gods circulated in a secular and perhaps irreverent garb at the time. We must assume then that some of these popular tales found their way into the epic texts that grew larger and larger, though in the absence of evidence (and due to the chronologies established under the distorting influence of the AIT), we are at present unable to trace this process even approximately. Since the Flood legend is attested in the *ŚB*, a more popular and slightly different version may have been in circulation finding its way eventually into the epic *MB*.

The flood-legend seems to have been known in Saptasindhu at c 3000 in two versions. In *ŚB* we find the simpler, shorter version with the bare essentials of the tale; here the Seven Seers and the seeds of creatures are missing and the new beginning is made through Iḷā, the divine embodiment of the essence of sacrifice. The version in the epic (as we have it) is more elaborate, more literary (eg "he threw the fish *candrāṃ suśadṛśaprabham* which shone like moonbeams": 185, 11; etc) and therefore later; but is has the 7 Seers, who are obviously the 7 hotṛs of Manu in *RV* X 63, 7, and this detail makes the essential tale early. Two more substantial differences are the inclusion of all seeds of creatures *bījāni sarvāṇi* and the identity of the fish as Brahmā in the epic version (both absent from the other). The appearance of Brahmā is undoubtedly late but the seeds are probably original just like the 7 Seers (see § 17, end).

16. Now comes the critical question: was there interaction between the Vedic legend and the Mesopotamian one, or borrowing, and which way did the influence run?... It is quite possible that the legend appeared independently in Saptasindhu and Mesopotamia. However, if there was interaction or borrowing, then the influence ran from Saptasindhu to Mesopotamia. This latter conclusion is based on two considerations.

To begin with, the Flood, like the Seven Sages, is a PIE theme. It is well known in Greece where the survivors are Deucalion and his wife Pyrrha, whose son Hellēn subsequently became the progenitor of all Hellenes (=Greeks): some traces are found in Hesiod (White 1935: 154-7), more in Plato (*Timaios* 22A; *Laws* 677A) and more in other authors (Kerényi 1982: 226; *GM* p38; Vitaliano 1977: 156-60). The Greeks may have borrowed it from the NE but the legend appears also in Avestan, in the Scandinavian and Russian lore and in the Celtic tradition of Ireland. So it is an inherited mythological motif. The *Edda* has a flood early on: only the giant Bergelmir and his wife survived in their *luðr* 'box-mill' (1996:11). All these traditions are later than the Vedic and Mesopotamian attestations and add nothing further to our understanding but do stress the IE pedigree of this mythologem. Since this legend is PIE it could not have been borrowed by the Indoaryans from the Mesopotamians.

It may be argued that the AIT is true, and that the Indoaryans lost this legend and borrowed it from the NE c 1300-1200. This is utterly unlikely but, in any case, there is another aspect for consideration. The Vedic tradition is not encaged in gross material forms and its deities are not such anthropomorphic (or zoomorphic) figures as in other mythologies, like those of Mesopotamia, Egypt or Greece. In the hymns and in later texts we find abstractions, qualities and essences to a greater degree than concrete characteristics and actions. Thus there is creation with gross materials as in the *RV* hymn to Viśvakarman X 81 or the dismemberment of Puruṣa in X 90 but also, and more often, with subtle forces like *māyā* or *asuratva* through will, inner vision and meditation as in the *nāsadīya* X 129, or in X 190, and in the upanishadic formulas *sa aikṣata* 'he envisioned', *so'kāmayata* 'he desired', *sa tapo'tapyata* 'he meditated/ brooded or practised austerity' in *Bṛhādaraṇyaka Up* I, 2, 5-6. Thus the Vedic mind, even if only in few and select individuals, could conceive and accept that Manu and the Seven Seers took with them on the boat the seeds of creatures and that through *tapas* Manu would be able to create anew all the creatures including *devas* and *asuras* (*MB* III 185, 49-52).

The Mesopotamians, on the other hand, do not display a similar capacity for abstraction: there is nothing like *mahā́d devā́nām asuratvā́m ékam* 'single is the great god-power of the gods' (*RV* III 55 refrain) or the One that breathed without air, of itself, prior to existence and non-existence (X 129). The creation of men in *Atrahasīs* requires gross materials like clay and blood, specialist gods like Nintu (Jacobsen 108), who is the great goddess Ninhursag now in her aspect of womb-goddess or divine midwife, and concrete actions as when "She pinched off fourteen pieces (of clay)/... seven pieces on the right/seven on the left" and "She covered her head/.../ Put on her belt..." etc (*MM* 16-7). In the *Enūma Elish* Marduk creates the universe from parts of Tiamat, deification of Mother-chaos, again in very concrete terms (*MM* 255-7), like the dismemberment in the *Puruṣa Sūkta*. Consider also the Mesopotamian need for temples and statues of gods, whereas the rigvedic people had none and were content to know their deities by their attributes (and as expressions of the One) and made their offerings on any patch of ground strewn with sacred grass. The Tablet of Destinies (symbolic but solid) is another example of the Mesopotamian concrete concepts. Thus the Mesopotamian mind apparently could not deal in abstract entities like Iḷā (in the *ŚB* version) or the Seven Seers (in the epic) or a sacrifice that creates a new generation of humans or the mere 'seeds' of creatures.

17. Quite important, if not crucial, is the element of the "seeds of creatures". It is found in all the Indic relevant versions except that of the *ŚB*. The question naturally arises: is this a native motif or has it been borrowed from the NE legends? Before dealing with it, let us see how the Mesopotamians treat and develop this theme. In the extant legend Ea instructs his chosen one: "Leave possessions, search out living things/ Reject chattels and save Lives/ Put aboard the seed of all living things into the boat" (*Gilgamesh* IX, i: *MM* 110)[14]. The essential instruction here seems to be "Put aboard the seeds of all living things". But the poet seems to have a difficulty with this: how would Atrahasis/ Utnapishtim gather all the seeds of creatures and

[14]A slightly different translation of these two lines reads: "Abandon possessions and look for life/ Despise worldly goods and save your soul." *Epic of Gilgamesh* 1988, Penguin Classics, cited by Hancock 1995:202. Yet another translation says: "Reject the corpse-like stench of wealth./ Choose to live and choose to love; /.../ Be moderate as you flee for survival/in a boat that has no place for riches./ Take the seed of all you need..." Yet here too the survivor puts aboard silver, gold and the rest, contrary to the divine instruction (Jackson & Bigs 1993). There are other variant translations.

subsequently create anew the creatures and then promote civilized life with just "seeds"?... So in the boat are brought silver and gold, domesticated and wild animals, relatives and all kinds of craftsmen (*MM* 111-2). For the same reasons the boat is made quite big so as to be able to contain all these creatures[15]. The Mesopotamians have even less faith than the Hebrews. Noah is content to gather into his ark pairs of all living things and to start afresh with divine help. Atrahasis needs in addition precious metals and various craftsmen. Another telling detail is that while the two Vedic texts speak of a flood or of ocean and billows, the Mesopotamian legend enlarges with darkness, winds, storms and torrents. So the tale becomes more realistic, again in a concrete fashion.

The motif "seeds of creatures" in the *MB* version seems to be native. For instance, in *RV* V 53, 13 seer Ātreya prays to the Maruts for *bī́jam-ákṣitam* 'seed imperishable' for progeny and wealth and long life. No doubt the Mesopotamians too knew of seeds but the point is that the Vedic poets did not need to borrow this; they had 'indestructible seed' in their native tradition and obviously could adapt this to the needs of Manu's survival through the flood. If they had borrowed this motif (assuming the Mesopotamians had 'imperishable seed'), they would not have ignored all the other interesting details in the Mesopotamian material. On the contrary, they would have elaborated even further the description of the decks and the various animals' accommodation as well as the arts and skills

---

[15]In a private communication to me (4/11/02), A George, Prof of Assyriology in University College, London, wrote: "'Seed of all living creatures' in *Gilg* XI means a living representative of each type of animal, in my view. It was clearly not imperishable, for special arrangements had to be made to preserve it from destruction by the flood. I do not know of other evidence for animals. The "seed of kingship" was, according to a common expression, eternal: this reflects a political ideology in which kingship was established by the gods in the remote past as the proper method of human governance and thus expected to be a fact of human life for ever."

of the craftsmen or Seven Seers. In the Indian epic generally the tendency for accretions and expansion is all too obvious. The extant epic version of the Flood has some obvious accretions which are, however, natural developments or elaborations of native elements. One such type is the description of Manu's asceticism: he is standing on one foot with arms raised, with head bent and eyes unblinking for ten thousand years (*MB* III 185, 4-5). This is a recognizably late development of an earlier yogic element in the Vedas and certainly not Mesopotamian. Other later elaborations—but always within the native tradition—are various poetic touches, one of which was noted earlier, the fish shining like moonbeams; another one is "the boat buffeted by hurricanes—like an excited, unsteady woman"[16]. Yet another addition is the revelation that the fish is god Brahamā (the divine embodiment of the 'holy power' *brâhman*). What were these "seeds of creatures" and how did Manu manage to preserve them in his small boat? One can only speculate that they were forms of knowledge held in mind/consciousness that would be uttered into material existence by the power of the Word. This too is a common theme in the Vedic texts.

All these elaborations are decidedly *not* in the Mesopotamian texts. The Indian bards developed and added elements of their own native tradition. They accepted the efficacy of the great spiritual powers of Manu and the 7 Seers who could by the potency of the Word in prayer stop rivers, defeat enemy-armies, make the sun and fire to burn and create worlds anew. So they were essentially concerned to bring Manu's boat safely through the cataclysm and, later, to introduce god Brahmā as the saviour in the form of the fish while Manu's miraculous spirituality would generate the new worlds.

---

[16]J van Buitenen translates, perhaps more correctly(?) "like a drunken whore" but this is not a very apt simile for the vehicle carrying the progenitor and the 7 Seers.

First conclusion

18. These four test-cases show that the Vedic people did not borrow from the Mesopotamians. Borrowers were the latter, if there was borrowing. We can envisage, for example, some Indoaryans transmitting to the Sumerians a (confused?) version of the Flood-legend c 2800-2600. Or perhaps the Sumerians understood it imperfectly and disseminated it among themselves in a confused manner. The Vedic legend was diversified into two. One was that of the Seven Sages who, combining the fish's role of protector and saviour and the Seers' supernatural powers to re-create and re-civilize, became the Mesopotamian Seven Craftsmen/Counsellors in the strange garb of the fish. The other was that of the flood and the survivor with his (seeds of) living things. It is quite possible that the Mesopotamians had indigenous forms of these myths and grafted onto them the Vedic material elaborating them further, because, as I indicated above, they could not comprehend fully how a Sage could revitalize and regenerate all the creatures of the world only with "seeds". Let us now proceed with more parallels.

Other mythological affinities

19. The four test-cases show that the Vedic people did not borrow from the Meopotamians. If there was borrowing, the latter were the borrowers. We now proceed wih more parallels. Interesting is the **number 432000**. This of course is the number of years in the Kaliyuga in the Puranic reckoning. De Santillana and von Dechend pointed out long ago that "Berossos made the Babylonian Great Year to last 432000 years" while "it is also the number of syllables in the *Rigveda*" (p 162; see also Kak 2000, ch 5 and McEvilley, ch 3). Here again the Mesopotamian culture would seem to be indebted to the earlier Vedic tradition. But here it could be argued that the Indic material is of c 500 CE while Berossos is of the 3rd cent BC. However, while the Purāṇas as we have them are late, they may (and in several cases do) contain very old material.

20. We need note also the theme of humans springing out of the soil. In the text *Creation of the Hoe* god Enlil fashions the first hoe and with that breaks the hard crust of the earth out of which emerge the first humans like plants (Jacobsen, p 103). This is reminiscent of *AV* hymn III 17, 3 where the plough *lāṅglala* digs up a cow, a sheep, a chariot-frame (or a horse) and a lusty, fat girl; it reminds faintly also of Sitā both in *RV* IV 57, 6 and in the *Rāmāyaṇa Bāla-Kāṇḍa* where she emerges from the furrow.

21. The Sungod's boat. In Mesopotama Śamaś/Utu traverses the sky in a boat and is depicted doing so in extant seals (Black & Green 44-5), like the Egyptian sungod Re where the mythologem is much more complex. Many other gods have boats and at their festivals their statue (or image) is placed on a boat and paraded thus. In a country with two large rivers (as also in Egypt with the Nile) this seems very natural. Even Ninurta the Sumerian wargod par excellance (and god of fertility) travels in a boat.

Travelling by boat is not at all common on the part of gods in Vedic texts. But we cannot ignore *RV* VII 88, 3-4 where sage Vasiṣṭha sails with Varuṇa in the god's boat into the middle of the (sky-?) ocean. Varuṇa is no sungod but he is closely associated with him: in *RV* I 50, 6 sungod Sūrya is identified with Varuṇa; in VII 87, 5 Varuṇa has fashioned and placed the sun in the sky (also V 85, 2); he holds the sun there or draws it along (V 62, 2 and 66, 7; VII 87, 1 and 88, 1). It is only one small step away to have the god of ocean-and-waters Varuṇa (who actually has a boat and who guides the Sun in heaven) carry the latter across the sky on a boat. Something like this (but without Varuṇa) happens in the *AV* hymn XVII 1, where the sun (*āditya* in st 25 and *sūrya* in st 26) is said to be on a boat of a hundred oars. However, already in RV VI, 58, 3, Pūṣan, the glowing aspect of the Sungod (*āghṛṇi*), the guardian of paths, who often travels on a goat-drawn car, moves in the aerial ocean with his fleet of golden ships. The motif of the Sungod travelling in a boat is thus well-established in the Veda.

The motif appears in Greece also. Usually the Greek sungod Apollo (or Phoibos = V *bhaga*) travels in the sky on a horse-drawn carriage and so does Helios (=V *sūrya*) in the hymns to these two gods (White 1935:340-1, 458-9)—and as Vedic Sūrya and Savitṛ do. However in a fragment of early Mimnermus (also in late Stesichorus), Helios passes along the ocean (in the night, and before sunrise) from west to east in a golden winged vessel fashioned by Hephaistos (Onians 1988:251, n 11). This motif may have come to Greece from the NE (Egypt rather than Mesopotamia). But it could just as feasibly be IE, retained in some parts of Greece but forgotten in the regions of Homer (eastern Aegean) and Hesiod (Boeotia). If it had come from the NE, we would expect to meet it in Homer since his epics contain much NE material (Kazanas 2001b; Burkert 1992). That it is not known in other IE branches (eg Celtic and Germanic) is not surprising since they did not retain a definite Sungod as found in the Greek and Vedic traditions, which, especially the latter, preserve many more IE elements. So this motif of a sun-boat, quite accordant with that of celestial waters, may well have been PIE.

22. In the *RV* the sun is often described as a **bull** (eg III 61, 7; VII 88, 1; etc); so is Agni (I 140, 2; II 35, 13; etc); so is of course Indra, the mighty god of thunder-and-lightning (I 32, 7; VII 20, 5; etc). In Mesopotamia the bull is associated with and is the emblem of Adad (Sumerian Iškur), the storm-god who also has the lightning (Black & Green, 46-7; *MM* 316); the clouds are described as "bull-calves". Sometimes the animal is associated with the moon-god Nanna/Suen (Black & Green 47). In the *RV* also the moon-god Soma is often mentioned as a bull (IX 2, 6; etc, etc). In *RV* IX (5, 1-2; 27, 3-4; 70, 5-7; etc) Soma is repeatedly described as a mighty and unconquered bull in heaven reminding us of the Bull-of-

Heaven whom goddess Ishtar brought down to punish Gilgamesh for offending her but whom Gilgamesh and Enkidu killed (*MM* 80-2: tablet VI, iii-iv). In *ŚB* I 1, 4, 14 Manu has a miraculous bull whose snorting kills demons and foes and this gets sacrificed. It is worth noting here that the Bull "appears as one of the incarnations of Verethraghna", the Avestan equivalent of Indra (Macdonell 1898:150). In Greek mythology Zeus, in the form of a bull, carries off Europa while Dionysos also is described as a "bull-god" (Kerényi 109); Talos, the Sun, is also called *Tauros* 'the bull' (*GM*, 92, 7.) (However, the Greek bull may not be IE, or not wholly so, since the cult of the bull was common in Crete before the advent of the Mycenaeans.) With the Celts of Gaul too in pre-Roman times the bull has great importance (Larousse 240) represented as a divine animal in monumental iconography; A and B Rees, in speaking of the "great bull" in Ulster (Ireland), cite G Dumézil to the effect that the animal "symbolizes the warrior function both in Rome and in India" (1995: 124). So the bull-figure as a god is PIE and certainly does not derive from Mesopotamia. Harappan seals often depict a vigorous bull (and sometimes bull-man).

23. If there is a mighty bull there is bound to be a **Cow-of-plenty** also. In the Vedic texts Aditi herself, mother of the Ādityas, is spoken of as a cow (*RV* I 153, 3; etc; *VS* XIII 43). In another form, Pṛśni, the spotted cow, is the mother of the Maruts. But we meet also the cosmic cow in *RV* I 80, 3, III 55, 1 etc; also as cow Audhumla nourishing universal man Ymir in the Scandinavian *Edda* (1996:10)—and thus having a PIE identity. The cow as Cow-of-Plenty appears in Iranian, Irish and Norse legends (Koppers 1936:320-7) as well as Vedic. The *dhenuḥ kāmadughā* 'Cow-of-Plenty' is found in *AV* IV 34, 8, granting all desires in heaven.

In the Mesopotamian pantheon Ninhursag(a), the supreme lady and mistress of the gods (*Belet-ili*) has the cow as her symbol (*MM* 326), as does Inanna/Ishtar (Black & Green 53); the latter is goddess of love and war, daughter of the moon-god (and appearing as the morning- and evening-star: see also Kak 1996). In a different tradition Ishtar is said to be daughter of An, the Skygod (*MM* 326). Jacobsen writes: "... a tradition ... saw the power in the sky as both male and female and distinguished the god An (Akkadian *Anum*) from the goddess An (Akkadian *Antum*) to whom he was married. According to that view the rains flowed from the sky goddess' breasts, or (since she was usually envisaged in cow shape) her udder—that is, from the clouds" (p 95).

In Jacobsen's passage there are interesting and revealing details. Skygod An/Anu is like the Vedic *Dyaus* (*div/dyu/dyo*) both masculine and feminine. Just as Anu has progeny with Antu (but also others, including his daughter Ishtar, who bore Shara 'hero of Anu'), Dyaus is invariably coupled with Mother-earth Pṛthivī. Then the rains flowing from the skygoddess's breasts or udders ("envisaged in cow shape") is an image of very common incidence in the Vedic texts: in *RV* I 92, a hymn to the Dawn, we find the cow and breast and udder in stanza 4; in I, 164, 26 and after we find cow, calf, milk, heavenly stream, rain-cloud etc; cf also I, 64, 5-6 and X, 100, 11, etc, and *VS* II, 16.

24. Just as significant is the theme of creating the worlds out of the **dismemberment of a divine being**. The *Puruṣa sūkta* (*RV* X 90) deals at length with this theme. It seems to divide into two parts: the first part (stanzas 1-5) resembles the *Nāsadīya* hymn X 129 in that an unknown Being is said to manifest with its one fourth as the cosmos and be immanent in it, yet, at the same time with its other three parts, the Being remains beyond or transcends the cosmos. Then, part two (stanzas 6-16) describes the sacrificial dismemberment of manifest (anthropomorphic) Puruṣa (born of Virāḷ) who was born of the first Puruṣa (st 5) and the creation of different worlds and creatures from his members.

In the *Enūma Elish* Marduk fights, defeats and kills Tiamat, the mother of the older generation of gods, a kind of Vedic Aditi. Here she has a gigantic, monstrous form with four eyes, a horn and a tail but she is not necessarily a dragon-serpent, as some have claimed (for details see Heidel 1969:83-8). She has spawned serpents and during the fight as well as during the final deadly blows of Marduk and her dismemberment, she reminds one of a repulsive demonness: Marduk sliced her in two making the sky and earth; with her liver he made the zenith and from her eyes the rivers Tigris and Euphrates and so on (*MM* 255-7). This epic is a glorification of Marduk who slays a demonic monster then creates the world and its hub, the country between and along the two rivers, and thus becomes the new King of the gods. However, beneath this version lurks a different story where Tiamat was a primal Mothergoddess, consort of Apsu: she gave birth to the good gods (those that now fought against her), cared for her offspring and probably willingly offered herself originally to the cosmic sacrifice that generated the worlds (Heidel, ibid; Jacobsen, 187).

The Indoaryans would not have borrowed because the divine dismemberment must go back to the PIE era, since the Scandinavians preserved the similar myth of the dismemberment of the first giant-being Ymir (=V *Yama*) by which the gods made the world (*Edda* 10ff; Kazanas 2001a:280). In Greek mythology Hesiod gives the castration of Ouranos from whose blood and organs spring up different divine beings (*Theogony* 176ff; White 1935): this seems to be an amalgam of the IE myth (Vedic Puruṣa, like Scandinavian Ymir, and perhaps Indra hacking up Vṛtra to release the waters and bring out the sun in *RV* I 32) and of various NE versions like Kumarbi castrating Anu. The IE theme is very old. So in this case, again, the Mesopotamian presentation is very crude but, as was said, contains hints of an earlier finer version, which has subtler affiinties with the Vedic culture.

25. Significant is also the motif of the **tortoise** or turtle. Jacobsen summarizes (p 132) the extant portion of a Sumerian myth in which Ninurta, wargod son of Ellil but also god of fertility, desired to gain control over the much larger area of the Apsu and after an adventure with the thunderbird Imdugud generated an enormous flood-wave against Enki, the god of fresh-waters and wisdom, and his temple. Enki created a turtle and placed it at the entrance of the Apsu. When Ninurta appeared the turtle quickly dug a pit and pushed the wargod into it! This is, of course, quite an extraordinary tale. Turtles undoubtedly existed in South Mesopotamia and it is not surprising that this animal should play some role in a cosmic myth where ambition and violence (Ninurta) turns against wisdom (Enki). What is extraordinary is that this proverbially slow-moving animal should dig a pit "quickly" and push a god in. I can only suppose that the myth was originally different and the turtle functioned more as a guardian stemming perhaps the flood and thus saving the temple (and the world?).

The tortoise is not a very a common motif in world mythology (apart from a Siberian tale, S Thompson, 1989, has very few entries under 'tortoise'), but, as one would expect, it has its place in the Vedic tradition. Long before the *Kūrma Purāṇa* with *Viṣṇu's* second avatāra in tortoise-form, the name of one of the 7 Seers 'Kaśyapa' means also 'tortoise' (=*kūrma*, *kacchapa*). In the *AV* Kaśyapa is often identified with Prajāpati (eg XIX 53, 10) while in *ŚB* VII 4, 3, 5 Prajāpati becomes a tortoise and then in VII 5, 1, 1 produces all creatures. In the (*White*) *Yajurveda* the tortoise is said to enter into the altar and be elevated as "master of waters" (*VS* XIII 31). S Kak mentions the kūrma-shaped altar showing its structure (2000:13, 15-7)[17]. In the *Jaiminīya Brāhmaṇa* again the *akūpāra* 'limitless' tortoise finds the earth, a firm resting-place, in the ocean (*JB* III 203, 273) and so foreshadows

[17]Kak's cognation of *kaśyapa* with Greek *kassiopeia* (a queen and mother of Andromeda in Greek mythology who after boasting of her beauty was made into the well-known constellation), is implausible both for semantic and phonological reasons. Kaśyapa does not have this astronomical connection and the Kassiopeia constellation does not remotely look like a tortoise. Vedic **ś** usually appears as Greek **k** or **p** as in V *aśman* Gk *akmōn* 'stone', *aśvaikko/hippo* 'horse', *daśa deka* 'ten' etc.

Vīṣṇu's incarnation. Thus, while I would not at all preclude an indigenous Mesopotamian legend involving a turtle, I would at the same time maintain a strong suspicion that some influence came from Saptasindhu. Note too that the turtle was the emblem of Enki/Ea (Black & Green 1995:179), who was god of wisdom and creativity like Prajāpati.

26. Connected with the world "Beyond" (underworld or heaven) is **the motif of eating (or abstaining from) certain food-stuffs there** which will bind the eater to the Underworld or make him immortal in Heaven. We noted this motif earlier in the Mesopotamian legend of Adapa, one of the 7 Sages, when he went before Anu in heaven but, on the earlier advice of his patron-god Ea, refused to take the bread and water (of immortality) offered to him (§ 10). In the Greek myth of the abduction of Persephone by Hades, god of the Underworld, she eats pomegranate seeds and when her mother Demeter finally reclaims her, Persephone can remain with her only for six months and then must return to Hades (Kerényi, p 239-40). A similar motif is found in the Japanese myth of Izanagi, a kind of creative-god and father of creatures, who seeks his beloved Izanami (his sister/wife and mother of gods and islands) in the Underworld but she cannot leave that realm because she has eaten its food (Larousse, p 407).

This theme is also found in the Vedic tradition, in the Naciketas legend. A simple if elliptic version is in the *KU* (I, 1-9) which becomes a philosophical treatise explaining the fire-ritual of Naciketas as a means of practical knowledge and discipline leading to union with the Supreme Self and immortality. The kernel of the story is found in *Taittirīya Br* III 11, 8 and in *RV* X 135 (where, however the child in Yama's abode is not named). In the Upaniṣad, Naciketas himself chooses to go to Yama's abode and remains without food and water for 3 nights. In the Brāhmaṇa, however, he must go to Yama at the express instruction of a divine voice—and *not eat anything there for three nights*. This may be a coincidence with the Mesopotamian story where Ea instructs Adapa (*MM* 186) or, as I think, the latter is an adaptation of the Vedic motif. In both the mortal figure returns to man's world, but while the Vedic legend stresses positive values (self-abnegation, faith, acquisition of true knowledge) the Mesopotamian one suggests trickery on the part of Ea (or Anu?), and the powerlessness and ultimate failure of even a supposed sage like Adapa.

Magical and ritual practices

By this are meant simply omens, divination and various apotropaic and catharctic practices involving incantation and other forms of ritual.

27. Divination. Dalley suggested that the art of bird-augury, as attested in a Greek inscription of the 6th century, derived from Mesopotamia (1998:100). I pointed out that the Greek and Mesopotamian texts she compared are in fact quite different and that she is probably wrong since this kind of divination was practised quite early on in the Vedic culture and west of Greece among the Celts (Kazanas 2001b: sect I and IV). Indeed bird-augury is attested in *RV* hymns II 42 and 43 taking the *Kapinjala*, a kind of heather-cock, as birds of good or bad omen, depending on the direction from which they call: if the call is from the right or south of the house, then it is auspicious. Dalley cites the omen: "If many eagles keep flying over a city, the city will be besieged." (The Greek omen is: "If [a particular bird] flying from right to left disappears from view, [the omen] is favourable...").

In the Vedic texts many phenomena serve as omens, particularly in the Brāhmaṇas: the movement of cows; the clarity or otherwise of the sacrificial fire; a dream of making a neckband or garland; meteors and lightning, and so on (Kazanas, ibid). However, hepatoscopy, that is the inspection of liver and entrails, is not evidenced even in late texts, whereas it was common practice in Mesopotamia (Jacobsen, 84; Oppenheim 207ff; Burkert 46-51).

28. Demons, ghosts etc. In Mesopotamia there are evil spirits and ghosts that cannot find rest in the Netherworld (Jacobsen 12-3; Oppenheim 109-203; Burkert 65-6), take possession of men and cause bodily or mental illness. There are also monsters, dragons and serpents like Humbaba, the guardian of the forest in *Gilgamesh* (*MM* 21: Tablet V, i) or the monstrous offspring of Tiamat in the *Enūma Elish* (*MM* 237: Tablet I). The *AV* hymns are full of demonic creatures like Takman "god of yellow hue... son of Varuṇa" (I 25, 2-3) or *rakṣasas* and *piśacas* that assume animal, insect or deformed human shapes (VI 37, II; VII 6, 13; etc; cf also *RV* I 133, 5, VII 104, 10, etc); for such creatures pestering houses or causing mental disorders see *AV* IV 36, 8; IV 37 II; V 29, 5-9; etc. We must not forget also Vṛtra, the dreadful dragon/demon whom Indra kills and releases the waters.

In Mesopotamia these demonic figures are often said to effect their torments by enveloping humans with a net or by binding them with fetters and there are texts praying for release (Onians 1988:364, 372, with references). Similar concepts are found in India too. Very common is Varuna's *pāśa* 'noose, fetter' which binds threefold and even sevenfold the sinner in the *RV* (I, 24, 15; VI, 74, 4; VII, 75, 3; etc). Varuṇa and other gods are frequently implored to forgive the transgression and remove the noose(s), as in I, 24, IV, 12, 4, etc. Indra too has a net with which he vanquishes foes (*AV* VIII 8, 5-8). (In later texts we find also Yama carrying a noose like a hunter, as in the story of Sāvitrī, *MB* III 281, 8). In these texts we find also that the noose is woven by the gods (*AV* VIII, 8, 4) or by Fate (*Rāmāyaṇa* VII, 37, 9). In the *ŚB* XIII 6, 2, 20 a rope-maker is consecrated to Fate; here we should note also the term *guṇa* as 'thread, rope, quality, attribute, type', suggesting that "attributes" are "threads" woven into a pattern of "type" or of life.

These concepts—noose, Fate and release—are well attested in other IE traditions. In the earliest Greek texts we find the gods binding individuals or embattled groups with a rope or noose (*Iliad* 13, 347-60; *Odyssey* 22, 268ff; etc) while the lot of a man's life is "woven" by Fate, as in Plato's famous myth of the three Fates, Clotho, Lachesis and Atropos (*Republic* 616Cff); people pray, of course, to gods for release (*Iliad* 23, 262ff; *Odyssey* 5, 394ff). Similar ideas are found among the Iranians, Germans and Celts (Onians 1988:353-7, 363, 381). Since the broader idea of Fates or gods "weaving" a man's life-pattern is absent in the Near East, it would hardly be possible that these beliefs and cultic practices were borrowed by all these different IE peoples.

29. Protection. Many and various means for protection against these demonic forces (and for purification) were used by the Mesopotamians: spells, votive offerings, amulets of all kinds, even effigies, today's "voodoodoll" (Burkert, 60-1, 65-7, 82, 87, 110). It should not come as a surprise that all such means, with some variants here and there, are amply presented in the Veda. The *Atharvaveda* (and much of the Sūtra literature) abounds in various protective, expulsive, offensive and retaliatory means: spells (V, 31, 1; etc; also, the verses from *RV* I 23, 22 and X, 97—"O Waters, carry off whatever sin is in me..." etc—are another such incantation); amulets of all kinds (I, 16, 3; etc, etc); use of plants (IV, 7; VIII, 7, 3; etc) and ointments of all kinds which are sometimes genuine medicinal remedies (IV, 9, 8; etc); carrying round of fire (VIII, 64, 1); and of course water for all occasions. Another feature in these practices is the making of effigies (out of wax and other substances) which are melted, buried or pierced through. These are made by women also and one description is in *AV* X, 1, 1-3, which also has incantations for protection; most of them can be and are placed in wells or cemeteries (V, 31, 8). More details are found in the Sūtra texts (Keith, p 389).

Oppenheim mentions foundation deposits (p 26) while J Black and A Green refer to them together with building rites (p 46) and Burkert distinguishes (pp 53-5) between two types of these during the construction or consecration of a house, temple or other building, both in the Near East and Greece: one type consists of precious metals and/or stones, guardian figures and tablets with inscriptions; the other consists of animal sacrifice and libations. The first type, essentially an extension of the second, is unknown in the Vedic tradition, which, as was said earlier (§ 16), did not at that early period show much concern with material objects. However, a beautiful Hymn (*AV* III, 12) describes the consecration of a house invoking gods Savir̥, Vāyu, Indra, Br̥haspati, the Maruts, and Bhaga 'Bestower of fortune'. Offerings are made of milk, corn, jars of purified butter and curdled milk, honey and water. In later texts, the Sūtra-literature, a black cow or a white goat may be offered and in this Keith finds a similarity to "the black cock killed at the foundation of a new house in Greece" (p 363). So here we have another affinity.

30. Purification. Burkert mentions that branches of special trees are used in purification as evidenced in an Akkadian poem: "a remarkable young [man] holding in his hand a tamarisk rod of purification... the water he was carrying he threw over me, pronounced the life-giving incantation and rubbed [my body]" (p 60-1, square brackets original). Of course in the Veda we find the use of the plant *Apāmārga* 'which-drives-away' (*AV* IV, 7; etc) as well as of other plants (*AV* VIII 7, 3ff; etc); they are used against diseases, evil dreams and any other form of real or supposed pollution.

"Anything left over from the purification must be carefully disposed of" writes Burkert (p 62). We find the same practice in the Vedic tradition: all remnants of the rite must be burnt completely and whatever is left must be buried secretly (*ŚB* III 8, 5, 9ff); then all get washed and the last traces of uncleanness flow away with the running water.

More details and examples are found in Kazanas 2001b. Indeed many more could be cited, but enough has been given here to show that there are many Vedic parallels in this sphere also.

We turn now to another area of possible influence.

31. The Origin of Kingship has its own common mythology in the two traditions.

Jacobsen delineates the emergence of the king as an important "savior-figure... exalted above men" (p 79). In many tales the human ruler challenges even the authority of the gods—as when Gilgamesh disregards Enlil and kills the god's giant forester Humbaba (*MM* 63, 73-4), or rejects Inanna/Ishtar's advances insulting her (*MM* 77-9). Then comes a development whereby An/Anu is supreme (p 95), but holds his distance and does not intervene much. The other gods hold appointments under his authority: eg Enki has the duty to keep the river-mouths clear, enrich the sap in plants, make dense the clouds and so on, while Ellil has charge of all the winds (p 85). Then ultimate power is seen to rest in "the Assembly of the Gods" and this becomes the "highest authority in the Mesopotamian universe" (p 86). Jacobsen stopped at this point, but it is obvious that there is a further development in *The Epic of Creation* where Marduk becomes king of the gods, supreme ruler, after he defeats Tiamat and her army of gods and monsters. Heidel points out that the epic is "not only a religious treatise but also a political one" (1969:11) because in exalting Marduk as creator and ordainer of the universe and so on, the poem praises Babylon (and her king) stressing her supremacy over other cities (ibid). So here, as in earlier times, the King on earth is a reflection of the King in heaven. Oppenheim stresses "the divinity of kings" whose name was often written with the determinative DINGIR 'god' (1977:98).

In *RV* X 173 the king is elected (or re-elected, in other cases) by the people *viśas* but is established steadfast in sovereignty *rāṣṭra* by steadfast Indra (then by Soma and other gods, including king Varuṇa). Two hymns in the *AV*, III 4 and 5, are even more explicit in that the people, the 5 tribes including princes, chariot-makers and metal-workers, elect the king, who has the blessing of the gods, Agni, Aśvins and so on. The origin of kinship is in *AB* I, 14: the gods were losing the war against the demons so they elected Soma as their king and thus conquered all quarters. In *TB* I, 5 the tale is repeated but here the assembly of the gods make a sacrifice to Prajāpati, the supreme creator-god (like Anu), and he sends his son Indra, endowed with brilliance and royalty to lead and rule them.

I find no evidence that the democratic principle of electing the king was ever practised in Mesopotamia as it was in Saptasindhu. Here we must bear in mind that in those ancient times the chariot- and metal-workers were not necessarily uneducated and unintelligent people: even late Lawbooks allow the *vaiśya* class of producers, artisans and traders to study the Vedas (but not teach), so they may have been of high quality and with good, broad knowledge. Otherwise all elements are very similar in the two cultures. Here, we may have independent development but the (overplayed) Assembly of the Gods in Mesopotamian texts may well be an elaboration of the (underplayed) occasional gods' assemblies in the Vedic texts.

Also, the *Epic of Creation* may derive from the *TB* tale. For just as Prajāpati sends his son Indra to lead the gods against the demons so Anshar (another creator skygod) sends his grandson Marduk against Tiamat and confers on him all power (*MM* 242-4). This epic may be late (1st millennium) or from c 2000 (*MM* 228-9) or from the 16th century from the reign of the Kassite king Agum-Kakrine (*MM* 229) when, much literary activity took place (see § 43, below). Be that as it may, the Vedic material is much older.

Here I stop. No doubt further researches will produce more parallels in this field but now we must turn to a different area.

Language, Writing, Mathematics, Astronomy and Peacocks

32. Starting with lexical similarities we should note the possible connection of Sanskrit (=S hereafter) *mleccha* and the Mesopotamian (=Mp hereafter) *meluhha/melukha*. To this we could add another cognation given by Sethna—S *karpāsa* (>Prākrit *kapāsa*) and Mp *kapazum* 'cotton'. These sound quite valid. As cotton was cultivated in the ISC but not in Mesopotamia until much later (see n 22), we must take it that the Mp *kapazum* is a loan from S *karpāsa*. For this loan there is the indubitable archaeological evidence.

There may be more, as yet unknown or unverified. Frawley for instance thought (1991) that *Iḷā* is cognate with *Ela-m*, the name of the region east of Sumer and that *iḍ/iḷ* 'libation, (sacred) speech' and goddess *Iḷā* are linked with "the most important Mesopotamian name for the Divine... 'Il' " and also Hebrew *El* or *Elohim* 'God the Father' (pointing out that *Elohim* is a plural neuter, which indicates that originally it was a plurality of gods); he also connected god *Ashur* of the Assyrians and Egyptian *Asar* (=*Osiris*) with S *asura* (=*Avestan Ahura*) and both √*as* 'be, live' and √*ās* 'sit, exist, abide' (pp 268-84). Some of these ideas he repeats in his 2001 study (pp 27-9). One could add some more hypothetical cognations (See also Frayne 1993; Whittaker 1998)[18]: S *muh-yati* 'be unconscious, deluded' and Egyptian *mhy* 'be negligent'; S *ap* 'water' (loc pl *apsú* 'in waters') and Mp *ab/absū* 'fresh-waters'; S *dhāman* 'abode' (cf Greek *ana-thēma* 'offering') and Mp *temen* '*foundation*' (?Greek *temenos* '(sanctified) site'); S *cakra* (cf Greek *kuklos*) 'wheel' and Mp *gigir* 'wagon'; S *sapta* Mp *sebit-/ti/tu* 'seven'; one might also suggest tentatively S *māyā* and Mp *me* 'creative power/knowledge'; and so on.

However, all such cognations seem fortuitous and arbitrary. Only if one knew Sumerian/Akkadian (or whatever

---

[18]G Whittaker argues, not very convincingly, that the Sumerians were not indigenous but were preceded by an IE people in the area. This is not, of course, impossible but that an IE people should have moved into this region so early seems improbable. Others thought Dravidians moved from India to Elam and Mesopotamia (references in McEvilley pp 238ff). However if more evidence were to be accumulated, one or other proposition would be acceptable.

relevant NE language) as well as Sanskrit, would one be able to make such comparisons convincingly. Assyrian god's name *Ashur* may be cognate with S *asura* but experts on Mesopotamian culture say that this deity's name probably grew out of the name of, and in parallel with, the city *Aššur* (Black & Green 1995:37). So all such comparisons and etymologies must be laid aside until much more is known about the subject[19].

33. While lexical elements (except for very few cases) are rather uncertain, there are **poetic elements** or devices which are common. That there should be stock epithets in both literatures can be ascribed to independent development. The examples in the *RV* hymns are numerous: *ugra* 'fierce' of Rudra (II 33, 9), *somapā* 'soma-drinker' of Indra (II 12, 13), *urukrama* of Viṣṇu, *jātavedas* of Agni etc, etc. In Mesopotamian poems these are much fewer: eg in *Atrahasīs* "warrior" Enlil, "far-sighted" Enki, "wise" Mami (*MM* 9-35). As in the *RV*, Mesopotamian similes are varied and some are very lyrical or expressive: "splendour like the stars of heaven" and "His face was like that of a long-distance traveller" (*MM* 290, 53). But there is one curious device common to both poetries which reveals close contact: this is when a character (a hero or god) speaks to himself. The common formula here is "speaking to one's heart/spirit" as in *MM* 96, 105 and in *RV* VII 86, 2 or X 129, 4.

34. When we turn to the material means of transmitting language, ie **writing**, we find that there is considerable uncertainty about its origins in Mesopotamia. Writing appears

---

[19]Burkert mentions the Greek/Vedic cognates *pelekus/paraśu* 'axe' and connects them with Akkadian *pilaqqu* which, however, means 'spindle, dagger' (1992:37). Mayrhofer (under *paraśu*) rejects this connection and proposes Altaic **paluqa* 'hammer' and Burushaski *baluquá/bulqá* 'big/ small hammer'. This may be correct but we must not ignore Sumerian *balag* 'axe'; so the connection with Mesopotamian seems to me quite valid. Burkert mentions also (p 37) the cognates Greek *smaragdos*, Mycenaean *pa-ra-ku* and Sanskrit *marakata* 'emerald' and connects them with Akkadian *baraktu* and Aramaic *bar'qa*.

simultaneouslyor so it seems—at c 3000 in Egypt, South Mesopotamia and the ISC. The Egyptian hieroglyphic style can be separated from the other two because it is quite different from them; the material upon which the hieroglyphs are inscribed is also different—stone, not clay tablets. Harappan and Mesopotamian scripts and materials have similarities. In his extensive survey of the different stages of writing (1992:55-102, esp 70) J Bottéro writes: "We do not have apodeictic proof of the priority of this discovery, only a solid mass of indications" (p 87). Saggs is even more explicit in rejecting Denise Schmandt-Bessarat's theory that writing in Sumer developed from prehistoric *tokens* (=small marbles or stones in different shapes, some having holes or incisions) via *bullas* (=clay balls containing tokens), numerical tablets and then protocuneiform tablets (1989:63-5); he states: "Either the invention of writing took place not in southern Mesopotamia but in some other place not yet excavated; or else, the earliest writing material was not clay but something perishable" (p 63). Michalowski again argued that protocuneiform was an invented technology that appeared on the scene quite suddenly, though not unrelated to earlier recording technologies (tokens etc) which were all practised concurrently (1990:54-8). Susan Pollock states that there has been no resolution to the divergent views on the subject (1998:166).

That writing made a sudden appearance is indicated in the native legend or historical text of *Enmerkar and the Lord of Aratta*, mentioned in § 8 above. In this text (transl and ed by Kramer 1952), the king of Erech/Kullab (=Uruk) Enmerkar communicates through a messenger with the lord of Aratta and engages in trade with that city—sending wheat in exchange for carnelian and lapis-lazuli. After the third journey of the messenger, we find a strange passage suggesting that Enmerkar was the first man to use writing on clay tablets. He did so because the herald for some reason (length of message?) was "heavy of mouth" and unable to repeat the message (II 498-507). That so momentous an event should be introduced so cursorily is quite baffling. Following a French secondary authority, Frawley proceeds to suggest that "the origin of Sumerian writing had some connection with Aratta [in the north-west Punjab] and might have been borrowed from there" (2001:227).

Although Kramer's translation of the text contains no overt suggestion of any borrowing or influence from Aratta, nonetheless Frawley's idea is not without merit. It is possible that writing started in the ISC before Sumer. Back in 1998 JM Kenoyer, expert on the ISC, in an interview said that inscriptions have been found there which may be as early as 3300 (1998:29). More recently there have been reports (Internet, Press) of inscriptions from 3500 (see Dr R Medow's view, *BBC News* on the Internet; McEvilley, p 242). All this, of course, requires further study and confirmation. Additional investigations may well prove that writing emerged independently in Sumer and in the ISC, but at present there is nothing to preclude writing coming to South Mesopotamia from Saptasindhu together with other goods, material and cultural.

35. The Mesopotamian debt to Vedic **Mathematics** seems to be more certain—at least according to the view of A Seidenberg, a distinguished American mathematician and historian of science. I have no training in Mathematics and can only accept his word and mathematical proofs. He argued (1962 and 1978) that there is "a single source" for the two distinct traditions in ancient Mathematics, that of the algebraic or computational and that of the geometric or constructive (1978:301). He examined the mathematical data and concluded that this 'original source' was either 'Vedic Mathematics' as formulated in the *Śulbasūtras* or an older system very much like it—rejecting the idea of Babylonian originality or the derivation of Vedic Mathematics from Babylon c 1700 BC (1978:304, 307, 310, 318-9) or from Egypt (1962:515). He states of this original source:

> "its mathematics was very much like what we see in the *Sulvasutras* [*śulbasūtras*]. In the first place, it was associated with ritual. Second, there was no dichotomy between number and magnitude ... In geometry it knew the Theorem of Pythagoras and how to convert a rectangle into a square. It knew the isosceles trapezoid and how to compute its area ... [and] some number theory centered on the existence of Pythagorean triplets ... [and how] to compute a square root. ...
>
> The arithmetical tendencies here encountered [ie in the *Śulbasūtras*] were expanded and in connection with observations on the rectangle led to Babylonian mathematics. A contrary tendency, namely, a concern for exactness of thought ... together with a recognition that arithmetic methods are not exact, led to Pythagorean mathematics. (1978: 329)

Sanskrit scholars, Seidenberg writes, did not give him a date for the *Śulbasūtras* as far back as 1700 BC. The earliest they would have given is 600, if that. He felt therefore obliged to "*postulate* a pre-Old-Babylonian source for the kind of geometric rituals we see preserved in the *Sulvasutras*, or at least for the mathematics involved in these rituals" (1978:329). However, there is no general acceptance of Seidenberg's views and more research will be needed.

36. I am now fairly certain that many sūtra texts belong to the first quarter of the 3rd millennium, if not earlier in a more primitive form. Obviously cities like Harappa, Kalibangan, Mohenjorado, Dholavira etc, with their straight streets, square blocks, large buildings, domestic and urban water-supply, "way ahead of those of any other civilization of their time", and "main drainage system" (McIntosh 2001:100-1), etc, indicate town-planning, and town-planning requires knowledge of geometry, precisely the sort of "constructive" mathematics contained in the Śulbasūtras. Although Seidenberg may have been wrong, I find nothing remarkable about the Śulbasūtras being early or the Mesopotamians borrowing (from) them. An additional consideration will help here. One of Bṛhaspati's sūtras states: "A privy, a fireplace, a pit or a receptacle for leavings of food and other [rubbish], must never be made very close to the house of another man (XIX 26)." This sounds like a regulation to control excesses from pressure due to increasing population and the beginning of urbanization. This situation arose probably c 3000-2600 when the ISC was in its early urban phase, before town-planning was established generally.

37. David Pingree, and many another before him, thinks that Indian **astronomy** or astrology, or at any rate the study of celestial phenomena that were regarded as ominous and somehow influencing human life, derived from Mesopotamia (1998). He finds A Parpola's "interpretation of the inscriptions in Harappan seals as recording, in a Dravidian language, an astral religion related to an alleged counterpart in Mesopotamia... too hypothetical and unsubstantiated for us to consider it further" (p 127)[20]. He then takes as his basis the text MUL.APIN which is assigned to c 700, possibly back to 1000 (p 125, 127) and indicates correspondences with Vedic texts. He finds similarities in the lists of 18 constellations in the path of the Moon in MUL. APIN and the 27 or 28 nakṣatras in Vedic *AV* XIX 7, 2-5, *Taittirīyasaṃhitā* IV 4, 10 and *Taittirīyabrāhmaṇa* I, 5 and III, 1 and thinks that the association of deities with the nakṣatras in India "seems totally arbitrary and unexpected" but the Mesopotamian belief that the constellations are manifestations of gods and goddesses is not so (p 127). Why the Indian nakṣatra/deity relations are arbitrary but not the Mesopotamian ones is not at all clear to me, but Pingree gives no further explanations. He then refers to "the ideal year of 360 days divided into twelve equal months" being the same in both MUL.APIN and *RV* I 164, 11 and *AV* IV 35, 4; the same holds for the intercalary months in the real lunar calendar: here Pingree finds that such divisions serve specific purposes in the Babylonian tradition but not in the Vedic

[20]He cites Parpola's *The Sky-Garment*, Helsinki 1985, and *Deciphering the Indus Script*, Cambridge 1994. We too shall ignore Parpola's conjectures.

one—which seems a most astounding statement since any and every calendar serves the very obvious purpose of signalling days and months not only for religious festivals and rituals (in the Vedic culture too) but also for simple routine chronology. Pingree mentions also that in a "later liturgical calendar recorded in a Vedic text" (ie *kauśitakibrāhmaṇa* 19, 2) the practice of reckoning the months from the new moon and of adding an extra month before the New Year is one followed in the Babylonian calendar (p 128); this however can hardly indicate borrowing from Babylon since, as Pingree notes only one paragraph earlier, different Vedic texts reckon months sometimes from the full moon and sometimes from the new moon, exactly as in the MUL.APIN!

38. There is absolutely nothing in Pingree's evidence and arguments to demonstrate a west-eastward movement of influence[21]. His conviction that the Vedic culture is the borrower stems obviously from the AIT and the old mainstream chronologies assigning the *RV* to c 1200, the other Vedas to c 1000 and so on (see n 1, above). Although the MUL.APIN is at the very earliest c 1000, nonetheless Pingree cites evidence of translations into Hittite and Elamite which give us a date in the mid-second millennium. But since we have evidence now that the Aryans are indigenous to Saptasindhu and the *RV* is from before 3100 (and some hymns much earlier), then any similarities must be taken to indicate a westward movement as we saw with other cases. Apart from the aspects discussed in the previous section on Mathematics, an additional consideration is the astronomical references in the *MB* which, as N Achar demonstrated in 2001, belong to the year 3067 (see Kazanas 2002a). If the Aryans were in a position to make such accurate observations at 3067 then they were well ahead of the Mesopotamians in this science and all correspondences that hitherto indicated

[21]It may be that in later times, whether with Buddhist texts of the last centuries BC or with Hindu texts well into the Common Era, India borrowed through Iran (Pingree pp 130ff) but this does not concern us in this paper.

Vedic borrowing, thanks to the warped old chronologies, must now be reversed. Thus, in this sphere again the debtor is Mesopotamia—and § 37 gives additional confirmation. For a scientist's treatment of the Vedic evidence, confirming my view, see S Kak 2003.

39. Oppenheim writes: "both the **peacock** and the chicken passed through [Mesopotamia] on their way westward[;] the Sumerians called the chicken 'the bird from Meluhha' and the Syrians called it the 'Akkadian bird' "(p 317: my square brackets). As we saw earlier (also below), the Mesopotamians called Meluhha the Saptasindhu; so chicken and peacocks came to the Near East from the ISC.

In relation to this, of great interest is the view of B Brentzes which I have been unable to see in its original publication but whose significant part is given by SS Misra (1992). Now Brentzes is an invasionist who found (independently of Oppenheim's statements) some archaeological evidence that links the NE with Saptasindhu: this is the representation of the peacock in Iran and countries of the NE as early as "the late 3rd millennium" in Elam ("two figured poles from Susa with peacock symbols"). It is pointed out that "the earliest examples are known... from Mohenjo-daro and Harappa: two birds sitting on either side of the first tree of life are painted on ceramics" (pp 11-2). The transmission to Syria and Palestine (and Sassanian art in Iran) was ascribed to the Aryans in the NE , Kassites and Mitannis c 1600. And Brentzes concluded : "So we are forced to accept the Indo-Aryans in what is now Iran , especially Eastern Iran before 1600 BC were under the Indian influence for such a long period that they could have taken over the peacock veneration. In that case they could not be part of the Andronovo culture, but should have come to Iran centuries before, at the time when the Hittites came to Anatolia."

Misra comments: "Thus, Brentzes has supplied us with a very important archaeological evidence and he has shown with cogent arguments that Indo-Aryans were in India much before the second half of the 3rd millennium BC and that they moved to Iran and Iraq [=Mesopotamia] from India and influenced them culturally" (1992:13; my square bracket). Albright and Dumont too state that peacocks were exported from India to Mesopotamia at the latest c 750 (1934:106, n 6)[22]. Here now, we have another undoubted case of influence from India to Mesopotamia.

External inter-relations

40. I have shown that as regards the internal evidence of the Indic and Mesopotamian legends the latter is the more likely one to have borrowed from the former. The external inter-relations between the two cultures seems to confirm this likelihood.

CA Hromnik discussed (1981) the Indian influence on sub-Saharan, eastern and southern Africa from early to modern times suggesting that Indians introduced, among other things, the fat-tailed sheep into the region before the 5th cent BC (p 40) and started gold-mining "on and around the south Zambezi plateau" as early as 1000 BC (p 45). R Austen examines maritime trade through the Indian Ocean by means of the *dhow* boat, but only in the period after 150 CE; he refers briefly to some studies dealing with earlier periods (p 12 and 25, n 14) but mentions Hromnik nowhere. Clearly more research is needed in this area. However, early trade-contacts between India and Mesopotamia are well established.

BB Lal presents (1997) ample evidence for products from the ISC found in various sites of Mesopotamia (Ur, Kish, Nippur etc) suggesting that there were trade exchanges from 2600 onwards (182-5). This is significant since

[22]The same two writers state that "wool-bearing trees", ie cotton, from India were planted in Assyria c 700 (1934:108, n 5; also Oppenheim 1977: 94). McEvilley writes, "In Mesopotamia the obelisk of Shalmaneser III (around 860 BC) shows imported Indian elephants" (p 5). These are late attestations, of course.

Mesopotamian literary activity is thought to begin only a little before c 2800, though of course oral tradition would be older. Lal presents ample evidence of Harappan products at Bahrain and Oman in the Persian Gulf and in Tepe Yahya near the South coast of Iran (185-7). All this indicates that there was a sea-route connecting the ISC and southern Mesopotamian. "That there did exist land-routes through which the Harappan objects were disseminated is rather self-evident from the occurrence of etched carnelian beads at Shah Tepe and Hissar [in central and north Iran], in levels ascribable broadly to c 2300-1800 BC" (188). Now on the basis of the Mesopotamian text *Enmerkar and the Lord of Aratta*, H Saggs thinks that "perhaps by 2750 BC direct trading between states, by organised caravans, was taking place" (1989:130). Aratta was "a notable source not only of gold and silver, but also of lapis-lazuli and carnelian" (ibid). Saggs thinks that Aratta contained perhaps Sahr-i-Sokhta (in Afghanistan: ibid). However, D Frawley rightly points out that such identifications are hypothetical and unnecessary since the epic *MB* (VIII 44-5) actually refers to the region Aratta in northwest Punjab (2001:224, 226). So the Mesopotamian text describes trading with a region (kingdom, major city?) in the ISC—definitely at c 1700 and perhaps 2700 (see Saggs, ibid). Lal thinks—tentatively—that the countries Dilmun, Magan and Meluhha, whose ships berthed in Agade (=Akkad) as stated in a document of King Sargon c 2350, correspond to Bahrain, Oman and Saptasindhu (195-7). G Roux on the other hand has little hesitation in accepting these identifications, shown explicitly on the first Map in his book (1992: Maps). Equally certain of this is Harriet Crawford (1994:148). Frawley reminds us that "KD Sethna has shown with much evidence that Meluhha, pronounced 'Melukha", derives from 'Malekha", which is Prakrit for Mleccha" (2001: 227). Lal suggests also that a small community of Harappan merchants might have been established in one or more of the large Mesopotamian cities (1997:192); Crawford also accepts the possibility of such "colonies" (1994:148)[23].

It is not beyond the bounds of possibility, surely, that at this early period, c 2700, and perhaps before,not only material goods but also cultural ideas travelled from Saptasindhu to Mesopotamia.

41. The Hittites were certainly established in central and south-east Anatolia in "the land of Hatti" by 1900 (Gurney 1990:13-5; Dunstan 1998:160-1). It is not clear what and how much of the IE heritage the Hittites brought with them initially because the early centuries of their history are unknown to us. They were conquerors setting up a kingdom (c 1650) that developed into a powerful empire lasting down to c 1180. Yet their mythology (which surfaced in written texts from c 1600) preserved few IE elements. The Hattis, as they were known by their neighbours, retained the names of only 3 gods (Agnis, D-Siu and Inar = V Agni, Dyaus and Indra respectively) and the slaying of the serpent-dragon by Inar and the Weathergod (Kazanas 2001a:§ 4c); the castration of Anu by Kumarbi may be related to or even derived from Indra's slaying Vṛtra and other relevant castration-material

---

[23]On the strength of other modern writings of the 1960's and 1970's McEvilley accepts the establishment of such a colony and even points out that a reciprocal Mesopotamian settlement in India seems to be absent or less prominent (p 240). However, not being content with this situation and, wishing to show that the Mesopotamians were the dominant power commercially and culturally, cites DC Snell (1997:28), who wrote "The ... Mesopotamians had contact with the periphery mainly to trade for or to seize raw materials, and in that contact they may have influenced the people they confronted." True, but Snell does not mention India, and Mesopotamia's "periphery" is (according to the maps McEvilley helpfully provides) the Caucasus in the north, Syria in the west, Arabian desert in the south and Elam and Iran in the east. True, the Mesopotamians showed aggressiveness and seized both raw materials and regions, but their trade with far-distant ISC could only have been peaceful and costly since the latter, rich in natural resources, needed very little or nothing from Mesopotamia (McIntosh 2002:169-172).

(Kazanas 2001b, § VII, 6). Their language may have retained some archaic features but it alone among all the other IE branches lost the feminine gender and all 4 commonest of relation words—'father' (V *pitṛ*, Gk *pater*, Gmc *fadar* etc), 'mother' (V *mātṛ*, Gk *mātēr*, Gmc *mōdor* etc), 'daughter' (V duhitṛ, Gk *thugater*, Gmc *tohter*, etc) and 'son' (V sūnu, Gk *huio-*, Gmc *sun-*); even Tocharian has cognates of all four. Nonetheless, it is possible that the Hittites brought with them much more IE lore which they gradually forgot or altered beyond recognition[24], but some of which found its way into the legendry of neighbouring people. To use T Burrow's judgment of Tocharian, we can say of the Hittite culture that it underwent "profound and far reaching ... changes strongly suggestive of alien influence" since it had "travelled [long and] far from its original home" (1973:10, my square brackets).

Something similar may be said of the Kassites also who came from the east and set up their own kingdom (shortly before or after) c 1600 ruling Mesopotamia for about 400 years. They too brought little IE material as far as can be ascertained from the extant texts but with a significant difference: their language had elements that proved to be of pure Indoaryan provenance and some of their gods and kings had, again, Indoaryan names—like Indaš/Indra, Bugaš/Bhaga, Maruttaš/Marut-as etc (Oppenheim 1977:338).

[24]The myth of the missing god Telepinu may be a fusion of the Vedic myth of Saraṇyū's disappearance and the Mesopotamian myth of fertility-god Dumuzi's death. Unlike Saraṇyū who is daughter of Tvaṣṭṛ and marries the Sungod Vivasvant, Telepinu is masculine and the son of the great Sungod; in the Hittite legend the Sungod gives a feast and invites all the gods and then Telepinu disappears while in *RV* X 17, 1-2 Tvaṣṭṛ gives the feast and Saraṇyū jolts away. Saraṇyū arranges to leave behind her substitute thus seeming to return. Unlike Dumuzi, Telepinu does not die but returns after a period and restores the fertility cycle. These myths are obviously connected with that of Demeter and her daughter Persephone in Greece, but this would take us far from our immediate concern. (For a discussion of the Telepinu-myth see Gurney 152-5; for the text, Pritchard 1958:87-91 and Hoffner 1998:15-20).

A little later another people of a similar Indoaryan descent, the Mitannis, established their own kingdom in North Mesopotamia (and part of today's Syria); they too had some clear Indoaryan linguistic elements and kings' and gods' names (Sutarna/Sutaraṇa, Tušratha/Tveṣaratha, Šuriaš/Sūrya, Maruttaš/Marut-as etc: Burrow 1973:27-9). A highly significant feature here is that under the Kassites' rule in Babylonia, especially under Agum II in early 16th century, there was "a surge of literary invention, collection and recording" (*MM* 47, 229; Heidel 1965:13-4; Roux 1992:251). This might have been a period when new ideas of Vedic descent entered into the Mesopotamian culture and other NE ones.

Conclusion

42. The material discussed in the preceding sections shows that the Vedic Mythological ideas and motifs **have** correspondences in other IE branches and are therefore of PIE provenance. Consequently they cannot be said to be loans from the NE. Different types of evidence suggest that the borrowing was done by the Mesopotamians. I suspect the opposite view prevailed until now because of the wretched AIT and its very recent dates for the Indoaryan culture. Once the AIT is removed and the ISC is seen as a material expression of the anterior Vedic Tradition this problem is also solved. The commercial travels and colonies established by the Indians in Mesopotamia in the 3rd millennium as well as the presence of Kassites and Mitannis (who are linguistically of Indoaryan descent) in the NE show how the east-west influences may have been transmitted. It is also possible that the Indoaryans may have sent civilizing missions much earlier. But, as I said in § 3, we must not rule out the possibility that we have shared elements of a much earlier culture, common to Indians, Mesopotamians and other peoples.

Eight: **Vedic & Egyptian Affinities**

1. Argument. There are more than 20 motifs/themes exhibiting close affinities in the religious texts of the Vedic and Egyptian peoples. Some like the Sungod's boat (§ 11), the Water as a primal cosmogonic element (§ 5), the Cow of plenty (§ 21) and the sacred Bull (§ 22) are common to the Mesopotamian culture too (paper Seven). Some are quite extraordinary and occur only here with some weak echoes in other Indoeuropean branches: the lotus-born one § 3, the eye running off § 4, etc, including many elements in the famous Isis-Osiris tale § 16-18. These affinities are close and suggest either a common origin for both cultures or cross influences. However, most of the motifs, including the Isis-Osiris and Yama tales, have correspondences in other IE[1] traditions: this

---

1 Abbreviations.

AB = *Aitareya Brāhmaṇa*; *AU* = *Aitareya Upaniṣad*; *BD* = *Book of the Dead*; Bibl = Bibliography; cent = century; *CT* = *Coffin Texts*; *CU* = *Chāndogya Upaniṣad*; *GEL* = See Bibl; *GM* = See Bibl; *GPA* = See Bibliography; *IE* = *IndoEuropean*; ISC = Indus Sarasvati (=old 'Indus Valley') Civilization; *JIES* = *Journal of Indo-European Studies* in Bibl; *KU* = *Kaṭha Upaniṣad*; L = Latin; Lth = Lithuanian; *MM* = See Bibl; *MSD* = See Bibl; *MU* = *Muṇḍaka Upaniṣad*; NE = Near East(ern); par(s) = paragraph(s) within a section/spell of, eg, *PT*; *PIE* = ProtoIndoEuropean; *PT* = *Pyramid Texts*; S = Sanskrit; *ŚB* = *Śatapatha Brāhmaṇa*; *TB* = *Taittirīya Brāhmaṇa*; *TS* = *Taittirīya Saṃhitā* (of the Black Yajur Veda); *TU* = *Taittirīya Upaniṣad* ; *VI* = See Bibl; *VS* = *Vājasaneyī Saṃhitā* (of the White Yajur Veda).

Helps to the reader.

sign § = section or paragraph in this study, unless other; sign [...] = square brackets indicating my own intervention in citations; sign > = becomes; sign < = derives from.

fact suggests that the motifs are inherited in the Vedic texts and not borrowed from Egypt. Thus we must conclude either that Saptasindhu, the land of the Vedic people, influenced Egypt or that both cultures derive or borrow from a third unknown one. The former case is difficult to determine as there is no firm evidence for an early contact between Egypt and Saptasindhu. Consequently, without entirely ruling out the possibility of Vedic influences on Egyptian culture, we must assume a devolution from an older unknown civilization (§ 30ff).

2. Introductory. Direct connexions between India and Egypt are not attested in any period before Hellenistic times, in other words, before Alexander's thrust into NW India in 328 which thereafter opened up traffic between India and Egypt. In fact, direct maritime trade between India and Egypt is attested only in the second half of the 1st cent BC—after Hippalus discovered the periodic changes of the Indian monsoons (Miller 1998). This was through the port Berenike, founded by the Ptolemies in the 3rd century and later used extensively by the Romans; it was located on the Egyptian Red Sea coast, about 500 miles south of Suez. We may conjecture that, much earlier, after reaching eastern Africa by c 1000 (if Hromnik 1981 is correct), Indian merchants sailed north, along the African coast, then along the south coast of Arabia, then through the straits of Aden and up into the Red Sea; for this there is, of course, no textual or archaeological attestation. It is well attested that there were Indian communities in Egypt in Roman times (Sedlar 1980:81). Indeed, these may go back several centuries to the period when Indians served as soldiers in the Persian armies that conquered Egypt in 525 in the reign of Cambyses. Even earlier (long before Buddhist, Jain and Ājīvika mendicants wandered so far in the west, according to McEvilley's extravagant conjectures, 2002), some Mitannis and Kassites, apart from the princesses who married Tuthmosis IV and Amenhotep III, could have come into Egypt in the mid-second millennium. Earlier still, the Hyksos 'rulers-of-foreign-lands', who invaded Egypt c 1670 and established in the north region Dynasties 15 and 16, may have been Indoaryans (David 1993:145), but this is uncertain. We may even hypothesize that the Indian merchants, who had established their colonies in Mesopotamia in the Sargonic period c 2300 or even c 2400, could have driven caravans accross the Arabian desert to Egypt.[2]

However, all these considerations, apart from being largely hypothetical, suffer from a major drawback and cannot explain the undoubted similarities of more than twenty religious ideas, themes and motifs in the Indian and Egyptian cultures. Even if all the early contacts are shown to have actually taken place, they are too late. At the latest, the first *Pyramid Texts* are dated c 2400-2350 but they are at this time so developed and evidently so taken for granted by the Egyptians that we must allow them several generations up to 200 years and perhaps more. This brings us to c 2550, the date when the very earliest Indo-Mesopotamian contacts are evidenced. Now, although Osiris himself is not attested epigraphically before c 2450, goddess Hathor is and consequentlly Horus (Hart 1995:14). Thus some version of the Osiris-Isis-Horus legend was current in early dynastic times c 3000-2700. The early Vedic texts, including the early Brāhmaṇas belong to a period before 2800, and the *RV* well before 3100. Consequently, Egyptian ideas could have influenced early Vedic concepts only if there had been contacts at c 3200, and Vedic ideas could have influenced Egyptian concepts through contacts at c 2800. In the present

---

[2]Various artefacts from the ISC found in Egypt (and indeed Cyprus and Crete) and assigned to the late 3rd millennium are too meagre and do not necessarily suggest direct trade-exchanges. Even McEvilley admits that the extant archaeological evidence (some mummies at Lothal and cotton sheets in Egypt) for Indo-Egyptian direct contacts is inadequate and resorts to similarities of ideas (pp 259-260), most of which are so tenuous and implausible that I have not examined them.

state of our knowledge, we must rule out any significant contacts before 2400.

In these circumstances all we can (speculatively) state is that Indic ideas could have influenced Egyptian concepts contained in texts later than the PT—the *Coffin Texts* perhaps and, more certainly, the *Book of the Dead*. But here we meet two difficulties. First, many concepts in the *CT*, *BD* and other literature, are demonstrably copies or developments of concepts already largely present in the *PT*. Second, most of the significant Egyptian parallels to Vedic concepts are found in the *PT*. Before going any further, let us examine the major correspondences.

Here also, as I did with Vedic-Mesopotamian cross influences (paper Seven), I shall seek IE parallels for the Vedic motifs. Wherever such IE parallels are found, then the Vedic motif should be taken to be inherited from the PIE period and therefore not (necessarily) indebted to the Egyptian culture.

Mythological Parallels

3. The Lotus-born one is an extraordinary and, as far as I know, unique motif, common to both cultures.

In *PT* 264 Sungod Re rises with a gleaming lotus flower at his nostril. In *CT* 197 this "redolent flower" is identified with Re, the great god within the flower, and worshipped as god Nefertum in Memphis (Hart, 16). In the iconography the child Sungod rises out of the lotus-flower (Hart 16; Silverman 31).

In the Vedic tradition, long before the legend of Brahmā, Creator-god, arising from the lotus on Viṣṇu's navel, as the latter lay on the serpent Śeṣa on the Primeval Ocean, in the *Ṛgveda* we meet at least twice the lotus-blossom as a matrix. First, hymn VI 16, 13 says that Agni is brought forth by rubbing from within the lotus in the sky: this is probably an image for the flash of lightning. Second, VII 33, 11 says that the great seer Vasiṣṭha is born from a lotus upon which the gods placed the sperm-drop (*drapsa*) of Mitra-Varuṇa by means of the divine holy-power (*brâhmaṇā*). Agni, the Firegod, is of course often identified with the sun; this theme continues in the Yajurveda texts (eg *VS* XI 29; *TS* V 2, 6, 5) and *ŚB* VII 4, 1, 8-9 and X 5, 2, 6. The motif of the child and the lotus is found again in the *VS* II 33 (the boy wreathed with lotuses).

A somewhat different tale comes from the Irish Celts: here, king Math and his magician counsellor Gwydion conjure out of the oak-flowers the maid Blodeuedd (=she of the flowers) who becomes the wife (unfaithful later) of Lleu, the bright hero (Rees 1995:50-51)[3]. In Scandinavia, three gods, Odin, Vili and Ve, raised out of an ash-tree and an elm the first pair of human beings, Ask and Embla (Crossley-Holand 1993:5). In Greece, Aphrodite, born of the sea-foam out of the blood of the genitals of Ouranos, is said in a later variant legend to have sprung from a scallop- or cockle-shell (Kerényi 1982: 70); but another old legend says she is daughter of Zeus (or Ouranos) and Dionē, the goddess within the oak-tree (GM 50). Then in Hesiod's *Works and Days* (144-5) the third race of men spring out of ash-trees. Obviously, the idea of a flower-born or tree-born deity or human is not uncommon in IE mythology, even if the lotus is confined to the Indoaryan branch.

4. The Creator's eye running off is, for me, an even more startling mythologem.

The *Puruśa Sūkta* (*RV* I, 90, 13) says that from the eye of universal Man was generated the sun and from his mind the moon. In many *RV* hymns we read that the sun is the eye of gods: of Viṣṇu in his third stride, I 22, 20; of Varuṇa I 50, 6; of Mitra (and Varuṇa) I 115, 1, VI 51, 1, etc. In VII 77, 3, Uṣas, the Dawngoddess, is said to bring the eye of the gods and lead on the beautiful white horse. In the Funeral hymn X 16, 3 the eye of the dead man goes to the sun. In *AB* III 2 we read "The eye comes into existence first when man comes into

[3]See also paper Seven: § 2.

existence" and gets perfected with reciting a hymn to Mitra-Varuṇa. In *Kauṣītaki Br* 29, 1 we read this curious passage: "they say 'The eye came; it was a serpent; thus did poison come to the priests; he [ie the priest] used these (verses) connected with (Soma) the purifying, and repelling poison, in praise'." There are many other images and motifs regarding the eye in the Yajur Veda (White and Black) but the most relevant one is in *ŚB* XIII 3, 1, 1-2: here, the eye of creator-god Prajāpati swells, falls out and becomes the horse; by means of the Aśvamedha, the horse-sacrifice, during which a horse is let loose to wander then is brought back (cf *RV* VII 77, 3 above), the gods restore it to its original place and thus Prajāpati becomes complete again. This passage is repeated almost verbatim in *TS* V 3, 12. In several places in this Saṃhitā of the Black Yajurveda the eyes are connected with the sacrificial rite (I 1, 13; II 6, 2; VI 1, 5; 4, 10 etc).

In the Scandinavian tradition the Vanir cut off wise Mimir's head and sent it to the Aesir, who preserved it and lord Odin gave it power of speech for prophesying. Thus far we have the familiar IE theme "the severed head", like that of Celtic Bendigeidfran's head, Greek Orpheus's head, and Vedic Dadhyañc's head. Then, to gain additional wisdom, Lord Odin placed his eye as a pledge on Mimir's well (*Edda*, 17). Here we have again an eye that is removed and, since it is given as a pledge only, may return to Odin, the All-father. In Greece, again, Lamia, beautiful daughter of king Belus (son of god Poseidon and Libya), had the gift of *removing and replacing her eyes at will*—a gift bestowed on her by Zeus; later she became a terrible blood-sucking, child-eating demonness, *emp(o)usa* (*GM* 205, 189; *GEL*). Thus the motif can be said to be IE. (For more one-eyed figures in IE legendry, like the Greek Cyclops, Vedic Rudra, Irish Cu Chulainn, etc, see Das 2002 with references.)

The Eye of Horus appears frequently in the *PT*, the eye which Seth damaged during their fighting and was restored by Thoth's wisdom. This is identified with the Solar Eye repeatedly. The mythologem under discussion appears in CT 80 and in later texts: Atum speaking says, "the human beings who came forth from my eye which I sent out while I was alone with Nu in lassitude". Commenting on this TR Clark writes: "Initially God seems to have had only one Eye—a mysterious entity which is separable ... and is sent out ... to seek Shu and Tefnut who ... are lost in the immensity of the Abyss. The Eye finds them and brings them back to their father who proceeds to regenerate them as the life and order of the universe" (pp 45-7). A slightly different version appears in a later text (*Bremner Rhind Papyrus*, with material from c 1200): "My Eye followed them [ie Shu and Tefnut] for many ages,/they departed from me ... they brought back my Eye with them./ Whereupon I rejoined my limbs. I wept over them—/and thus mankind came into existence from the tears that sprang from my Eye./ Then it became enraged against me, when it returned and saw/that I had put another in its place,/replacing it with a brighter one" (Clark, 91). Then the Eye is transformed into a cobra on God's forehead—as it does on the Pharaoh's forehead defending him (ibid, 92). There are other variants and details but I would stress the separation of the Eye and its return making the High God whole again; also its identification with the Sun (*CT*, 342: Clark, 95-6).

In both traditions the Eye seems to represent the sun and the Creator's vision of the whole world. In both it gets detached then is brought back and the Creator is made whole again. The Vedic texts present the Eye as a poisonous serpent (=the "evil eye") to be repelled through praise and the purifying power of Soma that brings a transformation in the priests; in the Egyptian text it gets enraged then transformed into a cobra and placed on the forehead. Some scholars regard the aśvamedha-sacrifice as the (annual) renewal of the sun (Kak 2002a:51-2). The similarities are many and close.

5. Water is a primal source in the Heliopolitan cosmogony of Egypt (David 2002:81ff; Lesko 1991:88ff)).

Out of and in this unlimited Water, Nun 'father of the gods', arose Atum/Re who engendered Shu and Tefnut, then came the other gods and the Cosmos.

In the Veda, the One indescribable Source of all is not water but That One *tad ekam* (*RV* X, 129). But water appears as the celestial ocean which surrounds earth in several *RV* hymns (III, 1, 12; VII, 49, 3; etc), and X, 121, 7-9 mentions 'high waters' *āpaḥ ... bṛhatīḥ*, perhaps symbolizing the state of unmanifest energy (=*tamas*, *salila*, *tuchya* in X, 129, 3) from which manifestations arise. *AV* XII, 1, 8 says that the Earth *pṛthivī* is floating upon the water-flood *arṇava* and that she herself was originally *salila* (=water? fluctuating energy?) However, another view is given in *RV* X 82, 5-6. Here, in st 5, the Waters *āpaḥ* received the 'first seed' *gárbham prathamám* (but we are not told whence) and in them "all the gods saw one another". Then, in st 6, the gods are said to 'come all together' *samagachanta* therein. The implication is that at this cosmogonic stage the gods are all united/combined within the Waters (or within the "primary seed" in the Waters) and then emerge as separate individualities[4]. So, here, the parallel to the Egyptian concept is fairly close. But later texts say that "Verily, in the beginning this [world] was water" (*ŚB* XI 1, 6, 1).

However, this theme also is IE. In Greece, Homer records an old tradition that Ōkeanos (=Ocean) is the primal progenitor of gods (*Iliad* 14, 200; cf also 14, 244) and surrounds the world on the shield of Achilles (ibid: 18, 607). This idea may, as some claim, come from NE sources. But a similar concept is found in the Scandinavian *Edda* (pp 10-11): here, "at the beginning of time, when nothing was" except

[4]Here Th McEvilley brings in Mesopotamian and Egyptian creation myths and finds that the "waters wherein all gods are gathered together ... is a forbear of Anaximander's Infinite in which opposites lie mingled" (p 302). This may be true in a sense, but the rigvedic gods are not exactly "opposites" and in the *RV* hymn, st 6, the seed, the water and gods and all other things, arise from and rest upon the navel of the Unborn One *ajásya nābhau*.

"the mighty gap" Ginnugagap, the celestial rivers (see parallel with the *RV*, § 25) flowed into this "gap" or "void", became ice (natural in that northern region) and thence arose Ymir, the cosmic person from whose dismemberment all the creatures were produced. Then in Celtic myths, Manannán is son of the Ocean (Lyr) and himself god of the sea(s) spawning offspring everywhere and giving immortality to the gods (Crossley-Holland, p 189; Rees, pp 31, 39, 139).

In Mesopotamia, cosmogony began when Apsu 'freshwater' and Tiamat 'seawater' mingled (*MM* 233).

6. Creator's seed-spilling. The *PT* 527 says that Atum proceeded to masturbate and from his ejaculation were born Shu and Tefnut. This act, *CT* spell 152 says, happened while Atum was still in the Water-abyss and *CT* 80 explains that Shu is Life and Tefnut is Order. In another text (*PT* 600) Atum spits out Shu and coughs out Tefnut, but this we put aside.

In *RV* I 71, 8 we read that "When *tejas* (=energy, heat, lustre) filled the Lord of men for increase, Dyaus (=the Skygod) laid down the bright seed (*śuci rétas*) that was spilt"; with this Agni created a host of youths (the Aṅgirases or Maruts). This motif of seed-spilling, sometimes combined with incest, is fairly frequent in post-rigvedic texts (eg *AB* III, 33-4; *ŚB* VII, 5, 2).

7. Separation of heaven and earth. Writes Clark: "Shu is both light and air, and as the offspring of God he is manifest life. As light he separates the earth from the sky and as air he upholds the sky vault" (p 45). Indeed, in *CT* IV, 235, Shu himself addresses Atum-Re saying "I am that star which came forth... I am that space which came about in the waters, I came into being in them, I grew in them". This is how manifestation comes about together with the separation of sky and earth. Shu and Tefnut generate the next pair Nut and Geb, Sky (fem) and Earth (masc). It was thereafter the function of Shu (with the help of 8 spirits) to keep Sky and Earth apart—who, it is hinted in some spells, were in an incestuous sexual union, or perhaps formed an androgyne, a bisexual entity.

Here Vedic Indra resembles Shu. True, he does much more than the Egyptian god but he covers perfectly Shu's three attributes or functions. In the *RV* several gods are said to hold up the sky (Agni IV 6, 2; Varuṇa and Mitra V 62, 3 and VI 70, 1; etc), but Indra is both aerial and solar. He generates heaven and earth (VIII 36, 4) and stretches them apart (VIII 3, 6). He supports heaven (III 49, 4; etc) filling all space between earth and heaven (IV 16, 5; etc) and this is his aerial aspect—in that he occupies *antarikṣa* the atmosphere and in that he has Vāyu, the wind-deity, for his car (IV 16, 5). In his solar aspect he generates the Dawn (III 31, 5; etc) and the Sun (II 12, 7) and, indeed, is the Sun Sūrya (IV 26, 1; etc) naturally dispelling darkness with his brightness (VI 17, 5). He is also called *Savitṛ* the one who impels life and action (II 30, 1) and "Lord of all that moves and breathes" (*viśvasya jágataḥ prāṇataś pátiḥ* I 101, 5). Indra is an IE deity (Das 2002; paper Three).

In other IE legendry there is no clear account of the separation of sky and earth. Only in Hesiod's *Theogony* Earth and Ouranos (=Skygod) mingle and generate gods, then separate; and then Kronos, one of their children, castrates Ouranos who subsequently fades out of the picture (White: 866-944). In the same work, Atlas supports the sky standing at the western borders of the earth (White 116).

PT spell 509 mentions "the ramparts of Shu". One of Shu's symbols is "the four pillars of heaven" (Budge 1988:148); spell 76 of the *CT* says that Shu "bound together the ladder of Atum" and made eight *ḥeḥ* (=supporting divine spirits) "from the emanation of his limbs" to hold up "the chambers of the sky" (Lesko, 94). Indra suports the luminaries in heaven (I, 6, 1-3) and has the group of 8 Vasus (VII 10, 4 and 35, 6) as well as the Maruts for assistants (V 42, 6) but also Soma in supporting heaven with a pillar *skambha* (IX 74, 2); the Sun (with whom Indra is identified) also holds heaven and earth in place "with imperishable pillars" *ajárebhiḥ skámbhanebhiḥ* (I, 160, 4).

8. Eight divinities is an unusual group-number but we find them in both cultures.

We met above, the 8 *ḥeḥ* who helped Shu support the sky in the Heliopolitan theology. The cosmogonic version from Hermopolis in the south has creating agents which are 8 spirits of the primeval Abyss of Nun—the Ogdoad. In *PT* 301 only two pairs are mentioned but later texts give four pairs (Lesko, 35; Clark 55).

In the Vedic tradition also we have a group of 8 vasus (=the bright ones) connected with light and Agni. Here the names, which appear in post-Vedic texts (see MSD under vasu), are of no significance and no rigvedic mythologem relates to them. But there are also the 8 ādityas, sons of Mother Goddess *Aditi*. These are sometimes 6 (*RV* II 27, 1) and once 7 (IX 114, 3) but the later Vedic texts make them 12 and identify them with the months. The hymn *AV* VIII 9, 21 and the *TB* also give them as 8—Mitra, Varuṇa, Aryaman, Indra, Bhaga and so on; of the eighth one, Vivasvan or Mārtāṇḍa (=the Sungod) we shall speak anon. Here Aditi and Nun correspond.

In *PT* 301 the two pairs Niu and Nenet and Amun and Amaunet are said to protect the gods (see also Lesko 1991: 94). In *RV* II 27, 4 the Ādityas support what moves and stands and protect the whole world and the god-power itself *asurya*.

Since the number eight is not found much in significant motifs in other IE mythologems (Gk, Gmc etc) here we may assume an independent development in both cultures.

9. The Cosmic Egg is another interesting motif—appearing also in Greek Orphism. The Ogdoad swimming in the primordial Ocean Nun created, according to the Hermopolitan tradition, an egg from which sprang the Creator-god. There are different versions of the tale in different spells and in one of them (*CT* 223) it is closely linked with Shu as air and light: "I am that egg which was in the Great Primeval One [=Nun], I am the keeper of that great support that separates Geb from Nut." Other references to the Egg are present in the *CT* (eg 714) and the *BD* (eg 85). In *PT* 408 the speaker (=pharaoh) requests that "you two... may give birth to me, who am in the egg". It is not said who the two are nor whether it is the Cosmic Egg; but we can assume that here the King identifies himself with Shu or Re breaking out of the egg.

In *RV* X 72, 9 Aditi brings the eighth Āditya last: he is *Mārtāṇḍa* 'sprung from a dead egg' that is Vivasvan or the Setting Sun who will be reborn anew, for the life and death of other creatures too. Hymn X 121, 1 says that in the beginning [of manifest creation] rose Hiraṇyagarbha 'the golden embryo', the one manifest Lord of what came to be. A later passage in *ŚB* XI 1, 6, 1-2, says: "Verily, in the beginning this [world] was water... The waters desired a way to be reproduced... When they were heated up a golden egg was produced... In a year's time... Prajāpati [=Lord of creatures, Creator-god] was produced therein... He broke open this egg...".

The Mesopotamian culture has no trace of a Cosmic Egg. We find one only in Orphism in Greece, but since this appears in texts of the fifth century and after and since it does not appear in other IE traditions (Slavic, Germanic etc), there can be no certainty that this motif belongs to the IE heritage; the Greeks could have borrowed it from Egypt. On the other hand, since the name *Orpheus* is cognate with Vedic ṛbhu (and Germanic 'elf') and the severed head (of Orpheus) is also an IE motif, perhaps the Cosmic Egg is part and parcel of the general Orphic mythology and so an inherited motif. RB Onians cites the Finnish *Kalevala* where the cosmic Egg is thrust upon the waves by Watermother Ilmatar (1988:177). The difficulty here does not seem insoluble. No early direct contacts are attested between the Finnish and the Greek or Egyptian peoples. But Finno-Ugrian has many loanwords from Vedic (V *nāma*, F *nime* 'name'; V *udhar*, F *utar*, Mordwin odar, Čeremis *vodar* 'udder'; V *svasar*, F *sisar*, Mord *sazor* Čer *šužar* 'sister'; V *vasana*, Hungarian *vaszon* 'garment, cloth'; V *surā*, Hung *sör* 'strong drink'; V *chāga*, Mord *śeja* 'goat'; V *śata*, F *sata*, Lapp *cuotte*, Mord *śaco* '100'; etc: all from Burrow, 1973: 23-7, who writes of the Indo-Iranian common period following the Aryan Immigration/ Invasion Theory)[5]. So I am inclined to think that the Finns borrowed the 'cosmic egg' from the Veda.

10. The sun-bird. We have just mentioned *Mārtāṇḍa* who, in the Veda is the sun about to set and then be reborn next day "for procreation and death" (*prajāyai mṛtyā́ve*: *RV* X 72, 9)—his own as well as other creatures'. In VII 63, 5 the sun is likened to a flying falcon; in V 47, 3 he is called a bright-red bird (cf also I, 164, 14 and 26; also X, 123 and 177). This motif may be IE since we find an echo of it in the Celtic tradition in Ireland, where the "bright hero" Lleu (possibly the older Britannic Lugh, god of light) flies in the sky as an eagle (§ 71).

In Egypt, Atum is essentially unmanifest and manifests as the Sungod Re, appearing under many names and titles (for morning, midday and late afternoon); in this he is called *Kheprer*, or *Khepri* the one who crawls accross the sky and is signified by the scarab hieroglyph (Clark, 41; Silverman 1991:36-7). Like Mārtāṇḍa who is also the skybird (born out of the dead egg), Atum as Re manifests as the Bennu-bird Phoenix (dying and being reborn) to herald the visible creation (Clark, 37, 39, 79; Hart 1995:16-7).

This image may be an instance of independent indigenous development in both traditions.

11. The Sungod's boat. In Egypt the theme of Re travelling accross the sky in a boat is a major and complex one. Other gods are also in the boat, especially the Heliopolitan ones (Isis, Osiris and so on) and the soul of the

---

[5]This Theory has bedevilled Indology since about 1850. Some other scholars and myself have been arguing against this theory (known as AIT) positing 4500 as the very latest possible date, if that, and a *RV* in the early 4th millennium BC; the Iranians moved out of Saptasindhu into their historical habitat and so, perhaps did the other IE branches (see § 31).

devotee often aspires to embark on it. Otherwise, both Mesopotamian and Vedic texts have it and it was examined in paper Seven § 21. In *RV* VII 88, 3-4 sage Vasiṣṭha sails with Varuṇa in the god's boat; *RV* VI 58, 3 shows god Pūṣan, the glowing aspect of the Sun, to sail in the sky-ocean with his fleet of golden ships; and *AV* XVII, 1, stanzas 25, 26 have the Sungod moving with his 100-oared boat. The motif appears also in Greece (paper Seven: § 21; Onians 1998:255).

12. The enemy serpent threatening or upsetting the natural order is a worldwide motif: it is part of the mythologem 'god/hero slays serpent/monster', common to almost all IE branches—and to Mesopotamia.

In Egypt several texts, *PT, CT, BD, Book of Am-Duat* (Hart, p 54; Hornung 1999:38) etc, refer to Re who has to fight and overcome the hostile Serpent "the Slippery One" in his journey through night. The motif is depicted frequently in the iconography of tombs and the vignettes of papyrus-texts.

In the Veda the hostile serpent/dragon, embodying darkness or evil, is represented preeminently by Vrtra whom Indra slays and releases the waters. It is a very common theme and will not detain us in IE traditions (Apollo against Tuphoeus, Thor against Midgar-serpent, etc). But it has two other aspects that deserve some attention—as below.

13. The Fair Enchantress. Spell *CT* 154 says that once the Serpent surprised Re and ensnared him by assuming the form of a fair curly-haired maiden. No further details are given but this (lost) legend belongs obviously to the genre of the enchantress or temptress. This motif probably belongs to a world-wide motif: we find it both in Mesopotamia and in the Vedic culture. In *Gilgamesh* the wild man Enkidu is created by goddess Aruru out of a divine image infused into clay to be a match for king Gilgamesh.The king hears of the wild man's existence and sends a harlot to seduce him which she accomplished thoroughly over a week (*MM* 56). In the Vedic Tradition, in both epics (*MBh* III, 110-3, and *Rāmāyaṇa* I, 65, 16) a young seer Ṛśyaśṛṅga is seduced by a whore for different reasons and in different circumstances. But much earlier, in *RV* I.179 Lopāmudrā eventually seduces her aging husband Agastya who would not respond to her approach while in *RV* X, 10, Yamī attempts but fails to seduce her brother Yama.Thus the theme is well attested in Indic texts.

14. The wise, creative Serpent. In Egyptian texts, the Serpent was originally an aspect of the High God co-existing with him in the Waters of Nun. *PT* par 1146 says "I am the Provider-of-Attributes, serpent with many coils" and *CT* IV 321 says "I bent right round myself, I was encircled in my coils, one who made a place for himself in the midst of his coils". *BD* spell 175 says that Atum will destroy all that he has created and will become again "the Old Serpent who knew no man and saw no god." Another text, the *Bremner Rhind Papyrus*, says that the High God created snakes and worms in the Primeval Waters (Clark, 91); this is supported by *CT* 98 which says that these were formed in the Creator's eye and represent the original forms of the morning stars.

In the Vedic texts there is no such cosmogonic Serpent. On the other hand, there must have been a complex legend about a divine, benevolent Serpent *ahi*. In the *RV* there are several references to a deity *ahi budhnya* who is born in and rests at the bottom of the waters (VII 34, 16). It is generally agreed that the waters are celestial or atmospheric and that Ahi Budhnya is an aerial deity. It should be noted that Agni in the midair is called a raging *ahi* (I, 79, 1). Ahi Budhnya is probably the basis for the post-Vedic thousand-headed Śeṣa which lies on the Waters and upon which rests Viṣṇu. But there are several intermediate references. A notable reference occurs in *AV* hymn VIII 10, 29: it mentions a serpent deity *Takṣaka* 'fashioner/creator'. Then, we find oblations offered to serpent deities (eg *VS* I 5, 4; etc) and the striking statement "the serpents are these worlds" when *ŚB* VII 4, 1, 25ff explains the Sarpanāma (=Serpent-names) formulas. So there could well have been a complex Serpent mythologem now lost; even so, the surviving details show many correspondences with the Egyptian motifs.

The serpent/snake is of course a common motif in the IE traditions.

15. Creation through the Word. The Egyptian texts speak of creation taking place through the Word and sound—a doctrine taken up early by the Judaic tradition where in *Genesis* God creates the worlds by speaking. *CT* spell IV 321 which mentions the Serpent and its coils together with Atum adds that the High God devised "the utterance" whereby manifestation will come about. But a more complete description is in the Memphis Theology where god Ptah is the mighty Great One who created all gods through speech and pronounced the names of all things (Lesko 1991:95-6).

The idea of creating through the Word is, of course, prominent in the Vedic tradition. In *ŚB* XI 1, 6, 3, when Prajāpati emerged from the Cosmic Egg, he spoke: the sound *bhūḥ* became the earth; the sound *bhuvaḥ* became the atmosphere; the sound *svaḥ* became the sky. In *VS* III 1, 1 Prajāpati creates different classes of creatures through desire, penance and speech. And *RV* I 164, 35: *brahmā́yaṃ vācáḥ paramáṃ vyóma* 'this holy-power is the highest heaven of Vāk, [goddess of] Speech'. This *śabdabrahman*, or this Logos doctrine, as it is generally known (from John's Gospel I, 1), acquires great prominence in the Upaniṣads and post-Vedic literature. But Vāk, the deity of Speech, is already quite prominent in the *RV* (X, 71 and 125; VIII, 100, 10-11; I, 164, 35).

16. Osiris-Asura and Yama. While the name of Osiris *ausir/wsir* and Vedic *asura* have phonetic resemblance , it is impossible to find any Vedic *asura*, god or demon[6], who

---

[6]Initially the word *asura* meant 'lord, high-god' but later (even in the later hymns of the *RV*) it came to denote a demonic being. It is connected with *Ahura* 'Lord' in Iranian and perhaps with *Aesir* (plural), the gods in the Scandinavian lore.

resembles Osiris in the slightest: none of them is killed and reborn to become King in the realm of the dead. However, there are striking similarities between Osiris and Yama.

1) Yama is the son of Vivasvat (=aspect of the Sungod) and Saraṇyū (*RV* X, 17, 1), daughter of Tvaṣṭṛ, a god who shapes forms (*RV* I, 188, 9; etc).

2) He has a twin sister Yamī who approaches him erotically wanting to have his child but is repulsed (*RV*, X, 10; see above § 13).

3) There are two more twins, the horse-deities Aśvins. The later texts *Nirukta* and *Bṛhaddevatā* tell how Saraṇyū disappeared after the birth of Yama and Yamī taking the form of a mare but Vivasvat found her, became a stallion, mounted her and thus were born the Aśvins. (A fifth brother, Manu, survivor of the flood, can be disregarded for the purposes of our comparison here.)

4) Yama dies. The Vedic texts give no details but one hymn suggests that he gave up his body in some sacrificial act for the sake of the gods (*RV* X, 13, 4).

5) In *Maitrayaṇī Saṃhitā* I, 5, 12, Yamī mourns her brother and is unable to forget him. (Time was then one endless day [=eternity?].)

6) The gods create night so that Yamī can forget, and she does so as 'tomorrow' *svastana* comes about [=measured, linear time?].

7) Yama is the first mortal to find the path to immortality (*RV* X, 14, 1-2) and become King of the dead in heaven.

8) He has two dogs *śabala* 'brindled' and *śyāma* 'black' (*AV* VIII, 1, 9) who guard the path and watch the dead who come to his realm (*RV* X, 14, 10-12).

9) He and the gods drink together beside a tree in *RV* X, 135, 1.

Now, the Osiris legend has affinities with every one of these nine points. But before indicating them, I should stress that Yama is a thoroughly IE figure. His name appears as Yima in the Iranian Avesta where he is king of an underworld paradise; in later Iranian texts he has a twin sister Yimeh and from their union emerge the first humans. As 'Ymir' the name appears also in the Scandinavian *Edda*, where he, as a Cosmic Person, is dismembered by gods and his parts become parts of the world. His mother *Saraṇyū* appears in the Mycenaean religion as *Erinus* and in later Greek legendry as the Arcadian *Erinus* (Kazanas 2001a and Paper Three). The latter was goddess Demeter in the form of a mare trying to eschew Poseidon's erotic harassment but he became a stallion and from their union were born a noble horse and a daughter (Kazanas 2001a:283; also paper Three). In Greek legend we also find the two pairs of twins one of the females being beautiful *Helenē* (Helen of Troy) whose name also may be cognate with *Saraṇyū*. Her two brothers, Castor and Poludeukes, are semi-divine heroes, sons of Zeus, who save people from shipwreck and aid their sister when she is in danger; one of them is expert with horses—like the Aśvins. Then, just as the Aśvins accompany Sūryā, the Sungod's daughter to her wedding, so the (Sky-)god's sons *Dievo Sūnelai*, in the Baltic tradition, save from drowning the Sunmaiden and escort her to safety. The twins and the horse-motif appear also in Slavic, Germanic and Celtic myths. The only major motif missing in the other IE branches, except Iranian, is Yama's kingship in the realm of the dead. Even in this area, the Greeks have a detail, if the name of the watchdog *Kerberos* in Hades is cognate with Yama's dog *śabala*.

17. In the corresponding Egyptian cult, Osiris is indeed the king in the realm of the dead and the Foremost of the Westerners, ie of those who enter the Afterlife or Netherworld in the Western Horizon (*PT* pars 759, 1298). Like Saraṇyū, his grandmother Tefnut ran away from her brother-husband Shu and her father Atum and disappeared in the Primeval Waters so that Atum sent his Eye to find her (§ 4). Then, there are the two deities, Wepwaet, the wolf-god opener of the path, and Anubis, the jackal-headed god, who escorts the dead to the Judgment Hall. But there are four major differences:

a) Osiris is a vegetation-god as well, connected with the Nile inundation and the rejuvenation of the plants. Here, there may be a remote affinity with the tree where Yama and the gods meet and drink (above, point 9).

b) Osiris does marry his twin sister Isis and, after she recovers and revivifies his corpse, she conceives their son Horus. Here, we have some intriguing details. It may be, as Macdonell suggests on the basis of the Iranian legend (1898:173), that in the original IE tale brother and sister did unite but that the rigvedic seers innovated and cleared Yama of the guilt of incest; this is supported by the fact that in *RV* X, 135, 1, Yama is addressed as "our father", which, unless it is a mere metaphor, implies that Yama had as his progeny the human race—a fact acknowledged in later texts (eg *TS* VI, 5, 6, 2). But the use of metaphor is very common. On the other hand, neither Osiris nor Horus are in any Egyptian text said to generate mankind.

c) There is no equivalent of Seth, the evil brother, nor of Nephthys, another sister, in the Vedic legend.

d) Osiris is King in the Netherworld and represents the night-aspect of the Sungod, whose creative day-aspect is Re, while Yama is king of the dead in the luminous and highest region (*RV* X, 14, 8; IX, 113, 7-9; also *AV* IX, 5, 1-8; XI, 4, 11; XVIII, 4, 3) and is clearly connected with the radiant day-aspect of the sun (*RV* I, 83, 5 and 163, 1-3). Here, points 5 and 6, above, bring in the creation of night and 'tomorrow' in the Veda. This motif seems to be connected with the Osiris legend, for *BD* spell 17 has Atum, identifying with Re ("I was Atum... I was Re...") say, "To me belongs yesterday, I know tomorrow"; here the gloss adds, "What does it mean? As for yesterday, that is Osiris [;] as for tomorrow, that is Re".

18. An additional link at this juncture is provided by Varuṇa. Apart from the Sun and Agni, Yama is closely associated with this god too. Thus they are both the horse in *RV* I, 163, 3-4, which is also the sun; then, on reaching heaven, the dead see these two kings, Yama and Varuṇa together (*RV* X, 14, 7).

Varuṇa is not only the High God of moral order. Often in conjunction with Mitra, he is also connected with the sun (*RV* I, 24, 8; VII, 87, 1-5; etc) and the seasons and months (I, 25, 8; VII, 66, 11). Streams, rivers and waters generally flow according to his ordinances (II, 28, 4, V, 85, 6; VII, 64, 2), he is surrounded/clothed with waters (VII, 49, 3; IX, 90, 2) and, of course, bestows abundant rain (V, 63; 85, 3-4; VII, 64, 2). In I, 24, 7 he sustains the Tree which has roots above and branches-rays downward, the Tree of Life or the *Axis Mundi* or Cosmic Tree; through this and bedewing the earth and pasturage, he is evidently linked with fertility and vegetation. He also encompasses the nights (VIII, 41, 3) and in post-rigvedic texts he is especially connected with the night (*TS* II, 1, 7, 4; VI, 4, 8, 3) while Mitra with the day.

Thus Varuṇa supplies those traits of Osiris which are missing in Yama. And, of course, Varuṇa is an *asura* (*RV* VII, 65, 2; VIII, 25, 4) and furnishes the possible linguistic connexion with the name *Wsir* 'Osiris'.

19. What can we make of all this information?

We cannot say that the Vedic Tradition borrowed from the Egyptians. Varuṇa is well established in the *RV* and appears in the *Avesta* as Ahura Mazda while his name is cognate with Greek *Ouranos* 'Sky-god'. Yama appears in BkI and BkX of the *RV*, ie the middle and late strata—not in the early hymns. But, then, the mythology associated with him is so well attested and widespread among the other IE traditions, Iranian, Greek, Baltic and Scandinavian, that we cannot entertain the notion of Vedic borrowing even as a remote possibility, unless the transmission from Egypt occured before the dispersal of the IndoEuropeans—a notion equally difficult to accept.

Did the Egyptians borrow, then? This seems possible but not easy to demonstrate. The only indication supporting such a transmission from the Veda to Egypt is the fact that, as we noted (§ 2), there is no archaeological or epigraphical evidence for the existence of Osiris before the *PT* or, say, 2500. The serious difficulty here is that we have no evidence for any direct contact between India and Egypt at so early a date; another consideration is that even if Osiris is an importation, since the Osiris legend in the *PT* is so well established that it appears in fragments comprehensible to the Egyptians themselves, the importation must have taken place much earlier, perhaps c 2700 or 2800. It is possible that at, say, c 2700 the Yama-Varuṇa-Asura concepts came to Egypt and were grafted onto the cult of a local deity combining the attributes of vegetation and inundation. But this is pure speculation, of no value.

Another conjectural alternative is that the various Yama-Varuṇa-Asura-Osiris concepts started long long ago as a single mythologem common to Egyptians and IndoEuropeans then developed indigenously along divergent lines. But then could the absence of evidence for Osiris for several millennea before the *PT* be fortuitous?... As this seems highly improbable, the issue remains, at present, irresolvable.

20. The Falcon. Horus, the son of Osiris and Isis, holds little interest for our purposes, but the Falcon with which he is identified is of interest. Even while pregnant, Isis describes the foetus in her womb as a falcon: "A falcon is within my womb" (*CT* 148). In iconography Horus is invariably depicted with the head of a falcon and the bird becomes another emblem for kingship found, in iconography, perched on the shoulder of some pharaohs. The same *CT* spell says Horus as the Falcon reached the end of the horizon having passed the gods of Nut [=the sky] and gone further than the gods of old. Thus this god-bird brought "the ways of eternity to the twilight of the morning". Having gone beyond the power of Seth who represents the disruption of "cosmic order" (*ma'at*), the new king has put disorder under his feet heralding a new dispensation. (See Clark, 213-7.) However, the Falcon is at first a messenger carrying news of Horus to his father Osiris in *CT* 312. Here it is also said to be Horus's soul and thus becomes a generalised symbol for the soul (Budge 1988:90).

In the *RV* also we find a bird which flies to heaven: it is the *śyena* 'hawk, eagle' or *suparṇa* 'the bird of strong wings' or 'of fine feathers'. (See the discussion about the Mesopotamian and Vedic eagles in paper Seven, §§ 5-7.) This bird fetches the drink *soma* from heaven (especially in IV 26 and 27 but also in other hymns, eg VIII 95, 3; in III 93, 6 from a mountain). The bird brings the drink to Indra usually. In IV 26, 4 the drink is brought to Manu, the progenitor, and in IV, 19, 13 it is brought to the seer Vāmadeva; here some scholars think the Falcon represents Indra. In VII 15, 4 the falcon is identified with Agni—probably as the sun. In IX 67, 14-5 it is the drink Soma itself (and the god) that is identified with the śyena. In X 92, 6 the Maruts (and perhaps the Rudras) are described as the śyenas of Dyaus, the Skygod. In X 114, 5 the bird *suparṇa* is said to be one but the poets devise many images in speaking of it. The Vedic bird is thus a bird in its own right but represents several deities and the One-which-appears-as-many. Hymn IV 26, 1 provides another aspect suggesting a more complex legend. The śyena is guarded in 100 *purs* (=magic strongholds, hard as metal), imprisoned by demons, as some think (Geldner, vol 2, 455) but the bird somehow does break free and fetches down the Soma. Here it is taken by some to represent the soul. The complete legend is lost to us.

Later Vedic texts continue to refer to the Soma-bringing bird (eg *VS* V1, vi 32). One of the shapes of the altars is that of a falcon and *TS* V 4, 11 says: "[The sacrificer] who desires the sky should pile in hawk shape; the hawk is the best flier among birds; verily becoming a hawk he flies to the world of heaven". Then, *ŚB* XII 7, 1, 6 says that the *śyena* is the courage in Indra's heart; so in XII 3, 4, 3-4, the sacrificer prays that the falcon will bear him to well-being. The *AU* II 1, 5 takes the *RV* IV 26, 1 and interprets the image of the falcon as the spirit of the seer Vāmadeva which is imprisoned in the womb *garbhe* yet breaks free and attains liberation. Thus it is that the bird represents the soul as well.

The falcon is a common bird in Egypt and India so its use as a poetic image and religious symbol may have developed independently. But that it should, in both cultures, develop into a symbol for a god (Egyptian Horus, Vedic Indra/Agni), for a messenger (bringing joyful news in Egypt, bringing exhilerating soma in India) and for the soul going to heaven, must be more than a coincidence. We find no such (triple) symbolism in Mesopotamia or the related IE legends; but the IE pedigree of the bird cannot be doubted.

21. The Cow. The heavenly Cow-Mother-Goddess *mḥt-wrt* has greater prominence in Egypt than in Mesopotamia, the cow being one of the oldest sacred animals there. The Cow-goddess best known to us was Hathor. The spots on Hathor's image of spotted cow were the stars in the sky. *Ḥat-Hor* or *Ḥwt-Ḥr* means 'Mansion-of Horus' and this suggests that this name at least was later than Horus. Hathor as well as Isis suckled Horus in some texts and this act shows that she was identified with Isis; indeed, she was identified with numerous goddesses (Budge, 1988: 228-32). In *The Destruction of Mankind* (Lesko 109-111; Clark 181-5) Nut herself becomes a cow and takes on her back Re who is now aged and tired of the world; in this same text the Eye assumes the form of Hathor and proceeds to slay mankind. A later hymn (in Hathor's temple at Dendera) praises both cow and goddess: "O beauteous one, O cow, O great one,/ O great magician, O splendid lady, O gold/queen of gods!" (Lichtheim, vol 3:108).

The Vedic (and Mesopotamian) Cow-goddess was examined earlier, in paper Seven, § 22: Aditi the mother of the gods Ādityas is a cow in *RV* I, 153, 3; *VS* , XIII, 43 etc; a cosmic cow appears in *RV* I, 80, 3 and III, 55, 1, etc. (A cosmic cow appears in the *Edda* and nourishes universal man Ymir; it appears in Iranian legendry also.)

22. The Bull. The worship of the Bull was common in Egypt at all periods and practically in all districts. Classical sources refer to two cults: the Apis-Bull in Memphis embodied Osiris, Ptah and, later, Seker, god of the Memphis underworld; the Mnevis-Bull of Heliopolis embodied Re and Osiris. Both cults went back to early dynastic times but there were others (Budge, 73-5).

The Vedic (and Mesopotamian) Bull was examined earlier in paper Seven, § 21: gods Agni of fire (I, 40, 2, etc) and Indra of thunder and lightning (I, 32, 7, etc) are described as 'bull'. The bull appears in Iran, Greece and elsewhere as a sacred animal.

23. Dog, Jackal, Wolf. The Dog, worshipped at Cynopolis was often confounded with Anubis, the jackal-god. The latter conducted the souls of the dead; he was the official embalmer and Guardian of the Scales on which were weighed the hearts of the dead in the Hall of Judgment of Osiris. Then there was the Wolf-god *Wepwaet* "the opener of the Roads" who assisted Anubis in guiding the souls.

In the Vedic tradition the jackal is hardly ever mentioned (eg *RV* X 28,4; *VS* XXIV 32). The wolf is mentioned more frequently but is to be kept off (eg *RV* X 127,6; *VS* IX 16). As regards the Dog, this animal had no divine aspect as such nor a cult. But Indra had Saramā, which pursued and located the thieves of cattle and then Indra recovered the animals (*RV* X 106); Saramā is not expressly said to be a bitch in the *RV* but is so taken by subsequent texts (*Nirukta* XI 25). However, *RV* has two more dogs, those of Yama the guardian of the dead in heaven (*RV* X 14, 10-12). Descendants of Saramā, with the epithet *Sārameya*, they are called *śabala* 'brindled' and *śyāma* 'black': they guard the path of the dead to Yama's abode (§ 16, end). "It is possible that they were conceived as going among men, and taking to the abode of death [in heaven] the souls of the dead" (Keith, p 406).

24. The Ram or Goat. In Egypt, it seems, ram and goat were regarded as one and the same for cultic purposes. There were two Ram-gods, one at Mendes (Tet or Busiris, at the Delta) and one at Elephantine (first Nile-catarract, south). Because of their strength and virility the sacred animal at

Mendes, Hermopolis and Lycopolis were used by women for sexual intercourse (Budge, 1988:75). The Ram-god at Elephantine was from early times worshipped as the Ram-headed god Khnum who was portrayed as a Potter-god fashioning mankind out of clay. But before this, he was also a Water-god who was said to bring the Nile into Egypt (Budge 173-4).

There is no distinct Ram-god in the Veda, but Indra is several times called "that much invoked Ram" (=meṣa: *RV* I 51, 1; 52, 1 etc). In addition, there is *aja ekapād* usually rendered as 'One-footed Goat', which does not mean much exactly, but this deity is five times invoked together with Ahi Budhnya, the Serpent of the Deep, and once (*RV* X 66, 11) with the ocean, river Sindhu and floods. So this deity may have been connected with the waters. More important, however, is its connection with *aja* 'the Unborn One' or "goat" who established the six regions of space (I 164, 6) and holds Earth (I 61, 10) and Heaven (VIII 41, 10) and has all the worlds supported on its navel (X 82, 6).

25. Nile-Sarasvatī: river in the sky. LH Lesko cites a hymn to the Sungod in which the god is praised for having "placed a Nile in the sky/that it might descend for them and make waves upon the mountain" (1991:108). RO Faulkner writes of "the celestial river, equated by the Egyptians with the Milky Way" (1985:90).

The Indoaryans also had their celestial river, Sarasvatī, which was also the "best river" (*RV* II 41, 16) on earth and flowed pure "from the mountains to the ocean" (VII 95, 2). But she was also a great goddess and hymn V 43, 11 invokes holy Sarasvatī to flow from high heaven while VI 61, 11 says that she has filled the firmament. The Greek and Scandinavian mythologies have celestial rivers, so it is an IE motif.

26. The Pit of Nonexistence. J Baines, Professor of Egyptology at Oxford, wrote (1991:151): "Old Kingdom sources are compatible with belief in a judgment [after death]... Belief in a judgment might therefore have been integral to religion in all accessible periods." Indeed, several decades earlier Wallis Budge had written: "The Memphite theologians speak of a celestial court which preceded that of Re or Osiris, for they tell us that the earth-god Gebb sat in judgment" (1988:280). Clark cites spell *CT* 312 which changes an older text "before the Divine Court which sat down to judge in the presence of Geb" into "before the Divine Court which sat down to judge before Geb (*earth*) *and Re* (*sun*)... *on earth and in the sky*" (Clark, 164: my italics showing the addition). But Osiris had already become the great Judge of the dead. In the Hall of Judgment close to the Scales sits the monster Am-mit with head of crocodile, body of lion and backside of hippopotamus: it would gobble up any condemned person, body and soul. But there were also hells in the Underworld where the damned were immersed in pits of fire and consumed out of existence. To quote Baines again: "Evil people who are-found wanting in an ethical judgment after their death are cast out of creation" (ibid 129).

RV hymn VII 104 is a prayer to gods Indra and Soma to punish evil-doers, sorcerers and fiends. Stanza 9 prays that seducers and corruptors be delivered to the Serpent ahi- or to the "lap of Annihilation" *nírṛter upásthe*. Stanza 3 wants the evil-doers hurled into "the pit, the bottomless darkness" from which they will not come up again. Similar references are found in II 29, 6, IV 5, 5, IX 73, 8-9 and X 152, 4. There is no explicit mention of Judgment but only some such action would have sent the good to heaven and the wicked to the pit. Judgment is mentioned overtly in *Taittirīya Āraṇyaka* VI 5, 13. *ŚB* XI 2,7, 33 correlates the sacrificial altar with the Balance in the other world and advices the sacrificer to touch the right edge of the altar so that his good deeds will go into it and rise with the oblation. Hell is mentioned explicitly in *AV*

XII 4, 36 *nāraka- loka-* and in hell goes a murderer in *VS* XXX 5. Punishments and tortures in hell are depicted in *Kauṣītaki Br* XI 3 and *ŚB* XI 6, 1 (people being cut up or eaten up).

27. Afterlife in Heaven. Here we shall ignore mummification. Otherwise, first the Pharaoh, then the nobles and later commoners aspired to unite with God—but always a particular god: Re in his barque, Osiris, Horus, Amun, even Khnum; or being in some god's company, or among the stars. (Eg see spells *PT* 215 king-Atum; 250 king-Sia; 412 king among the stars, Orion, Sothis, Morning Star, etc; *CT* 42-3 king-Osiris; 75 king-Shu; etc; for Khnum, *BD* 36; etc.)

As regards the Vedic tradition, we saw earlier (§ 20) that the man who aspires to go to heaven should, apart from anything else, sacrifice with a falcon-shaped altar. Many passages in the *RV* (and later texts) indicate that, except for the evil-doer, the soul goes to Yama's abode in heaven (X 14, 8), to the Sun or among the stars. Thus the ancestral Fathers "adorn the sky with the constellations" (*RV* X 68 11); those who practised tapas 'penance, austerities' have gone to heaven or to the Fathers who guard the Sun (X 154, 2 and 5); and the liberal givers dwell with the Sun (X 107, 2). But, of course, in the Vedic Tradition we find also reincarnation and divinization or Selfrealization with true immortality (Kazanas 2005a).

28. There are, in fact, **many more parallels** that could be cited. The realm of magical practices in both cultures provides spells against snake-bites, diseases and other calamities: both used ritual, the elements of fire and water, amulets and plants and figurines. There is also the annual rejuvenation of the king and of the Sungod (in Egypt Amun-Re). Then, there is the concept of Cosmic Order, *ma'at* in Egypt and *ṛta* in Saptasindhu as well as the actual social structure and the scales weighing in Afterlife good and bad deeds; and so on. However, a detailed discussion of all these points (which I leave for a future study) would add many pages to this study without helping us to understand better whether, and when, there had been early contacts between the two cultures and any cross-influences.

29. One more point needs to be made. Attempts appear at times to connect Indic languages (sanskritic or dravidian) with Old Mesopotamian or Egyptian. In the next section 30 I refer to a paper on Vedic and Mesopotamian cross-influences in which I examined some of these alleged linguistic affinities and showed them to be wrong. Here I shall advert to an article by BZ Szalek (2005) who lists parallels between Old Egyptian and Tamil or Telugu. Apart from several duplications which make the items look many more than they actually are, the list contains Tamil *muti-ya* 'to die' which is obviously linked to S √*mṛ*, *mṛtyu*, *mriyate* 'dying, death, is dead' etc; *piri-ya* 'to depart' which is linked to S *pre* or *pra-yā* 'depart, go forth'; *tapi*, *tapana* 'be hot, heat' which are linked to S *tap*, *tapana* 'burning, heating'. All three Sanskrit roots (and stems) have perfectly matching IE correspondences: S *mṛ* = Gk *a-mbrot-o*, L *mors*, *mortius*, Lth *mirtis*; etc. S -i, *yā* = Gk *eisi/eiti*, L *it*, Lth *eiti/joti*, Irish *ath*, etc. S *tap* = L *tepeo* , Irish *tē*, Slavic *top-lu*, etc. Thus here also borrowing by the Indic peoples must be ruled out. However, my view here is rather impressionistic as I have no real knowledge of Dravidic languages.

30. My earlier discussion of Indo-Mesopotamian parallels (paper Seven)[7] showed that, contrary to hitherto prevalent theories, it is rather the Mesopotamians who were culturally influenced in the main, although influences in the other direction should not be ruled out, particularly as regards iconographic material. It may be argued, that such a conclusion is based on unacceptably early dates arbitrarily given to the Vedic texts and that this does not stand in the mainstream view of the AIT and a *RV* composed c 1200-1000. Such an argument, however, ignores two important facts. First, the evidence for the early dates is strong and convincing, in contrast to the AIT which, in truth, has not a

[7]The references § 4 etc, below in this section, are to this publication.

solid leg to stand on—other than mechanical repetition. Second, the nature of the parallels themselves. To take the first example of the horse-sacrifice (§ 4), only obstinacy and prejudice would insist that the Veda borrowed. The Veda has a rich horse mythology which is totally absent in Mesopotamia; moreover, it is attested in various forms in other IE traditions but is lacking in Near Eastern ones. Other IE mythologems are that of the eagle ascending to heaven (§§ 5ff), the Flood (§ 11) and the dismemberment of a divine being (weak in Greece but strong in Scandinavia: § 22). My close analyses of these mythologems and others, like the bull (§ 22), the cow (§ 21) or the origin of kingship (§ 30), show that the Vedic legends contain no distinctly Mesopotamian elements. All these pieces of evidence demonstrate clearly that the Veda is not the borrower. Then, there are the tell-tale pieces of the Mesopotamian text *Enmerkar and the Lord of Aratta* (§§ 33, 39) and the transmission of the peacock (§ 38). Moreover, Berossos tells us that the ancient arts and sciences were not discovered by gifted Mesopotamians but were brought from elsewhere; his figure of 432000 years for a Great Year (§ 18) stands arbitrary and isolated, while it forms a valid detail in the larger Indic system. Thus, if there was borrowing (and obviously there was), then the borrower was Mesopotamia—first c 2600, perhaps, and then c 1600.

31. The situation with Egypt is different. Some of the parallels are remarkable and unique, like 'the lotus-born one' (§ 3), 'the eye that runs off' (§ 4), 'the Cosmic Egg' (§ 9) or the Yama-Osiris correspondences (§ 16ff). Then, egyptologists admit that the sudden birth of an almost full-blown culture in Egypt ushering in the Pyramid Age presupposes a previous period of development in the centuries, say, 3000-2700, yet no traces of such development have been found (David 2002; Emery 1991). On the other hand, the simple culture in Saptasindhu and its development into early, mature and late ISC shows, according to all specialist archaeologists, an uninterrupted continuity from at least the early 5th millennium to mid-sixth century. Thus, since the Vedic people had knowledge of mathematics and astronomy (paper Seven) which found expression in the material culture of the ISC, one is tempted to suggest that the influence for the sudden outburst of the Egyptian civilization came from Saptasindhu, especially since no other comparable culture is in evidence in the late fourth millennium. But precisely here both archaeological and textual evidence fail us in not indicating any direct contacts. We are left only with speculation that, perhaps, some Indoaryans, in obedience to the dictum in *RV* X, 65, 11 that they should spread the Aryan laws/usages all over the earth *áryā vratā̃ visṛjánto ádhi kṣámi*, went to Egypt for this purpose. However, future archaeological work may present a new picture in Egypt.

32. There are other speculative alternatives. It is always possible that the Egyptians developed their own civilization within a few decades through sheer native inspiration. We could moreover follow those writers who offer evidence that the Sphinx was sculpted in the 11th millennium (Bauval & Hancock 1996; West 1993) and that that culture lay dormant with few unobtrusive expressions for some seven millennia. But then we still have to account for the parallels in their own and the Indoaryan religious concepts and legendry. These are not two or three isolated motifs or images that could come to anyone: they are many and some of them quite remarkable. So there must have been a contact of some kind some time before 2700.

In the recent 1990s CE, Indian marine archaeologists discovered on the seafloor of the Gulf of Cambay certain stone-structures and many artefacts suggestive of a large town that had been submerged: this was dated at c 7000. That a town-port might have existed there and then, and sank into the sea because rains and floods caused a rise of the sea-level is not impossible, nor that contacts with other cultures including Egypt took place at that period. But many serious archaeologists doubt the dating and, indeed, the submarine ruins may be of a much later date (Hancock 2002:169-197). We must await fresh evaluations and, perhaps, fresh data; for we must have in mind the *RV* which knows of no large urban structures but does know of the domesticated horse and of copper-metallurgy. Since there is no evidence for horse-domestication and copper-smelting much before 5500, this date sets the upper limit for the bulk of the *RV*, at least in the form we have it: earlier dates suggested for the *RV* are not at present tenable[8].

Another alternative is to suppose a moreorless unified PIE cultural continuum extending in the 8th or 7th millennium from Saptasindhu to the Pontic Steppe with various non-IndoEuropean speaking peoples moving in and out of this at different dates (Kazanas 2003). This widespread culture had contacts and exchanges with the near East from the Caucasus and Anatolia down to Egypt before breaking up and the different branches going to their respective historical habitats. Others again might prefer Out-of India movements at different moments of that distant past (see also Hock 1999), although such movements cannot be easily traced archaeologically and linguistically to the N-W extremities of Europe—except for the Gypsy migration in historical times (Fraser 1995). Personally, I lean towards the last view since the difficulties for any other PIE locus of dispersal are many more and greater (Kazanas 2003).

---

[8]Copper objects (pins, knives, beads) have been found in S-E Anatolia, Syria and S.Iran from c 7000-6500 but without any evidence of smelting, only hammering and perhaps melting (Saggs 1989:197-8). Even if we allow knowledge of melting (not smelting) to the *RV* and this sets an upper limit c 7000-6500, **we still have to meet the limit of the domesticated horse**. The spoked wheel poses no problem; for Vedic *ara* could well have denoted segments of a solid wheel rather than separate spokes. The different words for 'spoke' in the IE branches (eg Gk *aktis*, L *radius*, Gmc *spāce/spēke/speihha*) suggest that the spoke as we understand it was developed after the dispersal of the IE speakers. The technology for a separate-spoke wheel might not have been developed before 4000-3500 but we cannot theoretically preclude carts with solid wheels in the 5th millennium or even earlier.

However, all this speculating is not particularly fruitful. We simply have to rest with the admission that we do not know—unless and until new data appear. But, on the basis of the present state of our knowledge, we can state with confidence that, as regards the parallels discussed, the Vedic Tradition did not borrow from Egypt any more than from Mesopotamia. Rather, if anything, it is the other two cultures that borrowed.

33. What I find most noteworthy in the study of these three ancient civilizations is the presence of the One as the First Cause or Primal Source of all phenomena. This presence is nowhere explicit and certain in the Mesopotamian texts but, nonetheless, as Bottéro noted, it is inferable from some of them (2001:74); it is clearly discernible as Atum or Nun in the early Egyptian texts (Assman 2001:119); it is, of course, clearly articulated in the *RV* and, moreso, in later Vedic texts—even amid the kaleidoscopic multiplicity of deities (see Upanishads and Kazanas 2005a). It is not easy now to explain why this knowledge of the One Primal Cause was forgotten or gradually covered over by polytheism in the Near East. One can only speculate that it seems easier to worship one divinity, or many, having definite form(s) in natural phenomena and thereby being more readily approachable, than one unmanifest, inconceivable and therefore unapproachable Power. It seems also that in the IE branches as well as in the Near East the oral tradition was not so efficiently organized as in Saptasindhu. Both in the linguistic and the cultural areas the Vedic Tradition retained many more inherited elements than the other IE branches (Kazanas 2001, 2007b). As stressed earlier, the Egyptians and Mesopotamians obviously turned their attention to the more concrete aspects of culture, buildings, artefacts and iconic representations, whereas the early Vedic culture was more concerned with theoretical (mathematics and astronomy) and spiritual (the Unity of Being) considerations.

It is obvious, then, that when religiophilosophical thought was formulated in proto-historical times, at least as we find it in Saptasindhu and the Near East, it contained both polytheism and monism (or monotheism). Since there is no earlier textual attestation of polytheism exclusive of monism, the latter cannot be said to be a "development" from polytheism, animism and the like, as experts in these fields claim. On the contrary, on the basis of the evidence presented in the foregone discussion, I propose that modern notions (very popular in the 20th cent) about shamanism, fetihism, animism, polytheism and other beliefs found among "primitive" or "aboriginal" people do not represent truly early beliefs but rather offshoots (devolutions or degenarations) of a more ancient system having as its primary principle the Unity of Being, clearly illustrated in the first phase of the Vedic Tradition. Consequently, iconographic and other archaeological material from the cultures of the Stone Age (see Rudgley 1998) might be much more correctly interpreted not by the prejudices and superstitions of the 20th century but under the light of the ideas contained in some ancient texts examined above and particularly the *Ṛgveda*.

Nine: **Indo-European Linguistics and Indo-Aryan Indigenism**

0. Abstract. This paper examines the general IE[1] issue and argues in favour of Indoaryan indigenism against the AIT (Aryan Invasion/Immigration Theory) which has been mainstream doctrine for more than a century. The extreme positions that there was no PIE[1] language or that this language is as currently reconstructed are refuted: the evidence suggests there was a PIE language but this cannot be reconstructed and all efforts in this reconstruction are misplaced. Since they are in no way verifiable, they should not be used as evidence for historical events. It is admitted even by rabid Indian nationalists that humans came to India from Africa sometime in the Pleistocene, and now there is evidence of change in the skeletal record of the region indicating that a new people may have entered c 6000-4500[2]; even so, if these people were the IAs, they must, surely, be regarded as indigenous by 1700. Recent genetic

[1]IE = IndoEuropean; PIE = ProtoIndoEuropean; IA = Indoaryan(s). A large section of this paper is a revised version of a talk given at a Conference at the Center of Indic Studies, University of Massachusets, in June 2006.

[2]All dates are BCE except where stated otherwise. Dates in brackets, eg (2001) denote a publication by a modern author which will be found in the Bibliography.

I use the name Saptasindhu simply as a *bahuvrīhi* adjective. The 7 rivers are frequently mentioned in the *RV*—1.32.12; 34.8; 35.8; etc, etc. In the *Avesta* it is said that the Old Iranians had, before settling in Iran, been to various places and one of them was Haptahəndu. I take it that *Haptahəndu* indicates Saptasindhu, a name which has been frequently used by others before me.

studies do not suggest any entry of IAs within the last 10,000 years but state that the European peoples came out of South Asia after 50,000 BP. Apart from such studies, other kinds of evidence and arguments will be used in full to demonstrate indigenism.

Indoeuropean and ProtoIndoEuropean

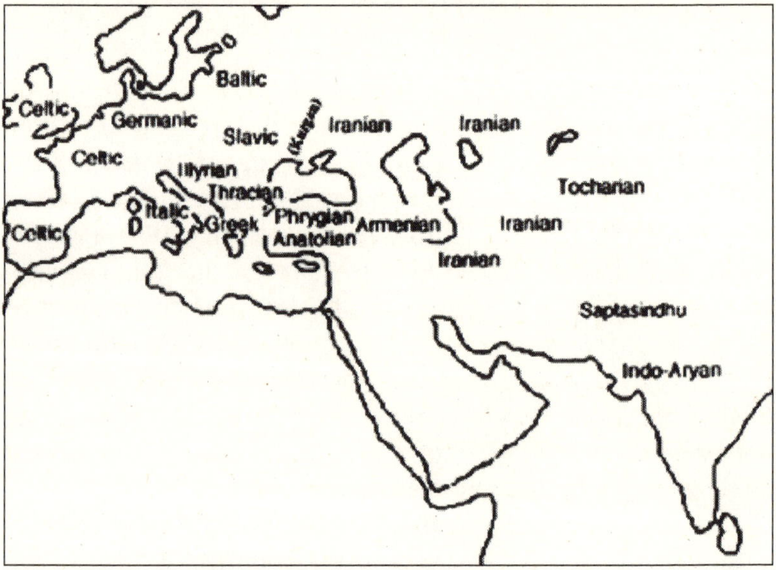

Map of IE languages

The map shows the location of languages broadly, not peoples or races; it is a modification of the map used by JV Day, 2001, p xiii.

1. Let us first see the ensuing discussion in its natural historical context.

American archaeologist J Shaffer had the courage to call the AIT of India "a myth" (1984). The development of this "myth" which had obtained mainstream status in academia is well traced by E Bryant (2001), J Day (1994) and J Mallory (1973). Here suffice it to say that having started as a linguistic theory, it soon acquired biological undertones involving more or less obvious ethnic/racial prejudices (Bryant 2001; Trautmann 1997; Shaffer 1984). Before the Nazi "aryanism" of the 1930's, the AIT was used by colonial politics as is obvious in British Prime Minister Baldwin's speech in Parliament in 1929: "Now after ages ... the two branches of the Aryan ancestry have again been brought together by Providence... By establishing British rule in India, God said to the British, 'I have brought you and the Indians together after a long separation ... it is your duty to raise them to your level as quickly as possible ... brothers that you are'"! God's ways were no longer so mysterious.

The linguistic theory which c 1800 CE sought to account for the similarities between Sanskrit, Greek, Latin, Germanic etc, contained the notion of an IE family of languages and a PIE mother-tongue. The literature on the subject is increasing enormously year by year. Hereafter I shall refute first the rejection by some scholars of a PIE tongue and even a family of IE languages and then the claims of others about the nature of PIE and its alleged "reconstruction". There is sufficient evidence to show that there had been a unitary PIE language and civilization but not enough to enable us to go very far with reconstructions. In any case, in the absence of people speaking PIE and of recognizably original texts, the reconstruction of the language—even if it were possible, which it is not—would be pointless and wasteful of other people's money. E Leach wrote that after the discovery of the ISC (=Indus-Sarasvati Civilization) "Indo-European scholars should have scrapped all their historical reconstructions and started again from scratch. But this is not what happened. Vested interests and academic posts were involved" (1990).

'Vested' interests and academic posts are still involved and will continue to be involved because the human ego is not educated to let go of claims that are shown to be untrue, despite much trumpeting to the contrary. At the same time, although this phenomenon may cause and has caused considerable delay and darkness on the path of progress, it cannot ultimately prevent the establishment of true knowledge. A good case in point is the so-called "Copernican revolution" which, in general terms, ousted the Ptolemaic geocentric system of the heavens that had beclouded knowledge for some 18 centuries since Aristotle, and brought the heliocentric system which had been known by Greek naturalists (especially Aristarchos of Samos) even before Aristotle (Kuhn 1970, Koestler 1954). For many decades after the publication of Copernicus's work *De Revolutionibus...* in 1543 the mainstream savants of the day concocted more and more epicycles of the planets to account for the mathematics involved and the new observations. Eventually, after about a century the old model collapsed: more and more naturalists abandoned it in favour of the new heliocentric system. Similar concoctions, like the astronomical epicycles, are being produced in the field of Indology but with the new genetic studies (§ 19) the issue of indigenism can no longer be easily refuted.

2. The IndoEuropean family. That the IE family of languages is not a "family" is by no means a recent view, though it is not as old as the initial hypothesis that there is a "family" and a unitary PIE civilization and language. We love to speculate and set up theories and models—the more elegant the better. The human mind does not ordinarily seem to like gaps and emptiness. So it hastens to fill a gap in knowledge with some hypothesis. Then others raise objections and set up a different or even an opposite theory and so on. Thus, we speculate about everything raising one theory after another to keep mind and pen occupied. Here is an example out of myriads. A. Speirs writes (1978:26) "The principle of economy of hypothesis requires us to assume or at least to test the proposition that the labio-velars were PIE phonemes which in the PIE period shifted to labials and dentals in some circumstances, lost the labial element in others..." etc. We have the theory of a PIE, then the theory of the existence of labio-velar phonemes (§ 6, end), then speculation about what happened to these imaginary entities. Of course theories are useful because they become a tool for further research so long as one does not cling to the theory and argue that this is the one and only truth. Thus from the first half of the 20th c several scholars began to doubt the existence of PIE. I give a selection of them: Bonfante 1931; Walder 1936; Trubezkoy 1939; Pisani 1949/71; Morgan Keeley 1992; Marcantonio 2002/05. There are many more, all doubting that what are described as IE branches (=Sanskrit, Greek, Germanic, etc) are offshoots of a unitary PIE. One of the explanations is that the similarities in these so-called IE branches are due to chance and have no further significance. Now, some fortuitous similarities in lexical items are not merely possible but quite probable—and this could apply to languages outside the IE family. But we are hardly justified in evoking "chance" or "accident" when we meet 25 undoubtedly cognate stems present in three or more IE branches accross Eurasia and designating the very same parts of the human body: eg eye, nose, tooth, jaw, breast, knee, foot, flesh, heart, blood etc. We find also at least 15 stems of equally certain cognation in three or more branches denoting relations and functions like brother, chief, carpenter/ fashioner, daughter, father, husband/master, man, mother etc (see § 3b). Then could it possibly be accidental similarity that we find accross Eurasia but not in the N-East S *lobha* 'longing', L *lu-/li-bido* 'desire', Gmc *lufu/liubi* and Sl *ljubi* 'love' or S *mās* Av *māh-*, Toch A *mañ*, Gmc *mona*, B *menuo* Sl *meis-ic* all 'moon' and Gk *meis/mēn*, L *mens-is* and C *mī* 'month'?

Perhaps, yes, it may be, as others have suggested, that borrowing or waves of diffusion, sporadic or whatever, or convergence through long/repeated contact, are responsible for the similarities and cognations (Trubezkoy 1939). But how probable is this? ... It may be probable that 10, 20, 50 perhaps lexical items of everyday common use travelled accross Eurasia at different times and in different directions. But this involves grave difficulties since the similarities and cognations in three or more IE branches run into many hundreds. Beyond this, there are close similarities in inflexion and conjugation and also in many social and cultural aspects (always exclusive of other non-IE peoples). Moreover, these similarities are not evident at all in Near Eastern languages.

Another objection raised is that common grammatical features appear only in S, Av, Ht, Gk and Italic. These branches, it is said, formed a closely related group that developed these common features. This is fallacious because, to take just one isogloss, while S and Av are səṭem, Ht, Gk and Italic are *kentum*. Moreover, as we shall see in § 3 both lexical items and grammatical features (nominal and verbal endings, reduplication, etc) are spread right across the IE spectrum and are not confined to the group of S, Ht, Gk and Italic.

3. Let us look in detail at some of the difficulties involved in diffusion-waves and the close group.

(a) All Near-Eastern languages are—but for negligible exceptions which are easily accountable as borrowings—unaffected by these hypothetical waves or long/repeated contacts. Yet, roughly speaking, they are located in between Tocharian, Sanskrit and Iranian in the east and Greek, Italic, Germanic, Baltic and Celtic in the west. Some studies that claim elements "shared by Indo-European and Semitic" (eg Levin 1991) and Greek and Semitic (Burkert 1992) show very clearly that the "shared" material is utterly insignificant in comparison with the correspondences in IE branches.

(b) The obviously cognate words (=similar in sound and sense) in three or more IE branches are far too many for random or deliberate borrowing. Taking these very criteria, ie presence in three branches and designation of more or less the same (relatively) invariable entity, quality or activity, I easily collected about 500 stems (Kazanas 2007). Some are common to all or most branches and many to more than three. Eg:

1. arm: S *bāhu*; Av *bāzu*; Gk *pēchus*; Gmc *buog*; Toch A *poke*.

2. belly: S *udara-*; Av *udara-*; Gk *hoderos* (=gaster); L *uterus'* (venter?); B *vēderas*.

3. brother: S *bhrātṛ*, Av *brātār-*; Gk *phratēr* (=member of brotherhood); L *frāter*; C *brathir*; Gmc *bruodar*; B *broter-*; Sl *bratrŭ*; Toch A *pracar*.

4. clan, tribe: S *jana/jāti*; Av *-zana-/-zantiš* ; Gk *genos* (*phulē*); L gens (*tribus*); Gmc *cynn/kyn*.

5. to desire/love: S *lubhyati*; L *lub-/lib-et*; Gmc *liufs/lufaρ*; Sl *ljubiti*: 'loves'.

6. eyebrow: S *bhrū* ; Av *brvat-*; Gk *o-phrus*; C *brūad*; Gmc *brūn*; B *bruvis*; Sl *brŭvĭ*; Toch A/B *pärwān*(*e*).

7. flesh: S *māṃsa*; Gmc *mimz*; B *meisa*; O *Prus mensā*; Sl *meso*; Alb *mish*; Arm *mis*; Toch B *misa*.

8. heel: S *parṣṇi*; Av *pāsna-*; Ht *parsna-*; Gk *pternē*; L *perna*; Gmc *fiersn*.

9. jaw: S *hanu*; Av *zānu-*; Gk *genus*; L *genu-* (back-tooth); C *gen*; Gmc *cin/kin*; B *žan*-das(?); Toch A *śanw-em* (fem dual).

10. knee: S *jānu*; Av *žnu-*; Ht *genu*; Gk *gonu*; L *genu*; Gmc *kniu*; Arm *cun-r*; Toch B *keni-*.

11. nose: S *nas-*; Av *nāh-*; L *nārīs*; Gmc *nasa*; B *nosis*; Sl *nosĭ* .

12. palm (of hand): S *pṛtha*; Ht *paltana*; Gk *palamē*; L *palma*.

13. reward: S *mīḍḥa*; Av *mīžda*; Gk *misthos*; Gmc *mizdō*; Sl *mĭzda*.

14. shoulder: S *aṃsa*; Gk *ōmos̄*; L *ume-rus*; Gmc *ams*; Arm *us*.

15. tooth, molar: S *jambha*; Gk *gomphos*; (*B ̃žam̃bas* 'sharp edge';) Sl *zǒbŭ*; Toch A/B *kam/keme*.

16. woman: S *gnā/jānī*; Av *jani-*; Gk *gunē*; Gmc *cwene/qino*; Sl *žena*; Arm *kin*.

Note that there are some 40 stems designating parts of the human body which are the most invariable of all words since people have their bodies in all places and conditions and can hardly confuse eyes with ears or breasts with cheeks. One might dispute 10 or 15 of them but 25 at least are certain cognations.

The question now arises: Why should, say, the Baltic-speakers give up their native non-IE word for 'belly' (assuming it was different) and adopt *vēderas*, changed from the IE stem used by the Greeks (*hoderos*) or the Romans (*uterus*)? Or, why would the Germanic-speakers give up their own non-IE word for 'jaw' and adopt *cin/kin*, changed from the IE stem used by, say, the Celts (*gen*) or the Romans (*genū*)?... Well, yes we can hypothesize successively at question mark after question mark, but at some point we must stop this easy way of escaping and get down to facts and sound reasoning. Yes, indeed, there may be some few freaky examples of inexplicable borrowing. But in the end the answer is—there is no ostensible reason whatever. Such changes could come about on a large scale only through contact with a superior (and literate) culture or through conquest and coercion. Otherwise, there must be a genetic relation.

(c) The similarities extend to genders, verbs and terminations. I take some random examples. Consider:

(i) The forms and endings of the 1st and/or 3rd sing of the non-reduplicating Perfect of the verb 'to know':

S	AV	Ht	Gk	L	Gth	B(OPr)	Sl
*ve**da***	*vaē**δa***	—	*Foi**da/e***	*vī**di(t)***	*wai**t***	*vaī**di**-*	*vě**dŭ***

Ht has only a Periphrastic Perfect which is formed with the nom/acc of the neuter participle plus the auxiliary *har-ak-* 'to have' as in *markan har-ak-* 'to have cut'. Cf similar periphrasis in S *vidām as-/kṛ-/bhū-* 'to have known'. This example of Perfect as given in the forms above implies a whole conjugation in existence in all these branches and this precludes borrowing or a limited group

(ii) The same should be said for many more, like the following verb 'one is' (3rd pers sing):

S	Av	Ht	Gk	L	Gth	B(Lith)	Sl
*a**sti***	—	ē**šzi**	es**ti**	es**t**	is**t**	ẽs**ti**	jes**tū**

(iii) Consider the endings for, say, 1st and 2nd plural Pres Active of 'carry'

S	Gk	L	Gth	Sl
*bharā**mas***	*phero**men***	*feri**mus***	*baira**m***	*bere**mŭ***
*bhara**ta***	*phere**te***	*fer**tis***	*bairip*	*bere**te***

(iv) The present participle active of the verb 'to eat'

S	Ht	Gk	L	OE
*ad-**ant**-*	*ada-**anz**-a*	*ed-**ont**-*	*ed-**ent**-*	*et-**end**-e*

This too precludes borrowing or the limited group.

Here all the examples above show a wider spread including Gmc, B and Sl. Thus the notions of borrowing and of the limited group are nullified. The same is demonstrated in the noun example that follow. More on this at the end of this section in paragraph (d).

(v) Take the sing Gen for 'father' (using 'mother' for Sl); note that in some branches like S this is also Abl.

S	Gk	L	Gth	Sl
pitus/r/ḥ	*patros*	*patris*	*fadars*	(*matere*)

vi) And the sing Gen for 'dog'

S	Ht	Gk	Lth	OIr
śunas	*kūnar*	*kunos*	*śums*	*coin*

vii) Also sing Gen of 'cloud'

S	Av	Ht	Gk	Sl
nabhasas	*nabaŋhas*	*nepisas*	*nepheos* (*nephous*)	*nebhese*

Note that these examples also exclude chance similarity and the narrow group. Now let us examine oblique cases other than the Gen.

viii) Consider the word for 'name' in sing NVA and Loc and Pl NVA.

	S	L	Gth	Sl
Sing NVA	*nāma*	*nōmen*	*namō*	*imę*
Loc	*nām(a)**ni***	*nōmi**ne***	*nam**in***	*ime**ne***
Pl NVA	*nām**ā(ni)***	*nōmi**na***	*nam**na***	*ime**na***

Note that Gk has *onoma* for NVA, *onoma-t-**i*** for Dative (=Loc) and Pl NVA *onoma-t-**a***. So here too, no narrow group!

Some of the above examples are taken from Misra (1968), Held (1997), Szemerényi (1996) and Clackson (2007). Here, all these similarities can be due neither to accident nor contact and diffusion.

It may be argued that other languages (usually reconstructed Proto-this and Proto-that) show certain affinities (nominal or verbal terminations) but these are very few and very tenuous and do not prove borrowing or convergence due to long/repeated contact. They may be due to accident that is independent native change, or to inherited memory from a distant common past. The similarities in the IE branches have sufficient divergence to show that they are not direct borrowings and sufficient similarity to show that they are devolutions from common original forms. Moreover, intermediate Near Eastern (non-IE) languages do not have these elements.

(d) Some of the features in (b) and (c) may not occur in statistically significant numbers, as Angela Marcantonio has argued (2002, 2005), but this is not a significant objection. It is generally assumed that statistics is a vital constituent of the "scientific" method. It is not realized that the scientific method is not applicable to many areas of human life and that, in any event, it is as much dependent on inspiration and luck on the one hand, and as much liable to blunder on the other, as any other "method" (Pert 1997; Cohen 1985; Beveridge 1968). In any event, in the area under discussion, the proper "scientific" approach would be to ignore rigidity, regularity and uniformity since the linguistic and cultural changes occurred in diverse ways and certainly under no observable law as we shall see in §§ 6-7.

Then, statistics is a purely quantitative factor that has no bearing on quality or significance—matters which require different criteria[3]. Statistics and numbers here must give way to more important considerations like the improbability of so many similarities resulting from sheer accident or from various diffusion waves. Apart from subjection or migration and the like, it is most improbable that, in normal circumstances, any ancient people would adopt the foreign linguistic features examined in (b) and (c), which in some cases would make speech extremely difficult. Consider the complexities alone in the conjugation of the reduplicating verbs in Greek (in *-mi*) and in Vedic. In historical times the tendency for languages is to become simpler, more streamlined by analogy and more synthetic with prepositions and auxiliary verbs. Consider also the difficulty mentioned in (a) that all such similarities are absent in Near-Eastern languages.

It may be and has been claimed that some languages or groups of them have innovated: eg Sanskrit, Greek and Latin (and less Hittite) spent time together and thus developed their highly complex verbal system to the exclusion of Germanic, Baltic etc. Such generalizations are entirely conjectural, unproductive and, since they don't embrace all relevant facts, totally unconvincing. First, no IE language in the historical period is known to develop from a simple to a complex inflective state, as has just been said; the contrary is observed in the cases of (various Afro-Asian languages, too) Vedic, Greek, Latin and, even, Old English which devolved into a simpler non-inflected language increasingly using prepositions and auxiliary verbs. Second, there are lexical

[3]Take as example the hospital. Here the patients are far more numerous than the doctors. Numerically they are more significant but it is the doctors who do the truly significant work, restoring health.

items and isoglosses that are shared by groups other than Sanskrit, Greek and Latin; thus palatalization separates Sanskrit from Hittite , Greek and Latin and joins it to Slavic and Baltic. Third, certain grammatical features join together Sanskrit Greek and Baltic—like the sigmatic Future; moreover, the reduplicated Perfect is found in Germanic as well as Sanskrit, Greek and Latin but not Baltic. To these should be added nominal inflexional features like neuters of the *nāma/nomen* type (in § 4, c, viii) which are shared by Sanskrit, Latin, Gothic and Slavic (but Gk has stem *onoma-t-*). Thus the notion of a group consisting of Sanskrit, Greek and Latin (and Hittite) must be abandoned. Otherwise, we must also wonder whether Slavic, Baltic and Germanic also started innovating just like Sanskrit in the same areas (by sheer coincidence!) and then suddenly stopped. Such claims, therefore, are valueless.

4. Another important type of evidence for a unitary PIE civilization is the presence of identical or very similar **cultural features** in the different branches.

(a) The spread of theonyms is our first consideration. We find a Firegod with the same or cognate name in three branches and nowhere in non-IE languages: thus V *Agni*, Ht *Agnis*, Sl *Ogon* (and variants)—while the stem for 'fire' (but not the theonym) appears as L *ignis*, Lth *ugnis* and Iranian *dašt-aγni-*. The name of another god appears as V *Aryaman*, Mycenaean *Areimene* (and probably later Gk *Arēs*), C *Ariomanus* (in Gaul)/ *Eremon* (in Ireland) and Gmc *Irmin*. The Skygod is V *Dyaus*, Ht *[D]Sius*, Gk *Zeus/Dia-*, L *Ju*[*s*]*-piter*, Gmc *Tīwaz* and South Russian *Divŭ*. One Rain- or Thunder-god is V *Parjanya*, Sl *Perenŭ*, B *Perkunas* and Gmc *Fjorgyn*. Then the Sungod is V *Sūrya*, Gk *Helios*, L *Sol* and B *Saule*—while the stem for 'sun' appears as Gmc *savil/sol*, Welsh *haul* and Sl *solnce* (and variants). The Dawngoddess is V *Uṣas*, Gk *Ēōs*, L *Au*[*s*]*rora*, Gmc *Eos-tre* (=Spring)—while the stem for 'dawn' appears as B *aušra* and probably C *gwawz* (paper Three). Surely all these agreements are not accidental.

(b) Many religious, ritualistic practices are shared by several IE branches. A well-known one is the horse-sacrifice, found in one form or another in India, Greece, Rome, Germania and Ireland (for details see Andersen 1999). But they share also several customs and legal practices (eg prohibition of incest, division into five tribes or demes/ regions, etc), apotropaic and purificatory rituals and, of course, divination (Dumézil 1952, 1954; Puhvel 1970; Kazanas 2001 for Greek and Vedic).

(c) Poetics too is a feature common in IE branches. Here we must exclude Hittite poetry which falls wholly within Near-Eastern traditions and has very little or no relation to IE forms and themes. Moreover, since Latin poetry imitates largely Greek prototypes (epic, lyric, drama) and Celtic, Germanic etc are again largely imitative of Latin and Greek forms (Watkins 2001), comparisons here must be made between Greek and Indic materials. In Vedic and Greek poetry we find three types of stock epithet: the Greek ones are all culled from *Iliad* 1 and the Vedic ones from the *Ṛgveda*. (Much of this comes from Kazanas 2001a.)

(i) Vague adjectives like Gk *dios* 'bright, divine', *diogenēs* 'nobly born', *megathumos* 'big-hearted'; etc. Corresponding Vedic ones are *daivya* 'bright, divine' (RV 1.35.5; 2.33.7), *ugra* 'fierce, mighty' (2.33.9; 10.34.8), *ṛtavan-* 'holy, observing order' (2.35.6; 7.61.2); etc.

(ii) Epithets denoting a specific feature that could be used of anyone but are applied only to a hero or divinity: eg Gk Hera 'of white hands' *leukolenos*, Athena 'of blue/grey eyes' *glaukopis*, Acheans 'of fine greaves' *euknēmis*; V *somapā* 'somadrinker' could be used of any god but is applied only to Indra (2.12.13; etc), *jalāṣa* 'cooling' used of Rudra (2.33.7, 7.35.6), *jātavedas* 'all-knowing' of Agni (1.44.1; 4.3.8), etc.

(iii) Epithets used of one figure (hero or deity) and denoting a specific feature thereof: Gk *asteropētēs* 'who throws the bolt' for Zeus, *hekēbolos* 'aim-attainer, farshooting' for Apollo, *polumēchanos* 'of many devices' for Odusseus; V *gṛhapati* 'lord of house' for Agni (1.45.1), *vajrin* 'he of the bolt' for Indra (7.49.1), *urugāya* 'far-going' for Viṣṇu (1.154.1) etc.

(iv) Then there are items of a common lexical stock (again in the *Iliad* and the *RV*): V *śravas/śruta* = Gk *kleos/kluto* 'fame(d)'; V *uru* = Gk *euru* 'wide'; V *āśu* = Gk *ōku* 'swift'; V *patnī* = Gk *potnia* 'reverend lady'; etc, etc.

(v) In Vedic poetry we meet strict metre like Anuṣṭubh (4 lines of 8 syllables) with an iambic cadence in the second and fourth unit, or *Gāyatrī* (3 lines of 8 syllables) but also within these strict metrical lines rich alliteration. In Greek and Latin poetry we find different metrical units (iambus, anapaest, hexameter etc) while in Germanic we find alliterative lines with loose metre.

All these features, except for rare recurring epithets, are not found in ancient Near-Eastern literature.

d) Common incidents, motifs, themes in religion (=mythology). A most interesting motif is that of **the goddess who becomes a mare** and a pursuing god turns into a stallion and mounts her: from this union comes a twin-pair or some other marvellous creature. In the Vedic tradition we have Sungod Vivasvat who becomes a stallion to mount his run-away bride Saraṇyū who had turned into a mare and later gave birth to the twin Horsegods Aśvins (*RV* 10.17.1-2; *Bṛhaddevatā* 6.162ff). In Greece (Pausanias VIII.25.5), Poseidon chases Dēmētra Erinus (=V *Saraṇyū*?) then both take on equine form and later Dēmētra gives birth to the beautiful horse Areion and a daughter Despoina. Finally in Norse legends (*Edda*, 35-6), Loki, the god of tricks and transformations, becomes a mare to attract from work the giant-mason's stallion, Svadilfari, then gives birth to wondrous Sleipnir, the eightlegged swiftest racer in the world, given as gift to Odin.

Another motif is that of the heroes or **divine youths who rescue** the Sunmaiden from a dangerous situation or become her companions. In India it is the Aśvins (saviours of men from tempests and other calamities) who accompany Sūryā the Sun-maiden, even to her wedding. In Greece it is the *Dioskouroi* 'Zeus's lads', Castor and Pollux (also saviours and expert horsemen) who rescue their abducted sister Helenē. Among the Lithuanians it is the *Dievo Sūnelai* 'the [sky-] god's lads' who rescue and escort the Sunmaiden *saules dukterys*.

A third example is the unusual motif of **the thigh-born child**. In Greece we meet the mythologem of Dionusos being born from the thigh of Zeus. In one version Semelē asked Zeus to appear in all his brilliant glory while she was six-months pregnant with his child; he did so, blazing away with his lightning and Semelē was burnt up. But then Hermes rushed and saved the embryo and stitched it within Zeus's thigh. The earliest attestation is in Euripides's *Bachai* 88-100 (*kata mērōi de kalupsas* 'having covered [the embryo] within the thigh' 97) which means c 420. In the Indian epic *Mahābhārata* Bk I, 169-71 there is the story of a radiant brahmin lady who fled from some cruel warriors carrying her child in her thigh; they found her but then the child issued out of the thigh blazing like the sun and blinded them. Here it may be claimed that the Indian tale is late and perhaps borrowed from Greece. But in the much earlier *Jaiminīya Brāhmaṇa* (III, 199), which would be 5th c at the latest, the child Kutsa is born from Indra's thigh: no details are given here, but Indra was, like Zeus, the storm-and-lightning god (Kazanas 2004c:46-49).

Let us take a fourth and final motif—**the severed head.** In Norse legendry, Odin preserves wise god Mimir's head (cut off by the Vanir) to consult it in times of danger and doubt (Davidson 1981:146). In the Welsh tradition the family of Lyr preserve Bendigeidfran's head (MacCana 1983:78). In Greek myths Bellerofon holds Medusa's head which still has the power to turn the onlooker into stone; then, Orpheus's head, after the Maenads tore him to pieces, floated down the river Hebros still lamenting and at Lesbos was installed as a shrine of prophecy. In India, in the *RV*, the Aśvins substituted sage

Dadhyañc's head with that of a horse to obtain secret knowledge and when Indra cut off the horse-head they reinstated the original. (See Macdonell 1898:141-2.)

Many more such motifs and parallels will be found in Kazanas 2001a, 2004c, all of which appear, as expected, with divergences in the east (=India) and in the west (Europe), but do not appear at all in intermediate Near East; these also suggest a common origin.

5. The aspects examined in §§ 3-4 indicate clearly that there is sufficient evidence to justify the claim for a unified PIE civilization which had a definite location somewhere in Eurasia before 6000 BC. It is generally assumed that 'civilization' means tools, large buildings, statues and paintings, ornaments, vehicles, weapons of war and other material artefacts. But civilization can flourish without advanced technology and artefacts, such as we find in Ancient Mesopotamia and Egypt: it can develop and thrive on elementary technology and very simple agriculture for a very long period of centuries and millennia. The difficulty will be that without the material evidence we don't know that there had been an advanced civilization. R Rudgley cites a modern scholar, Prof Yoshinory Yasuda who found "a marvellous principle" for civilization which is "respect for and co-existence with nature" and added: "Civilization begins to appear when a workable system for living, that is a proper relationship between men and nature, is established in accord with the features of a given region". Yasuda wrote this in regard to the Jōmon culture in Japan beginning c 10,000 BC (Rudgley 1998:31-33). No doubt there are many more definitions. One definition that is interesting because very unusual in directing our attention inwards is by A West who wrote about Ancient Egypt: "In a civilization, men are concerned with the quality of the *inner* life rather than with the *conditions* of day to day existence... a concern... to master greed, ambition, envy" (1993:6-7). Then, Plato's first ideal society is a community with simple agriculture, animal husbandry, essential crafts and trade (exchange), feeding on barley-bread and bulbs, drinking wine in moderation and singing hymns to the gods (*Republic* 370cff). The PIE civilization may have been of this nature with a "proper relationship between men and nature" and perhaps "a concern to master greed, ambition, envy" as their highest aspiration.

The evidence we have examined indicates clearly a unitary PIE civilization. The same evidence has sufficient diversity to show just as clearly that this civilization, wherever it was located (and this could have been an extensive area), lost its unity as, at a first stage perhaps, some sections of its population in different regions began to lose their pristine character deviating from the original norm and developing distinct linguistic and cultural peculiarities. At a second stage, again, different sections, large or small, successively moved away to new areas and eventually, settled to their respective historical habitats—Celts, Germans, Greeks etc. In this they influenced and were influenced by other cultural groups they encountered on the way or at the locus of settlement. Some lost many aspects of their original PIE culture, others lost most (at different indeterminate periods) and still others retained only meagre linguistic elements. Hence the considerable diverse cultural groups which, mainly through linguistic studies, have come to be known as the IE branches.

6a. Proto-Indoeuropean? From the linguistic fossils in the IE branches modern scholars have reconstructed what they claim to be the forms of words in the PIE language. They even call it a "science"; but it all seems wishful thinking. I have argued elsewhere (especially paper One) that reconstructions of Protolanguages are unreliable because they are conjectural and unverifiable: even if they happen to be right, we shall never be certain of this. O Szemerényi admits that reconstructions are used to facilitate comparisons, using one word instead of many IE variants, and cites

Hermann's statement that "complete forms (eg *deiwos [=S *deva-s*]) cannot be reconstructed at all, only single sounds, and even these are meant as approximation only" (Szemerényi 1996:33; my square brackets). Twenty years earlier Burrow had said much the same: "in the case of Indo-European it is certain that there was no such unitary language which can be reached by means of comparison ... the Indo-European that we can reach by this means was already deeply split up into a series of varying dialects" (1973:11). More recently, exhibiting scepticism like mine, X Tremblay writes (of various IE branches but mainly Iranian): "la grammaire comparée est en réalité *radicalement* incapable de discriminer entre parenté divergente ... et parenté convergente" (2005:63). This does not stop comparativists from reconstructing PIE forms and evince considerable faith in their 'scientific' reconstructions. And here we meet a serious instance of a conflict/divergence between thinking and acting that indicates great confusion.[4]

Now, let me take a simple example as starting point. Although I often use Rix's *Lexikon der indogermanische verben...* (eg § 17, below), I cannot but agree with A Marcantonio's critique of his methodology in taking often only 2 similar stems which, indeed, may be loans or may be devolutes of one stem in two closely related branches, eg Baltic and Slavic or Germanic. The examples I gave earlier (§ 3b) all have three or more cognations and encompass eastern and western branches. So, to start with, many stems may not be Proto-Indo-European and all such reconstructions are obviously pointless and utterly misleading.

Linguistic changes (vocabulary, accidence, spelling etc) are not subject to universal laws. The way English has changed from 1100 CE is quite different from the way French or Greek changed, even though some aspects are general

---

[4]A deep and wide inconsistency between thought and action must indicate something is amiss.

and common (loss of inflexion, increasing use of auxiliaries etc). Now, while certain general phenomena have some regularity and invariability and thus may be said to approximate the nature of "law" within documented and defined periods of changes in any one language or in relationships within a group of languages (like the IE), nonetheless all such phenomena have exceptions and, in any case, are specific to the particular period of the language or group of languages under examination. Marcantonio (2005) rightly criticizes many aspects of these so-called "laws"[5]. The changes in Vedic, Greek, Germanic and other languages differ enormously among themselves: eg the various forms of 'be/become' as in S √*bhū* (>*bhava-*), Gk *phuomai*, L *fui*, C *buith*, Gmc *be-* etc. Then again, Gk plosive *ph* became a fricative *f* as is the Italic *f*. How or why did the original initial consonant—whatever it was—change into these sounds? Linguists don't know. One comes across various hypotheses but there is no sure knowledge—because there is no documentation. The changes occurred in particular, if not precisely determined places, periods and peoples and

[5]She points out that, eg, there are 36 sound-rules governing consonantal differences between Latin and Germanic but only 34 attested parallels to support them. Marcantonio is, however, much too rigid in laying down her four criteria for scientifically determining genuine correspondences. Her 2nd criterion—that "a given sound in language A can correspond with only one sound in language B, or perhaps two (similar) alternatives in language B" contains an assumption which is untrue, the assumption that languages change uniformly. Changes in different languages are neither uniform nor parallel, as she herself points out (Marcantonio & Brady 2005), and therefore one can't rely on such strict correspondences. Ultimately one must rely on "naked eye" as she puts it, or "impressionistic" perceptions. If some regular sound-correspondences can be established, all well and good; but they should not be taken as absolute and exclusive of other alternatives. Thus Gk *theos* 'god' could well = L *deus*, S *deva*, and S *dvār* 'door' could well = Gk *thura*, Gmc *dawr/tor* etc. Marcantonio cites also S *napāt* 'offspring', Gk *nepodes* 'children, offspring', L *nepōs* 'nephew' and Gmc *nefo* 'nephew, relative' and takes exception to the sound d in Gk *nepodes* (pl with unattested sing) observing that it should—according to the specific "law"—be **t**. Well, as I said, the changes were not uniform and one must rely on one's discrimination, not "laws" nor statistics, though both are often useful.

stopped there. If linguists don't know how or why these changes occurred, then they most assuredly cannot know from existing material what the original forms were. It may be legitimate to make guesses and postulate certain forms (for the sake of convenience). But to proceed then to regard these entirely hypothetical forms as factual and use them in further comparisons with other hypothetical forms or build upon them structures and employ them as arguments in discussions about historical events seems to me wholly unacceptable.

6b. Consider a different example. In Greece, in the late 1970's an Act of Parliament imposed reforms in the spelling, accent and accidence of Modern Greek. Nobody could have predicted these changes 100 years earlier just as nobody could have predicted at c 900 CE the changes in English that would come with the Norman Conquest or later, after Chaucer. All such changes have no regularity, constancy or universality and are of the nature of accident—not law—due to social factors. If we can have no reliable predictions about future developments we can have no reliable reconstructions of forms in past periods before documentation: so also most emphatically Hock 1991. Reconstructions are futile, wasteful exercises.

Another obvious inconsistency is the reconstruction of three dorsals which are thought by many to be unnecessary (Szemerényi 1996; Sihler 1995; Lehman 1993; Speirs 1978) and one of which, the labio-velar family, is unpronounceable! How on earth can anyone pronounce as one unitary sound k^w or g^wh which contain both a guttural/velar and a labial element? One simply can't, however neat it looks on paper. To state that labio-velars exist in *Latin* (and other languages) is an assertion of no value. Certainly, we have L *qu-a-*(*lis*/ etc) and in English *qua-*(lity) and Italian *quando* etc. But in every case we have three separate, successive sounds: velar *q* (pronounced **k**), a glide vowel **-u-** and a vowel; in no case do we have a single, unitary consonant. In fact, the phonemes **qu**- do not differ from L **cu**-(lpo). If it is claimed that L **qu** is pronounced **q-v-** then, again we have two distinct sounds—the velar **q/k** and the labial semivowel **-v-**. Sanskrit also has *kva*, *dva*, *śva* etc: these can be pronounced only as separate successive sounds not as a single one. Attempts at describing how these hypothetical phonemes are pronounced (eg Clackson 2007:49-51) are theoretical and of no practical value. Please, try yourselves! Also to pronounce the monstrosity **dhg^{w}hec* 'to perish'! (For other unpronounceable examples see, for instance, Watkins 2000, 2001; Clackson 2007.)

A final point about laryngeals, which are wholly unattested except in Hittite (a language whose IE character is much decayed, being smothered by other neighbours rich in laryngeals). Let us consider the example of H_2 (or h_2 or ∂_2). This appears in PIE **dhugH$_2$ter* 'daughter' (Fortson 2004: 204): appears as a in Gk *thug**a**tēr*, but as *i* in S *duh**i**tar*. However, Av *duγδar* (Hale 2004:748) or *duxtar* (Fortson, 204) has neither *a* nor *i*. So what was the form in Proto-Indo-Iranian?... Not known. Old Avestan has *pta* for 'father' but later *patar* and *pitar* (Mayerhofer *KEWA*, vol 2, 277); this is S *pitṛ*, Gk *patēr* and L *pater* (Fortson, 23, 276) all allegedly from PIE **pH$_2$ter*. But, again, what was the from in Proto-Indo-Iranian?...Unknown. First of all consider that unlike S (which has many cognates from √*duh*), Av *duγδar* and Gk *thugater* stand isolated without related stems in their languages. Then, as M Hale observed, the *i* was not an invariable feature of Proto-Indo-Iranian (2004:748). The cognates for 'father' expose yet another inconsistency. L has also *Ju*[*s*]*pitar* with *i* as well as *pater* in the selfsame phonetic environment and B Fortson offers no explanation at all (2004:23, 33, 253, 261; also *Marspitār* 276, 406). A further difficulty sprouts out from S *pitr*. We mentioned already that Av has *pta*, *pitar* and *patar*, despite the selfsame phonetic environment. But according to IEnists S should have **phitṛ*! Because according to the IE "reconstruction"-system, the laryngeal H_2 becomes *i* in S but also aspirates the previous consonants. Thus PIE *$*stH_2to$* > S *s**thi**ta* 'one who has stood' and PIE *$*pletH_2$-* > S *pra**thi**man* 'width'. However, *pitṛ* has no aspirate *ph*! Those disparate phenomena show most flagrantly that these IE "reconstructions" and "phonetic laws" are anything but satisfactory.

7a. A most interesting aspect of Indoeuropean Linguistics is the root and the vowel gradation or *ablaut* system (or apophonie). Indoeuropeanists adopted an hypothetical five-grade ablaut from Greek. Now, the only language that has roots is Sanskrit. To begin with, the word 'root' does not strictly translate the S *dhātu* 'layer, element, constituent, seed-form'; nor can a "root" exist as an independent and generative element of a plant as a seed can. But putting this aside, only Sanskrit has roots and a proper vowel gradation. **All other IE branches have stems, not roots as such.** Like every other modern IE branch English has no actual working concept of root. (Of course 'act' in English can function as a root and generate '***act***-ed, ***act***-ing, ***act***-ion, ***act***-ivate, in-***act***-ively' etc, but 'act' itself comes ultimately from Latin.) Greek had verbs, and scholars say that nouns derive from the verb-stem: eg *che-ō* > *che-u-ma* 'a flow/stream'; *cho-ē* 'pouring, libation', *cho-a-nē* 'melting pot'; *chu-ma* 'the fluid', *chu-s*-is 'shedding', *chu-tra* 'earthen pot'; etc. Even if we took *che-* as the root, it is difficult to see how this develops into *cheu-*, *cho-* and then *chu-*! One realizes how inconsistent Greek is when one considers two similar verbs: *deō* 'bind' > *de-ma* 'band, rope', *de-s-is* 'the binding together', *de-s-mos* 'bond', (*dia-*)*dē-ma* 'ribbon round hair' —but no *deu-*, *do-* and *du-*; *pne-ō* 'blow, breathe' > *pne-u-ma* 'blast of air' (later 'spirit'), *pne-u-s-/pno-ē/pnoi-a* 'blast, breeze, breath'—showing unexpected *pnoi-* but not *pnu-*! If one examined other similar verbs (*bdeō, zeō, keō, xeō, neō* etc) one would find even more bizarre changes in the stem. There is no regularity; moreover the vowels change from palatal *e* to labial *u/o* etc without rhyme or reason.

Sanskrit has three gradations in the development of the root-stem: eg √*cit* 'being conscious of' >*cet-aś* 'mind, intelligence' or *cet-a-ti* 'he/she realizes', *a-cait* 'realized' (aor), *cait-anya* 'consciousness' etc ī always changes to *e* and *ai*, never to *a* or *u/o*. Similarly radical *u* → → *o* → → *au* and *ṛ* → → *ar* → → *ār*. Now, *ṛ* sometimes will give *ra/ri/ru* but will never become *i/e* or *u/o*. Thus there is the basic grade of the simple vowels *a*, *i*, *u*, *ṛ*, *ḷ* (though some roots have a 'developed' vowel), the strong (*guṇa*) grade *a* (same), e, *o*, *ar*, *al* and the fully developed one (vṛddhi) *ā*, *ai*, *au*, *ār*, *āl*. This triple gradation has its equivalent in Vedic cosmology and philosophy where we find three main world-levels—heaven, midair and earth (*svar*, *antarikṣa* and *pṛthivī*)—and causal or natural, subtle or mental and gross or material. As nouns and verbs are generated from the root, the radical vowel changes according to constant regulations (except, as was said, in the case of *ṛ* which is somewhat unstable). This process is absent from other IE branches. (And, as we see in Greek, it is utterly confused. Modern studies since, say J Kurylowicz (1956), O Szemerényi (1972) *et al*, rationalize but also tacitly acknowledge this fact.)

After Brugmann had turned against Sanskrit and favoured Greek (1912-16), comparativists adopted a five-grade ablaut from Greek *patēr* 'father' and *eupatōr* 'good father' in incredible disorder (Szemerényi, p 84):

i) *pa-ter-a* (acc sing) where—*ter-* shows ***e*** as the basic grade (to be distinguished from S *e* which is long and second grade).

ii) *eu-pa-tor-a* (acc sing) where—*tor-* shows the **o**-grade (again to be distinguished from S *o* which is long). But note that, unlike the Sanskrit series, here we have a different noun declension and sound-family: *e* is palatal and *o* labial!

iii) *pa-tr-os* (gen sing) where—*tr-* shows the zero or nil grade! But here we have in fact syncopation or loss of vowel (*lopa* in S).

iv) *pa-tēr* (nom sing) where—*tēr* shows the long-vowel grade (**ē**).

v) *eu-pa-tōr* (nom sing) where—*tōr* shows the long *ō* grade (**ō**-mega).

Obviously there is neither rhyme nor reason in all this. More importantly, the ablaut occurs in the affix -t-*r*- not the root stem. This series, if it can be considered such, might have some validity if it occurred in one noun or one verb and if it followed some principle(s) that governed the same changes in many other nouns or verbs. Szemerényi gives instead the following examples stating that "Very often only full grade [ie the vowel *e*], o-grade and zero grade are attested" (p 84):

a) *leip-ō* (pres) *le-loip-a* (perf), *e-lip-on* (aor) 'leave'

b) *derk-omai* (pres), *de-dork-a* (perf), *e-dr-akon* (aor) 'perceive'.

c) *penthos* (neut nom sing), *pe-ponth-a* (perf), *e-path-on* (aor) 'grieve'.

Here one cannot but wonder at this astonishing presentation, which merely increases the disorder. Here we have more bizarre phenomena. First, the vowel-change occurs in the stem, not in affixes or terminations, as above. Then *leip-* and *derk-* are verbs but *penthos* in (c) is a noun! Then the zero grade is not syncopation or disappearance of the vowel as in (iii) above, but a different vowel ***–i*** in (a) and ***a*** in (c). Another difficulty is the dipthong *ei* in (a); for we find also *eu-pa-**teir**-a* (nom sing fem 'she of a noble father') and we now do not know whether this is full grade as with ***leip**-ō*, or a sixth grade according to the five-grade presentation above[6].

But what principles govern these so-called vowel-grades in Greek? In fact there are no principles such as we have in Sanskrit! Clackson writes at length about the

[6]Here too we have examples showing apparently great confusion as noted in § 7.

significance of the root but does not give a single example in PIE or any branch of a root generating primary and secondary derivatives as in Sanskrit (2007:65-9, 187-191). This issue and others like the obvious problems of reconstructed sounds, especially consonants, I have discussed at great length elsewhere (Kazanas 2004b) and we need not therefore spend more time with them. A quotation from Burrow should suffice here: "Chiefly owing to its antiquity the Sanskrit language is more readily analysable and its roots more easily separable from other accretionary elements *than any other IE language* (Burrow 1973:123, 289, my emphasis).

7b. By way of conclusion, let me repeat that PIE cannot be reconstructed at all from the available data in the known IE branches. The comparative efforts fail as a science miserably, because they employ far too many "laws" which at the same time have far too many exceptions and discrepancies. One of the worst aspects is the reconstruction of words that, as we saw, look very nice on paper but cannot be pronounced—like **nekʷts* 'night' or **dhghm̥ma* 'on the ground' etc. The positive sciences have as their final testing ground Maths and the reality of the material world. What corresponds to this in the linguistic/phonetic field is sound, *pronounceable sound*! If the lexemes we produce are unpronounceable, then our system is wrong.

A linguist not involved in IE comparativism, R Nixon (Professor of Linguistics at Australian National University) points out sharply (1997:46) that R Hall reconstructed the Original for the Romance languages (Italian, French, Spanish etc) but this was only a partial approximation to Latin, though some elements were correct. F Southworth made a similar study of the various Indoaryan languages and his result also was only a partial approximation to Sanskrit. Nixon points out that each scholar knew the respective original language. Nixon's implication is that not much of the PIE reconstruction could be correct when the IEnists do not and cannot know the PIE since there are no documents in the PIE languages. Enough said on this subject.

Indo-Aryan

8. Having held and taught for more than 18 years, but without investigating, the received doctrine that the IE branches dispersed from the South Russian or Pontic Steppe (as per Mallory 1997, 1989; Gimbutas 1985, 1970; and others), and that the IAs had entered Saptasindhu c 1500, I began to examine these mainstream notions thoroughly and c 1997 abandoned them. I decided that no evidence of any kind supported them; on the contrary, the evidence showed that by 1500 the IAs were wholly indigenous and that the elusive IE homeland was very probably Saptasindhu and the adjacent area—the Land of Seven Rivers in what is today N-W India and Pakistan; this area could well have extended as far northwest as the Steppe.

Apart from the (recent) genetic studies, which at that time were not so well-known nor so secure (see § 19, below) the decisive evidence for me now is the antiquity of Sanskrit indicated by its inner coherence and its preservation of apparently original PIE linguistic features (like the dhātu, five families of phonemes, etc) and cultural elements (eg § 4). The Vedic language as seen in the RV alone, despite much obvious attrition and several innovations, has preserved many more features from the putative PIE language and wider culture. This was due to its well attested and incomparable system of oral tradition (papers One, Three and Kazanas 2004b) which preserved the ancient texts fairly intact (*RV*, *AV*, etc) and continued even into the 20th c. An oral tradition of this kind cannot be maintained by a people on the move for decades if not centuries over many thousands of miles, as the AIT proposes. Such a tradition could be preserved only by a sedentary people where the older generation would have the necessary leisure to pass the communal lore to the younger one[7].

9. I was not of course the first to come up with such a view. On the strength of Sanskrit many European scholars in the early 19th c thought India was the original homeland (Mallory 1973:26-9). Even after scholars rejected India in the later 19th c and began to adduce different urheimats from the Baltic to the Balkans rewriting Indian (proto-)history, there was a succession of Indian scholars, mainly, who maintained the indigenist view in one or other form: Rao 1880; Shri Aurobindo 1914; Dhar 1930; A Das 1971 et al. Indeed, in recent years also many publications advocated indigenism: Sethna 1992; Elst 1993, 1999; Talageri 1993, 2000; Frawley 1994 and with Rajaram 1997; Feuerstein et al 1995; and others. In fact, more and more scholars in the West have re-examined the issue and rejected the mainstream view advocating instead a movement Out of India into Europe: Schildman 1994, 1998; Elst 1999; Friedrich 2003, 2004; Danino 2007. Here we must add the fact that since 1984 there is full consensus among archaeologist specialists in the area that the ISC has unbroken continuity (Lal & Gupta 1984; Allchin 1997; Kenoyer 1999; Shaffer & Lichtenstein 1999;

---

[7]In a private communication, Nov 2004, Mallory mentioned the Jews who wandered much and long and preserved their traditions of the *Old Testament*. If we take the Hebrew traditional orthodox view (which is by no means accepted generally), the Judaic people had literacy certainly since the time of Moses (c 1300-1100?) and most probably since their stay in Ur of the Chaldees c 1700-1600 (*Genesis* 11), since the Mesopotamians had literacy for more than a millennium earlier. So we can't say that the Jews maintained an oral tradition during their long travels. Then, the Jews mention constantly the (mis-)adventures they had and the different people they met on their travels. If we assume that the IAs had their oral tradition even as (according to the AIT) they travelled from the Steppe to Saptasindhu, what was it they were transmitting? The Vedic texts were composed (it is universally agreed) in India. So what were they transmitting before?... Why is there not one mention in the Vedic texts of dangers, mishaps and alien people met on the way—as we find in the Judaic texts? There is no such mention for the simple reason that, unlike the Jews, the IAs did not migrate. See discussion in paper Three.

McIntosh 2002; Possehl 2003). Thus the mainstream strident cries of warning about "fundamentalists, nationalists, revisionists" in India and their colleagues in the West (Witzel 2003; Huld 2002; Kuzmina 2002) are seen to be either hollow slogans or echoes of those slogans; for neither the indigenist scholars mentioned above nor the archaeologists specializing in the ISC and insisting on its unbroken continuity down to the 6th century belong to this (non-existent) band of bogies. I benefited from all of them.

Nonetheless, the AIT persists. Several linguistic arguments have been adduced to prop up this fanciful theory one of them being the (loan-)words in the *RV* language which were allegedly borrowed from other languages met by the IAs on their way to and at Saptasindhu. A closely related argument is the alleged common Indo-Iranian period during this journey to Saptasindhu[8]. Good examples of a combination of these two arguments are found in M Witzel 2001, 2005 and F Kuiper 1991. RS Sharma too makes the exaggerated claim that Vedic is "a mixture of Munda and Dravidian words with the Indo-Aryan language" (2004:142) which is linguistically an absurd statement. But that 4% of the Rigvedic vocabulary might consist of loanwords (as these controversial studies claim), or even 6% or more, surely should not be surprising since the IAs did not live in a vacuum and there must have been peoples with different languages around them. However, this pet linguistic subject of Witzel's has been attacked by RP Das (1995 general critique), by Krishnamurti (2003:37-8 mainly against Dravidian cognations) and paper One[9]. Recently even (non-indigenist) HH Hock questioned all supposed borrowings finding them unconvincing (2005:

[8]A common Indo-Iranian period there definitely was but this, according to a different view, is to be found in Saptasindhu whence later the Iranians left.

[9]Witzel's earlier views on these loans and Bryant's emphasis on linguistic argument (2001) have been contested by me in various articles; article 2002b is paper One herein.

286)—and he happens to be a most eminent comparativist. In any case, no amount of arguing along these lines gives of itself any actual dates even approximately and the direction of movement can more reasonably be the reverse. There is B Sergent who, although not at all an indigenist, argued in favour of a movement from Central Asia north-westward (1997). Also, Johanna Nichols, an eminent Indo-European linguist, found on purely linguistic grounds that "the locus of the IE spread was ... somewhere in the vicinity of ancient Bactria" (1997:113)—which is only a stone's throw away from Saptasindhu. Linguists will continue to disagree violently among themselves about the original locus (from the Baltic to the Balkans and to Bactria), about the direction of the movement and about the date: some give a late period somewhere c 3000, others an early one, in the 7th millennium (Misra 1992)—and all these disagreements on exactly the same linguistic data! I ignore all such linguistic arguments and conclusions since they are so contradictory. I ignore also the results from the reappearence in Gray & Atkinson (2003) of the discredited method of glottochronology. The situation is in no way improved by claims that "I am right' and allegations that "the others are wrong". We must bear in mind also that all such arguments involve "reconstructed" proto-languages which are sheer conjectural affairs and therefore inadmissible in any impartial court of law.

10. Horses and chariots One of the best known comparative linguists of our times, Hans Hock, pointed out repeatedly (1999, 1996) that several dialects spoken in N-W India travelled north-westward at different times in the Common Era, the most notable one being that of the Gypsies in the early centuries CE (see also Fraser 1995). Hock stated that Indoaryan indigenism and even the Out of India Theory could theoretically be possible, provided the distribution of the IE isoglosses was accepted and the Vedic language was seen to be a devolved form of Proto-Indo-European—facts which I certainly accept fully. But he opted for the mainstream doctrine (=the AIT out of the Pontic Steppe) because of the archaeological evidence of horses and chariots arriving in Saptasidhu in bulk after 1700 BCE (1999:13). Thus he supports the spread of the Kurgan culture (as do also Allchin B and R, Gimbutas, Kuzmina, Mallory, Parpola, Witzel et al), even though the cranio-skeletal evidence for this diffusion is very limited according to J Day (2001). Hock also mentions that it is simpler to have one movement into India rather than many out of it to account for the diversity and chronologies of the spread of the various IE branches. But this is rather self-contradictory since, as he wrote (1996, 1999), the Indoaryan language left India north-westwards three times in the Common Era and generated new dialects and the Gypsies did reach the north-west extremity of Europe into England; so Indoaryan could have done the same in the misty past BCE. Besides, the ancient IAs could, in the Out of India scenario, have left in a sizeable mass, stayed in a location in Baluchistan/Afghanistan (or even the Steppe) for some time, then, successively, in groups, moved away in diverse directions. We need not make a problem out of this rather simple affair. (But I have argued in other papers that we must not preclude the possibility of a broad IE continuum from the Kurgan steppe down to Saptasindhu at a very early period from which, within which and into which occurred various undetermined movements.)

On the matter of horses and chariots, Hock was misinformed, I like to think. The evidence of horses and chariots proves the very opposite if examined with a modicum of attention. As one authority put it, "the horse was widely domesticated and used in India during the third millennium BCE over most of the areas covered by the Indus-Sarasvati [or Harappan] Civilization" (Pande 1999:344; the square brackets original). I myself collected much evidence for horse-finds in different ISC (=Indus-Sarasvati Civilization/ Culture) sites in a papers of 2003, § 10 (pp 196-7): thus one may further consult Kochhar (2000 pp 186, 192), Chakrabarti

(1999), Lal (1997), Sharma (1996 p 17), Thomas et al (1995), Dhavalikar (1995:116-7), Allchin & Joshi (1995:95), Rao (1991) and, necessarily, Sharma (1980:110ff). M Danino's paper 'The horse and the Aryan Debate' is a more recent addition to this literature (2006c). These publications show abundantly that the true horse, *Equus ferus* and *Equus cabalus*, was present in its wild state in India from c 17000 and there is much evidence now for the domesticated horse in the Mature Harappan period. Moreover there are several terracota figurines of this animal from different ISC sites as reported by Lal (2002) and Tharpar & Mughal (1994).

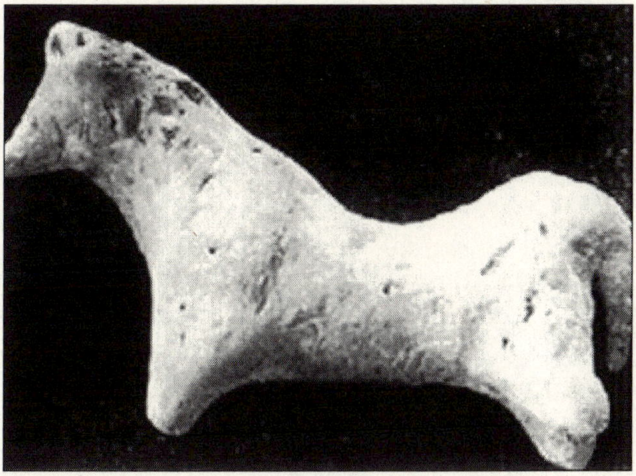

Lothal: Terracotta horse, Mature Harappan

As for the chariot, S Piggott established the presence of a sophisticated type of vehicle with "one or two pairs of wheels with their axles ... from the Rhine to the Indus by around 3000" (1992:18).

Archaeological evidence does not consist only of the actual remains of buildings, weapons, tools, chariots etc. Pictures, reliefs, toys and figurines of these things are also evidence. Many years ago HK Sankalia had pointed out that the six-spoked wheel appears on seals and signs of the alphabet (1974:363). SR Rao found at Lothal "terracotta wheels ... with diagonal lines suggesting spokes" (1973: 124). This representational practice seems to have been widespread, for S Piggott mentions similarly marked wheels found in the Karpathian Basin from the Earlier Bronze Age (1983:91-92). In his recent study, Lal presents four terracotta wheels (from Mature Harappan sites Banawali, Kalibangan, Rakhigarhi) with spokes painted on (2002:74, Figs 3.28ff). The Harappans had the technology for making spoke-wheels (Kazanas 1999:33; Basham 1954:21).

Finally, it was A Parpola, an inveterate adherent of the AIT, who identified the figure on Harappan seal No 3357 as representing simplistically a man with outstretched arms standing on two six-spoked wheels (of a chariot) realizing that this was "a later invention of the Aryans' (1969:24). The later notion that it is a potter on two wheels is obviously far-fetched and, in any case, the wheel is spoked (Sethna 1992)! LS Rao has recently presented many more finds of models of terracotta toy wheels with spokes from Harappan locations in *Purātattva*, vol 36 (pp 59-66), 2006.

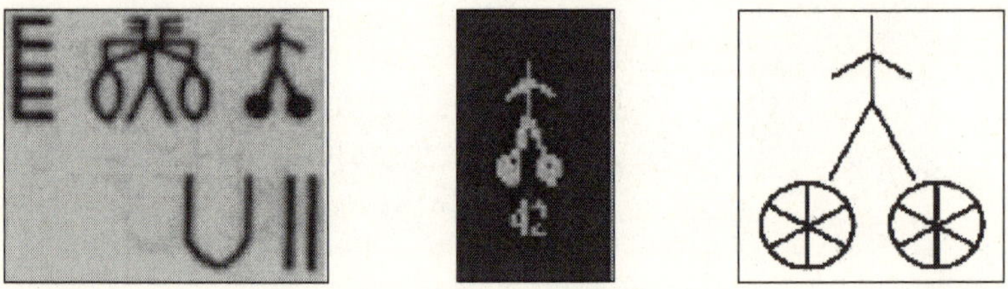

Spoked Wheel

Rakhigarhi: Terracotta wheel with pointed spokes

Kalibangan: Terracotta wheel with pointed spokes

11. The question of course is whether there were spoked wheels before 3000 since the *RV* uses the word *ara* which is usually translated as 'spoke' (1.32.15; 5.58.5; etc). We don't know. Some Indian scholars approach the issue strategically and say that Rigvedic hymns with *ara* are later intrusions from the second millennium when the spoked wheel was quite common. This is possible of course, since we know that some hymns are later interpolations. However, there could have been spoked wheels as we know them even at c 3200 and before. But then again, *ara* need not mean 'spoke'. It could mean a section of the (solid) wheel. After all, different IE branches have a different stem for spoke (Gk *aktis*, *knēmē*; L *radius*; Gmc *speca/speihha*, etc) which suggests that spokes were developed after the dispersal (in the 6th or 8th millennium, or whichever). So *ara* could well have meant something other than spoke and only later acquired the meaning of 'spoke', as we know it now. The spoked wheel poses, in fact, no problem for dating the *RV*. There are other more clearcut types of evidence which are examined below.

The usual objection is that there are no chariot remains from that period. Here, there is the double assumption that *RV* chariots are necessarily like near-eastern ones of, say, 1500, or the Androvo c 1900, and that there should be remains. But why assume that the *RV* chariots are like the near-eastern ones? The only real-life vehicle in a race that we know is in 10.102 and this is pulled by oxen not horses while 1.123.1 alludes to a 'broad chariot' *pṛthū́ rathaḥ*! Elsewhere in the *RV* the chariot *ratha* is described as being *bṛhat* 'tall, big' (6.61.13), also *variṣṭha...vandhura* 'widest... seated' (6.47.9), *trivandhura* 'three seated' (1.41.2; 118.2; 7.71.4; 8.22.5; etc) and once even *aṣṭavandhura* 'eight-seated' (10.53.7)! These are all **rathas** and hardly like the near-eastern battle-chariots. Then again, there are no remains of chariots in India from 1500 or 1000 or 700. So, on the strict AIT thinking, we should say no chariots were brought in by the alleged IE entrants either.

12. Harappan features absent in the *RV*. The Harappan or Indus-Sarasvati Culture has certain characteristics which help to define its uniqueness. A number of these features are absent from the *RV* and this absence indicates that the *RV* is pre-Harappan. Arguments *e silentio* are not decisive since absence of evidence is not always evidence of real absence. But in this case the features are far too many. (Some of these were noted by Sethna, 1992.)

a) *iṣṭakā* 'brick'. The *RV* mentions as building materials metal, stone, mud and wood but not 'brick', which was the basic material in Harappan constructions. This is found in post-Rigvedic texts: the word *iṣṭakā* is not in the *RV*. Archaeologists write of the early Harappan or Ravi phase (ie 3300-2800): "These early settlers built huts made of wood with wattle-and-daub" (K Kenoyer and RH Meadow 2007:125). This is the common habitation in the whole of the *RV*. Brick-walls came later, as Kenoyer pointed out much earlier: these appear after this early phase, ie after 2800 (Kenoyer 1997/2000:56). The dates 3300-2800 BCE are different from those given by SP Gupta who places this early phase c 3700 and before and calls it Hakra-Ravi (2007:223).

b) Urbanization is wholly absent in the RV. There certainly was "nomad pastoralism" as mainstreamers emphasize repeatedly but there were also agricultural settlements (a fact which mainstreamers underplay or do not mention). The hymn to Kṣetrapati 'Lord of the Field/Soil' (4.57) alone should suffice but also the girl Apālā refers to her father's *urvarā* 'fertile field' (8.91.5); then there are many cultivation implements *khanitra* 'shovel', *lāṅgala/sīra* 'plough', *sṛṇī* 'sickle', etc. Moreover, there is weaving with loom, shuttle, warp and woof (*RV* 1.134.4; 1.3.6; etc, etc) and metallurgy with smithies of sorts (4.2.17; 5.9.5; etc). Such activities imply settlement.

Some writers think the Rigvedic and Harappan cultures converge (Gupta 2005, Bisht 1999, Lal 1998, Singh 1995). As evidence is cited the word *pur-* which denotes 'city, citadel, fort, town' as its Greek and Baltic cognates 'polis' and '*pil*(*i*)s' do. This is a very general misconception. In the *RV pur* never means anything other than an occult, magical, esoteric defence or stronghold which is not created nor ever destroyed by humans as we saw earlier as in 'Ṛgvedic Pur', paper Four. The ISC cities had regular blocks, large buildings, also domestic and urban water-supply (McIntosh 2001:100-101; Gupta: 2007:235) the *RV* knows nothing of all these. There are references to *oka*, *gṛha*, *dama*, *dhāma* etc, all of which can denote any type of 'home/house' (made of wood and mud), or the thousand-pillared mansion of kings Mitra and Varuṇa in the sky (2.41.5; 5.62.6: probably suggested by sunrays streaming down through clouds; for not even ISC cities had such mansions!). These most certainly do not indicate any urbanization: neither brick- nor stone-walls are mentioned nor other features found in the ISC towns.

Such rigvedic settlements are pre-urban as known in the mature Harappan. "These are found spreading from Taxila in the northwest through the eastern foothills of Baluchistan through Rajasthan and Haryana via Punjab, Sindh and Kachch. All this presupposes the existence of a very strong internal network which was fully operational by 3000 BC" (Gupta 2007:214).

The words for 'council' *sabhā* and *samiti* are also cited by some scholars but, surely, any community can have a council of elders without urbanization. Allusions in the *RV* to chiefs/kings *rājā* and overlords/emperors *samrāṭ* also do not show urbanization since such offices can just as easily exist in rural communities. (The Red Indians in North America, nomadic and rural tribes, had local chiefs and overlords.) Pathways and/or roads (*path-*) also have been mentioned as crossing or branching out, but these too can be just as easily seen in a rural context. (For all these claims see Singh 1995; Bisht 1999 and Lal 2002, 2005.)

c) Fixed altars or hearths are unknown in the *RV* but common in the ISC cities. The Rigvedic altar is a shallow bed dug in the ground and covered with grass (eg *RV* 5.11.2,

7.43.2-3; Parpola 1988:225). Fixed brick-altars are very common in post-Rigvedic texts.

d) Many cities were abandoned and fell to ruination after 1900 BC when the Harappans began to move eastward because of the drying up of the Sarasvatī and of the more general desiccation due to tectonic disturbances and climatic changes. The *RV* knows nothing of such ruins even though, according to the AIT, the IAs moved through these regions c 1700-1500 (in small waves, settled there, in the midst of deserts, and wrote the hymns which praise the mighty Sarasvatī!). Some attempts have been made to read hymn 1.133 with its *arma-ka* (=of unknown meaning, really) as a description of a ruined city (eg Burrow 1963, Rao 1991:32) but, in fact, the hymn mentions no ruined buildings, no fallen walls and no materials such as wood, stone or bricks! It is a ghostly scene of frightful desolation, peopled only with unfriendly she-fiends and demons (*yātumati*, *piśāci* and *rakṣas*). In sharp contrast the Old English poem *The Ruin* contains such persuasive details of the ancient remains (from Roman times?) that some scholars think it refers to the town of Bath (Mitchell & Robinson 1996:252-5).

e) No cotton *Karpāsa* appears in the *RV* although this plant was extensively cultivated in the ISC and the fabric was exported as far as Egypt in the middle of the 3rd millennium while the Mesopotamians adopted the name as *kapazum* (? from *prākṛta kapāsa*). The *RV* has 'skin' *eta* (1.166.10; *ajina* in *AV* 5.21.7 etc), 'wool' *avi* (*RV* 9.78.1) and *śāmulya* (10.85.29) and numerous terms for clothing and weaving but no mention of cotton. Be it noted that *karpāsa* is the only word for cotton in Sanskrit. It is found first in the sūtra texts, in Gautama's (1.18) and in Baudhāyana's (16.13.10) *Dharmasūtra*. Now, although cotton seeds were found at Mehrgarh period II, c 5000, none were found in subsequent periods. Cotton cultivation appears only in the Mature SSC, after 2500. Thus the sūtra texts can be placed at this period at the earliest, ie c 2600.

f) Silver *rajata* also makes no appearance in the *RV* though gold and copper are well attested and silver is plentiful in the ISC. The word *rajata* occurs in *RV* 8.25.22 and it denotes a steed or a chariot 'shining white'. Only in later texts is it used singly (*AV* 5.28.1) or with *hiraṇya* to denote 'silver' or 'white gold' = 'silver' (see *Vedic Index* 2:196-7 and Lubotsky 2:1169).

g) Rice *vrīhi* too is absent from the *RV* although it appears in various sites of the ISC from at least 2300 (and in the Ganges Valley from the 6th millennium)[10]. The *RV* knows only *yava* 'barley'. Rice becomes important in post-Rigvedic ritual and the more general diet. Some writers argue that the *RV* has food-preparations of rice like *apūpa*, *puroḷāś* and *odana* (Talageri 2000:126-7). This is possible, of course. All three are in post-rigvedic tradition said to be rice-preparations (though *apūpa* is given as flour-cake in most texts and 'wheat' in Lexica). But *odana* is primarily a water or fluid preparation (*ud-*) and *odatī* 'refreshing, dewy' is an epithet of Uṣas, the Dawngoddess. Since *vrīhi* 'rice' does not appear in *RV* (but does appear in *AV*) and rigvedic yava is from the earliest tradition accepted as 'barley', I take it that the rigvedic people had barley and not rice.

h) Literacy is not known in the RV. Some scholars think it was known and cite *RV* 10.71.4 or *AV* 19.72 (eg Kak: 2003, Frawley 1991).

RV 71.4a says: *utá tvaḥ páśyan ná dadarśa vắcam, utá tvaḥ sṛṇván ná śṛṇoti-enām* 'seeing indeed (utā) one sees not Vāk [and] hearing indeed one hears her not'. Vāk is the

---

[10]Private communication from SP Gupta, Chairman of Indian Archaeological Society (June 2006). See also Sharma 1980 for rice in the Ganges basin in the 5th millennium and R Tewari et al in *Purātattva* 2006 (vol 36:68-75) for rice, again in the Ganga basin, north-east, in the district Sant Kabir Nagar (UP) in 7th millennium. These locations are too far from Vedic Saptasindhu but it seemss likely that by 3000 the composers of the AV had become acquainted with rice *vrīhi* and later this grain was cultivated in the ISC too.

mighty goddess of Speech (or Language) through which all things excellent and pure were manifested (*níhitam-āviḥ*, stanza 1). What st 4a-b says is that some people see and hear but, in fact they don't know Vāk (a) and the goddess reveals herself to those [she chooses] as a well-dressed, loving wife to her husband (b). There is not a single hint in all eleven stanzas that there is writing. In fact st 11 says that some sing (*gā-*) the psalms and prosper and some brahmins utter (*vad-*) knowledge and thus deal out (*vi-mā-*) the measures/regulations of sacrifice; there is no suggestion of writing: it is all oral. *vāc* means 'speech, utterance', never writing.

D Frawley thought that a passage in *AV* 19.72 may refer to writing: 'From whichever receptacle *kośāt* we have taken the Veda, into that we put it down'. Books in ancient India consisted in collections of palm-leaves or strips of birch-bark and were kept in boxes (1991:249). Whether this is enough to establish knowledge of writing is doubtful. The word veda is 'knowledge' generally and not necessarily one of the three Vedas which in any case were transmitted orally. The word *kośa* could refer to some (metaphorical) non-material storing-place, eg memory, lower mind (*manas*) higher mind (*cetas, bodha,* both in *AV*) etc. In any case, there is no other passage even remotely hinting at writing.

Words like *likh-*, *lekha*(*-na*) and mainly *lipi* (Pāṇini 3.2.21) denoting 'writing' are not in use before the sūtra texts. The vast corpus of *Brāhmaṇa*, *Araṇyaka* and *Upaniṣad* texts have not a single hint about writing and so create an enormous gap between the AV and the sūtra period. Someone would have made a reference to writing somewhere in all these texts! So, writing was known in the ISC and the sūtras but not in the *RV*.

True, *Aitareya Āraṇyka* 5.3.3 has both *ul-likhya* and *ava-likhya* and at first sight one might think these are references to writing particularly as they occur in a context about study (Deshpande 1966). But this very context, in fact, disallows the meaning "writing". For the text says "the student should not study/learn (*adhīyīta*) ... after "writing" (*ul-likhya*); if the student does not learn in conjunction with writing, then when would he do so? Moreover, the wider context stresses memorizing from the guru's utterances; again, if there was writing, it would have been mentioned and memorization would not have been stressed. (See Falk 1992 with full references). So, in fact, there are no allusions (*likh-*, *lip-*,) with the meaning 'writing' before the Sūtra-texts.

i) The *RV* has no allusions to artistic iconography—paintings, relif representations, statue(-tte)s or seals, all so common in the ISC. (The *RV* 4.24.10 asks "Who will buy this my Indra" and this is thought by some to refer to a statuette, but this could be a transfer of favour and it is the only reference in the whole *RV* without the use of any word for statue or icon.)

13. Now all the fore-mentioned features are found in post Rigvedic texts—the Saṃhitās, the Brāhmaṇas and fully in the Sūtra literature. For instance, brick altars are mentioned in *Śatapatha Brāhmaṇa* 7.1.1.37, or 10.2.3.1 etc. Rice *vrīhi* is found in *AV* 6.140.2; 7.1.20; etc. Cotton *karpāsa* appears first in Gautama's (1.18) and in Baudhāyana's (14.13.10) *Dharmasūtra*. The fact of the convergence of the post-Rigvedic texts and the Harappan culture was noted long ago by archaeologists. B & R Allchin stated unequivocally that these features are of the kind "described in detail in the later Vedic literature" (1982:203).

If we had a case of 2 or 3 items we could bypass them saying indeed that absence of evidence is no evidence of absence; but the items are many and the absence of the building material *iṣakṭā* in the *RV* (against the presence of wood, stone, mud and metal) seems to me quite decisive.

We must also take into account that many iconographic motifs, Harappan artefacts, decorations or seals, show affinity with elements found in post-Rigvedic texts. Thus PK Agrawala (2005) draws attention to round-bottomed perforated pots from Harappan sites and a vessel (*kuṃbha*) with nine holes (*navavitṛṇṇa*) or 100 holes (*śatavitṛṇṇa*) mentioned in *Śatapatha Br* 5.5.4.27 and *śatatṛṇṇā kumbhī* 'a pitcher with 100 perforations' in 12.7.2.13. These and other similar descriptions echo the White Yajurveda (*Vājasaṇeyī Saṃhitā*) verse 19:87 'a pitcher with 100 streams'. Such vessels were used for ritual sprinkling. A second parallel is furnished by the two-horned bovine-like animal, duplicated and facing itself, (on a Mohenjodaro) seal with long necks and the pipal tree growing out of their juncture. This corresponds (writes Agrawala) to the two-headed cattle dvāyā in *AV* 5.19.7. Agrawala mentions other parallels of a two-headed tiger and a two-headed bird (2005:10-13). Thus it is indeed the later Vedic texts that have parallels with the Harappan arts and crafts, not the *RV*.

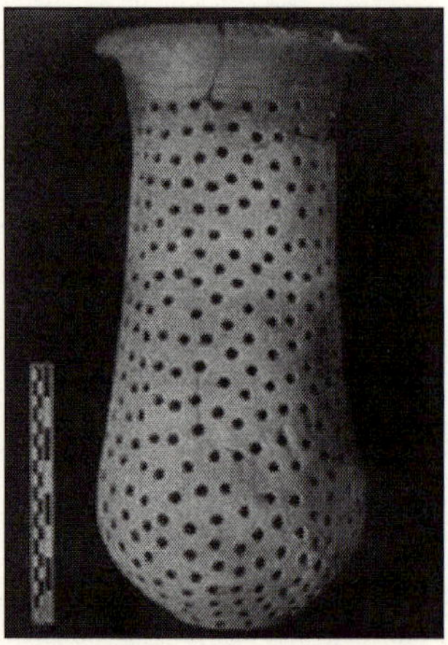

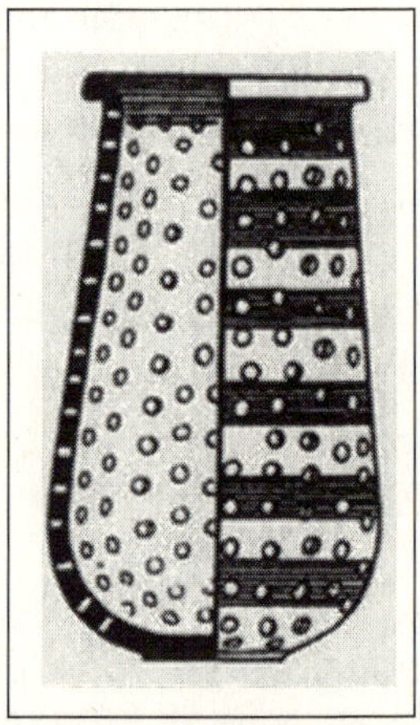

Pot with 100 perforations: *Śatapatha Br* 12.7.2.13.

dvāyā in *Atharvaveda* 5.19.7. *OM?*

N Rajaram follows a similar line of investigation (2005) and adduces iconographic motifs from Harappan seals but does not distinguish between Rigvedic (or early Vedic) and post-Rigvedic (or late Vedic) periods and cultures. Thus he cites the aśvattha-tree foliage and the horse and links them to the RV disregarding the fact that these are not exclusively Rigvedic and therefore could be simply from a post-Rigvedic period. Moreover he cites the svastika and the sign of sound OM, both of which are, as he states, from post-Rigvedic texts. It is also doubtful that the seal-sign which is horizontal, depicts the symbol for OM, which should be upright, anyway. (But, of course, the seal could be seen as upright since we don't know what the symbols indicate.)

It is an astonishing phenomenon but some scholars make the extraordinary claim that because these items are not in the RV, this text must be post-Harappan (Witzel 2001; RS Sharma 2004)! Thus, blithely and illogically they put the proverbial cart before the horse and—and push!

On this score, then, the bulk of the RV, is pre-Harappan, or 3000+. This, of course, could well be the very early proto-ISC (=Harappan culture) starting at c 3800 (Gupta 2007:214; see § 12b).

14. Some Brāhmaṇas comment on or give explanations of incidents in the Rigvedic hymns. For example, the *Aitareya Br* 7.13.33 narrates extensively the story of *Śunaḥepa*, alluded to briefly in *RV* 1.24.12-13 and 5.2.7, while the *Śatapatha Br* 11.5.1 comments on the the Pururavas and *Urvaśī* love story given elliptically in dialogue form in *RV* 10.95. Another point to note. Some legends in the *RV* remain unexplained. For instance, who was Bhujyu whom the Aśvins saved from a tempest (1.116.3-4; etc) and how did he find himself in that predicament? The later texts say nothing more. Or, take the birth of Indra; was he an unwelcome child to Aditi and did he commit parricide (4.18.1ff; etc)? Again, the Brāhmaṇas tell us nothing. Obviously such exegetical texts would not have been composed until the understanding regarding the older texts had lapsed: this implies many centuries.

What is the date of the Brāhmaṇas? Well, S Kak ascribes the *Śatapatha* to the early third millennium (1997, 1994) saying that the Pleiades/Kṛttikas not swerving from the east, as is stated in this *Brāhmaṇa* (2.1.2.3), could only occur c 2950 BCE. Narahari Achar (Prof Astrophysics, Memphis, USA) using computer and planetarium apparatus arrived at a date c 3000 pointing out that SB Dikshit had arrived at similar conclusions 100 years earlier but was ignored by Western scholars (1999): these scholars really had no knowledge of astronomy. BB Lal too thought that "astronomical calculations (re *Aitareya Br*) would place the *RV* in the fourth millennium" but did not then adopt such a date only because he could not judge the evidence (1997:286).

So we could again place the *RV* easily before 3000.

15. The *Bṛhadāraṇyaka Upaniṣat* has three *vaṃśas*, ie list of teachers, each comprising 65-70 names. The first 4 or 5 are names of gods in the normal Indic way which ascribes the beginning of every human activity to some deity. Let us take the mainstream date of early sixth century for this text (say 550) according to the AIT premises and let us take 60 teachers giving to each one an average of 15 years, though 20 and 30 would be more realistic. This exercise has now been tilted very heavily in favour of the AIT and mainstream views because, in truth, in this text we read "I ask about that upanishadic Person (*aupaniṣadaṃ puruṣaṃ pṛcchāmi* 3.9.26) which indicates that there was a traditional upanishadic teaching about Puruṣa as a spiritual being (=Self) and this aspect we meet in the *Atharvaveda*. However, let us bypass this point. These calculations (60×15=900 plus 550) give us a date c 1450 for the inception of the doctrines in this Upaniṣat. The chief doctrine is that the self of man (*ātman*) is the same in all beings and the same as the Self of the universe (*brahman* 'Mystic Spirit' or 'Absolute'). We should also bear in mind that the teachers' names are quite different from those of the seers of the *RV* hymns as given by the native tradition. Following others, M Witzel thinks these lists "rest on typically weak foundations" (2001, § 19) but this is a typically weak subterfuge because the results of calculating the number of years prove how unrealistic the AIT chronologies are! Let us see, then.

The Upanishadic doctrine of the identity of the individual self and the universal self, in the formulations *ayam ātmā brahma* and *ahaṃ brahmāsmi* 'the Self is the Absolute' and 'I am the Absolute', should be known, then, c 1500 or 1300 or 1200, when, according to the AIT, the *RV* was composed. Yet, quite surprisingly, this doctrine is totally unknown in the RV in these terms (although enunciated differently) and begins hesitantly to appear in the *AV* (eg 10.2.32-3; 11.4.23; etc). Consequently, the *AV* should be placed at least c 1600 and the *RV* c 1800, always following the AIT assumptions. But the *RV* is composed, even according to Witzel (2005:90), in Saptasindhu, yet the IAs do not appear in this area before, at the very earliest, 1700, and the *RV* gets composed after several centuries!

This is one of the comical paradoxes that the mainstream chronology refuses obdurately to resolve. Yet, on the grounds given in §§ 12-13 above, we saw that the *RV* should be assigned to the 4th millennium, say around 3600. Now subtracting two hundred years for the *AV* hymns and the start of the Upanishadic doctrine and a further 900 or 1000 years (for the teachers) we should place the early Upaniṣads at the start of the period of the Mature Harappan, ie 2500 (with the *ātma-brahman* doctrine having come down orally) and the Sūtra texts immediately after. These dates satisfy yet another requirement. The word for cotton *karpāsa* is first used in the Sūtra texts as we saw in § 12e above and the cultivation of the plant (although seeds of it were found in much earlier periods) gets well established c 2500. All these dates are, of course, approximate.

16. Astrophysicist Achar pursued his **palaeo-astronomical research** into the Mahābhārata epic also, examining astronomical references in Books 3, 5 and 18. His sky map showed that all these converge in the year 3067. (Achar 2003; see also paper One). Achar acknowledged that, in 1969, S Raghavan had arrived at the same date. Now, it is obvious that the *Mbh* had acquired many accretions over many centuries and that it was streamlined stylistically perhaps first in the 2nd millennium and finally at about the start of the Common Era. It is obvious that it contains much late material like 2.28.48-9, which mentions Rome and Antiochia (*romā* and *antakhī*): this could not be earlier than 300 BCE since Antioch was founded in 301. On the other hand, the frequent use of the bow and, moreso, the use by Bhīma of a (tree trunk as a) club show much more primitive conditions.

Thus the war took place in 3067 and the core of the *MBh* in poems and songs was laid down in that year. This and the native traditional view that the Kali Yuga came at 3102 are both correct, according to Achar. He pointed out that the Kali Yuga had no full force until the death of Kṛṣṇa which occurred 35 years after 3067, at 3032 (private communication June 2006); but immorality had set in already, as is shown by the unjust behaviour of the Kauravas and some reprehensible acts during the war itself. Surely no bards (compilers or redactors) in the 3rd cent CE or the 3rd cent BCE could possibly know the star and planet positions relative to the *nakṣatras* or the zodiac signs of the year 3067. The astronomical references examined by Achar (and Raghavan) are so numerous that chance coincidence has to be discarded (Achar 2003). However, that the war took place in 3137 and bards began to sing of these events two generations later should not be precluded. Personally, I still tend towards the traditional view of the War taking place in 3137. The Megasthenes report (from c 300 BCE) of the ancient kings from 6000+, surviving in Arrian and other classical writers, supports these long periods of the past (paper One). Then, deterioration in behaviour would have started in the *sandhyā* transitional period before the onset of the Kali Yuga—when also the Kṣatriyas passed away. Here a question remains: how did the astronomers (and Āryabhaṭa especially) determine the date for Kali Yuga as 3102? Is there an answer?

17. The Sarasvatī river furnishes useful literary and archaeological evidence for dating the *RV*. It is a mighty river extolled in all Books of the *RV* except the fourth. It is *nadītamā, ambitamā, devitamā* 'best river, best mother, best goddess' (2.41.16); it is swollen and fed by three or more rivers *pinvamānā sindhubhiḥ* (6.52.6); it is endless, swift moving, roaring, most dear among her sister rivers; together with her divine aspect, it nourishes the Indoaryan tribes (6.61.8-13). In 7.95.2 the river is said to flow pure in her course "from the mountains to the ocean" *giribhyaḥā samudrāt*. Then 7.96.2 and 10.177 pray to the rivergoddess for sustenance and good fortune while 10.64.9 calls upon her (and Sarayu and Indus) as "great" and "nourishing". Clearly then, we have here, even in the late Bk 10, a great river flowing from the Himalayas to the ocean in the south, fed and swollen by other rivers and sustaining the tribes of the IAs on its banks—not a river known in the past or in some other region, or a river now considerably shrunk (Witzel 2001)[11].

Some scholars claim that here *samudra* does not mean 'ocean' but confluence and especially the place where a tributary flowed into the Indus (eg Klaus 1989 and Witzel

---

[11]The mainstream view (Witzel's really) that the Vedic river is merely a memory of the Iranian Haraxvaiti which belongs to the common Indo-Iranian period, when the Iranoaryans lived together in Iran before the IAs moved further southeast (according to the AIT), is no more than modern myth-making. Mainstreamers often invoke Occam's razor (ie that the simpler solution is more probable) but here they forget it and prefer their own complex scenario.

2001). The last point can be discarded since there is not the slightest hint elsewhere that the Sarasvati flowed into the Indus—in which case the Indus and not Saraswati would have been lauded as the best river (2.41.16) We can also aver with full certitude (as the *Vedic Index* does under *Samudra*) that the rig-vedic people knew the ocean (see paper Five, above; also Prabhakar 1994). The meaning 'terminal lake(s)' adopted by Witzel is entirely fanciful. In his Dictionary M Mayrhofer gives for *samudra* only 'confluence' and 'ocean/sea' (1996 *EWA*). And the Vedic poet would certainly have used (not *ā samudrāt* but) ā *sarobhyaḥ* 'to the terminal lakes' maintaining his – ∪ – – cadence. This phrase would then have indicated clearly the alleged fanciful etymological connection of the name *Saras-vatī* 'she who has (terminal) lakes'. The name means rather 'she who has swirls and currents', since the primary sense of √ sṛ (>*saras*) is 'movement' (*gatau*) or 'flowing, leaping, rushing'.

Please, consider also that the Vedic **-s-** is inherited from PIE, according to all IEnists, whereas Avestan **–h-** is a devolved, not PIE, sound. Vedic √ *sṛ* has many primary and secondary cognates like *sara*, *sarit* etc. Now Avestan has no cognates for √ *sṛ* and its products, and the Avestan noun for lake is *vairi-*, while *vār-* is 'rain(-water)' = S *vāri*(?). The stem *hara-* (cognate with Vedic saras) occurs only in the river name Haraxvaiti. Consequently, it is the Iranians that moved away from the Indoaryans as, indeed, is shown by their memory of having lived in a location they called *Haptahəndu* = Saptasindhu. The root *sṛ* has cognates in other IE branches, Gk *hial-*, Latin *sal-*, Toch *sal-* etc as is shown by Rix 1998. Now, it would be ludicrous to claim that the IAs left the common Indo-Iranian habitat, as per the AIT, moved into Saptasindhu and turning the *Haraxvaiti* name into *Sarasvatī* gave it to a river there to remember their past while they proceeded to generate the root *sṛ* and its derivatives to accord with other IE languages. Occam's razor, which here is conveniently ignored by AIT adherents, commands the opposite: that the Iranians moved away, lost the root *sṛ* and the name Sarasvatī in its devolved form *Haraxvaiti* was given it to a river in their new habitat. This, together with the fact that, like Greek, Avestan has no obvious system of roots and derivatives (as Sanskrit has), should be enough to question if not refute various IEnists' claims that Avestan retains older forms of nouns and verbs and that therefore the Indoaryans were with the Iranians in Iran in the common Indo-Iranian period—before moving to Saptasindhu. One should also note that these linguists rely entirely on linguistic facts amenable to a reverse interpretation and ignore other aspects—literary, mythological, archaeological and genetic (for which see § 19).

The river Sarasvatī in Saptasindhu is thought to have dried up almost completely by 1900 (Allchins 1997:117; Rao 1991: 77-79). In previous years it had lost tributaries to the Indus in the West and the Ganges in the East. Is there any evidence that it flowed down to the Indian (or Arabian) ocean at any earlier period?

G Possehl examined (1998) all the palaeoenvironmental and geological data relevant to the Sarasvatī river and concluded that the river could have flowed down to the ocean only before 3200 at the very latest and, more probably, before 3800! He re-stated his finds in his study of 2002 (pp 8-9). P-H. Francfort has been just as certain of a date 3600-3800 in his survey of 1992.

All this helps us place the passages ascribing the grandeur of river Sarasvatī at a date before 3200 at least. (For more recent scientific investigations through satellite showing the course of the old Sarasvatī reaching the ocean see Sharma JR et al 2006.)

18. In a recent publication **Dr S. Levitt** (of New York), who is by no means an indigenist, examined the development of the "early Indic tradition" and the development of religion in ancient Mesopotamia.

After comparing several elements in the Vedic and Mesopotamian religions, Levitt concluded: "We can date the early Indic tradition on the basis of comparable points in ancient Mesopotamia. By this, the Ṛgveda would date back to the beginning of the third millennium BC, with some of the earliest hymns perhaps even dating to the end of the fourth millennium BC" (2003:356).

However, unaware of Levitt's paper, I myself made at about that time a very detailed comparative study of Vedic and Mesopotamian religious (mythological) motifs, published in *Migration and Diffusion* vol 24, 2005[12]. In this I showed that since more than 20 motifs in the Vedic texts had close parallels in other IE branches (eg the horse mythology, the skyboat of the Sungod, the Flood, the elixir from heaven, the creation of cosmic parts from the dismemberment of a divine being, etc) and were therefore of Proto-Indo-European provenance, they could not have been borrowed by the Vedics from the Mesopotamians as is usually alleged (McEvilley 2002; Dalley 1998) but must be inherited and therefore older than the Mesopotamian (Sumerian, Babylonian etc) parallels. Since the Mesopotamian culture (starting with old Sumerian) surfaces c 3000, the Vedic motifs must be earlier. Most of these have no parallels in Ugarite, Hebrew and other intermediate Near-Eastern cultures.

Thus again we arrive at a date before 3000 for the bulk of the *RV*.

19. Since, according to the preceding discussion we must now assign the (bulk of the) *RV* to c 3200 at the latest and since the *RV* by general consent was composed around the Sarasvatī, then it follows that the IAs were ensconced in Saptasindhu by 3200 and that the ISC was a material manifestation of the early oral Vedic tradition expressed in the RV. This issue was treated by me extensivey in preceding papers and no more need be said now. I should only add that, in fact, more and more scholars in the West have re-examined the issue and rejected wholly or in part the

[12]This was badly printed and the Sanskrit transliterations are unreadable! A revised version was published in *Adyar Library Bulletin* 2007. This is now paper Seven in this volume.

mainstream view advocating instead a movement Out of India into Europe: Schildmann 1998; Klostermaier 1998, 2000; Friedrich 2004; Hasenpflug 2006.(See also § 9, above.)

To all this I should add the increasing evidence from Genetics which declares that no substantial flow of genes occurred from Europe or the northwestern adjacent areas into India before 600 BCE. On the contrary, recent genetic studies show an outflow from India into countries west and north and Europe (Sahoo et al 2006; Oppenheimer 2003). M Danino has made a useful overview of the evidence produced by studies over the last 10 years in his paper 'Genetics and the Aryan Debate', published in *Purātattva* (2006b). Thus the Indoaryans are now shown to be indigenous to Saptasindhu and there is nothing to undemine my contention that the *RV* in its bulk is pre-Harappan. What I am arguing for primarily and most emphatically is the proposition that, since the only biological change is in the skeletal record of the area and occurs c 6000-4500 (paper One with references), if the Indoaryans made an entry it would have happened at that period; but by 1700 BCE they certainly were indigenous. Genetic evidence, however, suggests strongly now an Out-of-India scenario.

Cavalli-Sforza and his team state that "Indian tribal and caste populations derive largely from the same genetic heritage of Pleistocene [=10000 to 3 mya] southern and western Asians and *have received limited gene flow from external regions since the Holocene* [=c 10000 to present]. The phylogeography [=neighbouring branches] of the primal mtDNA and Y-chromosome founders suggest that these southern Asian Pleistocene coastal settlers from Africa would have provided the inocula for the subsequent differentiation of the distinctive eastern and western Eurasian gene pools" (emphasis and square brackets added; Cavalli-Sforza 2003).

Another geneticist, S Oppenheimer, offers independent confirmation (2003) that there was no Aryan entry, either male or female; he focuses on the M 17, or so-called "Caucasoid" (= Aryan!), genetic marker: "South Asia is logically the ultimate origin of M 17 and his ancestors; and sure enough we find highest rates and greatest diversity of the M 17 line in Pakistan, India and eastern Iran, and low rates in the Caucasus. M 17 is not only more diverse in South Asia than in Central Asia but diversity *characterizes* its presence in isolated tribal groups in the south, thus **undermining any theory of M 17 as a marker of a 'male Aryan invasion' of India**" (2003:152: my emphasis). He adds that this M 17 marker travelled from India or Pakistan (= our Saptasindhu) through Kashmir, Central Asia, Russia and then Europe after 40000 BP (p 154). Thus migration is from east westward.

A more recent study (Sahoo ... Endicot, Kivisild... Kashyap 2006) concludes: "The Y-chromosomal data consistently suggest a largely South Asian origin of Indian caste communities and therefore argue against any major influx, from regions north and west of India" (p 843); then again: "It is not necessary, based on the current evidence, to look beyond South Asia for the origins of the paternal heritage of the majority of Indians at the time of the onset of settled agriculture. ... our findings do support a local origin of haplogroups F* and H" (p 847).

However, all these finds are by no means final and we need to be cautious; but the indications now are that there will be no reversal. If there was a migration, this was most probably out of Saptasindhu and the adjacent region.

Why mainstreamers insist on the AIT is a mystery. Lord C Renfrew wrote of the AIT (1989:182): "this comes rather from a *historical assumption* about the 'coming' of the Indo-Europeans" (my emphasis). Then Edmund Leach wrote (1990): "Because of their commitment to a unilateral segmented history of language development that needed to be mapped onto the ground, the philologists took it for granted that proto-Indo-Iranian was a language that has originated outside India or Iran... From this we derived the myth of the "Aryan invasion"." These are the two legs of clay upon which stands the AIT and its variants.

Leach went further saying that after the discovery of the Indus-Sarasvati Civilization "Indo-European scholars should have scrapped all their historical reconstructions and started again from scratch. But this is not what happened. Vested interests and academic posts were involved" (1990). This is still true. But the new genetic evidence will soon perhaps force linguists to reconsider their theories. And we must not forget that there may well have been an IE continuum from the Steppe to Saptasidhu and the IAs did not move from their location. It is worth noting that S Zimmer admitted (2002) that (although himself a mainstream non-indigenist) he could not be certain of the exact location of the PIE homeland since the facts are so obscure in those far-off times. More recently, H-P Francfort, the eminent excavator of Shortughai, expert on Central Asia Oxus area (or BMAC) and N-W India, critiqued V Sarianidi, E Kuzmina and J Mallory and their theories about [proto-]Indo-Iranian movements through the Oxus region (2005:262-8); further on (p 283ff) he pointed out that the pantheon in the Oxus iconography has a dominant goddess and so does not tally with Iranian and Indoaryan religions: on the whole he is most reluctant to accept Indo-Iranians (or Aryans) passing through that area c 1800-1400 BCE. So even some mainstreamers have now serious doubts about the alleged Aryan immigration/invasion.

20. Does it matter whether the *RV* was composed in the 4th millennium or c 1000? whether the Indoaryans are indigenous or came to India c 1500? After all life goes on irrespective of such ancient events. So from one point of view, no, it doesn't matter. But from another, it does matter. First, it is the function of scholarship to establish and promote true knoweldge so that our life be regulated by this—not prejudices, partisan views (even patriotic but false) or pet theories. Second, Indian (proto-)history must be restored and revalued in a correct time-frame. It is sad, indeed, as Frawley wrote (2002 *The Hindu* June 18th), "to note how intellectuals in India are quick to denigrate the extent and antiquity of their history". Third, the *RV* contains ideas that are of great value to mankind and reveal, as other recent discoveries in prehistoric cultures (Rudgley 1998 passim), that so-called "primitive" people had much important knowledge that held them at a fairly high level of civilization enabling them to live in harmony with the natural processes (*ṛta*) of their environment. The *RV*, eg, preserves for us, from that so ancient period, the idea of a Primal Unity that is the First Cause of the universe and all its phenomena: not only in the *Nāadīya sūkta* and the *Puruṣa sūkta* (10.129 and 90) but also in 1.164,6; 3.55 refrain; 6.75.19; 8.58; 10.114.5 and less obviously in others. This concept is absent from all other IE traditions (Hittite, Greek, Roman etc) and may well have been an essential constituent of PIE culture lost in the other branches. Thus the Rigvedic IA culture (and perhaps PIE) consisted not so much of material artefacts but of inner knowledge and spiritual strength—*bráhma várma mamā́ntaram* 'the holy-power is my inner defence' *RV* 6.75.19.

Let us hope that the noxious AIT and all notions rooted in it will sooner rather than later end up in the only place they should be—the dustbin of History. Let us also hope that the RV will be re-examined not only for its historical information but its cultural ideas that will illuminate many other studies and disciplines in Ancient History, Anthropology, Civilization, Linguistics, Religion, Sociology, etc.

Ten: **The "Mainstream Model"**

"Mainstream model (or paradigm), "received wisdom", "established doctrine" and similar phrases are terms used to denote the prevalent, established idea accepted by academics in any field of study. Once established and having acquired the status of mainstram view and the inevitable respectability that cloaks it, this is very difficult to be dislodged. In this paper I examine the mode whereby any idea becomes the mainstream view.

In Indology, particularly in the area of (proto-)History, the mainstream model has been dominated for almost a century and a half by the AIT (=Aryan Invasion/ Immigration Theory). Now, for the last 10 years I have been publishing papers refuting this theory. Of course I am not the only one nor the first one. In modern times others did the same several years before me and continue to do so (eg Frawley 1991, 2001; Sethna 1992; Elst 1993, 1999; Talageri 1993, 2000; Danino 2006a, 2006b; etc). One difference is that I managed to have my papers published in accredited academic Journals, some of which are refereed (eg *Journal of Indo-European Studies or Indian Linguistics*) and so forced academics to attend to this problem once again.

Be that as it may, one scholar, AB Marathe, wrote in his review of a book in the *Annals* of BORI (2001, vol 82): "[T]he changing perception of the chronology of the Indian proto-history (see 'The *Ṛgveda* and the Indo-Europeans' vol 80 by Nicholas Kazanas, *ABORI* vol 80, 1999 pp 15-42) has not been taken into account. If it gets well-established, a fresh thinking on this subject may be necessary" (p 287). One hears and reads such remarks very often.

How does an idea (or whatever) get well-established?

First, I would suggest that "fresh thinking" on all matters of Indian proto-history is absolutely necessary. It is high time indologists (archaeologists, proto-historians, sanskritists, *et al*) in academia stopped parroting mechanically the inherited views that somehow attained the status of mainstream orthodoxy. A scholar must, if he/she is to perform this noble function, constantly examine and reexamine the views and assumptions entertained by himself/herself and others. If one is content with mere repetition and citation of sources (without a reasonable examination of these sources) then one becomes a mere pedant. The "noble function" of scholarship is to discover, defend and promote the truth of a subject, not to perpetuate partisan/patriotic views and pet theories.

Most academics, indoeuropeanists, indologists, sanskritists, historians et al, with the notable exception of archaeologists-experts in the Indus-Sarasvati Civilization, adhere to the AIT as regards India, not because they have actually examined the data and arguments for it but because it is easier to repeat mechanically what "authorities" like Gimbutas, Mallory, Parpola, Witzel et al, say or have said. In fact, the AIT has no data at all to support it and not one argument in its favour will hold water. This has been demonstrated very adequately by E Bryant in his 2001 publication: for every piece of evidence supposedly supporting the AIT he presents counter-evidence that shows the former to be fictional. The course by which this Theory (started as a mere proposition by M Müller) has been established as the mainstream view has been examined at length by Mallory (1973) and J Day (1994).

How does an idea or view really become well-established?... It may be, and usually is, assumed that this depends on its factual truth. This of course is not true.

An idea/view becomes "established" as the mainstream orthodoxy only because a number of people (and this need not be large) who hold a key-position—authoritative and therefore decisive—accept it and promote it. Such a view may be utterly wrong yet it may hold sway for decades and centuries.

It may be thought that such a mishap occurs only in fields where the subjective factor, as distinct from objective, measurable data, is predominant as happens in the arts or humanities (literary criticism, history etc). Not so. Wrong views have become mainstream orthodoxy even in the hard positive sciences like biology, chemistry and physics (Pert 1997, Cohen 1985, Kuhn 1970).

Let us look at some well-known cases.

First, before archaeology came to its own late in the 19th century, hellenists (=scholars dealing with the Greek culture) thought Homer's world in the *Iliad* and *Odyssey* was imaginary, totally mythological. It was H Schliemann, a retired German merchant with little learning but much faith in Homer and enough funds, who dug in north-eastern Peloponnese (Greece) and brought to the astonished eyes of the world the Mycenaean monuments (from c 1600 BC), the fortified palace and the vaulted graves with all the bronze and gold treasures they contained. Then followed Tiryns and other excavations (Taylour 1990).

A little before, in 1865 Gregor Mendel presented the accumulated results of his researches in heredity and experiments with peas to the Brünn Society for the Study of Natural Science. Brünn, now called Brno, was then the capital of Moravia, a region straddling parts of Czechoslovakia, Poland and Germany. Although the scientist-members of the Society did not understand Mendel's paper, nonetheless it was published along with the rest of the Proceedings for that year. As a matter of routine, copies of that publication were sent to over 100 learned institutions in London, Paris, Vienna, Rome, Petersburg, Upsala etc. Few people read it: they did not understand the significance of those invisible and undetectable "factors" or "particles" (today we call them "genes") which were responsible for heredity. Mendel died in 1884. Sixteen years later his paper was rediscovered together with its contents that had in 1900 been confirmed by H De Vries in the Netherlands and C Correne in Germany. Biologists (botanists, geneticists, et al) rushed to the library-shelves to read Mendel's paper (published in 1866) and most of them discovered that those pages in the Proceedings of the Brünn Society had not even been cut! Earlier the idea dominant in that field had been that of an "egg" containing the miniature of the creature (human being, hen, oak or whatever): this began to recede in the 1870s and 1880s. (For details see Iltis 1932; Gribbin 1985.)

We could examine many more instances where a wrong idea was dominant and impeded true knowledge and/or progress. I shall refer only to another well-known case—from Astronomy.

The geocentric model of the cosmos dominated European thinking for 18 centuries. It was Copernicus (N Koppernigk: 1473-1543) who wrote of the Revolutions of the Celestial Spheres (*De Revolutionibus...* 1543) demonstrating the heliocentric arrangement of our solar system. 50-60 years later Kepler and Galileo supported and developed further this system. Did the mainstreamers of those days clap "bravo" and shout for joy at this? No, far from it. Galileo was made by the mainstream orthodoxy (the eminent scholars and churchmen of the time) to renounce the heliocentric view *twice*—first in 1615 and then in 1633, even though by now the Florentine Inquisition had sanctioned his work, and he was confined to a villa for the next 19 years of his life. Kepler's popularization work was condemned by the Church in 1622, printers would not publish anything of his and he lost job and income for a period. Giordano Bruno, who also advocated the Copernican system, the plurality of worlds and the circulation of blood (ideas that would become common after 50 years), was burnt at the stake in Rome in February 1600. Copernicus himself escaped persecution because he had the sagacity to publish his book even as he was dying (in 1543) and dedicated it to the exceptionally liberal Pope Paul III admitting in the Preface that his ideas might be wrong. Nonetheless, the book was placed on the Index (ie it should not be read by devout Catholics) 33 years after its publication.

In the last 50 years of the 16th century Copernicus's *De Revolutionibus...* had only one reprint whereas in the same period the books of mainstream orthodoxy (Clavin's *Treatise...*, Melachthon's *Doctrine of Physics*, attempting to refute Copernicus, Paucer's textbook on geocentric Astronomy, Ptolemy's *Almagest* and Peuerbach's *Planetary Theory*) had altogether about 100 reprints (Koestler 1964: 194).

The odd thing about this story is that the heliocentric view was known in Europe long before Copernicus but, for various reasons, was totally ignored by the "established" dogma. Leonardo Da Vinci, the famous artist, engineer and naturalist (1452-1512), stated in his Notes that "The sun does not move" (Gombrich, 1995:294). So this information was known in Italy—unofficially—before Copernicus, who studied in Bologna, Padua and Ferrara during 1495-1503 and could well have imbibed the basic idea from those centres of learning, although there is no hard proof for this. In fact, much much earlier, *Aristarchos of Samos had given a heliocentric model in the 3rd century BC, ie 1700 years before Copernicus*, but none of the savants of his day (including the great Archimides), believed it or bothered to verify it and **for the next 18 centuries mainstream orthodoxy was the geocentric view:** this was formulated by Apollonius of Perga (also 3rd century BC), who followed Aristotle's world-picture of the Prime Mover and "intelligences" moving the concentric celestial spheres, then was developed by Hipparchus of Rhodes and completed by Ptolemy of Alexandria in the 2nd cent CE (hence, the Ptolemaic system).

Thereafter all kinds of absurdities were written about the heavens, the celestial spheres, the sub- and supra-lunar worlds, the fixed stars, the Empyrean, the Prime Mover and so on, which constituted the "established" view. And all the time the real knowledge was there and all those schoolmen, could, with some practical observation and sensible application of Mathematics, have found out that the Ptolemaic system was not true. But they did not: they preferred to argue about such weighty matters as how many angels could sit on the point of a pin or how the world was created by God from nothing (*creatio ex nihilo*)! (There were exceptions, of course). Even when the proofs were presented to them in black and white, hard and irrefutable mathematical demonstrations, they still rejected them preferring the comforts of the "established" dogma. Theology (and Church interests) decided what was acceptable.

I am not claiming to be another Copernicus or Mendel or Schliemann. What I am saying is that a wrong idea can be the mainstream orthodoxy for many decades or centuries and that scholars should neither accept mainstream doctrines nor dismiss new, controversial ideas all too readily. I myself adhered to and taught the AIT for some 18 years having imbibed it in my University years and not having bothered to study the evidence because I was not then interested in Indian protohistory. It was not easy to give up a view I had entertained for so long, but once the evidence was examined (and because I was not afraid of losing reputation, job and income) I felt I had little choice but to abandon the AIT and accept indigenism and a *Ṛgveda* of 3000+ BC.

How does a view get "well-established"? And I answer—only by acceptance.

The question facing sanskritists and proto-historians is, really, whether, by circumventing their own inertia, the comfortable security of repeating the mainstream dogma and any facile emotional reactions in favour or against, they can bestir themselves and actually examine, or re-examine, the factual evidence and decide for themselves. Let me explain further.

The AIT (now turned into "immigration") has been the established mainstream view, only because a decisive number of academics in key position accepted it in the last quarter of the 19th century. Until about then it was thought that N-W India or a neighbouring area had been the locus of IE expansion (Mallory 1973:26-29). Even after this date there were many dissenting scholars who continued to doubt the AIT or some of its aspects like late chronologies (Winternitz vol I, 270-288; Day 1994 passim). I have discussed these issues at length elsewhere (Kazanas 1999, 2001a, 2007) and so have others (Bryant 2001). Apart from the ethnic or racist prejudices involved (Bryant 2001; Trautmann 1997; Shaffer 1984), two other considerations were instrumental in establishing the AIT. I shall use the words of two Western academics: a) Edmund Leach wrote: "Because of their commitment to a unilateral segmented history of language development that needed to be mapped onto the ground, the philologists took it for granted that proto-Indo-Iranian was a language that had originated outside India or Iran... From this we derived the myth of the Aryan invasions" (1990). b) Lord Renfrew wrote (1989:182) of the AIT: "this comes rather from a historical assumption about the 'coming' of the Indo-Europeans". These are the two legs of clay upon which the AIT and its variants stand. Be it noted that neither "leg" furnishes any data for an entry. The entry and its date c 1500 BC are purely conjectural affairs. Yet this unhistorical theory has bedevilled Indology for some 120 years.

It has become very obvious to me that adherents of the AIT continue to argue mechanically, blindly, unreasonably simply to maintain their (untenable) position. Instead of looking at the data that have been presented in various publications since the mid-1980's, they ignore them wholly and continue to repeat the dogma or they resort to various irrelevant remarks. Thus at a Vedic Conference in Ujjain (Jan 2006) I met with two eminent professors from the USA and was drawn into heated discussions on Indoaryans origins and the *RV* composition date. One of them mentioned the palatalization of certain Proto-Indo-European consonants in Sanskrit—eg **ca** against Greek *kai* and Latin *que-* and refused to see that this, even if it were a historical actuality (which is by no means incontrovertible), did not provide dates since it could have happened in the 4th, 5th, 6th or 7th millenium BC. The other adduced three arguments. a) No remains of horses and chariots were found in N-W India before 1700—refusing to accept the numerous publications in India reporting remains of domesticated horse. (Remains of chariot were not discovered even from 600 BC!) b) One entry into N-W India is more credible than many out-flows from it—even though it has been repeatedly stressed (eg Hock 1996, etc) that at least three times in the historical period Indoaryan languages are known to have travelled north-westward out of India and one of them, the Gypsy or Romani idiom reached the United Kingdom. c) A few entrants into N-W India could have brought in the Vedic idiom—even though Vedic is an extremely difficult language and the toponymics (names of mountains, plains, lakes and rivers) are clearly Sanskritic and do not belong to another language (eg Dravidian) as we would expect for some of them if Vedic was an intruder and not native. All such arguments are expressive of prejudice and desperately try to maintain the mainstream dogma.

I am not denying that the Indoaryans may have come to India from some other location at an earlier period. Indeed, at c 6000-4500 BC there is a break in the skeletal record of the region (Elst 1999:233; Witzel 2001:9). If—and I repeat "if"—the Indoaryans did immigrate at, say, c 6000-4500 then, surely, by 1500 BC they have every right to be regarded as indigenous, and since the *Ṛgveda* knows nothing at all of the Indus-Sarasvatī Civilization which began to emerge c 3000, then it (or the large bulk of it) can have been composed only before that date (Kazanas 2001a, 2005b).

To say that the ISC (=Indus-Sarasvati Culture) is an expression of the Vedic tradition beginning with the *RV* and that the continuity flows on in historical times (albeit with some changes, loans and losses) is reasonable. To say that the *RV* reflects the ISC is to ignore many facts—and chiefly the fact that the *RV* does not know urban structures or ruins, bricks (*iṣṭakā*), fixed fire-hearths/altars, etc, ie elements prominent in the ISC and post-rigvedic texts. To say that the *RV* is post-ISC is to put the proverbial cart before the horse.

If Shri Marathe and others like him (after due consideration of the matter) accept "the changing perception of the chronology of the Indian proto-history", then this will get "well-established". If (again after due consideration) they don't accept it, then it will not get established. It is no good saying "if" and "when", wait for others to accept it and then get on the band-wagon.

Leach, Master of King's College (Cambridge, UK), went further in his critique of the AIT writing in the same study that after the unearthing of the ISC in the 1920's—"Indo-European scholars should have scrapped all their historical recontructions and started again from scratch. But this is not what happened. Vested interests and academic posts were involved." And here this distinguished anthropologist (he was knighted) touches a crucial spot and I agree. Personal interests played—and continue to play—an important role in keeping alive this utterly defective and deforming doctrine. Hopefully more and more indologists will re-examine this matter and their own psychological state. Indian scholars should stop denigrating their own proto-history, the depth and significance of its antiquity.

Helps to the reader

Sign § = numbered section in the different chapters.
[...] = square brackets indicating my own intervention in citations.
> = becomes.
< = derives from.

Abbreviations. Some of them like *RV*, *AV*, *PT* etc are indicated in the text. Others are given in the notes to the different chapters

AB	= *Aitareya Brāhmaṇa*	*MSD*	= See Bibliography
AIT	= Aryan Invasion/ Immigration Theory	*MU*	= *Muṇḍaka Upaniṣad*
AU	= *Aitareya Upaniṣad*	NE	= Near East(ern)
cent	= century	par(s)	= paragraph(s) within a section/spell of, eg, *PT*
CU	= *Chāndogya Upaniṣad*	*PIE*	= ProtoIndoEuropean
GEL	= See Bibliography	*ŚB*	= *Śatapatha Brāhmaṇa*
GM	= See Bibliography	*TB*	= *Taittirīya Brāhmaṇa*
IE	= *IndoEuropean*	*TS*	= *Taittirīya Saṃhitā* (of the Black Yajur Veda)
JIES	= *Journal of IE Studies*	*TU*	= *Taittirīya Upaniṣad*
KU	= *Kaṭha Upaniṣad*	*VI*	= See Bibliography
MM	= See Bibliography	*VS*	= *Vājasaneyī Saṃhitā* (of the White Yajur Veda)

Bibliography

Achar BNN 2003 'Date of the Mahābhārata War...' in *Quarterly Journal of the Mythic Society*, vol XCIV and Issue Nos 1-2.

2001 'Planetarium Software and the date of the *Mahābhārata War*' paper given in Montreal and sent privately to NK.

2000 'A case for revising the date of *Vedāṅga Jyotiṣa*' in *Indian Journal of History of Sciences*, 35.3 (173-83).

1999 'On exploring the Vedic sky with modern computer software' *Electronic Journal of Vedic Studies* pp 3-9.

Agarwal V 2006 'Is there evidence for the Indo-Aryan Immigration to India?' talk at WAVES Conference August. See <http://www.omilosmeleton.gr/english en_index.html>.

Agrawal A (ed) 2005 *In search of Vedic Harappan Relationship*, New Delhi, Aryan Books Intern.

Agrawal DP 2002 'Comments on "Indigenous Indo Aryans' in *Journal of IE Studies*, vol 30 (129-135).

Agrawala PK 2005 'Two Harappan Motifs & their Vedic Affinity' in A Agrawal ed (10-13).

Aklujkar A 1996 'The Early History of Sanskrit as Supreme Language' Leiden, Brill, in EM Houben (ed) *Ideology and Status of Sanskrit...*

Albright W & Dumont P 1934 'A Parallel between Indic and Babylonian Sacrificial Ritual' in *Journal of American Oriental Society*, 54 (107-128).

Allchin B & R — 1997 *Origins of a Civilization India*, Delhi, Viking Penguin.

1982 *The Rise of Civilization in India & Pakistan* Cambridge, CUP.

Allchin F & Joshi J — 1995 (Eds) *Excavations at Malvan* Delhi, Archaeological Survey of India (Memoir No 92).

Allen JP — 1988 *Genesis in Egypt* N Haven, Yale University Press.

Anderson ER — 1999 'Horse-sacrifice and Kingship' *JIES* vol 27 (379-393).

Anthony D & Vinogradov NB — 1995 'The birth of the chariot' *Archaeology* 48 (36-41).

Assman J — 2001 (1984) *The Search for God in Ancient Egypt* trans D Lorton, Ithaca, Cornell University Press.

Aurobindo Shri — 1956 *On the Veda* and *The Secret of the Veda* both originally 1914-20 in the Journal *Arya*, India; both in book form, India, Pondicherry (several edns).

Austen RA — 1987 *African Economic History* London/ Portssmouth, J Currey & Heinemann.

Baines, J — 1991 'Society, Morality and Religious Practice' in Shafer 1991 (123-200).

Baldi P — 1983 *An Introduction to the Indo-European Languages* Southern Illinois Univ. Press, Carbondale & Edwardsville.

Bauval R & Hancock G — 1996 *Keepers of Genesis* London, Heinemann.

Beveridge W — 1968 *The Art of Scientific Investigation* (1957 3rd ed) London, Heinemann.

Bhattacharji S — 1993 'Some common mythological motifs...' *Indo-Hellenic Journal* (India) vol 3 (3-14).

Bisht RS — 1999/2000 'Harappan and the *Ṛgveda*: Points of Convergence' in G Pande, ed (393-442).

Black J & Green A — 1995 *Gods, Demons & Symbols of Ancient Mesopotamia* Austin, Univ Texas Press.

Blažek V 2001 'On Baltic Theonyms' *JIES* 29 (351-65).

Bloomfield L 1933 *Language* NY/London, Holt & Company.

Bodewitz H 1999 'Yonder world in the Atharvaveda' *Indo-Iranian Journal* 42 (107-20).

Bottéro J 2001 *Religion in Ancient Mesopotamia* (1998) trans TL Fagan, Chicago/London, Univ Chicago Press.

1992 *Mesopotamia* (1987) transl Z Bahrani & M van de Mieroop, Chicago/ London, Univ Chicago Press.

Bottéro J et al 2000 *Ancestor of the West* Chicago, Chicago Univ Press.

Boyce M 1989 *A History of Zoroastrianism*, vol I (1975) 1989, vol II 1982, vol III with F Grenet (& R Beck) 1991, Leiden, Brill.

Branston B 1993 *The Last Gods of England*, London, Constable.

Brooks R 2001 'The Relation between matter and life' *Nature* 409 (Jan 18:409-11).

Brugmann K 1897-1916 *Grundriss der Vergleichenden grammatik der indogermanischen Sprachen* Strassburg, Trübner.

Bryant E 2002 'Somewhere in Asia and no more' *JIES* 30 (136-48).

2001 *The Quest of the Origins of Vedic Culture* Oxford, OUP.

Bryce T 2002 *Life and society in the Hittite World Oxford*, OUP.

Buck CD 1988 *Dictionary of Selected Synonyms...* (1949) Chicago, Univ Chicago Press.

Budge EA Wallis 1988 *From Fetish to God* (1934) NY, Dover Publ.

1898 ed *The Book of the Dead* 3 vols, London, British Museum.

Burkert W 1992 *The Orientalizing Revolution* Camb Mass, HUP.

Burrow T 1975 'The Early Aryans' in AL Basham (ed) *A Cultural History of India* OUP, Oxford.

1973 *The Sanskrit Language* Faber & Faber, London.

1963 'On the significance of the terms arma-armaka...' *Journal of Indian History* vol 4 (159-68).

Cardona G & Hoeningswald H — 1970 & Senn A *Indoeuropean and Indoeuropeans*, Philadelphia, Univ Pensylvania Press.

Cavalli-Sforza et al — 2003 'The Genetic Heritage of the Earliest Settlers...' American Journal of Human Genetics 72 (313-32).

Cavalli-Sforza L Menozzi P & Piazza A — 1996 *The History and Geography of Human Genes* Princeton Univ Press (1994).

Chakrabarti DK — 1999 *India: An archaeological History* Cambridge, CUP.

Chatterji SK — 1968 *Balts & Aryans* Indian Institute of Advanced Study, Simla.

Childe G — 1926 *The Aryans* London, Kegan Paul.

Clackson J — 2007 *Indo-European Linguistics: an Introduction* Cambridge, CUP.

Clark RT Rundle — 1993 *Myth & Symbol in Ancient Egypt* (1959) London, Thames & Hudson.

Cohen IB — 2001 *Revolution in Science* (1985) Camb Mass, HUP.

Coleman JE — 2000 'An Archaeological scenario for the "Coming of the Greeks" at c 3200 BC' JIES 28 (101-53).

Coomaraswamy AK — 1942 'Ātmayajña: Self-Sacrifice' *Harvard Journal of Asian Studies.*

Coomaraswamy AK et al — 1967 *Myths of the Hindus & Buddhists* 1913 NY, Dover Publications.

Cox Sir GW — (1882) 1963 *The Mythology of the Aryan Nations* Benares, Chowkhamba Sanskrit Series.

Crawford H — 1994 *Sumer and the Sumerians* Cambridge, CUP.

Cremo M — 2003 *Human Devolution* Los Angeles, Torchlight Publishing.

Crossley-Holland, K — 1993 *Norse Myths* (1980) London & NY, Penguins.

Dales G — 1966 'The Decline of the Harappans' *Scientific American*, 241 (92-9).

Dalley S — (ed) 1998 *The Legacy of Mesopotamia* Oxford, OUP.

1998 'Occasions and Opportunities I and II' in Dalley S ed 1998 (9-55).

1991 *Myths from Mesopotamia* Oxford, OUP.

Dandekar RN — 1967 *Some Aspects of the History of Hinduism* Poona, Univ of Poona Press.

Dange SA — 1967 'The Gaviṣṭi (Go-iṣṭi) and the Mehanā in the Ṛgveda' *Nagpur University Journal: Humanities*, Vol 22 (75-108), (India).

Danino M — 2006a *L' Inde et l' invasion de nulle part...* Paris, Les Belles Lettres.

2006b 'Genetics and the Aryan Debate' in *Purātattva*, vol 36.

2006c 'The Horse and the Aryan Debate' *Journal of Indian History and Culture* vol 13 (33-59), Chennai, India.

Darmesteter J — 1965 *The Zend-Avesta* (1883) Sacred Books of the East 4, 23, Delhi, M Banarsidass.

Das RP — 2002 'Indra and Śiva/Rudra' in (eds) RP Das and G Meiser *Geregeltes Ungestüm* Veröffentlichungen zur Indogermanistik and Anthropologie Bremen, Hempen Verlag.

1995 'Hunt for foreign Words in *RV*' *Indo-Iranian Journal* 38 (207-38)

Davaras C — 2005 'Bronze Age Crete and India' in *Indian Historical Review*, 32 (126-139).

David AR — 2002 *Religion and Magic in Ancient Egypt* London, Penguins.

1993 *Discovering Ancient Egypt* London, O' Mara Books Ltd.

Day JV — 2001 *Indo-European Origins* Washington, Institute for the study of Man.

1994 'The concept of the Aryan race in the 19th-century scholarship' *Orpheus* 4, 15-48.

de Buck A — 1935-61 ed *Coffin Texts* 7 vols, ed Chicago, Chicago University Press.

de Lubicz RAS — 1988 *Sacred Science...* (1961) Rochester (VA), Inner Traditions.

Deraniyagala S & Abeyratne M — 2000. 'Radiocarbon Chronology of Anuradhapura, Sri Lanka: a revised age estimate' in M Taddei and G De Marco *South Asian Archaeology* vol 2, Rome, Instituto Italiano per L' Africa e L' Oriente.

de Santillana G & Dechend H von — 1977 *Hamlet's Mill* (1969), Boston, DR Godine.

Deshpande GT — 1966 'Evidence of writing in the Vedic Age' in *Nagpur University Journal* vol 16(2).

Dembski WA (ed) — 1998 *Mere Creation* Downers Grove (IL), Inter Varsity Press.

Dhar L — 1930 *The Home of the Aryas* Delhi Univ Publications.

Dhavalikar MK — 1995 *Cultural Imperialism...* Delhi, Books & Books.

Dimock EC & Ramanujan AK — 1964 'Manashā: Goddess of Snakes' *History of Religion* 3 (49-70).

Dixon R — 1997 *The Rise and fall of languages* Cambridge, CUP.

Drews R — 1993 *The End of the Bronze Age: Changes in Warfare and the Catastrophe ca 1200 BC* Princeton, New Jersey: Princeton University Press.

Du Noüy L — 1949 *Human Destiny*, NY, Mentor, The New American Library.

Dumézil G — 1954 *Rituels indo-européens* Collection 'Etudes et Commentaires', vol 19, Paris, Klincksieck.

1952 *Les Dieux des Indo-Européens* 'Mythes et Religions' vol 29, Paris, PuF.

1950 'Dieux cassites...' *Revue Hittite et Asiatique* vol 11 (18-37).

Dundes A — (ed) 1988 *The Flood Myth* Berkeley, Univ California Press.

Dunstan WE — 1998 *The Ancient Near East* Harcourt Brace, Orlando Flo.

Edda — 1996 Snori Sturluson, London, Everyman (1987).

Edwards IE — 1992 *The Pyramids of Egypt* London, Hammondsworth, Penguins.

Ehret C — 1988 'Language change and ethnic shift' *Antiquity* 62 (564-74).

Eleutheriadou N — 1997 *Pelasgoi* (*The Pelasgians* in Md Gk) Athens, Kaktos.

Elizarenkova TY — 1996-7 'The concept of Water and the names for it in the Rgveda' *Orientalia Suecana* XLV-XLVI (21-8).

Elst K — 1999 *Update on the Aryan Invasion Debate* Delhi, Aditya Prakashan.

1993 *Indigenous Indians* Delhi, Voice of India.

Emenau M — 1980 *Language & Linguistic Area* California, Stanford Univ. Press.

1954 'Linguistic Prehistory of India' *Proceedings of the American Philological Society* 98 (282-92).

Emiliani C — 2000 *Planet Earth* Cambridge, CUP.

Epic of Gilgamesh — 1988 London, Penguin Classic.

Erdosy G — 1995 ed *The Indo-Aryans of Ancient South Asia*, Berlin, NY, de Gruyter.

Estell M — 1999 'Orpeus and Ṛbhu revisited' *JIES* 27 (327-333).

1985 'Primary and secondary homeland...' in *JIES* pts 1-2 (185-202).

EWA — see Mayrhofer.

Falk H — 1992 "Nollikhya Nāvalikhya" *Indo-Iranian Journal,* vol 35, no 1, pp 1-17.

1981 'Vedische arma' Zeitschrift der deutschen morgenländischen Gesellschaft 131 (160-71).

Faulkner RO — 1985[4] *The Book of the Dead* (1972), London, Trustees of the British Museum, revised edition.
1978 *Coffin Texts* (trans, 1973) London, Aris and Phillips.
1969 *Pyramid Texts*, Oxford OUP.
1966 'The King and the Star-religion in the Pyramid Texts' *Journal of Near Eastern Studies* 25 (153-61).

Feuerstein G, Kak S & Frawley D — 1995 *In Search of the Cradle of Civilization*, Wheaton/Madras, Quest Books.

Fortson B — 2004 *Indo-European Language and Culture* Oxford, Blackwell.

Francfort P-H — 1992 'Evidence for Harappan irrigation system' in *Eastern Anthropologist* vol 45 (87-103).

Fox A — 1995 *Linguistic Reconstruction. An Introduction...* Oxford OUP.

Francfort P-H — 2005 'La Civilisation de l' Oxus et les Indo-Iraniens et Indo-Aryens en Asie Centrale' in Fussman G, Kellens J, et al (below).
1992 'Evidence for Harappan irrigation system' in *Eastern Anthropologist* vol 45 (87-103).

Fraser A — 1995 *The Gypsies* Oxford, Blackwell.

Frawley D — 2002 'Witzel's vanishing ocean...' http://voiceofdharma.com/indology ReplytoWitzel.html
2001 *The Rigveda and the History of India* Delhi, Aditya.
1994 *The Myth of the Aryan Invasion* N. Delhi, Voice of India (new ed 2000).
1992 *Wisdom of the Ancient Seers* Salt Lake City, Passage Press.
1991 *Gods, Sages & Kings* Salt Lake City, Passage Press.

Frawley D & Rajaram N — 1997 *Vedic Aryans & Origins of Civilization* Delhi, Voice of India.

Frayne DR — 1993 'Indo-Europeans and Sumerians...' BCSMS, No 25.

Friedrich H — 2004 'A Diffusionist's view on the concept of "Language Families"' *Migration & Diffusion* vol 5, No 19 July-September (6-14).

2003 'Hebrew Ethnogenesis and Diffusion' *Migration & Diffusion* 4, 16 (Oct-Dec).

Frisk H — 1954ff *Griechisches Etymologisches Wüterbuch* Heidelberg, C Winter.

Fussman G, Kellens J, Francfort H-P & Tremblay X — 2005 *Aryas, Aryens et Iraniens en Asie Centrale* Paris, College de France, Publications de l' Institut de Civilisation Indienne.

Gamkrelidze TV & Ivanov VV — 1995 *IndoEuropean & the Indo-Europeans* Trends in Linguistics Berlin, Mouton.

1990 'The Early History of the IE Languages' *Scientific American*, March (110-6).

1985 'The Problem of the Original Homeland...' *JIES* 13 (174-84).

Gardiner Sir A — 1957 *Egyptian Grammar* (1994) Griffith Institute, Oxford.

GEL = Liddel HG & Scott R — 1996, *Greek-English Lexicon*: rev by Janes SH and McKenzie R with Supplement Oxford, OUP.

Geldner KF — 1951-7 *Der Rig-Veda* vols 33-36, Cambridge Mass, Harvard Oriental Series.

Ghosh E — 1933/83 *Studies on Rigvedic Deities* New Delhi, Cosmo Pub.

Gibbons Ann — 2001 'Modern men trace ancestry to African migrants' *Science* 292:1051-52.

Gimbutas M — 1985 'Primary and Secondary Homeland of the Indo-Europeans' in *JIES* (185-202).

1970 'Proto-Indo-European Culture' in G Cardona & H Hoeningswald & A Senn eds

GM = *Greek Myths* R Graves — 1977 (1955), 2 vols, Pelicans Hammondsworth.

Gnoli G — 1980 *Zoroaster's Time & Homeland...* Naples, Instituto Universitario Orientale (Series & Minores VII).

Gombrich Sir E — 1994 *The Story of Art* (16th edn) London, Phaidon Press.

Gonda J — 1963 *The Vision of the Vedic Poets* Mouton, Hague.

GPA = — 'Greek Philosophy to Aristotle' by N Kazanas in the PHISPC series (Forthcoming, Delhi, Centre for Studies in Civilization.

Gray & Atkinson Q — 2003 'Language Tree Divergence Time...' *Nature 426* (435-9).

Green MJ — 1996 *Celtic Myths* (1993) London, British Museum Press.

Gribbin J — 1985 *In Search of the double Helix* NY, Bantam Books.

Gribbin J & Cherfas J — 2003 *The First Chimpanzee* NY, Barnes & Noble.

Griffith RT — 1973 *The Hymns of the Ṛgveda* Delhi, Motilal Banarsidas.

Griswold HD — 1923 *The Religion of the Rigveda* London, H Milford.

Gupta SP — 2007 'City in Protohistoric India' in G Pande ed *Golden Chain of Civilizations...* PHISPC vol 1, pt 4, (pp 209-355), Delhi, Centre for Studies in Civilization.

2005 'The Saraswatī and the Homeland of Early Rigvedic Ṛishis' in A Agrawal ed (55-73).

Gurney OR — 1990 *The Hittites*, rev ed, London, NY, Penguin.

Hale M — 2004 'Avestan' in RD Woodard (ed) *The Cambridge Encyclopaedia of the World's Ancient Languages* (pp 742-763).

Hancock G — 2002 *Underworld* London, Penguin Books Ltd.

1995 *Fingerprints of the Gods*, London, Mandarin, Reed International.

Hart G — 1995 *Egyptian Myths* London, British Museum Press.

Hawkins J & Gell-Man M — 1992 *The Evolution of Human Languages*, Santa Fe, Addison-Wesley.

Heesterman J — 1993 *The Broken World of Sacrifice* Chicago, Chicago Univ Press.

Heidel A — 1969 *The Babylonian Genesis* Chicago/ London, Univ Chicago Press.

Held W, Schmalstieg W & Gertz J — 1987 *Beginning Hittite*, Columbus (Ohio), Slavica.

Hencken H — 1955 'Indo-European languages and archaeology': American Anthropological Association Memoir no 84.

Heskel DL — 1984 'Iran-Indus Valley connections' in BB Lal & SP Gupta (p 333-346).

Hiriyanna M — 1994 *Outlines of Indian Philosophy*, (1932) Motilal Banarsidas, Delhi.

Hitze A — 1998 'The Migrations of the Indo-Iranians...' *Akten der X Factangung der Indo-Germanischen Gesselschaft Sept 1996*, Univ Innsbruck.

Hock HH — 2005 'Philology and the historical interpretation of the Vedic texts' in EF Bryant and Lili Patton *The Indo-Aryan Controversy* London/NY, Routledge.

1999 'Out of India? The Linguistic Evidence' in J Bronkhorst & M. Deshpande (eds) *Aryan and Non-Aryan in South Asia*, Camb Mass, HOS (1-18).

1996 'Pre-ṛgvedic convergence' in Houben EM *Ideology and Status of Sanskrit* Leiden, Brill.

1996 'Subversion or Convergence?...' in *Studies in the Linguistic Sciences* (23, 2).

1991 *Principles of Historical Linguistics* (2nd ed) Berlin/NY, de Gruyter.

Hoffner HA — 1998 (ed Beckman GM) *Hittite Myths* Atlanta, Scholars Press.

Hopkins EW — 1898 'The Punjab and the Rig-Veda' in Journal of the *American Oriental Society* vol 19 (19-28).

Hornung E — 1998 *The Ancient Egyptian Books of the Afterlife* trans D Lorton, Ithaca, Cornell University Press.

1982 *Conceptions of God in Ancient Egypt...* trans J Baines, Ithaca, Cornell University Press (also London, 1983).

Hromnik C — 1981 *IndoAfrica* Cape Town Johannesburg, Juta & Co.

Hughes R & Rowe M — 1982 *The Colouring, Bronzing and Patination of Metals* Arts Council, Oxf.

Huld ME — 2002 'Linguistic Science, Truth and the Indocentric Hypothesis' *Journal of IE Studies* 30 (149-60).

Iltis H — 1932 *Life of Mendel* London, Allen & Unwin (The only biography.)

Ingalls DH — 1971 'Remarks on Mr Wasson's Soma' in the *Journal of the American Oriental Society* vol 91 (2), 188-191.

Jackson DP & Bigs RD — 1993 *The Epic of Gilgamesh* Wanconda (Ill), Bolchazy-Carducei.

Jacobi H — 1910 'The antiquity of Vedic Culture' *Journal of the Royal Asiatic Society* 456-67.

Jacobsen KT — 1976 *Treasures of Darkness* New Haven, Yale Univ Press.

Jacq C — 1985 *Egyptian Magic* Warminster, Aris & Phillips.

Jarrige JF & Meadow R — 1980 'The Antecedents of Civilization in the Indus Valley', *Scientific American* Aug (122-33).

Johnson W — 1980 *Poetry and Speculation of the Ṛgveda* Berkeley, Univ Calif Press.

Jordan P — 1998 *Riddles of the Sphinx* Glos (UK) Stroud Press.

Kak S — 2003a 'Vedaṅga Astronomy & Mathematics' paper presented at the Conference of the ICPR March-April in Delhi

2003b *How Old Is Indian Writing?* http://subhash-kak.sulekha.com/blog/post/2003/12/how-old-is-indian-writing.htm

2002 *The Gods Within* New Delhi, M Manoharlal.

2001 'Yājñavalkya and the origins of Purāṇic cosmology' *Brahmavidyā* vol 65 (145-156).

2001 'Mind, Immortality and Art' in *Mind, Man and Mask*, SC Malik (ed), Delhi, Aryan International (pp 16-27).

2000 'On the Chronological Framework for Indian Culture' JICPR special issue, ed GC Pande, *Chronology and Indian Philosophy* (1-24).

1997 'Archaeoastronomy & Literature' October issue of *Current Science*.

1996 'Vena, Veda, Venus' *Brahmavidyā*: *Adyar Library Bulletin*, 60 (229-39).

1996 'Indic Language Families and Indo-European' *Yavanika: Indo-Hellenic Studies* vol 6 (51-65).

1994 *The Astronomical code of the Ṛgveda* (new ed 2000) Delhi, M Manoharlal.

Kazanas N

2007 'Coherence & Preservation in Sanskrit' *Research Bulletin* of the Vishveshvarand Vedic Research Institute, vol 5.

2005a 'Philosophy & Self-realization in the *Ṛgveda*' in DP Chattopadhyaya (ed) *Self, Society and Science* PHISPC Vol XI, pt 2, Delhi, Centre for Studies in Civilization.

2005b 'The Ṛgveda and Harappa' in *Vedic-Harappan Relationship* ed A Agrawal, Delhi, Voice of India.

2004a 'Sanskrit & Proto-Indo-European' *Indian Linguistics* vol 65 (75-100).

2004b 'Homer, Hesiod and the Mahābhārata' in *Vishveshvarananda Vedic Research Inst Research Bul* vol 3.

2003 'Advaita and Gnosticism' in *Research Bulletin VVRI* vol 2 (43-112).

2002 'The Three Functions and Unity in the *RV*' *Journal of Indian Council for Philosophical Research* XIX, 1 (75-98).

	2001a 'A new date of the *Ṛgveda*' in GC Pande & D. Krishna (eds) *Journal of Indian Council of Philosophical Research* Special Issue, 79-108.
	2001b 'Archaic Greece and the Veda' *ABORI* 82 (1-42).
	2001c 'Indo-European deities and the Ṛgveda' *Journal of Indo-European Studies* 29 (257-93).
	1999 'The *Ṛgveda* and Indoeuropeans' *ABORI* 80 Pune (15-42).
Keith AB	1925 *The Religion and Philosophy of the Veda and Upanishads* 2 vols, Delhi, M Banarsidass, Harvard Oriental series, reprint 1989.
	1922 'The age of the Rigveda', *Cambridge History of India* vol I (77-113).
Kenoyer JM	1998 'Secrets of a Civilization' interview to N Denison, in *On Wisconsin*, Fall.
	1998 *Ancient cities of the IVC* OUP, Karachi.
	1997/2000 'The Ravi Phase: A new cultural manifestation at Harappa' in *South Asian Archaeology* (55-76) Rome.
Kenoyer JM & Meadow RH	2007 'The Early Indus Script at Harappa' in E Olijdam & RH Spoor (Eds) *Intercultural Relations between South & Southwest Asia* BAR International Series.
Kerényi C	1982 *The Gods of the Greeks* (1951) London, Thames & Hudson.
KEWA	see Mayrhofer M 1956-.
Kingsley P	1995 *Ancient Philosophy, Mystery and Magic*, OUP, Oxford.
Kittel F	1872 *A Tract on Sacrifice (yajña-sudhanidhi)* Mangalore, C Stolz.
Klaus K	1989 'Samudrá im Vedá': Deutscher Orientalistentag 1985, Würzburg, XIII, E von Schuler (ed) Ausgewählte Vorträge, Wiesbaden (364-71).
Klostermaier K	2000 *Hinduism* Oxford, Oneworld Books.
	1998 'Questioning the Aryan Invasion

Theory ...' *Iskcon Communications Journal* 6:1 (5-16). Republished in *International Quarterly of Indian Philosophy* June 2001 (63-78).

Knipe DM — 1967 'The Heroic Theft...' in *History of Religions* VI, 4 (328-360).

Kochhar R — 2000 *The Vedic People* Hyderabad (1997), Orient Longman.

Koestler A — 1964 *The Sleepwalkers* (1954) London, Penguins.

Kramer SN — 1952 *Enmerkar & the Lord of Aratta* Philadelphia, Univ of Pennsylvania.

Krishnamurti B — 2003 'The Dravidian Language' Cambridbge CUP.

Kuhn TS — 1970 *The Structure of Scientific Revolutions* (1962, 2nd rev ed) Chicago, the Univ Press.

Kurylowicz J — 1956 *L'apophonie en indo-européen* Breslau.

Kuiper FBJ — 1995 'On a hunt for possible objections' *IndoIranian Journal* vol 38 (239-47).

1991 *Aryans in the Rigveda* Atlanta: Rodopi (Leiden Studies in Indo European1).

(1967) 1974 'The Genesis of a Linguistic Area.' *Indo-Iranian Journal* 10:81-102. Reprinted in *International Journal of Dravidian Linguistics* 3:133-53.

1955 'Ṛgvedic loan words' in *Studia Indologica* (ed) Bonn, O Spies, (137-85).

Kuzmina EE — 2002 'Comments on Kazanas' *Journal of IE Studies* 30 (161-69).

Lal BB — 2005 *The Homeland of the Aryans* N Delhi, Aryan Books International.

2002 *The Sarasvatī Flows On*, Delhi, Books International.

1998 India 1947-1997: *New Light on the Indus Civilization* Delhi, Aryan Books Intern.

1997 *The Earliest Civilization* Delhi, Aryan Books.

Lal BB & Gupta SS — 1984 eds *Frontiers of the Indus Civilization*, Indian Archaeological Society.

Larousse — 1973 *New Larousse Encyclopedia of Mythology* London/NY, Hamlyn.

Leach E — 1990 'Aryan invasions over four millennia' in *Culture through Time...* (ed) E Ohnuki-Tierney, Stanford, Stanford Univ Press, (227-45).

Lehman WP — 1993 *Theoretical Bases of Indo-European Linguistics* New York, Routledge.

Lehner, M — 2001 *The Complete Pyramids* (1997) London & NY, Hamlyn.

Lesko LH — 1991 'Ancient Egyptian Cosmogonies' in B Shafer 1991 (88-122).

Lesky A — 1971 *Geschichte der Griechischen Literatur*, Bern/München, Francke Verlag.

Levin S — 1991 'Full and other key words shared by Indo-European and Semitic' in Lamb SM and ED Mitchell (eds) *Sprung from Some Common Source* Stanford (CA) Stanford University Press (166-177).

Levitt SH — 2003 'The Dating of the Indian Tradition' *Anthropos* vol 98 (341-59).

Lichteim M — 1973-80 *Ancient Egyptian Literature* 3 vols California, Berkeley University Press.

Littauer MA & Crouwel JH — 1996 'The Origin of the true chariot' *Antiquity* 70 (934-9).

Littleton CS — 1973 *The New Comparative Mythology* Berkley/London, Univ of California Press.

Lockwood WB — 1972 *A Panorama of Indo-European Languages*, as above.

1969 *Indo-European Philology...*, Hutchinsons London, Univ Press.

Lubotsky A — 1997 A Ṛgvedic Word Concordance *New Haven, American Oriental Society.*

MacCanna P — 1996 *Celtic Mythology* (1968) London, Chancellor Press.

MacCulloch JA — 1949 *The Celtic and Scandinavian Religions* London, Hutchinson Univ Press.

MacDonell AA — 1995 (1898) *Vedic Mythology* Delhi, M Banarsidass.
1916 *A Vedic Grammar for Students* Oxford, OUP.

Mack JE — 1999 *Passport to the Cosmos: Human Transformation...* New York, Random House.

Mahoney RWK — 1998 *The Artful Universe* Albany NY, State Univ of NY Press....

Mallory JP — 2004 Private communication to N Kazanas.
2002 'Indigenous Indo-Aryans: the Preservation and Total Distribution Principles' *JIES* vol 30, 170-182.
2001 'The IE language family...' (in **Md Gk**) ed AP Christides *History of the Greek Language* (in Md Gk) Institute of Md Greek Studies, Athens (135-41).
1997 'The Homelands of the I-Es' in R Blench & M Spriggs eds *Archaeology and Language*, London & N York, Routledge.
1989 *In search of the Indo-Europeans...*, Thames & Hudson.
1973 '*A Short History of the I-E Problem*' in *JIES* 1, (21-65).

Mann SE — 1984-7 *An Indo-European Comparative Dictionary* (2 vols), Hamburg, Helmut.

Marathe AB — 2001 Review of J Bronkhorst's *The Two Sources of Indian Asceticism* ABORI vol 82 (285-7).

Marcantonio A — 2002/05 'Linguistic Palaeontology: science or fiction?...in B Winsa (ed) *Finno-Ugric Peoples in the Nordic Countries* Proceedings of the 5th Roots Conference, Stockholm, Academia Tornedallensis (77-94).
2002 *The Uralic Language Family: Facts, myths and statistics*, Oxford/Boston, Blackwell.

Marcantonio A & Brady RM — 2005 'Evidence that Indo-European reconstructions are artefacts of the Linguistic method of analysis', paper delivered in Cambridge and sent to NK privately in Oct, 05.

2002/2005 'Evidence the missing concept in comparative studies' in M Fernandez Vest(ed) *Les Langues Ouraliennes Aujourd' huit* Bibliothèque de l' École des Hautes Études, Paris Librairie Honoré Champion (117-132).

Mayrhofer M — 1956/1996 *Kurtgefastes (KEWA) and Etymologisches Wörterbuches Altindischen (EWA)*, Heidelberg, C Winter.

McCall H — 1992 *Mesopotamian Myths*, London, British Museum.

McEvilley Th — 2002 *The Shape of Ancient Thought* New York, Allworth Press.

McIntosh JR — 2001 *A Peaceful Realm* Boulder (Colorado), Westview.

Meadow R & Patel A — 1997 'A Comment on horse remains...' *South Asian Studies* 13 (308-15).

Meillet A — 1922 *Les Dialects indo-européenes* (1908), Paris.

Melchert C — 1994 'The Feminine Gender in Anatolian' *Früh-, Mittel- und Spätindogermanisch* (231-44), Wiesbaden, Verlag.

Mendelssohn K — 1974 *The Riddle of the Pyramids* London, Thames & Hudson.

Menon YK — 1976 *The Mind of Adi Shankara* Delhi, Jaico Publishing House.

Michalowski P — 1990 'Early Mesopotamian communicative systems...' in A Gunter (ed) *Investigating Artistic Environments in the Ancient Near East* Washington DC, Smithsonian Inst Press.

Miller J — 1998 *The Spice Trade of the Roman Empire* Oxford, OUP.

Miller Jeanine — 1985 *The Vision of Cosmic Order* London, Routledge & Kegan Paul.
1974 *The Vedas: Harmony, Meditation and Fulfilment* London, Rider & Co.
1972 in Feuerstein G and Miller J *Yoga and Beyond* NY, Schocken Bks.

Misra SS — 1999 *The Date of the RV & the Aryan Migration* Pune, Univ of Pune.
1992 *The Aryan Problem: A Linguistic Approach* Delhi, M Manoharlal.
1968 *A Comparative Grammar of Sanskrit,* Greek & Hittite Calcutta.

Mitchel B & Robinson F — 1996 *A Guide to Old English* Oxford, Blackwell.

Mitchener JE — 1982 *The seven Ṛṣis* Delhi, M Banarsidass.

MM = Dalley S — 1991 *Myths from Mesopotamia* Oxford, OUP.

Morenz, S — 1973 *Egyptian Religion* transl A Keep, London, Methuen & Co.

Morgan Kelley E — 1992 *The Metaphorical Basis of Language.* New York, Lewiston.

MSD = Monnier-Williams, & Sir M — 1899 *Sanskrit English Dictionary*, Oxford, OUP.

Müller M — 1916 *The Six Systems of Indian Philosophy* London, Longmans (1908).

Murray O — 1993 *Early Greece*, Cambridge Mass, HUP.

Nichols J — 1997-98 'The Epicentre of the IE linguistic spread' and 'The Eurasian spread zone ...' in R Blench & M Spriggs (eds) *Archaeolology & Language* NY/London Routledge, vol 1, 122-148 & 2, 220-266.

Norman Brown W — 1966 *Man in the Universe* Berkeley, LA, University of California.

O' Flaherty WD — 1981 *The RigVeda: An Anthology* London & NY etc, Penguin Books.

OLD = Lewis & Short — 1982 *Latin Dictionary* Oxford, OUP.

Onians RB — 1989 *The Origins of European Thought...* Cambridge, CUP.

Oppenheim AL — 1977 *Ancient Mesopotamia* Chicago/ London, Univ Chicago Press.

Oppenheimer S	2003 *The Real Eve: Modern Man's Journey out of Africa* NY, Carroll & Graf.
	2002 *Out of Eden: the Peopling of the World* London, Constable.
	1998 *Eden in the East: The Drowned Continent...* London, Weidenfeld & Nicholson.
Otto R	1923 *The Idea of the Holy* Oxford, OUP.
Ouspensky PD	1953 *A New Model of the Universe* (1931) London, Routledge & Kegan Paul.
Owens G	1999 'The Structure of the Minoan Language' *JIES* vol 27 (25-55).
Palsule GB	1961 *The Sanskrit Dhātupāthas* Pune, Univ of Poona Press.
Panaino A	2002 'The Mesopotamian Heritage of Achaemenian Kingship' (35-49) in R Whiting (ed) *Symposium...* Helsinki, Helsinki Univ Press.
Pande GC (ed)	2007 *Golden Chain of Civilizations...* PHISPC vol 1, pt 4 N Delhi, Centre for Studies in Civilization.
	1999 *The Dawn of Indian Civilization up to 600 BC* New Delhi, PHISPC, Centre for Studies in Civilization.
Parpola A et al	1969 *Decipherment of Proto-Dravidian Inscriptions...* Copenhagen, Scandinavian Institute of Asian Studies.
	1988 *The Coming of the Aryans to Iran and India* Helsinki, Studia Orientalia.
Pejros I	1997 'Are correlations between archaeological and linguistic reconstructions possible?' As with Mallory 1997 (I:149-57).
Pert CB	2002 *Molecules of Emotion* (1997) NY/London, Scribner.
Piggott S	1992 *Wagon, Chariot and Carriage* London, Thames & Hudson.
	1983 *The Earliest Wheeled Transport* London, Thames & Hudson.
Pingree D	1998 'Legacies in Astronomy and Celestial Omens' in S Dalley ed 1998 (125-38).

Pizani V — 1971 (rev ed) *Glottologia Indoeuropea* (1949) Torino, Rosenberg & Sellier.

Pokorny J — 1959 *Indogermanisches Etymologisches Würterbuch*, Bern-Munchen, Francke.

Pollock S — 1999 *Ancient Mesopotamia* Cambridge, CUP.

Polomé EC — 1991 'Indo-European Religion and Indo-European Religious Vocabulary' in Lamb SM & Mitchell ED (eds) *Sprung from Some Common Source (*67-88) Stanford, Stanford Univ Press.

1994 'Isoglosses and the Reconstruction of the IE Dialectal Split' *JIES* vol 22 (289-305).

Possehl GL — 2002/3 *The Indus Civilization* Roman & Littlefield (Non-NBN); New Delhi, Vistaar Publications.

1998 'Did the Sarasvati ever flow to the Sea?' GS Phillips et al (eds). *Arabia & its Neighbours* (in *Honour of Beatrice de Cardi*) Turnhout, Brepols (339-54).

Possehl GL & Gullapalli P — 1999 'The early iron age in South Asia' in V Pigott ed *The Archaeometallurgy of the Asian Old World* Philadelphia, The Univ Museum (153-75).

Prabhakar CL — 1994 'The Ancients' Approach to the Ocean' *Quarterly Journal of the Mythic Society* vol 85, No 2 (30-45).

Pritchard JB — 1958 *The Ancient Near East* Princeton, Princeton Univ Press.

Puhvel J — 1994 'Anatolian: Autochthon or Interloper?' *JIES* 22 (251-88).

1991 "Whence the Hittite..." in M Lamb and E Douglas Mitchel (eds) *Sprung from Some Comon Source*, California, Stanford Univ Press.

1989 *Comparative Mythology* (1987) Baltimore, John Hopkins Univ Press.

1970 (ed) *Myth and Law among Indo-Europeans*, Berkeley, Univ California Press.

Pulgram E — 1958 *The Tongues of Italy* Harvard Cambr Mass, Univ Press.

Radhakrishnan S — 1953 *The Principal Upanishads* London, G Allen & Unwin.

Rajaram M-R — 1999 *Vedic Physics, Scientific Origin of Hinduism* Toronto, Golden Egg Publ.

Rajaram N — 2005 'Connections between Harappan Seals and the Vedic Literature' in Agrawal A 2005 (135-41).

Rao LS — 2006 'The Harappan spokedwheels...' in *Purātattva* vol 36 (59-67).

Rao R — 1880 'Puzzles for the philologists'in *Theosophist* I (305-8).

Rao SR — 1991 *Dawn & Devolution of the Indus Civilization* Delhi, Aditya Prakashan.

1973 *Lothal & the Indus Civilization* Bombay, Asia Publications.

Rau W — 1976 *The Meaning of pur in Vedic Literature* W Finck, Munchen (*non vidi*: cited by Bryant E 2001 & Witzel M 2001).

Rauling P — 2000 *Horses, Chariots and Indo-Europeans* Budapest, Archaeolingua.

Rees A & B — 1995 *Celtic Heritage* (1961), London, Thames & Hudson.

Renfrew C — 1999 'Time Depth, Convergence Theory and Innovation...' *JIES* vol 27 (258-93).

1997 'World linguistic diversity and farming dispersals' as with Mallory 1997.

1991, '*Before Babel...*' in *Cambridge Arch Journal*, vol 1.

1989 *Archaeology & Language* (1989) Penguin Books, Hammondsworth.

Rix H — 1998 *Lexikon der Indogermanischen Verben...* Wiesbaden, Reichert.

Roux G — 1992 *Ancient Iraq* 3rd ed, London, Penguins.

Rudgley R — 1998 *Lost Civilizations of the Stone Age* Century, London.

Saggs HWF — 1989 *Civilization Before Greece and Rome* New Haven/London, Yale Univ Press.

1995 *Babylonians* London, British Museum Press.

Sahoo S, Singh A, Kivisild T... et al — 2006 'A Prehistory of Indian Y-chromosomes' in *Proceedings of the National Academy of Sciences* (USA) vol 103, no 4, 843-8.

Sankalia HD — 1974 *Prehistory & Protohistory of India & Pakistan*, Poona, Deccan College.

Sarianidi V — 1999 'Near Eastern Aryans in Central Asia' *JIES* vol 27 (295-326).

Sauneron S — 1980 *The Priests of Ancient Egypt* trans A Morrisett, NY, Grove Press (also, trans D Lorton, Ithaca, Cornell University 2000).

Schildmann K — 1999 'Entzifferung der Burrows Cave Texte in USA und der Glozel Texte in Frankreich als Indus-Sanskrit Texte' in *Studia Orientalia und Atlantica*, Bonn.

1998 *β Indus/Burrows Cave USA-Deciphering* Bonn, Studia Orientalia et Indo-Attentica, Fascicle 1.

Schwartz JM — 2002 *The Mind and the Brain* NY/ London, Regan Books, Collin-Harper.

Sedlar JW — 1980 *India and the Greek World*, New Jersey, Rowman & Littlefied.

Seidenberg A — 1978 *'The Origin of Mathematics'* in *Archive...* , vol 18 (303-341).

Sergent B — 1997 *La Genèse de l' Inde* Paris, Payot & Rivages.

Sethe K — 1908-22 *Die Altägyptischen Pyramidentexte*, 4 vols, Leipsig, Universität Verlag, (and the posthumously published Translation... Gluckstadt, Hamburg, no date); see Faulkner RO.

Sethna DK — 1992 *The Problem of Aryan Origins* 2nd Ed, Delhi, Aditya Prakashan.

SGD = Stamatakos I — 1972 *Dictionary of Ancient Greek* (Md Gk) Athens, Pheonix.

Shafer BE — 1991 (ed) *Religion in Ancient Egypt* Cornell Univ, London, Routledge.

Shaffer JG — 1984, 'The Indo-Aryan Invasions: Cultural Myth and Archaeological Reality' in Lukacs JR (ed) *The People of South Asia: the Biological Anthropology of India, Pakistan and Nepal*, NY, Phenum.

Shaffer JG & Lichtenstein DA — 1995 'The cultural tradition and palaeoethnicity in South Asian Archaeology' G Erdosy (ed).

1999 'Migration, philology & South Asian archaeology' as with Hock HH 1999.

Sharma GR — 1980 *History to Protohistory: Archaeology of the Vindhyas and the Ganga Valley*, Allahabad, Allahabad University.

Sharma JR, Gupta AK & Bhadra BK — 2006 'Course of Vedic river Saraswati...' in *Purātattva* vol 36 (187-195).

Sharma RS — 2004 'Was the Harappan Culture Vedic?' in *Journal of Interdisciplinary Studies in History and Archaeology* (University of Allahabad) vol 1(2) pp135-144.

1999 *Advent of the Aryans in India* New Delhi, Orient Longman.

1996 *Looking for the Aryans* Hyderabad, Orient Longman.

Shendge MJ — 2001 'At the beginning of Philosophy in India...' *JICPR* special issue (eds) GC Pande & K Daya (145-161).

1994 *The Language of the Harappans...* New Delhi, Abhinava Publ.

Shouse B — 2001 'Spreading the Word, scattering the seeds' *Science* 294, 988-989.

Sihler AL — 1995 *A New Comparative Grammar of Latin & Greek* Oxford, OUP.

Silverman D — 1991 'Divinity and Deities in Ancient Egypt' in Shafer (ed) 1991 (7-87).

Simonov P — 1997 *Essential Russian Mythology* London/San Francisco, Thorsons.

Singh Bh — 1995 *The Vedic Harappans* Delhi, Aditya Prakashan.

Singh NK — 1997 *Vedic Mythology* N Delhi, APH Publishing Corporation.

Sparreboom M — 1985 *Chariots in the Veda* Leiden, Brill.

Speirs AG — 1978 *The Proto-Indo-European Labio-velars* Amsterdam, Hakkert.

Srinivasan LA — 1999-2000 'An Enquiry about Sumerian Words' *Mother Tongue* (109-118).

Stone A — 1997 *Ymir's Flesh* Loughborough (Britain), Heart of Albion Press.

Straus LG et al — 1996 *Humans at the End of the Ice Age* NY/ London, Plenum Press.

Swadesh M — 1955 'Towards greater accuracy in lexico statistical dating', *International Journal of American Linguists* vol 21 (121-137).

1953 'Archaeological and Linguistic chronology...' *American Anthropologist* vol 55 (349-352).

Szalek BZ — 2005 'On the relation of Ancient Egyptian to other agglutinative languages' in *Migration & Diffusion* vol 24 (6-18).

Szemerényi O — 1972 'Comparative Linguistics' in *Current Trends in Linguistics*, vol 9 (119-198).

1996 *Introduction to Indo-European Linguistics* (translated from German, 1990, with additional notes and references) Oxford, OUP.

Talageri SG — 2001 Reply to Witzel's critique at http://shrikanttalageri.voiceofdharma.com/

2000 *The Rigveda* Aditya Prakashan, Delhi.

1993 *The Aryan Invasion Theory* Aditya, New Delhi.

Taylour LW — 1990 *The Mycenaeans* London, Thames & Hudson.

Tewari R, Srivastava RK, Singh KK & Saraswat KS — 2006 'Further excavations at Lahuradeva, District Sant Kabir Nagar...' *Purātattva* vol 36 (68-75).

Thapar B & Mungal R — 1994 'The Indus Valley (3000-1500 BC) in A Dani & JP Mohen (eds) *History of Humanity* vol 2, London, Unesco/ Routledge (246-65).

Thapar R — 1999 *The Aryan Question Revisited* <http://members.tripod.com/ascjnu/aryan.html>.
1996 'The theory of Aryan race and India'; *Social Scientist*, 2 (3-29).

Thieme P — 1960 'The 'Aryan' gods of the Mitanni treaties', *Journal of the American Oriental Society* vol 41(301-317).
1953 *Die Heimat der Indohermanischen Gemeinsprache*. Wiesbaden, Akademie der Wissenschaften und der Literatur.

Thomas P et al — 1995 'Harappan subsistence patterns...' *Man & Environment* (India) 20, 2 (33-41).

Thompson SE — 1990 'The Origin of the Pyramid Texts...' *Journal of Egyptian Archaeology* 76 (17-25).

Thompson Stith — 1989 *Myth-Index of Folk Literature* (1932-35) Bloomington/London, Indiana University Press.

Thomson K — 2001 'The meaning and language of the Rigveda...' JIES vol 29, 3-4 (295-349).

Tilak L — 1893 *The Orion* Poona, India, Tilak Bros.

Trautmann TR — 1997 *Aryans & British India* New Delhi, Vistaar Publications.

Tremblay X — 2005 'Grammaire comparé et grammaire historique' in Fussman G, Kellens J, et al.

Trevelyan GM — 1972 *A Shortened History of England* (1942) Hammondsworth, Pelican.

Trubezkoy — 1939 Gedanken über das Indogermanen problem in *Acta Linguistica* 1 (81-89).

Vedic Index(VI) — 1995 (1912) by MacDonnell A & Keith A, Delhi, M Banarsidass.

Ventris M & Chadwick J — 1973 *Documents in Mycenaean Greek* , Cambridge, CUP.

Verbrugghe G et al — 1999 *Berossos & Manetho* Univ Michigan Press.

Vitaliano D — 1977 *Legends of the Earth: Their Geologic Origins* Indiana Univ Press.

von Buitenen J — 1973 *Mahābhārata* transl vols 1 & 2, Chicago/London, Univ Chicago Press.

Wadler A — 1988 *Der Turm von Babel* Wiesbaden, O Horrassowitz.

1936 *Germanische Urzeit*, Basel (reprinted Wiesbaden 1980).

Ward DJ — 1968 *The Divine Twins* Folklore Studies 19, Berkley, University of California Press.

Wasson RG — 1971 'The Soma of the Rigveda: What was it?' in the *Journal of the American Oriental Society* vol 91 (2) 169-187.

Wasson RG, Kranirisch Stella et al — 1986 *Persephone's Quest...* New Haven/ London, Yale University Press.

Watkins C — 2001 How to kill a Dragon: Aspects of IE Poetics OUP (1995).

2000 The American Heritage Dictionary of IE Roots (2nd rev ed) Boston/NY, H Mifflin.

Watterson B — 1993 *Introducing Egyptian Hieroglyphs* Edinburgh, Scottish Academic Press.

Werner K — 1989 'From Polytheism to Monism...' *Cosmos* vol 5, *Polytheistic Systems* ed G Davies, Edinburg Univ. Press (12-27).

1978 'The Vedic Concept of Human Personality...' *Journal of Indian Philosophy* vol 5 (275-289).

West AJ — 1993 *Serpent in the Sky* (1979 rev ed) Wheaton (III), Quest Books.

West ML — 1971 *Early Greek Philosophy and the Orient* Oxford, OUP.

White HE — 1935 *Hesiod and Homeric Hymns* Loeb Ed, Cambridge (MA), Harvard University Press & London, Heinemann.

Whitney WD — 1905 *The Atharva-Veda* Camb, Mass, HOS VII-VIII.

1885 *Roots, Verb-forms & Primary Derivatives...* Leipsig, London, Trübner & Co.

Whittaker G — 1998 'Traces of an early Indo-European Language in southern Mesopotamia' in *Göttinger Beiträge zur Sprachwissenschaft* Heft 1, Gottingen.

Wilson R et al — 2000 *The Great Ice Age* London, The Open University.

Winn SMM — 1995 *Heaven, Heroes and Happiness...* NY, London, Univ. Press of America.

Winternitz M — 1981-5 *Geschichte Der Indischen Literatur (1923)*: English trans by VS Sharma 2 vols (1981-83); 3rd vol by S Jha (1985) N Delhi, M Banarsidass.

Witzel M — 2005 'Central Asian Roots and Acculturation in South Asia' in Osada Tosiki ed *Linguistics, Archaeology and the Human Past,* Kyoto, Indus Project, Research Institute for Humanity and Nature.

2003 'Ein Fremdling in Ṛgveda' *JIES* vol 31.

2001 'Autochthonous Aryans' *Electronic Journal of Vedic Studies* 7-3, 1-93.

2001b Critique of Talageri's *Rigveda* in *EJVS* 7-2.

2000 'Horseplay at Harappa' with M Farmer in *Frontline* (Indian fortnightly) October 13 (4-13).

1999-2000 'Sumerian and Bengali...' *Mother Tongue* (119-140).

1995b 'Ṛgvedic History ...' in Erdosy G (ed), 307-52 (et al, eds) 1997 Rodopi; Atalanta/Amsterdam, *FBJ Kuiper*: *Selected Writings...*

1995 'Early Indian History' and 'Rigvedic History' in G Erdosy (ed).

Wolf FA — 2001 *Mind into Matter* Needham (MA), Moment Point Press.

Zide A — 1979 'A brief survey ... on the Indus script' in *Ancient Cities of the Indus* ed G Possehl, Carolina Acad Press, Durham (256-60).

Zimmer S — 2000 'The easy way to truth...' *JIES* 30, 192-201.

1990 'On Indo-Europeanization' *JIES* 18, 140-55.

Index